The Roman Market Economy

THE PRINCETON ECONOMIC HISTORY OF THE WESTERN WORLD
Joel Mokyr, Series Editor

A list of titles in this series appears at the back of the book.

The Roman Market Economy

. . . .

Peter Temin

Princeton University Press

Princeton & Oxford

Copyright © 2013 by Princeton University Press

Published by Princeton University Press, 41 William Street, Princeton, New Jersey 08540

In the United Kingdom: Princeton University Press, 6 Oxford Street, Woodstock, Oxfordshire OX20 1TR

press.princeton.edu

Cover art: Detail of cargo ship from road to market with trade symbols in mosaic. Roman, Ostia Antica near Rome Italy. Photo © Gianni Dagli Orti. Courtesy of Art Resource, NY. Cover design by Karl Spurzem.

First paperback printing, 2017.

Paperback ISBN 978-0-691-17794-6

The Library of Congress has cataloged the cloth edition of this book as follows:

Temin, Peter.
 The Roman market economy / Peter Temin.
   p. cm. — (The Princeton economic history of the Western world)
 Includes bibliographical references and index.
 ISBN 978-0-691-14768-0 (hardcover : alk. paper) 1. Rome—Economic conditions. 2. Rome—Economic policy. 3. Rome—Commerce. I. Title.
 HC39.T46 2013
 330.937—dc23

                                                                                    2012012347

British Library Cataloging-in-Publication Data is available

This book has been composed in Adobe Caslon Pro

Printed and bound by CPI Group (UK) Ltd, Croydon, CR0 4YY

For Charlotte

Contents

■ ■ ■

Preface and Acknowledgments   ix

1. Economics and Ancient History   1

Part I: Prices
Introduction: Data and Hypothesis Tests   27
2. Wheat Prices and Trade in the Early Roman Empire   29
3. Price Behavior in Hellenistic Babylon   53
Appendix to Chapter 3   66
4. Price Behavior in the Roman Empire   70

Part II: Markets in the Roman Empire
Introduction: Roman Microeconomics   95
5. The Grain Trade   97
6. The Labor Market   114
7. Land Ownership   139
8. Financial Intermediation   157

Part III: The Roman Economy
Introduction: Roman Macroeconomics   193
9. Growth Theory for Ancient Economies   195
10. Economic Growth in a Malthusian Empire   220
Appendix to Chapter 10   240
11. Per Capita GDP in the Early Roman Empire   243

References   263
Index   289

Preface and Acknowledgments

▪ ▪ ▪ ▪ ▪ ▪ ▪ ▪ ▪

This book presents a progress report in the process of understanding the nature of ancient economies. I am an economic historian who spent most of his academic career writing about modern and early-modern economies and teaching modern economics. Sometime before the end of the twentieth century, I became interested in ancient economies. If the Romans wrote all those letters and speeches and built all those roads and buildings, how did they get the resources to do so? Writing takes time and an education that enables a writer to express thoughts in historical perspective. Construction uses materials and labor that have to be organized and gathered for this purpose. How were people able to organize these activities and—to broaden our focus—build something as large and complex as the Roman Empire?

I read Finley's book, *The Ancient Economy*, when it came out over a quarter-century ago (Finley 1973), and more recent books over the years. I found they did not provide convincing answers to the questions I had raised, and I resolved to investigate further the economics of the ancient world. I published and presented papers to ancient-history conferences over the past decade that resulted from my curiosity. I offer the insights I gained from writing these papers and rethinking them now in light of subsequent research as a progress report that provides a view of the Roman economy that has become more popular—although not without controversy—than when I started on this quest.

I tried to learn a few of the languages needed by ancient historians, but I speedily realized that I would never be good enough to improve on the translations of experts. My comparative advantage—a term I explain more fully in the first chapter of this volume—is in economic analysis, not archaeology or text analysis. All scholars stand on the shoulders of those who have gone before, and I freely acknowledge my debt to the generations of ancient historians whose works I utilize. Even if I disagree with their analyses, I respect and envy their scholarship. I struggle also with modern languages, and my citations reflect my preference for English sources. If one has to choose one language for modern scholarship, it would be English, and I am fortunate to be a native speaker. If I repeat analyses published in other languages, I hope that readers will inform me.

I hope also that this book will be received better than my initial foray into ancient history. I wrote a research proposal for myself before I thought seriously about implementing it. I went to Oxford for a conference in 1999 and sent my proposal to a few Oxford people I knew or had arranged to meet. Economists laughed at my proposal at breakfast, and ancient historians laughed at it at lunch. They all assured me—for different reasons—that my proposal was unworkable. With that stimulus, I had to forge ahead! The proposal grew into my most well-known contribution to ancient economic history. It appeared as Temin (2001) in the *Journal of Roman Studies*, then under the editorship of an ancient historian who had laughed at me earlier. It set out a research agenda that was fulfilled in the chapters of the middle section of this book.

It may be wishful thinking, but I detect a movement toward an acceptance of modern economic concepts in the study of the ancient world in the past few years. When I started in this field, theoretical discussions of ancient history all started from Karl Polanyi and M. I. Finley. This is apparent in the extensive introduction to the reissue of Finley's book on its silver anniversary in 1999 (Morris 1999). Yet less than a decade later, *The Cambridge Economic History of the Greco-Roman World* was based more on Douglass North than Moses Finley. North, a Nobel laureate in economic history, emphasized the importance of economic institutions in determining economic performance. His work, together with other like-minded economists, has given rise to what is now called the New Institutional Economics (NIE). Almost all the essays in *The Cambridge Economic History of the Greco-Roman World* take their cue from the NIE, and the volume itself is organized by consideration of institutions. The essays on the regional development of the Roman Empire start from the premise that preexisting institutions affected how Roman expansion affected their economic activities (Scheidel, Morris, and Saller 2007).

From everything we know, prosperity in Greece and Rome extended beyond a royal family or clan into a larger group of people. I have tried to explore how the Roman economy functioned. I chose to focus primarily on the early Roman Empire because the scale of the Roman Empire was vast and the economy seemed to run amazingly well for a long time. It is one thing to run a small economy drawing small amounts of resources from a broad hinterland; it is much harder to involve millions of people into an integrated economic system. As Wickham (2005, 10) described it, "The Roman Empire was a coherent political and economic system, operating on a scale that has seldom since been matched in Europe and the Mediterranean, and never for so long." In addition, we have a lot of information about the economy of the early Roman

Empire when peace was more prevalent than war. The Roman information was generated by indirection, and we have to tease out economic information from sources designed for other concerns. This, of course, is the intellectual adventure: how to make sense of the fragments we have to understand the Roman economy.

It is a great pleasure to acknowledge the generous help I received from many ancient historians as I made this intellectual journey. Far from the haughtiness and clannish attitudes that I was assured typified ancient historians, I found them to be marvelously welcoming to an outside adventurer who took the effort to talk with them. Of course, not everyone agrees with me, and I regret that I have not been able to talk more widely with other ancient historians.

The first group is the small set of ancient historians who helped me get started: Alan Bowman, Rebecca Flemming, Martin Goodman, Joshua Sosin, and Dominic Rathbone. They were all happy to answer uninformed questions and correct elementary mistakes. Through it all, they were supportive of my quest, and Dominic coauthored a paper with me that gives chapter 8 its special texture. They remain friends today; Keith Hopkins, who also welcomed me and helped me, unfortunately died before I was prepared to write this book. To this initial group are added the ancient historians I met along the way, who have invited me to conferences, corresponded with me, and become welcome colleagues: Jean Andreau, Roger Bagnall, William Broadhead, Francois de Callatay, Richard Duncan-Jones, Paul Erdkamp, Peter Garnsey, Kyle Harper, William Harris, Christopher Howgego, Willem Jongman, Dennis Kehoe, Elio Lo Cascio, Michael McCormick, Ian Morris, Cécile Morrisson, Steven Ostrow, Walter Scheidel, Alice Slotsky, Richard Talbert, Koen Verboven, and Alan Wilson.

Economists Robert Allen, Elise Brezis, Victor Chernozhukov, Richard Eckaus, Bronwyn Hall, David Hendry, Joel Mokyr, Morris Silver, Nathan Sussman, and Joachim Voth also helped me along. MIT students Andrea Crandall, Julia Dennett, Edward Flores, Yerrie Kim, Brendan Sullivan, and Christine Yee helped me through MIT's Undergraduate Research Opportunities Program. David Kessler, a Harvard economics undergraduate who wanted to write a thesis on the Roman economy, turned into a coauthor of the papers underlying chapters 2 and 5. Eveline Felsten helped me with chapter 4. To all of the above, and to those I have accidently omitted, I offer my thanks and absolution from association with any of my errors and conclusions.

Portions of the book are derived in part from articles previously published in the *Journal of Roman Studies, Journal of Interdisciplinary History, Journal of Economic History, Economic History Review,* and *Explorations in Economic History.*

I want to thank particularly Emily Gallagher, my assistant at MIT, who helped me in myriad ways. I am grateful for financial support from the Simon R. Guggenheim Foundation and the Warden and Fellows of Nuffield College, Oxford, and for comments from the members of the Columbia Workshop on Economics for Ancient History organized by William Harris, Columbia University, June 2009. I also thank participants in the conferences I have been invited to for their comments on and discussion of my contributions. Finally, I thank my wife, Charlotte Temin, for her support, encouragement, and patience as I struggled to master a new area of research. Without her, it would have been much harder and lot less fun to write these papers.

The Roman Market Economy

Chapter 1

■ ■ ■

Economics and Ancient History

Ignorance is the first requisite of the historian—ignorance, which
simplifies and clarifies, which selects and omits, with a placid perfection
unattainable by the highest art.

—Lytton Strachey, *Eminent Victorians*

The reputation of the Roman Empire lives on long after the empire itself vanished. Roman literature, Roman archaeological remains, and Roman analogies—particularly now in our time of troubles—confront us at every term. Books like *Are We Rome?* trumpet the analogy, and less extensive allusions are frequent (Murphy 2007; Smil 2010). It often seems as if we are as familiar with the history of ancient Rome as much as of the recent history of the Western world.

While this was true in the late eighteenth century, as witnessed by the writings of our founding fathers, it is no longer so. Most of us do not study Greek and Latin in school, and we do not read the Classics in the original. Most of us know them only by allusion and summary. Classicists and ancient historians by contrast know the ancient languages and read ancient texts, but even they are subject to Strachey's critique. In particular, many accounts of ancient affairs neglect their economic aspects since most ancient historians have only limited training in the dismal science. The application of economic reasoning to ancient history is growing, but more ancient historians than economists are interested in ancient economies.

This book is a contribution to the economic analysis of ancient history from an economic historian who spent most of his academic career writing about modern and early-modern economies. Sometime before the end of the twentieth century, my interest in ancient economies turned from casual to serious.

This book is based on the papers that have resulted from the decade or so of research I have conducted into the economy of ancient Rome, updated and altered to fit into a coherent account. I hope to convince you of five points in this narrative.

First, economics provides useful insights into ancient history. Much of modern economics is devoted to the analysis of modern industrial economies and is not very useful to ancient historians. But the basic elements of economics, still taught in introductory economics classes, provide valuable tools. Supply and demand and comparative advantage allow historians to ask and occasionally answer a variety of questions that have plagued scholars for many years.

Second, ancient Rome had a market economy. There are many references to markets in ancient history, and it does not take much reading to see that they were ubiquitous. Focusing on markets allows us to ask how these markets worked, whether they were helped or hurt by the structure of Roman society, and how far they extended. I argue that markets knit the Roman economy together enough to call it a market economy.

Third, the Pax Romana stimulated Mediterranean trade. Shipping costs over sea were far less than over land before the Industrial Revolution and the advent of the railroad. Extensive Mediterranean trade promoted regional specialization, and comparative advantage worked to raise incomes across the Roman Empire.

Fourth, ordinary Romans lived well, probably better than any other large group—consisting of many millions of people—before the Industrial Revolution. They lived well as a result of extensive markets, comparative advantage, and technological change. True, the Industrial Revolution did not occur in Roman times, and conditions there were not propitious for this momentous change, at least in the form that it took in eighteenth-century Britain. But living conditions were better in the earlier Roman Empire than anywhere else and anytime else before the Industrial Revolution.

Fifth, we are learning more about the Roman economy all the time. Economics helps us ask new questions, and new information is coming to light all the time. Archaeology constantly provides new evidence of economic activity, and new questions suggest reinterpretations of previously known information. This book is a progress report on one part of an ongoing reinterpretation of the Roman economy being undertaken by many historians.

Consider two well-known Romans: Cicero and Trimalchio. They are quite different. One was a historical figure; the other, a fictional one. One lived through the start of the Roman Empire; the other was created a century later. Yet they are together in appearing regularly in the pages of modern ancient historians. It may be interesting to note how they are similar.

Neither of them was a member of a royal household. Often in the study of ancient empires we know only of royal families and their immediate helpers. Even for Rome, they are the most familiar figures, and there is a lot of Roman history that looks only at the emperors and their frequently dysfunctional families. It is uncommon to have abundant evidence of ordinary people long ago, and Roman times are unusual in having records of many ordinary people that have survived for two millennia. This gives us hope that we are not discussing just a tiny royal minority when we analyze records from the Roman Empire. True, most people were farmers and farm laborers who left few records, but even they have left records that have survived.

Both Cicero and Trimalchio were urban residents, in fact residents of Rome itself. Rome was a large city, perhaps a million strong. We need to be careful about that number as with all ancient numbers, but it seems clear that Rome was one of the largest cities that existed before the Industrial Revolution. The existence of this large city, as well as its smaller cousins, tells us that Roman agriculture was efficient enough to feed a lot of nonfarmers. I argue here that this accomplishment was achieved more by long-distance trade than through new technology; I will explain later in this chapter how trade improves incomes. In addition, large cities have their own ecology with lots of urban activities, from crafts to finance. The existence of these people raises questions related to their varied occupations, from how they were paid to whether they had contracts for their work. These questions will engage our attention in several chapters of this book.

Cicero and Trimalchio were both free men and Roman citizens (to the extent that a fictional character can be a citizen). Trimalchio was a freedman, and the *Satyricon* in which he appears satirizes the pretensions of freedmen in the early Roman Empire. Trimalchio was a member of the nouveau riche and subject to the time-honored ritual of being ridiculed for his inability to act like the scion of a respectable, that is, rich household. The ridicule comes from the fear of established people that newcomers will displace them in society, and a freedman contained that threat in ancient Rome. This implies that Roman slavery was far different from slavery in the antebellum United States with which it often is compared. The nature of Roman slavery will be explained further in chapter 6 on the Roman labor force.

Both men had urban occupations. Cicero was a lawyer who pleaded cases in Roman courts. For him to practice this profession there must have been laws and courts in which the laws were applied and tested. The existence of such a legal structure often is used today as a marker for modern societies and for economic growth in less-developed countries. Their existence in ancient Rome indicates that Rome had an important prerequisite for economic growth. The branch of economics that considers these prerequisites is known as the New

Institutional Economics (NIE), as I will explain in this chapter. Trimalchio was a merchant, and he recounts that he had to send out several ships that did not return until he sent our one that did return to his great profit. We learn from this story that there were private merchants, and they were common enough among the literate population for Petronius to assume that his readers knew what he was talking about. More evidence has survived about literary figures who did not like trade than about merchants themselves, so we have to infer their activities from a variety of sources. Chapters 2 and 5 approach this task from different directions. We also learn that being a merchant was a risky occupation, very different from the practice of agriculture. Some ways in which Romans dealt with risk are explained in chapters 5 and 6.

It should clear by now that we need some kind of framework in which to organize all these observations and questions about them. I propose that simple economic tools will help us in this attempt to organize our thoughts, and this chapter will explain a few important economic concepts and their applications to ancient times.

The economy of the early Roman Empire has been an object of study for at least the last century. The discussion has been marked by continuing debate, known sometimes as the primitivist/modern debate and at other times as the Finley debate, following M. I. Finley's famous Sather lectures, *The Ancient Economy*. Finley (1973, 22–23) declared that "ancient society did not have an economic system which was an enormous conglomeration of interdependent markets." He drew implicitly on research by Polanyi (1944, 1977) to oppose the views of Rostovtzeff (1957) within the field of ancient history and those of Fogel and Engerman (1974) in economic history, but he did not explicitly join their conceptual apparatuses. Morris (1999) summarized the debate fueled by Finley's dramatic lectures in his foreword to the twenty-fifth anniversary edition and argued that the controversy is still vigorous today. I hope to clarify the issues in this debate and even resolve the debate for the period of the early Roman Empire.

I argue that the economy of the early Roman Empire was primarily a market economy. The parts of this economy located far from each other were not tied together as tightly as markets often are today, but they still functioned as part of a comprehensive Mediterranean market. There are two reasons why this conclusion is important. First, it brings the description of the Roman economy as a whole into accord with the fragmentary evidence we have about individual market transactions. Second, this synthetic view provides a platform on which to investigate further questions about the origins and eventual demise of the Roman economy and about conditions for the formation and preservation of markets in general.

In his lectures and his subsequent "Further Thoughts," Finley (1999, 27, 182) called for models of the ancient economy. This is a good approach. But what does it mean to use a model of the ancient economy? A model is an abstract representation of reality. It is simpler than reality because it is created by social and natural scientists who can only conceptualize a few dimensions of reality at a time. Models typically are manipulated in order to reach conclusions, and they have to be simple enough for their formulators to manipulate. With the advent of computers, we can deal with much more complex models than before, but the most useful models often are the simplest.

Most economic models assume the existence of a market economy. The models show how institutions or other economic forces affect prices, quantities, and related variables in one or more industries or, sometimes, in the economy as a whole. The model provides a simplified description of events that can be repeated and discussed, and it allows economists to test *counterfactual* propositions. That is, the economist can ask what would have happened if the institutions or other economic forces had been different than they actually were. The resulting counterfactual history is not an account of events as they happened; it is a conjecture about what would have happened had history been different. The conjecture is conditional on the model. If the model is a poor one, the conjecture will be poor as well. And the conjecture is limited by the model; it can only track the variables in the model in the counterfactual world.

How can we tell whether a model is poor? This is a question that has energized generations of philosophers of science, and I will attempt only the most concrete answer here. A good model fits the observed facts more closely than a poor one. This apparently simple statement has several important components. First, any model depends on the facts behind it. If new data are discovered, models may need to be changed. Stated differently, good models are not made up out of whole cloth; they are distillations of the available data. One advantage of using a model is that it often suggests the need for more data to settle open questions and sets in motion data searches that have proven successful in many fields of economic history. Second, there must be a ranking by which one can tell which model fits the facts more closely than another. When there is an abundance of numerical data, modern statistics and econometrics provide tests that economic historians use. When the data are qualitative, as they generally are for the early Roman Empire, less formal tests have to be used. Third, no model is good in the abstract; it is better or worse than an alternative.

This last point is critical. Economics is a comparative science. The story is told of an economist who meets a colleague while walking across campus. The colleague hails the economist and asks, "How are your children?" The economist responds, "Compared to what?" This response, only slightly exaggerated here, is typical of economists. Economic models are supported by showing that they are superior to another, often called the "null hypothesis." The null hypothesis of most economics is that there is a well-functioning market, that prices are determined by supply and demand. This is a problem for the study of the Roman economy, because it is precisely this typical null hypothesis that needs to be tested.

I propose to test the hypothesis that there was a market economy in the early Roman Empire in two stages. I argue first that many individual actions and interactions are seen best as market transactions. I then argue that there were enough market transactions to constitute a market economy, that is, an economy where many resources are allocated by prices that are free to move in response to changes in underlying conditions. More technically I argue that markets in the early Roman Empire typically were equilibrated by means of prices.

I begin by presenting the alternatives to which market transactions are to be compared. The logical starting point, as for so much of this literature, is Polanyi. He provided a taxonomy of interactions that has been used widely. He asserted that "the main forms of integration in the human economy are, as we find them, reciprocity, redistribution, and exchange" (Polanyi 1977, 35–36). These forms describe different ways to organize the economic functions of any society. Reciprocity, as the term suggests, is a system in which people aim toward a rough balance between the goods and services they receive and that they give to others. The reciprocal obligations are determined by social obligations and tradition, and they change only slowly. This organization can be formalized, as in Malinowski's Trobriand Islanders, or simply followed with informal or implicit rules. Redistribution is a system in which goods are collected in one hand and distributed by virtue of custom, law, or ad hoc central decision. This system is present in units as small as households, where it is known as householding, as well as in the taxation levied by modern states. The essential characteristic is that a central authority collects and distributes goods and services. Exchange is the familiar economic transaction where people voluntarily exchange one or more goods for other goods or for money. Polanyi's categories appear frequently in books about various aspects of classical antiquity, from Peacock and Williams (1986) on amphorae to Jongman (1988) on Pompeii and Garnsey (1999) on food.

Polanyi's definitions of these different forms of integration are appealing, but imprecise. They suggest three models of interaction; we need to make them precise enough that we can choose between them. Pryor (1977) proposed tests in a study of primitive and peasant economies that can be used to differentiate Polanyi's forms of integration. Pryor distinguished between what he called exchanges and transfers. Exchanges are balanced transactions where goods or services are exchanged for other goods or services of equal value. This is the kind of behavior most often observed in markets. Transfers are one-way transactions where goods and services are given without a direct return. Grants, tributes, and taxes are all transfers. Pryor excluded "invisibles" from this accounting, so that taxes are considered to be transfers rather than an exchange of goods or money in order to purchase social order or military success. This exclusion is necessary because one can always hypothesize an invisible gain that makes all transactions balanced. In that case, there is no way to discriminate between different forms of behavior.

Pryor subdivided exchanges into those in which the ratio of goods or services exchanged can vary and those in which it cannot. The former may or may not involve money; the latter do not. He termed the former, market exchange; the latter, reciprocal exchange. The use of money is a good index of this distinction, as are changes in the exchange ratio over time. In the presence of money, changes in exchange ratios are expressed as changes in prices. Pryor divided transfers into centric and noncentric ones. Centric transfers are between individuals in a society and an institution or an individual carrying out a societalwide role. In the Roman context, large-scale centric transfers would be those with the Imperial authorities. If the grain to feed Rome were provided by taxes or tribute, this would be a centric transfer. If the grain were obtained by purchasing it with money, then this would be a market exchange.

These categories are observable, that is, they provide boxes into which activities and societies can be placed with confidence. They also correspond closely to Polanyi's forms of economic integration. Polanyi's first form, reciprocity, is composed of Pryor's noncentric transfers and reciprocal exchanges. His second form, redistribution, is accomplished by centric transfers. His third form, exchange, is characterized by what Pryor called market exchange. Pryor's project can be seen as a way to make Polanyi's classification empirically testable, not necessarily reaching Polanyi's conclusion that "price-making markets [are] the exceptional occurrence in history" (Neale 1957, 371).

This tripart schema corresponds also to a division of individual behavior (Temin 1980). People rely on a mixture of behavioral modes, choosing which one to use as a result of internal and external forces. These forces can be represented on two dimensions. One dimension measures internal forces along an index of personal autonomy. The other dimension indexes the rapidity of change in the external environment. When people are less autonomous and change is slow, they typically utilize customary behavior. When change is rapid and personal autonomy is neither very high nor very low, then people use command behavior. When personal autonomy is high and the pace of change is moderate, people employ instrumental behavior, that is, they have explicit goals in mind and choose actions that advance their plans. These different modes of behavior correspond to the three types of organization used in economic life. Customary behavior generally is used for noncentric transfers and reciprocal exchanges, that is, in reciprocity. Command behavior is typical of centric transfers, that is, redistribution. And instrumental behavior is used in market exchanges.

There consequently are two types of tests we can use to discriminate between the various kinds of integration. Prices are used in market exchanges, but not in noncentric transfers. They may appear in reciprocal exchanges, although they will not vary in response to economic conditions in that context. Variable prices then can be used as markers for the presence of market exchange. Phrased differently, we can infer from the existence of prices that market exchange more closely describes the interaction containing the prices than reciprocity or redistribution. Of course, we will need to make sure that these prices can vary over time to make sure that the prices are not simply stable markers of a noncentric exchange, that is, a specific type of reciprocity.

In addition, people will behave instrumentally in market exchanges, not customarily or by command, since these two modes of behavior are typical of reciprocal and redistributive organizations. Thoughts are observed far less easily than prices, although ancient sources often report the former more volubly than the latter. Nevertheless, we can ask when ancient authors describe their activities if they are describing instrumental, customary, or command behavior. We do so by comparing how well each model of behavior fits the described actions or the imputed thoughts. Phrased differently, we look at the incentives people have to continue their behavior.

The analysis so far tells how to find market exchanges in the early Roman Empire. But how many market exchanges are needed to make a market economy where most resources are allocated by prices that are free to move in response to changes in underlying conditions? There is no general answer to this question, for most economists deal with market economies and have no need to test its very existence. It is necessary to compare Rome with other economies to see the nature and extent of market exchanges in market economies. England and Holland in the seventeenth and eighteenth centuries, shortly before the Industrial Revolution, had economies that everyone agrees were market economies based on agriculture (de Vries and der Woude 1997; Mokyr 2009). Yet even in these market economies, a substantial part of marketed output was allocated by centric transfers rather than by market exchanges. Taxes in Britain were more than 10 percent of national income, and taxes in Holland were more than 40 percent of the income of unskilled laborers, of which about half came from excise taxes on goods consumed by workers. Some market exchanges also had characteristics of reciprocity and customary behavior. Large public works in both countries, primarily to drain land and (in Holland) contain the sea, were paid for by wealthy men, mostly but not exclusively large landowners. Nominal wages stayed constant for many years at a time in the market economy of early modern England, even though the price of grain fluctuated widely, suggesting that the "labor market" was at least partly an oxymoron; the employment relation often was reciprocal exchange (Phelps Brown and Hopkins 1981; O'Brien 1988; Floud and McCloskey 1997).

Even though there were extensive nonmarket transfers and exchanges, most resources in preindustrial Britain and Holland were allocated by markets. This can be seen by contrasting them with economies that were not primarily market economies. The feudal economy described by Bloch (1961) was a customary economy. Most transactions were made without prices as tenants worked on the lord's land part of the time and as vassals entertained lords to show their fealty. In addition, many transactions were centric transfers as tenants and vassals transferred resources—their labor or the produce of their tenants' labor—to lords in return for protection in the chaotic world of the medieval period. As obligations were written down and then commuted into money payments, the customary feudal economy developed into early modern market economies.

Centrally planned economies in twentieth-century Russia and China were command economies. Russian industries and Chinese farms were compelled to delivery quantities of goods according to a central plan. Prices in the Soviet Union were fixed for long periods of time. Planners expected firms to innovate out of the love of socialism. When that did not work, they set a higher, but still fixed, price for "new goods." Not surprisingly, many old goods were relabeled as new goods, and there was no increase in innovation (Berliner 1976). There were not even prices in the countryside of China until quite recently, as far as we can see, only production quotas. Only now that market reforms are being introduced are farmers selling produce for a price instead of delivering a quota.

There is no formal test to decide which kind of economy we are observing. The classification of these few economies should appear clear, which is why they were chosen. But for an economy about which we have fewer preconceptions we will need to ask several questions. Do the most important commodities, like food and lodging, have prices that move? Are there many transactions in which price appears to play a large part? Do prices move to clear markets? These questions will be answered affirmatively in succeeding chapters.

Before we get to that detail, we need to clarify the nature of what economists call markets and describe some useful economic tools. Markets were prominent in the ancient world; it will ease later discussions to clarify what a market is. The problem is that there is a popular definition and an economic definition, sowing confusion in historical discussions. The popular definition of a market is a place at which trade is conducted. The *Oxford English Dictionary* notes that the Roman forum was designated as a market in medieval writing. Markets now include fish markets, farmers markets, and supermarkets for food. In the modern world, most trade is directed via stores—distinguished from markets by having uniform, posted prices. Department stores arose in the mid-nineteenth century, and the initial function of prices was to let the store know how much the customer had paid and therefore the amount to be returned, not to inform the customer how much he or she would have to pay.

The stock market is located in a specific place on Wall Street, even though news of stock-market activity is all around us. It is considered to be a paragon of markets by economists because stock prices change the way competitive prices are expected to behave. Current prices embody all information about the stock to date. Future prices depend on future information and cannot be predicted. The best prediction of tomorrow's stock's price therefore is today's price. In mathematical terms, stock prices move as a random walk, that is, tomorrow's price is today's price plus a random (with today's knowledge) movement. I show in chapter 3 that agricultural prices in Hellenistic Babylon moved as a random walk, that is, that they behaved like modern market prices.

Now think of selling a house. We speak of putting our house on the market, but there is no place to take a house—and, of course, no way to take it even if there were such a place. The market in this case is a virtual or disembodied market. It is defined by the nature of the goods or services being sold rather than by where they are sold. This is the key to the economic use of the term, which focuses on the items being sold rather than the method of selling them.

People who anticipate buying or selling a house want to think about its price. To find a suitable range of prices, they look at the sale prices of other, similar houses. But what makes another house similar to this one? It might be location, the prime characteristic of all real estate, so that only local sales are relevant. Local sales might be those on the same street, in the same neighborhood, the same city, or the same country. They might be houses of the same size, or of the same age, or with the same kind of garden. They might even be houses of approximately the same putative value.

This highly ambiguous description is a key to how economists use the term *market*. All houses are in some sense in the same market, but some are closer substitutes for the house being sold than others. Economists argue roughly that houses are in the same market if the price of one affects the price of the other. This is the general idea, but the statement is not quite accurate. On one hand, the price of any single house cannot affect the price of any other in a perfectly competitive market, to be defined shortly, because there are so many similar houses in this kind of market that the sale of any one house has no effect on the market as a whole. On the other, the price of nearby apartments might affect the price of houses. We do not have to be very precise here; we stay with the idea of a market consisting of goods and services that compete with each other. The boundaries of such a market are unclear, and setting them provides employment for economists, but not for ancient historians.

Some historical cases are clear. The Romans dealt with the Chinese over the Silk Road, but travel was hard and long to get from one place to the other. Some goods were exchanged, and some imperfect knowledge of each party about the other went along the road, but the goods that were transported were hugely expensive at their destination, and the information was distorted. It is interesting to know about the Silk Road, but Rome and Han China were not in the same market (Liu 2010). "The two world empires remained hidden to each other in a twilight realm of fable and myth" (Bang 2009, 120).

Conditions on the Silk Road can be illustrated by the writings of Ibn Battuta, a traveler from the fourteenth century CE. He observed that Turkish tribes exported horses to India. The horse sold for about one dinar apiece in Asia, but for more than two hundred dinars in India (Gibb 1986, 145). It is unlikely that a price rise in Asia would affect the price in India. If the price doubled from one to two dinars, the price differential would hardly change. Prices differed by two orders of magnitude between Asia and India, and that shows that the two places were not in a common market. As shown in chapter 2, wheat prices around the Roman Mediterranean were all of the same magnitude, and very unlike the conditions of the Silk Road or fourteenth-century Asia and India.

Going from markets to a market economy adds another level of complexity to the discussion. When Hopkins (1978) described Rome as a slave society, he did not mean that everyone was a slave. Similarly, not every resource in a market economy is allocated through a market. In both cases, the terms indicate that slaves and markets were important, even dominant, institutions. In twentieth-century America—arguably the purest market economy in history—economists have estimated that one-third of economic activity in the United States today takes place within households, that is, in householding (Eisner 1989: 26). The proportion was even higher in the ancient world, but I argue that the economy of the early Roman Empire was a market economy because of the importance and prevalence of market activity (Temin 2001).

The consideration of societies can be made sharper by use of the New Institutional Economics (NIE). This body of thought grows out of a belated recognition by economists that institutions affect economic activity—and are in turn affected by economic pressures. Douglass North (1981; 1990) won a Nobel Prize for making this point over and over again. A paragraph in the earlier of these books says that Rome fell when it could no longer maintain property rights. This paragraph illustrates a weakness of the NIE. No ancient historian can take such a paragraph seriously. Was a decline in property rights a cause or an effect of the "decline of the Roman Empire"? How do you define or measure either of these concepts to find out?

We should not throw the baby out with the bathwater. The New Institutional

Economics helps focus attention on the institutions that govern activities in the ancient world, and it has given rise to some basic hypotheses that may be useful to explore when considering ancient institutions. For example, property rights have been found to promote economic growth by more systematic studies than North's. Acemoglu, Johnson, and Robinson (2001) made this assertion for modern colonies. They argued that colonies differed initially by the healthiness of European colonists. Where the Europeans survived, they brought with them European institutions. Where Europeans died frequently from new (to them) diseases, colonial leaders instituted what are called extractive institutions that did not guarantee private property, condoned bound service of various types, and enriched a small elite at the extent of the general population. Acemoglu, Johnson, and Robinson found that the effects of these initial conditions, indexed by European mortality, explain a substantial amount of income differences in former colonies today. This paper spawned an enormous literature, both because of its ideas and of a new indicator of institutions that avoided the chicken-and-egg problem in North's paragraph. (Economists speak of this chicken-and-egg problem as the identification problem, that is, the problem of identifying which is chicken and which is egg; see chapters 4 and 6.)

Another aid to economic activity is education. Like property rights, it often is hard to determine whether education is a cause or effect of economic growth and prosperity. The same goes for governments that keep corruption at a minimum and for the protection of intellectual rights, that is, the application of property rights to new discoveries. While all of these institutional factors raise similar identification problems, it is useful to set them out separately in order to see what kind of institutions dominated ancient societies. For example, chapters in Scheidel, Morris, and Saller (2007, part VII) describe regions of the Roman Empire, distinguishing them by their initial institutional background and making progress toward solving the identification problem. The western provinces contained few cities before the Roman conquest, and their economies were redirected after integration into the empire. The eastern Mediterranean provinces by contrast built on previous urban patterns, and Roman Egypt developed from its previous well-developed organization and its peculiar geography. Both Cicero and Trimalchio were educated, and they both worked in activities based on the existence of private property.

More difficult to measure but perhaps more important is the culture in which people operate. The Stoic tradition in Rome valued reciprocity in all actions. It made the fulfillment of contractual obligations a matter of personal honor. The effects of laws therefore were amplified by the actions of individuals. Even today, this informal culture promotes the smooth running of economic activities. Verboven (2002, 349) emphasized the role of the "moral economy" in Rome: "While conceptually reciprocity and market exchange may be opposed they not only coexist in reality but interact continuously. While the market economy profoundly influenced the operation of reciprocity relations and networks, the latter in turn influenced the market system." Reciprocity allowed people to engage in market activities in the expectation that the people they dealt with would fulfill their expectations and act to their mutual benefit. Although the NIE emphasizes the role of laws, the informal networks that underlie these laws are equally important. Wickham (2009, 31) records that these values were preserved by education as the Roman Empire declined, arguing that Roman literary culture held the empire together through shared knowledge and values. Laws, education, and culture are the institutions that make economies work well.

The importance of a shared culture in the modern world has been emphasized by Akerlof, a Nobel laureate for his work on asymmetric information, a key ingredient of the New Institutional Economics. He argued that people act to be connected to their chosen social group. They sometimes are forced into groups by virtue of their gender or race, but often people can choose their groups. Akerlof and Kranton (2010) illustrate this choice by an examination of high school students in the United States. The high school students divide into "jocks" and "nerds," who dress differently, talk differently, and associate largely with their own group. They argue that students have the ability to choose which group to join by considering the costs and benefits of the alternatives. Romans made similar choices when they chose to adhere to Stoic norms. The similarity is abundantly clear when comparing the Roman "economy of friends" and the efforts by the secretary of the U.S. Treasury in 2009, Henry Paulson, to work with his friends in the modern financial system to preserve their position as the global financial crisis spread (Verboven 2002; Paulson 2010).

There was far less information available to ancient people than to people in today's world. In fact, we may know more about the ancient economy than the ancients did, despite the paucity of evidence that has survived two millennia. The NIE focuses our attention on the lack of information and way that people try to deal with it. These concerns run through the following chapters, and in particular, chapter 5 on the grain trade is a contribution to the NIE. I will return to the problems of expensive information and asymmetric information—when one party to a transaction knows more than the other—many times. In order to explain a few basic economic tools, I assume in the rest of this chapter that information is freely available to all.

I also distinguish between personal and anonymous exchanges. The former is negotiated between a buyer and seller, possibly with a broker to facilitate the transaction. Most house purchases and sales, as well as most bazaar transactions, are of this type. Anonymous exchanges involve stated or posted prices that are available to any customers that come by. When we discuss the price of wheat in ancient Rome, we are referring to anonymous exchanges. Only if wheat had been sold in a bazaar for a different price to each purchaser would it be classified as personal exchange. In the abstractions of modern economics, all exchanges are anonymous.

One of the foundations of economic analysis is the separation of supply and demand. Both terms refer to schedules or curves relating the quantity supplied or demanded as a function of the relevant price. We have evidence of prices in the ancient world, and many of them appeared to vary as a result of changes in supply and demand. Some prices were fixed by administrative fiat of some sort, and some people were not aware of prices. I will discuss how to deal with the former; the latter can be dealt with by interpreting prices as an incentive to buy or sell. Economists speak of prices as shorthand for factors that provide incentives to supply or consume. University professors, for example, perform academic and administrative services for their departments and universities even when there are no explicit prices. The incentives to do so are informal, signifying reciprocity and customary behavior. Nevertheless, if the burden of doing these jobs gets large, professors will do less. If the rewards for these activities increase—say by enhancing chances for promotion or getting a better office—they will do more. This kind of enhanced price is harder to observe than a market price, but it functions in the same way.

We distinguish between supply and demand because it often is the case that different people are behind them. This was true particularly in Roman cities, where food was brought from farms located in the countryside and sometimes far away. It was true within cities when craftsmen made clothing or oil lamps for others to utilize. Robinson Crusoe, alone on his island, was both supplier and demander, but it even makes sense to distinguish him as producer (determining supply) and consumer (determining demand). The distinction helps to clarify the role of different forces affecting the allocation of resources even in such a simple economy (Temin 2012).

The quantity demanded generally increases when the price falls. At lower prices, people can consume more; their resources (in whatever form they take) go farther. In addition, people often want more when the price is lower; they may shift between goods to use more of the cheapest goods and leave some money left over for other things. If prices get much lower, then people may even think of new uses for a commodity. For example, the price of cotton fell dramatically in the Industrial Revolution, leading people to think of putting washable cotton sheets on the beds and cotton curtains on their windows.

These factors will differ in intensity for different goods, and economists use the concept of price elasticity to describe the extent to which the quantity demanded rises when the price declines. Unitary elasticity is defined to be when the proportional increase in the quantity demanded just equals the proportional decline in the price. Total expenditure stays the same. When the quantity demanded changes less than this, the demand curve is inelastic; when it changes more, demand is elastic. Demand is infinitely elastic if it is so elastic that even a very small change in price will lead to dramatic—even infinite—changes in the quantity demanded. In that case, the very high elasticity of demand keeps the price from varying. That is true in competitive markets, where the actions of any single person have no effect on the price. If the demand for houses, to return to the earlier example, is infinitely elastic, then the decision of any one person to put his or her house on the market will not have any effect on the price.

The quantity supplied generally increases when the price rises. As the price for a product increases, producers make and sell more. They can afford to use more inputs to produce their product, and they may enjoy greater return from the sale. The reasoning implicitly assumes that there are two inputs needed for production. Following a long tradition of classical economists, call them labor and land. If land is fixed, then increasing the number of workers will result in diminishing returns from each worker as more and more of them are added. It is diminishing returns that make the supply curve slope upward.

Supply and demand curves are shown in figure 1.1. Economists normally draw the quantity on the horizontal x-axis and price on the vertical y-axis, and I have followed that convention here. Since the demand curve slopes down and the supply curve slopes up, they generally cross. This is shown in the figure as happening at Q^* and P^*. What happens if the price is above P^*? The quantity of this good that producers want to sell is larger than Q^*, while the quantity that people want to buy is less than Q^*. Some of the goods produced will remain unsold, and producers will try to get rid of them. The easiest inducement for consumers to buy more is to reduce the price, and the price will fall if it is above P^*. Similarly, if the price is below P^*, people will want to buy more of the good than producers want to sell. Producers will see that they can sell almost as much as before—each individual producer may expect to sell as much as before—if they raise the price. It will rise as long as the price is below P^*. Only when the price equals P^* will it stay at that level. We therefore speak of P^* and Q^* as the equilibrium level of this market.

Why do economists use this framework? The first reason is to understand *changes* in prices or quantities. For example, the production of wheat increased in Roman times. Looking at figure 1.1, we see that the quantity is not likely to differ much from Q^* while the supply and demand curves stay the same. If the quantity of wheat produced rose substantially, we then can ask why it rose. We can ask if the supply curve, the demand curve, or both curves shifted to move Q^* to a new, higher level. Archaeological debates about innovations in agriculture focus on the supply curve, while thinking about feeding the city of

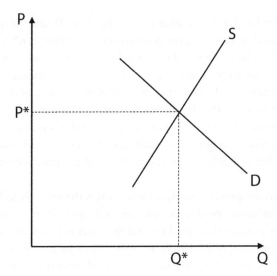

FIGURE 1.1. Supply and demand

Rome is concentrated on demand. Thinking about supply and demand enables us to integrate these disparate analyses.

Ancient historians may be wary of this framework because it appears to assume its conclusion. The motives imputed to buyers and sellers in the description of equilibrium assumed they were acting instrumentally and maximizing profits or satisfaction. Isn't that the same as assuming a market economy? No. Economic research into a variety of markets in industrial and agrarian economies has found that individuals today almost always want to better themselves. They act instrumentally to do so, although their actions often are constrained by the rules of society that are studied by the NIE so that they can improve their conditions a little, but not very much. The questions for ancient historians are largely whether the rules by which Roman society was organized were conducive or opposed to market activity. Supply and demand are useful even when rules did not seem directed toward economic affairs.

For example, a recent comparison of the supply and demand for wine and wheat in Republican Italy argued that there was not enough demand to support many large estates. It concluded that these markets were essentially competitive, earning limited profits for even large landowners and implying that "we must remove the aristocracy's formation of large, commercial estates from the central role they have long played in reconstructions of the social and economic developments in the middle and late Republic" (Rosenstein 2008, 23).

The forces of supply and demand operate even in reciprocity and redistribution. There are no explicit prices in these cases, but examples abound. The

Roman Senate gradually changed in the second century CE from a group of Italian senators to a group from the provinces (Eck 2000). The separation of supply and demand leads us to ask if this was due to conditions of supply (the scarcity of rich Italians) or instead to demand (a desire to have a wider representation in the Senate). Hopkins (1980) famously tried to estimate the GDP of the Roman Empire to show that the tax burden was light. He clearly was motivated by the presumption that rising taxation would have led to disaffection from the empire, that is, that it would have been harder to maintain the tax rate as its burden increased.

A second reason to use this supply and demand framework is to describe the way in which people made decisions. While the demand for Roman wheat might have risen, each Sicilian or Egyptian farmer would only have known what price—or tax rate—he faced. We have several surviving comments about the prevailing price of wheat, some in normal times and more in unusual ones. The presence of these prices indicates that both farmers and consumers knew what the price was. Since these prices typically were not for individual transactions, they also indicate the presence of anonymous exchanges. We have no way of knowing how widespread this information was, but the quotations suggest strongly that this was general information. It makes sense therefore to see farmers as facing a competitive market in which their output was too small to affect the price. They then made their choices on the basis of what they saw as a fixed market price, just as farmers do today. We can use the tools of a competitive market to analyze the behavior of Roman farmers, even though we do not presume that they—or many more recent farmers—consciously saw themselves in what we now call a competitive market.

A third reason is to examine administrative decisions to see if they were effective or not. For example, wheat was given away in early imperial Rome under the *annona*, the annual storage and distribution of wheat for the city of Rome, for free or a very low price. This price almost certainly was below P*, the price that would have prevailed if the wheat was bought on some kind of market. In that case, following the analysis of equilibrium, we expect that there should have been pressure from consumers for more free distribution than the authorities planned to give away. The program expanded over time, and this analysis provides one reason why it did.

Two extreme cases are often spoken of by economists. The first one is the infinitely elastic demand curve. As noted already, this is a characteristic of a competitive market, where there are many producers all trying to sell their products in the same market. Transport and transaction costs in the ancient world kept many producers from competing head-to-head with others, but the abstraction gives us a benchmark against which to evaluate what we observe. Given that there were lots of farmers, vineyards, olive presses, makers of oil lamps, etc., the assumption of a competitive market can be very useful. We can show that condition in figure 1.1 by making the demand curve horizontal.

The second extreme case is when supply is completely inelastic, that is, the supply curve is vertical. A vertical supply curve says that the amount supplied is independent of the price. Paying a high amount or almost nothing will not affect how much is supplied. The most prominent example of this condition is agricultural land. When the Antonine and Justinian plagues struck the ancient world, they decreased the number of farmers, but they had no effect on the quantity of farmland. With fewer farmers seeking to work on the same amount of land, the price of land fell. Since the fall did not affect the quantity of land, we speak of this price as a rent, that is, a price that does not affect the allocation of resources. The more inelastically a good is supplied, the more its price resembles rent.

Rent seeking in the NIE consists of activities designed to capture economic rents. They do not encourage productive activity, but rather contest the returns to inelastically supplied goods and services. A thief, for example, does not produce anything; he steals things. In other words, he changes the ownership of existing resources, which is known as rent seeking. If we undertake activities like locking our houses or hiring body guards to deter thieves or assassins, that also is rent seeking. These preventive activities redirect activities that could be productive into unproductive pursuits; locks and guards are only used if thieves try to steal our possessions or others want to harm us. The existence of rent seeking causes the costs of purchasing to exceed the return from selling it; this discrepancy gives rise to what we call transaction costs, which include both rent seeking and anything else—like transport or information costs—that introduce a gap between the selling and buying price.

The analysis so far has treated an isolated market. There are many markets, and we need to analyze what happens when different markets come into contact. Ricardo presented the theory of comparative advantage two hundred years ago; it has lasted as one of the most convincing argument in economics, showing how trade can benefit both partners. It is a simple theory, but it requires a little background to be understood. The theory of comparative advantage is so important that it has given rise to its own branch of economics: international economics. I will use the language of international economics here, talking of countries and regions trading with each other, but the analysis is only an extension of the supply-and-demand analysis already covered.

Every country has what economists call a production possibility frontier, or PPF. The PPF shows how much of any one good or service can be produced, given how much of the other goods and services are being made. This relationship is best seen in two dimensions, assuming that a country makes only two products. Let us call them wine and wheat. If we put wine on the vertical axis

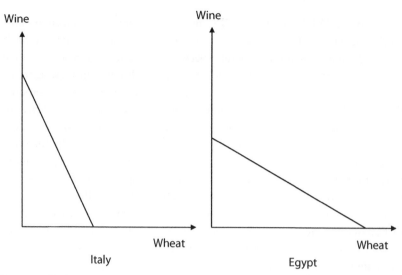

FIGURE 1.2. Production possibility curve

and wheat on the horizontal axis, we can draw a country's PPF. It will touch each axis where the country devotes all of its resources to the production of either wine or wheat, that is, if it specializes in one or the other. The PPF connects these two points. Ricardo assumed it ran in a straight line, assuming that the amount of wheat that needed to be given up to produce an extra unit of wine was not affected by the amount of wheat and wine being produced. He assumed there was a single input to production—call it labor—which was easily switched between the production of various goods. There was no second input like land and no diminishing returns like those introduced earlier to explain and upward-sloping supply curve.

This relationship is shown in figure 1.2. I show in this figure a PPF for each of two countries or regions that might trade with each other. The curves differ from one region to the other, even though both embody the same linear assumption. They differ in their slope. (The other possible difference—in height—will be discussed later.) One region, which we will call Italy, can make more wine more efficiently in terms of forgone wheat than the other region, which we will call Egypt. Egypt is well suited to growing wheat and needs to transfer a lot of resources from growing wheat to increase its wine production. The PPF for Italy therefore is steeper than the PPF for Egypt. (Note that another factor of production, land, has crept into the analysis to explain why countries differ.)

Consider the PPF for Italy. Where the PPF hits the vertical y-axis it shows how much wine would be produced in Italy if all the labor in Italy was used to produce wine. Where the Italian PPF hits the horizontal x-axis, it shows how much wheat would be produced if all the labor was used to produce wheat. If Italian agriculture is not completely specialized in wine or wheat, then total Italian production is shown by a point on the PPF between these extreme positions. The slope of the PPF shows the (constant) amount of one product that has to be forgone to produce more of the other. The ratio of the prices of the two goods is the *inverse* of this slope. Since Italy can make so much wine if it chooses to specialize in wine production, wine is cheap in Italy. The same reasoning applies to Egypt, where the PPF is flatter because Egypt is more suited to growing wheat. Wine therefore is more expensive in Egypt than in Italy because wine is scarcer—as represented by the flatter PPF.

It is the difference in the steepness of the PPF between the two countries that allows them to have comparative advantages and gains from trade. I have drawn the curves about the same level, but nothing rests on that. Assume for a minute that Italy is more efficient at producing both wine and wheat than Egypt. If the two PPF curves have different steepness, it still will be worthwhile to trade. For example, consider a lawyer who is the best lawyer in town and also the best typist. She has an absolute advantage over her secretary, even though the secretary has a comparative advantage in typing. The secretary can do a lot of typing for each unit of law services he omits, even though he does less legal work and typing than the lawyer in any time period. It makes sense for the lawyer to specialize in doing law and delegate her typing to her secretary, even though she is better at both. Despite the lawyer's absolute advantage in both activities, she still can gain by exploiting her *comparative* advantage in legal services.

Return to figure 1.2. If there is a market, then the price of wine in terms of wheat will be higher in Egypt than in Italy, since the PPF is flatter. If farmers cannot sell wheat on any kind of market, they will make the choice of product by comparing the relative outputs they can get from their limited resources. We can express this choice as expressing what economists call the "opportunity cost" of producing wheat or wine. That is the amount of the product *not* grown in order to produce the one that is grown. The opportunity cost functions exactly the way the price does in a market, and I use price as a generic term to include both market prices and opportunity costs. Egyptian farmers would like to produce wine due to its high price; the flat PPF shows that they cannot do so with Egyptian resources.

Now assume that trade is introduced between Italy and Egypt. Wine is more expensive in wheat units in Egypt because the opportunity cost of producing wine is larger than in Italy. Egyptians then will want to export wheat to get wine, which is relatively cheaper in Italy. Italians face exactly the opposite incentives. Wine can be produced easily in Italy, and the Italians will be happy

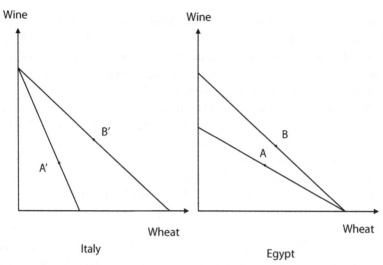

FIGURE 1.3. Effects of trade

to import wheat which is harder to grow (relative to wine). Trade will make both countries or regions better off.

The benefits are shown in figure 1.3. The price of wine was higher in Egypt before trade, and the price of wheat was higher in Italy. Once trade is allowed, both countries will have the same price ratio (in the absence of transport costs), which will be in between the initial price ratios in Italy and Egypt. The price of wine will fall in Egypt, allowing people there to get more wine for a given opportunity cost in wheat. Italy will use its resources to produce wine, getting its wheat by importing it. The initial consumption might have been at a point like A on the Italian PPF. With trade, Italy can now consume at point B, above the PPF and unobtainable without trade. Similarly, Egypt will use its resources to produce wheat and increase its consumption of wine and wheat from A' to B'. The price of wheat in terms of wine will fall in Italy, and rise in Egypt. The price of wheat in terms of wine, or of wine in terms of wheat, will be the same in both countries.

Adam Smith wrote that the division of labor was limited by the extent of the market. Trade extends the market between countries or regions and thereby promotes the division of labor. This is one way in which the extension of trade increases the earning of workers. Of course, if different regions or countries have resources unique to that locale, trade also allows these resources to be used for the benefit of the whole trading area (chapter 2).

Three extensions of this basic theory should be mentioned. First, what will be the new, common price of wine in terms of wheat? We know only that it must be between the original prices in Italy and Egypt, and the theory explained here does not contain enough detail to demonstrate where it will fall in this range. The position depends on the volume and elasticity of supply and demand for the two goods in the two countries or regions. In particular, large countries or regions that have large supplies and demands have much more effect on the eventual price than small countries. (This is where the height of the PPF is important.) When Britain was brought into the Roman trade network, it got many more gains from trade than the rest of the Roman world. Interregional trade benefits both regions, but taxes may offset form of the gains. For example, much of the wheat sent to Rome from Egypt was tribute. We clarify the effects of this tribute by dividing it into two parts. Trade improved access to all products in both Rome and Egypt. Tribute transferred some—or perhaps all—of this gain from Egypt to Rome.

Second, the model as stated assumes that there are no transport costs when trade is allowed. That is why the price lines with trade in figure 1.3 have the same slope in both graphs, indicating that the relative prices of wine and wheat were the same in Italy and Egypt. In antiquity, transport costs often were quite high, both because of the cost of transporting goods and because of administrative costs like duties and verification. If there are significant transport costs, the price ratios in the two countries will not approach equality. Instead, they will remain apart by the cost of the transport. If this wedge is large enough, it may preclude trade even if the costs of production in the two countries are different.

Transaction costs never completely eliminate trade. Very rare and expensive goods can be traded profitably even if transaction costs are high. Before the Pax Romana, jewelry and royal objects were traded around the known world. But high transaction costs prevented trade in cheaper goods, like wheat. Only when costs were low did trade extend to bulk commodities and the articles of common usage. This kind of trade flourished in the early Roman Empire, but it had existed earlier across the Mediterranean Sea. Two Phoenician ships sank in deep water during the eighth century BCE, each carrying four hundred amphoras of wine. Their documentation has been lost, and we do not know why they were sailing, but it makes sense to infer that the people who sent eight hundred amphoras of wine into the center of the Mediterranean were engaged in interregional trade (Temin 2006c).

The New Institutional Economics reminds us that transaction costs may be affected by institutions as well as transport costs. Trade requires not only shops or carts, but also ways to compensate prospective merchants for their efforts in bringing goods to strangers. The means of payments, the security of contracts— even implicit ones—are aspects of the institutions that promote trade.

Third, Ricardo drew the PPF as a straight line, but economists now generally draw it curving above a straight line. A convex PPF describes an economy in which there are diminishing returns to the production of wine and wheat. Here we consider two inputs to production, land and labor. If land cannot be transferred easily between different crops, there will be diminishing returns to labor in each activity. (This is the assumption that makes supply curves slope upward.) As the economy moves away from specialization in, say, wheat, it produces the first unit of wine by sacrificing only a tiny bit of wheat. In a position away from the axes where the economy is producing both wine and wheat, the economy has to give up a larger amount of wheat to free enough resources to make more wine. The gains from trade are the same as before with this complication, assuming that the internal price ratio of the goods differed initially in the two countries. The difference is that while countries will concentrate in the production of goods where they have a comparative advantage, they generally will continue to produce some of the other good as well. They will only specialize completely as shown in figure 1.3 if the cost structures in the two countries are very different.

Ricardo knew about diminishing returns; the rents to factors with inelastic supply curves often are known as Ricardian rents. But mathematics was not developed well enough two hundred years ago when Ricardo was writing for him to draw better diagrams. The necessary changes are shown in figure 1.4. In this diagram, the effect of land is shown directly as a cause of diminishing returns, not simply as a determinant of regional differences. The result is that the PPF for each region is curved. If all the labor is used for one or the other crop, there will be diminishing returns, and there will not be as much output as shown in figure 1.3. The initial price lines are now only tangent to the PPF at one point. That point shows where the PPF reaches the highest price line possible to maximize production at this relative price. As before, the initial points of production are labeled A and A'.

With diminishing returns, the effects of international trade are not as dramatic as before. As prices in both regions approach each other, each region moves along its PPF to reach the highest price line showing the new, international relative price. As before, consumption is now at B and B', above each country's PPF. Trade has allowed each region to benefit more than it could from using its resources in isolation. The basic insight of comparative advantage is maintained with this elaboration of Ricardo's theory.

There is, however, one important detail revealed by figure 1.4. Instead of going to a corner solution where each region produces only one product, each region goes only partway toward the relevant axis, to points C and C' in figure 1.4. Both regions specialize in the sense that they produce more of their export good, but they do not abandon production of their import goods due to diminishing returns in the export industry. In figure 1.3, each region was either isolated or completely specialized. In the more realistic figure 1.4, both regions

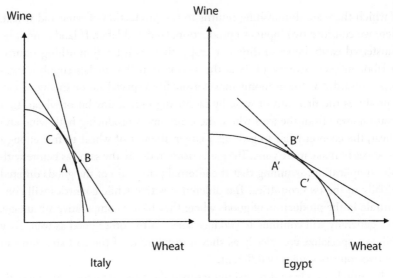

FIGURE 1.4. Effects of trade with diminishing returns

continue to produce both goods even after trade is introduced. Only if the production possibility frontiers are very different in the two regions or close to flat will there be complete specialization.

This is the form of comparative advantage taught universally today. Supply and demand curves provide tools for the understanding exchanges of individual commodities or services, whether through markets or other arrangements. The New Institutional Economics helps to evaluate the operation of markets. Comparative advantage provides a way to understand the economic interactions of regions, whether through markets or other kinds of transfers, illuminating the effects of the *Pax Romana*, the changing composition of production in Roman Italy, and economic expansion in the early Roman Empire. I show in the following chapters that a substantial part—perhaps most—of Roman exchanges were accomplished through markets, resulting in substantial improvements of living standards, particularly in Roman Italy.

Part I

· · ·

Prices

Part I

· · ·

Prices

Introduction

. . . .

Data and Hypothesis Tests

The Romans talked and wrote constantly about prices. It seems obvious that they must have been using these prices in their daily lives to leave us so many price quotes. Yet there has been doubt over the years whether the Roman economy was dominated by markets. I reviewed a small corner of this debate in chapter 1, and I turn in this section to documenting some of the assertions made there.

While there is lots of information about prices and transactions, there is little of what economists call data. Data, as economists consider it, consist of a set of uniform prices that can be compared with each other. Econometricians have developed many tools for extracting information from data, but they all depend on having some data to work with. The chapters in this section use econometric tools to analyze ancient data and discuss various problems that arise in this somewhat paradoxical effort.

The aim of data analysis is to test hypotheses. I defined markets in chapter 1; can we find evidence that markets existed in ancient times? There are many prices; were they used the way modern prices are used to signal the availability of items to purchase? And if conditions change, can we distinguish between possible causes for the change? Each chapter in this section confronts one of these questions and focuses on one major problem of dealing with ancient price data.

I test the proposition that extensive markets existed in the late Roman Republic and early Roman Empire in chapter 2. Even though there is a lack of data, there are enough observations for the price of wheat, the most extensively traded commodity, to perform a test. The problem is that there is only a little bit of data by modern standards. Consequently, I explain in chapter 2 why statistics are useful in interpreting small data sets and how one deals with various problems that arise when there are only a few data points.

To find a larger data set, I examined Hellenistic prices in Babylon in chapter 3. True, this is the wrong time and place for my main interest, but it is not far in either dimension, and a large data set has survived from Hellenistic Babylon. I can test more sophisticated hypotheses with this wealth of data. In particular, I look at price behavior to see if the prices moved over time in the way that modern prices appear to move. Even a large data set has problems, and the problem with this data set is missing observations. While there are lots of prices, they are spread over many years, and there are holes in the coverage of time. I propose a way to overcome the unevenness of the data and test whether these prices are records of market conditions.

I take a different tack in chapter 4. Instead of finding a coherent set of prices to measure Roman inflation, I take the scattered data that have survived to make an index of inflation. The index cannot describe the details of inflation, but it allows comparison between periods of time. In chapter 4, I test the hypothesis that the persistent inflation of the late Roman Empire came from political instability at the top of the empire. The test raises an important problem in going from correlation to causation; the problem is known as the identification problem: how can we decide what is cause and what is effect when looking at economic data?

I discuss the identification problem in chapter 4 and propose what economists call an identification strategy to suggest how Roman inflation got its start in the late second century. I then go behind the index of inflation I proposed to suggest how people living at the time might have experienced the apparently persistent inflation. I use regressions reminiscent of those in chapter 2 to set the stage for this explanation. Although there are scarcely more data in these regressions than in the ones in chapter 2, it is noteworthy that these are far less controversial among ancient historians. It may be that ancient historians do not object to regressions, but instead are reluctant to use these tools to settle traditional arguments in the interpretation of the Roman economy.

Chapter 2

■ ■ ■

Wheat Prices and Trade in the Early Roman Empire

Most ancient historians are comfortable with the idea that there were local markets in the late Roman Republic and the early Roman Empire. There are many documents attesting to purchases of local goods and services both in Rome and outlying areas. Any assertion that these local markets were tied together into a series of interdependent markets is more controversial, as noted in chapter 1. I use wheat prices in this chapter to test the proposition that many wheat markets across the Mediterranean were interconnected and interdependent.

The theory of comparative advantage described in chapter 1 implies that there were advantages to regional specialization in ancient Rome. The Romans put considerable effort into unifying the Mediterranean and clearing out pirates that impeded peaceful shipping. One purpose of that effort was to exploit the comparative advantage of different parts of the ancient world. As Erdkamp (2005, 207) noted, "Late Republican and early Imperial sources indicate that grain from almost the entire Mediterranean world arrived at Rome." As noted in chapter 1, this interregional trade made everyone better off, although taxes on the provinces may have concentrated the benefits onto Rome itself. I argue for integrated wheat markets in this chapter and explore the implications for Roman incomes in chapter 11.

I show first that there was an enormous amount of wheat moving around the Mediterranean in the few centuries surrounding the beginning of this era. Most of this wheat was being sent, carried, and received by private merchants. So far, this is not terribly controversial, and more details of merchant activities will be described in chapter 5. I then extend the work of Hopkins (1980), Rathbone (1991), and Wilson (2008, 2009b) to show that many markets in distant places were linked by prices, that is, that prices around the Mediterranean were determined by those in Rome. This relationship is very unlikely to be the result of chance. It provides new evidence of a set of interconnected Mediterranean markets. I use two overlapping data sets of prices from Rickman (1980) and Rathbone (2011) to reveal the extensive Mediterranean market and some of its limitations.

This view conflicts with those expressed by Erdkamp (2005). He argued that "the corn market seems largely to have operated within restricted, sometimes isolated regions" (Erdkamp 2005, 204). Although there is much to be admired in his book, he appears confused on this point. He noted that wheat prices were higher in Rome than in other cities, but also that "the degree of connectivity should not be exaggerated, even along the Mediterranean coasts of the Roman Empire" (Erdkamp 2005, 194–95). These two statements are inconsistent; wheat prices were higher in Rome precisely because many wheat markets around the Roman Mediterranean were highly connected.

Ancient historians have been misled by facile comparisons with early modern Europe. Persson (1999, 100) noted that "not until the mid-nineteenth century when the modern information and transport systems have emerged do we find evidence of swifter adjustment to shocks." Before then many European grain markets were subject to separate shocks and moved rather independently, as ancient historians claim did ancient grain markets. This comparison neglects the important geographic difference between the Roman Empire and early modern Europe. Trade within early modern Europe was over land, while the Mediterranean Sea was the center of the Roman Empire. It was far cheaper to ship goods by sea than over land before the advent of the railroad, and Rome had a far better chance of having an integrated grain market than early modern Europe.

Rome was a large city, probably the largest European city to exist before the Industrial Revolution. Its residents had to eat, and their diet was based on wheat, wine, oil, and dry legumes. Garnsey (1998, 240–42) argued that lentils, chickpeas, and broad beans were an important source of protein in the diet of common Roman people even if the bulk of their calories came from wheat. These products could not be grown in garden plots behind their houses; there was no room in a city. Some, particularly the legumes, might be grown near Rome, but there is abundant evidence that wheat was imported from Sicily, Spain, Egypt and North Africa. Oil also was imported from Africa and wine from Spain. There clearly was specialization of production around the Roman Mediterranean, and these agricultural products then were transported to Rome. How big was this transport of goods? It is even harder to find information on quantities than it is to find data on prices. The best we can hope to do is to make reasonable guesses about the magnitudes involved, focusing on grain since the evidence there is relatively most abundant. Given how large the city of Rome appears to have been, other food imports must have been large as well. That may be the only defensible statement, but I will try to be slightly more precise.

Hopkins (1978) suggested that the population of Rome was around 1 million. This estimate derives from *Rex Gestae*, stating that there were 250,000 free males over the age of ten in Rome around 1 CE. Hopkins expanded this estimate to 670,000 to 770,000 free people, with a preference for the higher figure. Adding an addition 70,000 soldiers and slaves brought the total to around 1 million. This remains the consensus estimate of Roman population, although it may be correct only to a single significant digit.

Brunt (1971) started from the number of free men receiving the annona, the free distribution of food in Rome, in 58 BCE, doubled the number to get the number of free men and women, and added 100,000 to 200,000 slaves. This provided a total of 600,000 to 840,000 people, and Brunt took the average, 750,000 as his estimate of the total population of Rome. Rickman (1980) started from the census of 5 BCE that reported 320,000 free adult males in Rome. He added 400,000 women and children and 200,000 slaves to bring the total close to Hopkins's estimate. Garnsey (1998, 191 fn. 26) and Scheidel (2004) also adopted Hopkins's estimate.

To go from the population to the consumption of wheat, we need an estimate of per capita wheat consumption. This measure appears less controversial than the size of the population, perhaps because it matters less to most historians. The range is between thirty *modii* per year as suggested by Garnsey (1998, 191) and forty modii per year as suggested by Rickman (1980, 10). This gives an annual consumption of wheat in Rome between 30 and 40 million modii a year.

Rathbone (2003b, 201) estimated that the average interprovincial ship of a medium size carried around ten thousand modii of wheat. He derived this estimate from "thin but nicely random" data and said that larger ships would have been used on the main large-scale routes such as the feeding of Rome. Using the average size of ships and the upper bound of Roman consumption to get a maximum number of trips, these estimates imply that it would have taken at least four thousand ship voyages to feed Rome every year. Since ships could make multiple trips in the roughly eight months a year when most trade took place, this implies that about 2,000 ships were needed to feed Rome. While we lack any good evidence on the total size of the Roman merchant fleet, this does not seem an unreasonable number.

The Romans ferried their grain from Ostia to Rome on barges that held about as much as an average sea-going ship. The trip, however, was much shorter, possibly taking only three days. It consequently would require a far smaller fleet of barges than of ships to bring wheat to Rome. River shipping may not have been much safer; almost three hundred barges were lost in a few days of 62 CE when two hundred sank in a storm at Ostia and one hundred more burned accidentally at Roman docks. Tacitus (*Ann*. 15) reported that there was no panic or even concern in Rome at this apparent disaster, and the supply of barges does not appear to have been a constraint on the transport of wheat to Rome.

Numerous large granaries in Ostia also provided a buffer for the market; grain could be stored if more grain arrived than was needed at Rome, and grain could be supplied from the granaries if ships did not arrive. Rickman (1971) described the granaries in detail. There were at least thirteen large granaries in Ostia, extending in size up to the huge and private *Horrea di Hortensius*, which covered 5,000 square meters. Rome clearly had developed the infrastructure needed to feed its large population.

Did the government operate all these facilities directly or were they the fruit of private initiative? The quick answer is that neither the republican government nor the early imperial governments were large enough to handle all this trade by themselves. Much of the process of feeding Rome had to be private. A more detailed answer involves considering government activities and comparing them with the total size of the wheat market.

The largest government activity was the annona. The government gave 60 modii per year to each male head of a household. The number of households receiving this largess is unclear, but it is generally thought to be between 200,000 and 250,000 during the reign of Augustus (Virlouvet 1995; Garnsey 1998, 236). That would make the total amount of wheat needed for the annona around 12 to 15 million modii. Taking the largest recipient population and the smallest total consumption, the annona used about half of the wheat imported into Rome. If the smaller recipient population and the larger total consumption are more accurate, the share falls to around one quarter. At least half of the wheat imported to Rome at the time of Augustus, and probably more, therefore was imported privately. Sirks (1991, 21) argued that the share of grain imported into Rome for the annona was even less, only around 15 percent, making the private share correspondingly larger.

The government transported the wheat for the annona privately. They let contracts to *societates* to provide wheat, and they offered inducements for private merchants to participate in this process. Claudius rewarded private merchants who used their own ships, carrying at least 10,000 modii, to import grain to Rome for five years in various ways. If the merchant was a citizen, he would be exempt from the *lex Papia Poppaea*, which penalized the childless. If the merchant was a woman, she could make a will without the intervention of a male tutor. And if the merchant was not a citizen, he would be granted citizenship. Hadrian extended these rewards by exempting any merchant devoting the greater part of his resources to the annona from compulsory services imposed by municipal authorities (Badian 1983; Garnsey 1988, 234; Sirks 1991, 63).

The limited size of the annona relative to the total food consumption and the government's use of private merchants to get the supplies for the annona imply that the grand bulk of the grain brought to Rome came by the agency of private merchants. But although the government was not active in the provision of wheat during normal years, it did intervene in the wheat market when there was a shortage. The government supplemented the annona with attempts to avoid the hardships of price spikes when supplies ran short. In 74 BCE, the government sold grain cheaply to offset the loss of wheat in Sicilian floods. In 57 BCE Pompey negotiated extra purchases himself, sailing from province to province in search of wheat. In 24 BCE Augustus gave four hundred HS (HS standing for *sestertii*, the common Roman brass currency equal to one-fourth of silver denarii) apiece to 250,000 people, allowing them to purchase wheat that was temporarily expensive. In 19 CE Tiberius placed a price ceiling on grain and offered to compensate merchants two HS per *modius*, equal to about 6.5 kilograms, suggesting that the price before his intervention was at least two HS above the price he thought people could bear. In 64 CE Nero set another price ceiling for wheat, this time at three HS per modius (Garnsey 1988, 195–222; Rickman 1980, 150–54).

Government interventions like these are summarized in table 2.1. It is clear that the government intervened in the wheat market from time to time, particularly under Augustus. It also is clear, even from what must be a partial list, that these interventions were intermittent. Even if we assume that these interventions are only half of the actual actions, the others being unrecorded in our sources, the years in which there were interventions were still clearly a minority. In most years the market for wheat was allowed to work on its own.

Erdkamp (2005, 256–57) concluded after surveying this mixed system that "free trade in the Empire's capital operated in the margins of a system that was characterized by public supply channels." Nonetheless, he acknowledged that prices rose when grain was scarce, official interventions like those in table 2.1 were abnormal, and the price at which wheat was sold in Rome ordinarily was free of government intervention. The periodic interventions shown in table 2.1 may have even improved the market in other years by creating anticipations that restrictions of supply would not be tolerated. If so, these interventions may have facilitated the operation of the private market by discouraging hoarding and other noncompetitive actions. The question then is whether the resulting actions of Roman merchants created an integrated set of wheat markets in the Mediterranean? Despite the absence of good price series, it turns out that there are enough prices to provide an answer.

TABLE 2.1.
Selected government interventions in the grain market

Date	Intervention type	Source
138 BCE	Rising prices lead tribunes to seek extra grain supplies.	Obsequens 22 (142).
129 BCE	Aedile arranges from grain to be shipped from Thessaly to Rome.	Plutarch, *Cato Maior* 8.1.
100 BCE	Feared shortage leads Senate to seek extra grain stock.	M. H. Crawford, *Roman Republican Coinage: Volume 2* (Cambridge: CUP, 1974), 74 and 616.
75 BCE	1½ *modii* distributed free per man given shortage.	Cicero, *Planc.* 64. Cicero, *2 Verr*, 3.215.
74 BCE	Aedile distributes grain at 1 AS per modius.	Pliny, *Hist nat.* 18.16.
66 BCE	Pompey tours Sicily, Africa, and Sardinia to secure extra grain in his capacity as grain commissioner.	Cicero, *Imp. Pomp.*, 34.
62 BCE	Cato's Lex Porcia raises grain outlay to 30 million HS or adds that much to the budget.	Plutarch, *Cato Min.* 26.1
58-56 BCE	Cicero appoints Pompey for grain supply, price falls.	Cicero, *Dom.* 10-12, 14-18; *Att.* 4.1; Cassius Dio, 39.9.3, 24.1; Cicero, *Q. fr.* 2.5; *Har. resp.* 31; Plutarch, *Pomp*, 49.4-50.2
49 BCE	Caesar distributes grain to starving Romans during the civil war (Garnsey 1988, 202).	Cicero, *Att.* 7.9.2, 4; 9.9.4; *Fam.* 14.7.3; Appian, *Bell. civ.* 2.48; Cassius Dio 41.16.1
24 BCE	Augustus gives 400 HS to 250,000 people.	*Res gest.*, 15.
24 BCE	Augustus gives 400 HS to 250,000 people.	*Res gest.*, 15.

TABLE 2.1.
(*continued*)

Date	Intervention type	Source
23 BCE	Augustus gives money and "12 rations" to 250,000 people. Tiberius also helps, and Suetonius says he "skillfully regulated the difficulties of the grain supply and relieved the scarcity of grain at Ostia and in the city."	*Res gest.*, 15. Suetonius, *Tib.* 8.
22 BCE	Augustus gives grain to many.	*Res gest.*, 5.
18 BCE	Augustus gives grain to at least 100,000.	*Res gest.*, 18.
11 BCE	Augustus gives 400 HS to 250,000 people.	*Res gest.*, 15.
5 BCE	Augustus gives 240 HS to 320,000 people.	*Res gest.*, 15.
2 BCE	Augustus gives 240 HS to 200,000 people.	*Res gest.*, 15.
6 CE	Augustus gives grain to many. Also expels some foreigners from the city to alleviate the crisis. (Garnsey 1988, 221)	Cassius Dio 55.22.3.
19 CE	Tiberius imposes price ceiling, gives dealers + 2 HS.	Tacitus, *Ann.*, 2.87.1.
51 CE	Claudius encourages merchants to sail in winter. (Garnsey 1988, 223)	Tacitus, *Ann.*, 12.43.
64 CE	Nero fixes price at 3 HS, *annona* suspended.	Tacitus, *Ann.*, 15.39.3.
189 CE	Commodus engages in price-fixing.	Herodian 1.12.2-4; Cassius Dio 72.13.2.

If there had been a unified wheat market, the main market would have been in Rome, where the largest number of potential consumers lived and the Roman government was located. In other words, Rome was where the largest supplies and demands for wheat would have come together and where the price of wheat consequently would have been set. The price would have varied over time as supplies fluctuated due to harvests across the Roman world, storms affected the cost of transportation, and government actions altered the value of the currency. Normal variations in supplies and demands elsewhere in the empire would have affected the price, although most fluctuations would have been small relative to the total production and the consumption at Rome. Most places outside of Rome would have had an excess supply of wheat, and the price would have been set in Rome where the excess supplies and the largest excess demand came together. When local places were isolated, there could have been excess local demand as well as excess local supply, that is, local famines as well as local gluts.

Under these circumstances, wheat outside of Rome would be valued by what it was worth in Rome. Wheat at Palermo in Sicily, for example, normally would be worth less than wheat in Rome because it would have to be transported to Rome to be sold. The price of wheat in Sicily would be the price of wheat in Rome less the cost of getting wheat from Sicily to Rome. This would be true almost always, but there undoubtedly were circumstances when it was not. If storms prevented the shipment of grain to Rome, the Sicilian price might temporarily deviate from the level set by the price in Rome. If a harvest failure in Sicily created a local famine, the price of wheat in Sicily would rise above the level indicated by the Roman price until new wheat supplies could be brought in. In the absence of extreme events like these, a unified market would keep Sicilian prices near the Roman price less the transportation cost.

The market is an abstraction, as noted in chapter 1; it is misleading to say the market would determine Sicilian prices. More accurately, competition would determine Sicilian prices if there was a unified market. If the Sicilian price of wheat rose above the Roman level minus transportation costs, it would not make sense for merchants to buy wheat in Sicily to sell in Rome. The amount of wheat demanded in Sicily would fall, and the price consequently would fall as well. If the Sicilian price of wheat fell below the Roman level minus transportation costs, merchants would increase the amount of wheat they would buy in Sicily, for they could make an unusually high profit by taking it to Rome and selling it there. Merchants would bid against each other, raising the Sicilian price as described for general supplies and demands in chapter 1.

Wheat at Lusitania in Spain would be worth less than wheat at Palermo because it was further from Rome. The cost of transporting wheat from Spain to Rome was larger than the cost of bringing it from Sicily, and the price of wheat in Spain correspondingly would be lower. The reasoning is exactly like that for Sicily, only the transport cost is different. But while each price is compared to that in Rome, the price in Spain would be lower than the price in Sicily if there were a unified market. In fact, wheat around the Mediterranean would be worth less than the price at Rome, with the amount less depending on the distance from Rome. We do not know the transport cost in any detail, but we are reasonably sure that it rose with distance. If there was a unified wheat market, therefore, the price of wheat would have decreased as one moved farther and farther from Rome.

All this sounds very abstract. But if it is not an accurate picture of the Roman world, we need to think of the relevant alternative. If there were not a unified market, if there were only independent local markets, then there would not be any relationship between local and Roman prices. There would be prices in local markets that would be determined by local conditions. The prices might move together at some times, if storms across the Mediterranean caused simultaneous harvest failures everywhere or currency debasements caused prices to rise everywhere, but they would not in general be related one to another; any single identity of prices could be a coincidence. If we find several wheat prices in different places, we can test whether the pattern we find is due to coincidence or an underlying market process.

It is hardly necessary for all merchants to be trying to arbitrage prices to bring them into relation with each other. Most participants in most markets simply do today what they did yesterday. Markets work when there are a few arbitrageurs that act as described here; Pompey, as he sailed around to find scarce wheat, was arbitraging prices. There is no theory of how many participants need to arbitrage prices to get to the equilibriums described in chapter 1. With modern computer technology, a few people with a lot of band width can make money and coax even large markets into equilibrium. They also can go broke if they guess wrong where the equilibrium is, as Long Term Capital Management did spectacularly in 1998. In ancient Rome, a dozen or two merchants in each market might have been enough to bring local prices into a relation with Roman prices.

The question is not whether one or the other of these ideal types was observed, whether there was an efficient market or that there were no factors unifying separate local markets. It is rather whether the historical experience lies closer to one end of a continuum than the other. The interventions noted for Rome in table 2.1 were echoed by local actions elsewhere around the Mediterranean. There must have been at least occasional local grain shortages and even famines. The question then is whether the normal state of affairs was one of interconnected markets, so that prices in different places typically were related, or one of separated and independent markets. In the latter case, we should not observe any systematic relationship between the location and the price of grain.

I approach this test in two steps, the first of which uses a small set of wheat prices from varied locations from Rickman (1980). This familiar sample provides a way to examine monetary integration at least provisionally. When dealing with fragmentary data it is necessary to collect a sample that is not determined by the desired outcome. Rickman was writing about the Roman wheat market, and he collected his sample to show habitual prices in different places. The sample, albeit small, therefore looks like a random sample. It is, in Rathbone's felicitous phrase, "thin but nicely random." We cannot be completely sure that the prices Rickman selected or that survived to be collected are completely random, but they may be as close to random as we can get for Roman history. The second step is to check these results with a new data set in Rathbone (2011). These data were collected to exhibit the surviving prices from around the Mediterranean. They overlap Rickman's sample, but the two authors made different choices in collecting data that allow us to delimit more precisely the extent of the Roman Mediterranean wheat market.

The Rickman sample consists of price pairs in outlying locations and in Rome at roughly the same time, accumulating six price pairs in almost two centuries ranging from the late republic to the early empire. This is not an overwhelming amount of evidence, but it is enough to test whether the patterns in the data are random or not. In each case the Roman price was subtracted from the price at the distant location to give a price differential. Wheat prices at Rome were subject to slow inflation according to Rickman (1980) and Duncan-Jones (1982). I characterize this period as having stable prices in chapter 4, with an allowance for slow and gradual price changes that can be documented here.

I describe the price observations in the order of their distance from Rome, calculated as straight-line distances on a map. This is only an approximation to the actual distance that wheat traveled, and this added randomness reduces the possibility of finding evidence of an integrated market. The closest price was from Sicily and came from Cicero's *Verrine Orations*. One of his accusations was that Verres did not transact business at the market price, even though he acknowledged its level in a letter (Cicero, 2 *Verr*. 3. 189). This observation, like most of the others, reports the prevailing local price in round numbers. Since the observation is general rather than the record of any transaction, it is likely to be only approximate. This casual quality of the data also militates against finding any systematic relationship between prices. It introduces more noise into any relationship of the prices being paid because of the unknown difference between the reported averages and actual prices.

The second price came from Polybius (34.8.7) in his discussion of conditions in Lusitania. As before, this is a general statement about the prevailing price. While it is good to have an average, the casual quality of the averaging process again adds noise into any comparison of prices in different places.

The third price comes from the Po Valley in Italy; it is another observation by Polybius (2.15.1). While this observation is closer to Rome than the first two prices, I made an exception to the general rule of measuring distance. The Po Valley was linked to Rome more by rivers rather than sea, although the transport of a bulk commodity like wheat may well have gone by sea (Harris 1989b). I calculated the distance in two ways that fortunately give the same distance. Diocletian's *Price Edict* fixed river transport prices at five times the level of sea transport, and I first took the cost of river transport from the Po Valley to have been five times as expensive as by sea. This evidence dates from over a century later than any of the other prices, but I assumed the ratio of sea and river transport costs remained constant over time as argued by Greene (1986, 40) and included the Po Valley in the price data by multiplying the distance from Rome by five. In addition, the distance by sea from the Po Valley to Rome is the same as the distance I calculated from the Diocletian Edict. The sea distance is not a straight line, and this observation therefore is slightly different from the others even if measured by sea. Despite the small sample, there is enough data to test whether this unusual attention to distance for this observation affects the statistical result.

The fourth price comes from an official intervention in the local market. An inscription records that the wheat price in Pisidian Antioch was high in a time of scarcity. The normal price was eight or nine *asses* (four asses equaled one sestertius) per modius; the acceptable limit price was one *denarius* per modius (*AÉ*1925, no. 126b). This inscription reveals several important aspects of the Mediterranean wheat market in addition to reporting the normal price. The need to damp down famine prices indicates that local markets were subject to local scarcities; they were not so well linked that wheat from elsewhere would be brought in instantly in response to a local shortage. The apparent success of such interventions, in this case limiting the price to double its normal range, indicates that many famines were not severe.

For Egypt, I preserve the spirit of Rickman's data but improve on his data since Rathbone (1997) reworked the sale prices that Rickman took from Duncan-Jones. I averaged seven Egyptian prices from the "famine" of 45–47 CE to get a price for Egypt. Rathbone argued that these prices were unusual, but the previous discussion suggests that they may not be far from average. We cannot know how unusual these prices were, and any special conditions introduce noise into our data. The Egyptian prices also come from agricultural areas, not from a Mediterranean port. The purported famine would have raised the price, but using country prices would have depressed it compared to those at a port. These offsets introduce added uncertainty into the accuracy of this observation since there is no reason to expect them to be exact offsets. The average of Rathbone's seven prices was seven *drachmae* per *artaba*. These prices in Egyptian currency and units were converted to HS per modius by following Duncan-Jones (1990, 372) and dividing by 4.5.

The final observation, from distant Palestine, is taken from Tenney Frank's *Economic Survey*; it too is an average of a few actual transactions (Heichelheim 1933–40, 181–83).

All of these prices were compared with roughly contemporaneous prices at Rome. Rickman argued that the price of wheat at Rome was between three and four HS per modius in the late republic, rising to five to six HS in the early empire. Duncan-Jones confirmed the general price level; Rathbone confirmed the inflation, at least for Egypt where the data are more abundant. The order of observations turns out to be almost chronological even though the order of exposition was by distance. There are six prices in almost two centuries. This is not an overwhelming amount of evidence, but it is enough to test whether the patterns in the data are random or not. In each case the Roman price was subtracted from the price at the distant location to give a price differential. More prices come to light all the time, but this "thin but nicely random" sample provides a way to answer the question at least provisionally.

The prices and the differences between the prices at Rome and the local prices are listed in table 2.2. The differences are all negative, consistent with the story of an integrated market and with general observations that agricultural prices were lower outside Rome (Garnsey 1998, 241). Wheat prices clearly were lower outside of Rome than in Rome itself. The straight-line distances from each location to Rome also are in table 2.2. I test whether the differences between prices in these provincial locations and the price at Rome were proportional to their distance to Rome. The value of a statistical test is that one can say with some precision how unlikely it is that the observed result would be found if the data were generated by pure chance. I describe how the data are only approximate. Each approximation introduces an added element of randomness into the data, increasing the probability that any observed pattern is simply noise.

The price differentials are graphed against the distance to Rome in figure 2.1. The results are quite striking; prices were lower in places further from Rome, and the price differentials appear almost proportional to the distance from Rome. These prices come from all over the Mediterranean and from various times in the late republic and early empire. If there were not a unified grain market, there would be no reason to expect a pattern in these prices. Even if there was a unified market, our inability to find more prices or more accurate transportation costs might have obscured any true relationship among the prices. Yet figure 2.1 reveals a clear picture.

TABLE 2.2.
Distance and prices for grain

Region	Distance (km) from Rome	Rome price (HS)	Province price (HS)	Distance-from-Rome "discount" (HS)	Year
Sicily (*Sicilia* province)	427	4.00 HS [a]	2.00–3.00 HS [c]	–1.50	77 BCE
Spain (*Lusitania* province)	1363	3.00–4.00 HS [a]	1 HS [d]	–2.50	150 BCE
Italy (*Italia* province), by river	1510	3.00–4.00 HS [a]	0.5 HS [b]	–3.00	150 BCE
Asia Minor (city of Pisidian Antioch)	1724	5.00–6.00 HS [a]	2.00–2.25 HS [e]	–3.13	80s CE
Egypt (region of the Fayum)	1953	5.00–6.00 HS [a]	1.5 HS [f]	–4.00	20 BC–56 CE
Palestine	2298	5.00–6.00 HS [a]	2.00–2.50 HS [g]	–3.25	15 CE

Sources: [a] Rickman (1980), 153–54.
[b] Polyb. 2.15.
[c] Cicero, 2 *Verr.* 3. 189.
[d] Polyb. 34. 8. 7.
[e] *Apigr.* (1925), 126b.
[f] P. Mich. II 1271.1.8–38.
[g] Frank (1933–40), iv, 181 and 183.

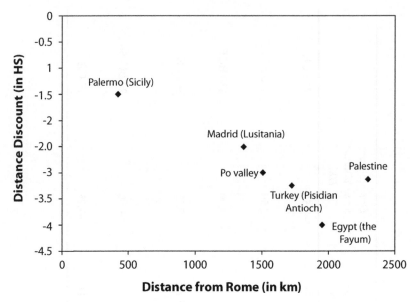

FIGURE 2.1. Plot of distance and Roman distance discount

It may appear as if the picture in figure 2.1 could only *suggest* such a story. It seems like a tiny bit of evidence on which to hang such a grand story of universal monetization and market integration. There is, however, a statistical technique that can be used to evaluate how likely it is that a picture like figure 2.1 could arise by chance. In other words, we can test the probability that the separate areas of the early Roman Empire were isolated and out of economic connection with Rome. Their prices would have been determined by local conditions, including perhaps the degree of monetization. There would have been no connection between the distance to Rome and the level of local prices.

This statistical technique is regression analysis. In this type of analysis we can evaluate the likelihood that there is a relation between the local price and the distance from Rome. We start by trying to draw a line that relates the price difference between the local price and the Roman price to the distance from Rome. We then adjust the line to make it the best description of the data in the sense that it minimizes the squared distance of the individual observations from the line. (We use the square of the distance to minimize the distance from points both above and below the line and to simplify the mathematics.) This process of regression analysis also is known as the method of "least squares," and the resulting least-squares line is the regression line. It is shown in figure 2.2.

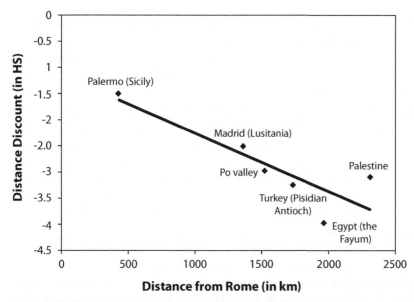

FIGURE 2.2. Relationship between distance and Roman distance discount

One of the values of regression analysis is that it generates tests of the hypotheses being tested. We can ask if an apparent relationship between the price discount and the distance from Rome is illusory, a result of observing only a few prices, rather than the result of a systematic process. In order to draw this line, we assumed that there was a relationship between the distance from Rome and the price discount. Regression analysis provides a test whether there is such an association in the data. This test tells us how unlikely it is for us to find a line like the one shown in figure 2.2 by chance. Assume that the prices we gathered from Rickman were randomly drawn from an underlying distribution of price observations. In another world, different prices could have survived from this same distribution. Taking account of the random quality of the observations we actually have, how unlikely is it for us to find the line in figure 2.2 by chance?

Regression analysis acknowledges that the slope of the line in figure 2.2 is not known with certainty. It is the best line that can be drawn with the data at hand, but it is subject to errors deriving from the incomplete sampling of the underlying distribution. In the jargon of regression analysis, the slope of the line has a standard error. If all the points in figures 2.1 and 2.2 lay in a straight line, then the slope of the regression line would be clear, and the standard error of the slope would be close to zero. If the points are spread out as they are in the figures here, then the line is not known as clearly, and there is a chance that the line has no slope at all, that is, that there is no relationship between the distance from Rome and the price difference.

The test is to compare the size of the slope, the coefficient in the regression, with the size of its standard error. If the coefficient is large relative to the standard error, then it is unlikely that the line was a random finding without support in the price data. On the other hand, if the coefficient is small relative to its standard error, then it is possible that even though the regression line has a slope, there is no underlying relationship between the price and distance. Statisticians call this ratio a t-statistic, and they have calculated tables that can translate t-statistics into probabilities that the line is observed by chance.

The tables take account of degrees of freedom, that is, the number of observations minus the number of coefficients. It takes two variables to define a line, its slope and its position (its height in the figures). With six observations and two variables, there are four degrees of freedom. Omitting the observation with river transport reduces the number of observations by one and the degrees of freedom to three. The t-statistic has to be larger with such few degrees of freedom than with more degrees of freedom to show that a given regression line is unlikely to be the result of chance.

One might think that the data—composed of only a few, badly observed values—are too poor for statistical analysis. Statistics are the best way of distinguishing signal from noise; they are particularly useful when there is a lot of noise in the system. They give us a precise sense of how unlikely it is that any putative pattern we think we observe would have been generated by random processes, that is, how unlikely it is that what looks like a pattern actually is noise. The value of statistics is that we can test a formal hypothesis, namely that wheat prices around the Mediterranean Sea were related in a simple way to those at Rome. We also can derive an explicit probability that this hypothesis is true, given the observations we have.

Errors in variables are a common problem in doing regressions. We often hypothesize a relationship between two variables—like the price in Rome and the price in Egypt—but cannot observe one or the other of them precisely. We then use a proxy such as the occasional price that happens to be mentioned in a surviving document. The errors introduced by such a procedure have been studied, and their effects are well known. The extra uncertainty introduced by using imperfect proxies reduces the explanatory power of regressions and tends to result in coefficients that are near zero; the addition of noise through imperfect observations makes the results look more like noise. The well-known scarcity of Roman prices therefore makes it very hard to find a pattern in them. When a pattern is found, however, it indicates both that there is a strong relationship between the prices and that the observations we have are reasonably representative.

Table 2.3.
Distance and distance discount regression results

	N	Constant	Distance	R^2
Distance discount	6	−1.150 (2.10)	−0.001 (3.41)	0.74
Distance discount (no Po Valley)	5	−1.116 (1.76)	−0.001 (3.01)	0.75
Log distance discount	6	0.125 (1.52)	0.002 (4.12)	0.81
Log distance discount (no Po Valley)	5	0.116 (1.26)	0.002 (3.78)	0.83

Absolute values of t-statistics are below the coefficients.
Source: Table 2.2.

Statistical tests are needed to tell if the observed pattern could be the result of chance. The results of four separate regressions of the price differential on the distance from Rome are shown in table 2.3. Since the transportation from Bologna was by river rather than sea, I was not sure that the correction for the relative cost of transport was accurate and tried the regressions both with and without the Bologna data point. In addition, in the bottom two regressions the price differentials are expressed in logarithms to measure the proportional change in them. Since there are no logarithms of negative numbers, the signs in the bottom two regressions are changed. The dependent variable is the premium of the Roman price over the local price instead of the discount of the local price from the Roman price.

Several conclusions emerge from these results. The R^2 shown in the final column measures the share of the variance of the price differentials that is explained by these simple regressions. Using the price differentials themselves, the regression explains three-quarters of the variation. Using logarithms of the differentials, the regressions explain even more. This result confirms the impression in table 2.2 and figure 2.1 that distance from Rome was a powerful explanatory factor in determining wheat prices around the Roman Mediterranean.

T-statistics are shown in parentheses beneath the coefficients in table 2.3, and they indicate whether the relationship between price differentials and distance was the result of chance. These statistics measure the probability that each coefficient is different from zero, taking account of the number of observations used to derive it as well as their variation. T-statistics above three indicate that there is less than one chance in twenty that the observed relationship between distance and price differentials was due to chance. In the more precise language normally used for regressions, the probability of observing the coefficients in the table if there were no relationship between the price of wheat and the distance from Rome is less than 5 percent in three out of four regressions and close to that probability in the fourth. The 5 percent value of the t-statistic for four degrees of freedom (six observations) is 2.8; for three degrees of freedom (five observations), 3.2. Higher t-statistics indicate lower probabilities that the observed relationship is the result of chance.

In other words, the regressions confirm with very high probability that there was a unified wheat market that extended from one end to the other of the Mediterranean Sea. Transport costs were roughly proportional to distance, and the effects of distance were larger than the idiosyncratic influences of particular markets and places.

The constant terms in these regressions were negative in the regressions for price discounts and positive in the regressions for the logarithms. They were not estimated as precisely as the relationship between distance and the price differentials, and they consequently could be the result of chance (as indicated by smaller t-statistics). Nonetheless, the constant terms are historically reasonable and indicate that not all costs were proportional to distance. There appear to have been other costs as well, albeit smaller and less well observed. These other costs were partly physical—the costs of transshipping wheat to and from seagoing ships—and partly administrative—port charges and taxes. Their presence does not detract from the effect of distance or the evidence in favor of a unified wheat market.

Finally, it does not make a difference whether Bologna is included or not. Removing this observation reduced our comparisons to five, but it did not affect the proportion of the variance explained or the evidence that the relationship of distance to price differentials was not random. The t-statistics take account of the reduction in the number of observations to calculate the probability that the observed correlation was due to chance. The logic behind this finding can be seen in figure 2.2. The observation for Bologna lies close to the regression line. Removing it therefore does not change the line.

These results can be extended with a new data set from Rathbone (2011), an expanded version of the data in Rathbone (2009). At first glance, this looks like a larger data set, with twenty-three observations and more power to test hypotheses. It turns out that the added data give us a way to clarify the previous results rather than to make a new start. We need first to consider how this sample was constructed. In Rathbones's words, they are the extant prices "which are significant for market behavior." In other words, they were not picked to prove a hypothesis, but rather to show what we know about Roman wheat markets. Again, thin but nicely random.

Eight of these observations are for prices at Rome. Rathbone recognized that the annona distorted the market at Rome, and he did not attempt to find a market price that prevailed in normal times. He presented high prices in severe shortages, although one of them is close to Rickman's Rome price, and state-subsidized prices. He did not follow Rickman and try to estimate an average from these very diverse prices. Without a set of prices at Rome, I used the prices elsewhere instead of discounting them from the Roman price. I added a time variable to account for the slight inflation visible in Rickman's data. The result is to lose eight observations and add a variable, decreasing the degrees of freedom by nine.

For other observations, I used the average where Rathbone provided ranges. I disregarded the few prices where Rathbone—ever cautious about data—added question marks to the prices or dates and a few prices from "extreme shortages." I also discarded the observation for Judaea as being too imprecise and probably irrelevant. The timing was given only as the second century CE, which is after the Judaean revolt. It is likely that the turmoil after the destruction of the Judean temple caused trade to be disrupted. In fact, the Talmud prohibited wheat exports (Heichelheim 1938, 182). The date and effectiveness of this prohibition are not known, but it suggests that the kind of price arbitrage discussed earlier in setting up the regressions was not operative after the revolt. (I did not inquire into the timing of my Judaean observation in using the Rickman data, but removing the Judaean price does not affect the results in table 2.3, although it decreases the degrees of freedom.)

I ended up with eight observations. I used them all and also tried omitting the observations on the Po Valley since the distance measure is problematical as noted already and an Egyptian price from the third century after inflation had picked up. The results are shown in table 2.4, where it can be seen that these regressions reproduce the coefficients on distance in table 2.3. The coefficients are the same size and known with the same precision. The regressions as a whole, however, do not have the same explanatory power as those from Rickman's data. Despite the overlap between the two data sets, there is more unexplained variation in this data set. In addition, when the two problematical observations are dropped, there are no more observations than in table 2.3. Since there is an additional variable, the degrees of freedom are like the second and fourth regressions in table 2.3 with only three degrees of freedom. As before, it is good that omitting these observations does not affect the results. The constant is larger than before because it includes an implied price at Rome in addition to any costs of taxes or transport to the city. The estimated inflation rate mysteriously is very large.

TABLE 2.4.
Distance and price regression results

	N	Constant	Distance	Time	R^2
Distance	8	34.8	−.009	.058	.42
		(5.77)	(2.13)	(2.15)	
Distance (No Po Valley or III)	6	46.6	−.016	.088	.46
		(4.60)	(2.30)	(2.09)	

Absolute values of t-statistics are below the coefficients.
Source: Rathbone (2011).

Several objections have been raised to this kind of test and its conclusion. The first objection is that prices were low outside Rome because coined money was scarce, not because transport to Rome was costly. This alternative cannot explain the prices in table 2.1. Coins may have been scarce in Lusitania at the time of Polybius, but coins were abundant in the eastern Mediterranean where the monetized Greek economy preceded the Roman one. Wheat prices there were lower than in Lusitania, as can be seen from the figures. Distance from Rome is a much better predictor of prices than coin scarcity.

A second objection is that the prices are unrepresentative because they are notional, biased because the observers had political motives, or unrepresentative due to price fluctuations. Such errors in the price observations may have been present, although Polybius was a very careful historian, not liable to falsify his evidence to make a rhetorical point. As noted already, such errors in recording the "true" prices introduce noise into the relationship between the price differential and distance from Rome. If there was a great deal of this distortion, any existing relationship might be obscured. Since the regressions show such a relation, it means that the relationship between distance and price was a strong one, visible even through the noise introduced by casual or distorted price observations.

More formally, we can think of the observed prices being determined by the true prevailing prices, which we observe with an error due to our approximation. Then the dependent variable we used in the regression is the true price differential plus an error. That error would add onto the error of the regression and result in a lower t-statistic and R^2. Given that they both are large, the data show that this rough assumption is quite good, that the observed prices appear to represent prevailing prices in a reasonable fashion.

Another related objection is that prices fluctuated during the year and observations may have come from different seasons. Again, this source of noise strengthens the results because the seasonal price variation introduces another source of noise into the hypothesized relationship. I suspect that the casual nature of the price observations has helped here. Travelers were told of the prevailing price, not sometimes the high price that obtains just before the harvest comes in and sometimes the low price following the harvest. The result appears to be a consistent set of prices. Phrased differently, while the few prices that have survived for two millennia are quite random, it is perverse to insist that any observed pattern has to be spurious. There does not seem to be a reason to throw out evidence from the ancient world on the grounds that the pattern must be as random as the observations.

Yet another objection to the use of these prices is that the argument is circular: I assume the data are sound because they support the hypothesis, but the test of the hypothesis requires the data to be sound. On the contrary, I assume that the observed prices are drawn from a distribution of prices in the late republic and early Roman Empire. I do not assume they are accurate or come from a particular kind of investigation or a particular time of year (as in the previous paragraph). I only assume that they are prices collected before anyone thought of doing a regression test. Given that I am sampling from the population of wheat prices, the t-statistic tells us whether there is a relationship between price and distance. There is no more circularity here than in any statistical test of a hypothesis.

Another objection is that the samples are tiny, only six price pairs or eight prices. The small samples are unfortunate, but no barrier to the test of this hypothesis. As noted above, the standard errors and t-statistics are corrected for degrees of freedom. Having few observations makes it easier to reject hypotheses, but it does not affect the validity of the test. We would, of course, like to have many more prices, but there are no more to be found at this time. The new Rathbone sample has hardly more useable prices, and it confirms the main outlines of the test.

Some of Rathbone's data come from periods of severe shortages, which also are noted in table 2.1. The few added observations do not give us more information on the frequency of these shortages, but they remind us that the Mediterranean wheat market was subject to events that increased the difficulty and cost of shipping wheat across the sea. The market worked in general, but there was not enough storage to smooth out the difficulties that arose from time to time.

Some objections are more emotional than rational. Erdkamp (2005, 256) talks of "the weaknesses of the grain market." This is not an economic term; perhaps it refers to the occasional shortages. Seminar participants have said that if one data point of this small data set was moved, then the result would disappear. But choosing data points to make a result come out the way you want it makes the process circular; a statistical test only is possible when the data are chosen for reasons other than influencing the result of a test. And Bang (2008, 31) stated dramatically:

> Peter Temin argued that Finley was quite simply wrong; the economy of the Roman Empire represented just such a conglomeration ["an enormous conglomeration of interdependent markets"]. This is an extraordinary claim. One might conceivably imagine that some markets had begun to be linked by middle- and long-distance trade. But to see the entire economy, spanning several continents, as organized by a set of interlinked markets is quite another matter. It is doubtful whether the mature eighteenth-century European economy, outside some restricted pockets, could be described in such terms.

The last sentence reveals a difficulty with references to early modern European economic history that is all too common among ancient historians. Bang reported staples of early modern trade practices—reports from agents, family networks, need for supercargoes, etc.—as if they precluded long-distance trade. He quoted the boilerplate at the end of a typical agent letter saying that prices vary over time as evidence that planning is impossible, and he decried the Roman failure to develop bills of exchange without understanding that the Roman universal currency area obviated the need for such bills. The best place to find a description of the relations between eighteenth-century international trade and the Industrial Revolution is Allen (2009b).

Bang also used an outmoded economic theory. He denied the presence of "Ricardian trade" by noting that complete specialization of Roman provinces did not take place (Bang 2008, 73–76). As shown in chapter 1, this is only a problem if Ricardo's original formulation is used and no notice is taken of two centuries of elaboration of comparative advantage. As shown in figure 1.4 of chapter 1, Ricardo's model still illuminates the principle of comparative advantage when we acknowledge there are two factors of production and the PPF is curved. The only difference is that the model used today allows for partial specialization if countries or regions are not too different.

This chapter presents evidence for the presence of a series of unified grain markets that stretched from one end of the Mediterranean to the other in the late republic and early empire. The extent of the Roman market has been debated exhaustively, but evidence to date has been restricted to local markets. The presence of localized market activity has ceased to be controversial, but the question of market integration is still alive. The evidence produced here demonstrates that there was something approaching a unified grain market in the Roman Mediterranean.

Government interventions in wheat markets summarized in table 2.1 make it clear that the market could not prevent shortages in Rome. The government intervened in the wheat market from time to time to lower prices and alleviate shortages, particularly under Augustus. It also is clear, even from what must be a partial list, that these interventions were intermittent. If these interventions are only half of the actual actions, the others being unrecorded in our sources, the years in which there were interventions were still clearly a minority. The market for wheat was allowed to work on its own in most years. In addition, if traders expected the government to interfere when famine loomed, they might have been discouraged from trying to corner the market in adversity. Government intervention therefore may have dampened speculation and made the underlying pattern of prices easier to see.

Of course, there also were local famines, and local areas were not always connected to the market in Rome. Rathbone recorded examples of isolated markets—with prices that do not fit this regression line—showing examples of prices not connected to the regular market. This test demonstrates that there were connections between far-flung Roman grain markets; only with more data will we be able to get a better idea of how often outlying markets were connected to the major consuming market in Rome.

This chapter illustrates the usefulness of regression analysis in ancient history; presenting existing information into a new format that offers the possibility of showing graphically the existence of a unified market, as in figure 2.1. It also provides a test of whether the observed pattern could have arisen by chance. Given the small number of observations, it always is possible that the pattern in figure 2.1 was simply a coincidence. Regression analysis allows us to quantify that possibility. The probability that the pattern in figure 2.1 was due to chance is about 5 percent, that is, one in twenty. This is a far more precise estimate of the probability that we are observing an actual relationship than has been available previously. Given the scarcity of data and the prevalence of shortages, it is clear that regressions can only help interpret existing data, not provide additional information to provide definitive answers to all questions, as will be seen again in chapter 4.

Finally, these regressions tested a very simple model of Roman trade, that there was a single wheat market across the whole Mediterranean. I tested this hypothesis with simple regressions with few degrees of freedom. Why should any ancient historian believe such a simple model and test? The purpose of a model is to provide an overall view of money and trade in Rome; it cannot explain every detail. Instead it provides an overview that helps our thinking. In this case, the regressions show that there were interconnected markets in the Mediterranean, but we also saw in the data that these markets did not work all the time or in all places. As expressed by Rathbone (2011):

Unsatisfactorily thin as the Roman wheat price data are, they seem to suggest a partially integrated market, determined primarily by regional productivity and demand on the one hand, and on the other by the ease or difficulty of transport. Basically the major coastal zones of the empire were linked into a hierarchical structure with the highest price band in Rome and Campania, where demand most exceeded production, a middle band in Sicily, the Greek cities and, to some extent, Judaea, and the lowest band in Egypt, which though not coastal was linked to the Mediterranean by the Nile, and where production most exceeded demand.

Rathbone sees a hierarchy where I see continuity, but we describe much the same conditions. He notes that the excess of demand over the supply of wheat was greatest in and around Rome, and he says other regions were "linked into a hierarchical structure." This is the structure of an interconnected set of Mediterranean markets that extended—with occasional interruptions and the probable exception of turbulent Judaea—from Egypt to Lusitania in the late Roman Republic and early Roman Empire.

Bransbourg (2012) provides additional evidence of the Mediterranean wheat market in a recent paper. He criticized the data shown in figure 2.1 and analyzed in table 2.4. His new statistical analysis, however, confirmed the negative relation between local wheat prices and the distance from Rome. Using six observations from coastal areas, he found the distance from Rome explained almost all the local variation in wheat prices; adding another half-dozen observations from places away from the sea maintained the explanatory power of the distance from Rome but explained less of the local variation.

Chapter 3

■ ■ ■

Price Behavior in Hellenistic Babylon

The previous chapter exploited a tiny data set of only a half-dozen observations. The prices in these observations appeared to be market prices, and I treated them as such. There was, however, no demonstration that they were market prices, that is, that they were the results of changing supplies and demands as explained in chapter 1.

One reason it has been hard to demonstrate the existence of ancient markets is that there is a paucity of ancient prices in the surviving records. Duncan-Jones (1982) and Rathbone (1997) collected prices for common articles in an agricultural economy—albeit one with many monuments and statues. Even though they found a large number of prices, the prices were spread over many commodities and even more years. One has only to look at the small number of observations found by these authors to realize that only the simplest of hypotheses can be tested. Hopkins (1978, 158) reported what he called "the largest single series of prices over time which we have from the classical world." The series contained seven hundred prices that slaves paid for their freedom, spread over the last two hundred years before the Common Era. Slaves, of course, were very diverse, and there were far fewer observations for any subsets of more similar slaves. He observed a rise in release prices over these years but could not test complex hypotheses.

In this context, Slotsky's (1997) report of what appeared to be a series of monthly market prices for six agricultural commodities for four hundred years in Hellenistic Babylon appeared to provide much more evidence of ancient market activity than had been available earlier. But although Slotsky argued that her observations were market prices, her interests were primarily historical and philological rather than economic. This chapter pursues the economics of these observations to answer two questions. First, were they market prices? Second, if so, what can their behavior tell us about the economy of the classical world? Babylon is not Rome, and the Hellenistic period preceded the Roman era. The paucity of Roman data has forced me to look a bit outside the time and place that is my main concern in this book in order to document the existence of market activity. At this point in our knowledge I can only infer that the conclusions in this chapter apply to the other chapters as well.

The price data come from a vast archive of astronomical cuneiform tablets from the ancient city of Babylon. This renowned site first gained importance in the beginning of the second millennium BCE and attained a preeminence in the ancient world which was to last for almost two thousand years. In the last seven centuries of the first millennium BCE, clay tablets, of which about twelve hundred fragments are known, were filled with almost daily astronomical and other observations written in the Akkadian language by observers specifically trained and employed by the Temple of Marduk in Babylon. Each day, scribes made entries on small tablets, recording on a single tablet information for periods ranging from a day or two to a few months. This was possible because clay can be kept soft and inscribable for up to three months (for example, by wrapping it in a wet cloth). At a later date, the scribes composed larger texts from these smaller ones, with the full-sized versions covering either an entire Babylonian calendar year or the first or last half of one (Sachs and Hunger 1988; 1989; 1996).

A typical half-year "astronomical diary" has six sections, seven in an intercalary year (that is, one with an extra month), each covering one lunar Babylonian month. Observations began with what was considered to be the beginning of the month—the first visibility of the new moon at sunset—and continued with the monthly progress of the moon among the stars and planets. Nightly and daily weather conditions were written down meticulously because they had an impact on visibility. Eclipses, equinoxes, and solstices; Sirius phenomena; and the appearance of comets (including Halley's comets of 234, 164, and 87 BCE) were recorded. At the end of the month, there was a final statement about the moon's last appearance, then a recapitulation of planetary positions at month's end, a list of the market values of six commodities that month, measurements of the changes in the water levels of the Euphrates, and anecdotal historical information.

These tablets are unique among documents pertinent to the study of ancient history. They are unmatched in magnitude, sequence, and detail. Because of the astronomical content, any evidence extracted from these texts—astronomical, meteorological, economic, and historical—can be dated with certainty. And the market quotations always were expressed in the same terms, quantities that can be purchased for one shekel of silver. (A shekel was a weight measure, not a coin.) In addition, values of the same six commodities were listed in a set order: barley, dates, cuscuta (called mustard in the early translations of the diaries and here), cardamom (originally and here called cress), sesame, wool.

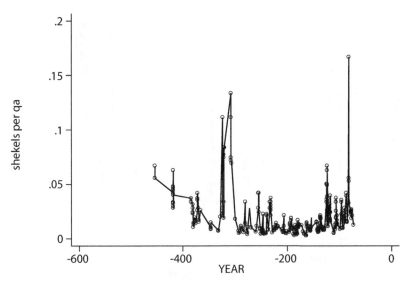

F"igure" 3.1. The price of barley, 464 to 72 BCE
Source: Slotsky (1997)

I study the data from 464 to 72 BCE, omitting one stray set of market values for 568 BCE. The data contain many missing values because of the many lost tablets and the large number that are damaged or broken. The commodity summary was inscribed close to the end of a monthly unit. The last month on a tablet was at the bottom of the tablet and in a particularly vulnerable position; there are many disconnected and broken passages, not to mention lost quotations. Tablet damage and loss was random from the point of view of prices. There are over three thousand observations—almost as many observations for each of the six commodities as Hopkins (1978) found for *all* slave freedom prices. The prices of barley and wool are shown in figures 3.1 and 3.2. Barley prices are measured in *qa* (close to a modern quart) per shekel (a standard weight of silver). Wool prices are measure in *mina* (close to a modern pound) per shekel.

Slotsky (1997) had no doubt that the market quotations were real market prices. The texts contained principally observed rather than predicted phenomena. The quotations appeared too irregular to have been computed according to some abstract principle. The pace of reporting commodity prices quickened and became erratic when they were volatile, and there were reports of interrupted or suspended commodity sales at these times. Slotsky analyzed these putative prices in the manner of an ancient historian and philologist, although she did use some statistics. I have used the tools of economics to ask

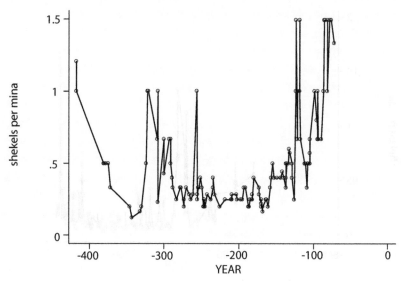

FIGURE 3.2. The price of wool, 464 to 72 BCE
Source: Slotsky (1997)

if these magnitudes behave like real prices. If so, what can we learn from them about the economy of the classical world?

Grainger (1999) and Van der Spek (2000) interpreted these prices as market prices. Grainger described long-run trends, and Van der Spek argued that prices rose in wartime. Grainger based his argument on bar graphs, while Van der Spek cited isolated prices, restricting his observations to wartimes and to the price of barley. Neither author subjected the data to any kind of formal tests.

In order to create a frame of reference, I compare the Babylonian prices with the price of wheat in England during the medieval and early modern periods. The price of wheat is a good standard of comparison for several reasons. The wheat prices are well attested and continuous for centuries, comparable to the Babylonian prices. They are the prices of an agricultural commodity from a primarily agricultural economy, as are the Babylonian prices. And they clearly were set in relatively free market conditions.

The first question is whether the Babylonian prices are market prices. To answer that question I need to consider what else they might be. The alternative is some sort of administered prices that indicate nonmarket activity such as tax collections or royal exactions of some other sort. If these prices indicated such an administrative activity, they would have been generated by some rule and would have followed a uniform pattern like the celestial movements also recorded on the tablets. Market prices, by contrast, move freely in response to changing conditions and would have exhibited a far more random pattern.

I therefore can test for market prices by looking for random movements in the data. I distinguish five types of movements to be examined.

1. Annual variation. I measure the year-to-year variation by examining yearly prices. Only the year in which prices were reported is relevant here, not the month. As can be seen from figures 3.1 and 3.2, the price series exhibit substantial annual variation. Prices, as we know from the modern world, also exhibit autocorrelation. In fact, they typically can be described as a random walk.

2. Long-run variation. I examine trends over time to see if prices exhibited persistent trends over the four centuries I observe. Administered prices could remain constant over time, but market prices are more likely to exhibit inflation or deflation over this long period. Grainger (1999) inferred long-run trends from bar graphs but could not test for significance in light of the short-run variation.

3. Short-run variation. Market prices react to unexpected events. Alexander returned to Babylon in 324 BCE and then died suddenly in 323, giving rise to lasting dynastic conflicts. These were events of great magnitude. If these observations are market prices, they may well have shown some effects. Changes in the supply of silver and any scarcity of goods resulting from Alexander's death both could have caused prices to rise. Van der Spek (2000) interpreted a price rise at this time as the effect of war rather than of other events.

4. Relative variation. The scribes recorded prices for six commodities. If the prices were administered, they should have preserved their relative magnitudes. It is a hallmark of administered prices even in modern times that they do not vary against each other (Berliner 1976). Market prices, by contrast, often diverge as there are changes in individual markets. Five of the prices I have are for crops, while wool is an animal product. If these are market prices, the price of wool could have moved differently from the price of crops.

5. Seasonal variation. Agricultural prices tend to have patterns that reflect growing conditions, both seasonal variation within years and yearly variations from weather changes. Crops were harvested at different times of the year in ancient Babylon, and there may not be uniform seasonal patterns. In addition, there may have been good and bad years for agriculture as a whole.

I use the annual variation of prices to test whether these prices were generated in relatively free markets. The prime characteristic of such prices is that they are not predictable in the short run. In other words the best prediction today of what a price will be tomorrow is the price today. The stock market today seems to be the best example of prices like these. The evening news reports whether prices went up or down. The news is based on the assumption that prices are autocorrelated, that is, that today's price is correlated with yesterday's price. It also is telling us what we could not have known yesterday, how today's price differed from yesterday's price. The change from yesterday was random from yesterday's point of view.

We speak of stochastic processes like this as random walks. The variable "walks" like a person, starting off from the results of the previous step and moving randomly to the next step. We therefore can express this movement in an equation that says that today's observation is equal to yesterday's observation plus a random movement. In the case at hand, today's price is equal to yesterday's price plus a random amount. It is possible to talk of a random walk with drift, as you can observe for prices in the midst of inflation or deflation. In that case, the randomness comes from the expected deviation around the trend, not simply from the previous price level.

In order to make the results intelligible and accurate, I make two changes in the price data as they are found on the tablets. They reported the quantity of barley, for example, per unit of currency. We are used to thinking about the units of currency needed to buy a standard unit of barley. I therefore use the inverse of the prices listed by the priests from the Temple of Marduk. I also use the logarithm of prices in order to reduce the effects of outliers in the data and to make the random movements independent of direction.

In order to deal with holes in the data, I have to expand the standard equation for a random walk. Despite the abundance of Babylonian prices, there are not prices for every year. There are more than three thousand observations, but they are for six commodities. That means about five hundred observations for each commodity, spread over roughly four hundred years, and there are not enough surviving tablets to provide observations for each year. To account for any possible trend in the prices, the trend needs to be multiplied by the number of years since the last observation. Since I am using the logarithm of the prices, the coefficient on the previous price needs to be raised to the relevant power.

I examine the first kind of variation through regressions of the following form:

$$\text{Log Price}_i(t) = \alpha + \beta_i^{\text{Lag}(t)} \text{Log Price}_i(t-1) + \varepsilon(t)$$

For modern prices with annual observations, Lag $(t) = 1$ for all years, and it normally is not expressed. As noted above, I calculated the price as the inverse of the volume or weight measure of each commodity described earlier.

Table 3.1.
Regressions of log prices on last year's prices

	Barley	Dates	Mustard	Cress	Sesame	Wool
Intercept	0.00047	−0.149	0.00027	0.0029	0.0031	0.010
	(0.392)	(0.495)	(0.750)	(0.967)	(0.861)	(0.455)
Log price−1	0.988*	0.988*	0.978*	0.979*	0.983*	0.996*
	(154)	(395)	(391)	(188)	(246)	(321)
DW	2.08	2.28	2.69	2.69	2.74	2.55
Obs.	127	120	99	104	109	99

Absolute values of t-statistics are below the coefficients. * = significantly different from zero at 1% probability.

The results of estimating this regression for each of the six commodities are shown in table 3.1. In each case, the constant is close to zero, and the coefficient on last year's price is very close to one. Taking into account the randomness of the sample of prices that have survived, as in chapter 2, the small standard errors of the coefficients show that the constant is not significantly different from zero nor the coefficient on the lagged price different from one. In plain English, the probability that the constant is different from zero or that the coefficients are different from one is less than 1 percent. These prices describe a random walk very much like that of modern prices.

I compare the autocorrelation in agricultural prices from Hellenistic Babylon with that in medieval and early modern English wheat prices to see if the degree of autocorrelation is the same. The analogous regression for wheat prices from 1260 to 1914 is:

$$\text{Log Price}_w(t) = -0.042 + 0.942 \text{ Log Price}_w(t-1) + \varepsilon(t)$$
$$(0.28) \quad (67.3)$$

Lag (t) has been suppressed since there are no missing years in the data and "t" in this expression always takes the value of 1 in this regression. The price of wheat for early modern Britain shows exactly the same kind of autocorrelation as the ancient Babylonian prices. The price of wheat after 1500 is shown in figure 3.3, using only part of the modern price series to approximate the time interval of the ancient one. The graph looks very similar to figures 3.1 and 3.2.

The existence of this stochastic process is a clear marker for market prices. The ancient prices behave like medieval and early modern prices, which in turn

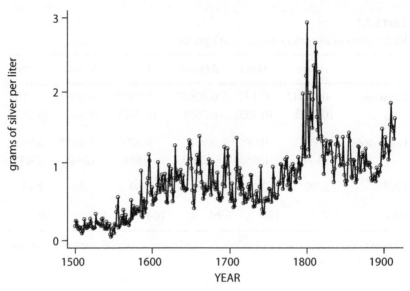

FIGURE 3.3. The price of wheat in England, 1500 to 1914
Source: Allen (2001)

share the time-series properties of prices today. Administered prices could not possibly have these properties. They would stay at or near some fixed level, or a level that changed deterministically over time; they would not behave as a random walk. In the regression, the constant should have been at the administrative level and clearly not zero, while the coefficient on the previous price would be zero. The data in figures 3.1–3.3 and table 3.1 therefore document clearly the market nature of agricultural prices in Babylon before and during the Hellenistic period.

To make the comparison more vivid, I show an administered price from eighteenth-century London in figure 3.4. The usury rate was binding at this time, and this figure shows the interest rate charged by a London bank to its customers. The usury rate was lowered from 6 to 5 percent in 1714, and the rate charged by the bank fell by the same amount. In a regression for the rates charged by the bank, the constant showed up as 5 or 6 percent depending on the date, and the coefficient on an unregulated interest rate—the return on government bonds—was effectively zero. To emphasize that these were actual rates, I added in a dotted line the average rate the bank charged, including loans that were made without any interest charge at all (Temin and Voth 2008).

This conclusion can be strengthened by analysis of the path of these market prices over time. As can be seen in table 3.1, the number of observations for each commodity fell from the observed five hundred or so to one hundred or

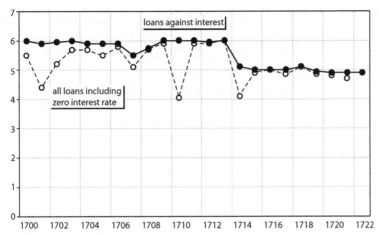

FIGURE 3.4. Two "average" interest rates, Hoare's, 1702–25
Source: Temin and Voth (2008)

slightly more in the annual regressions. This was the result of collapsing the data into annual observations and allowing for lags, and the remaining observations are quite sufficient to demonstrate the time-series properties of the ancient data. I used all the observations for the descriptive regressions described in the appendix to this chapter. These regressions summarize the movements of the prices in variations 2 through 5 and illuminate patterns shown in figures 3.1 and 3.2. See the appendix for regression specifications and partial results.

The results of estimating further regressions for each of the six commodities indicate that a cubic equation captures well the curvature of the price series. The presence of all positive coefficients appears to indicate steadily rising prices, but dealing with years before the Common Era is tricky. The years before the Common Era are negative, increasing from −463 to −71. As the years progress, getting closer to zero, the effect of a positive sign on a negative year diminishes, and prices turn upward. The prices of three commodities—cress, mustard, and dates—rose initially in the fifth century BCE, then fell until shortly after 200 BCE when they began to rise again. The prices of wool, sesame, and barley fell from the earliest years observed until reaching a minimum between 250 and 200 BCE, after which they too rose. Prices moved in various ways in early years, but they all rose with increasing speed after 150 BCE.

Grainger (1999) attributed this inflation to the breakdown of the Seleucid state. A lack of public order could impede trade and make goods scarce. But this argument about the demand for goods ignores the supply of money; an abundance of silver also could cause commodity prices in silver units to rise. We can clarify the problem by referring back to the supply and demand analysis in chapter 1. It is easiest to examine the supply and demand of silver, the units in which Babylonian prices were given. The price of silver is the inverse of the price of the commodities as noted earlier. When prices go up in inflation, the "price" of money, that is, silver, goes down.

Was this due to a shift in the supply or demand for silver? Grainger argued that the demand for silver went down because there were not enough goods to buy. People wanted goods and were willing to pay lots of silver for them. But what was happening to the supply of silver? We do not know much about the supplies of silver in this period, because most of our information comes from examining coins. Commerce in Babylonia was not based on coins, but rather on standard weights of silver. When Alexander introduced coins, they were weighed rather than counted (Powell 1996; Vargyas 2000). It is very hard to know how many coins were circulating, and even harder to estimate the volume of silver in use.

Alexander established a mint in Babylonia around 330 BCE when he first arrived. He then went to Persia and beyond, returning with treasure in 324, presumably including silver. But we do not know how he financed his expedition, and there is no evidence that the Persian treasure was made into coins (Mørkholm 1991, pp. 48–49). Conventional wisdom is that Rome was taking silver from the East in taxes and tribute. The Roman Republic was expanding its use of silver coinage in these years, and "silver drained out of Spain and the Greek world" to Italy and Rome after 200 BCE (Harl 1996, p. 39). It is unlikely as a result that there was an increasing supply of silver in Babylon. In addition, when Augustus reformed the Roman currency a century after the Babylonian price series ends, his coins embodied a gold-silver ratio of 12:1, valuing silver higher relative to gold than it would be valued later (Greene 1986, 49). This evidence does not suggest an abundance of silver in Rome at the end of our period, making a prior expansion of silver supplies in Babylon even more unlikely. Grainger's suggestion therefore appears to be a reasonable one.

A more rapid and more short-lived inflation took place in the years after Alexander's death. Prices rose dramatically and took about a generation to return to their normal trend. This price rise, clearly visible in figures 3.1 and 3.2, reveals the market nature of these prices, since episodic price rises are hallmarks of free markets. As with the later, more gradual price rise, the cause of this rise can only be inferred indirectly. It appears to be the effect of Alexander's unexpected death and the dynastic conflicts that followed.

If so, what was the mechanism? As in the more gradual later inflation, prices could rise either because agricultural goods were scarce in Babylon or because the stock of silver suddenly rose. Alexander brought back with him extensive plunder in 324 BCE. He did not coin this treasure, as noted above, but one modern author argued that he "released [his treasure] into circulation," dramatically increasing the supply of money (Patterson 1972). It is likely, however, that Alexander did not by himself give rise to this short, sharp inflation. Instead, competing claimants to Alexander's throne probably paid their soldiers from Alexander's treasure during the dynastic struggles that followed his death. Stolper (1994) described the political history of these years, showing that the dynastic conflicts continued for a long time. It is the continuation of these struggles that explains why prices stayed high for a generation after Alexander's sudden death. Of course, the inference that an increased supply of money caused prices to rise assumes that the prices in question were market prices determined in reasonably well-functioning markets.

The supply and demand model of chapter 1 has enabled us to distinguish between the two bouts of inflation in the Babylonian prices data. The swift inflation and deflation after Alexander's death was caused by changes in the *supply* of money, while the more gradual inflation starting in the second century BCE was due to changes in the *demand* for money. In other words, these two inflations were very different phenomenon with very different causes. One role of economics is to clarify the nature of the events that we observe. I discuss more statistical results in the following paragraphs; the regressions themselves are explained in the appendix to this chapter.

The analysis done here shows that agricultural prices in Babylon moved randomly from year to year, fell and rose again over the long run, and experienced severe market disruption after the death of Alexander the Great. These conclusions imply more general conclusions about ancient Babylon. There clearly were markets for agricultural goods that were operating continuously and giving rise to market prices. This suggests that there was a market economy in ancient Babylon. To reach a stronger conclusion about the economy as a whole, we would need evidence on the spread and influence of other markets as well as the ones analyzed here. I argue in this book that there was a market economy in the early Roman Empire by examining the nature of markets for commodities, land, capital, and labor. We lack this knowledge of the extent of market behavior in pre-Hellenistic and Hellenistic Babylon. We therefore can only be sure that there was a functioning free market in agricultural commodities.

The movements of these prices over time suggest conclusions about the politics of ancient Babylon as well. The severe disruption of prices after the death of Alexander confirms the views of those historians who have seen his death as the end of an era. The regressions tell us that it took almost a generation to restore stability to the agricultural markets in Babylon. They inform us that it was not a simple thing to restore order after a sudden shock like Alexander's death. The succession may have been decided quickly, but life did not return to normal for many years.

After order was restored with the establishment of the Seleucid dynasty, prices appear to have stabilized. But in the last two centuries before the Common Era, prices began to rise. As discussed earlier, this inflation may indicate a gradual breakdown of the government's ability to maintain stability as the Seleucid Empire gradually disintegrated. This price evidence, like that for the later Roman Empire, suggests that political and economic stability were becoming harder to achieve as time went on. A more complete analysis of the Roman inflation is presented in chapter 4.

The results of estimating equations for each of the six commodities revealed that the prices for different commodities differed from each other. There were trends in relative prices as well as trends in the price level as a whole. This again reveals agricultural markets in action. Only administered prices maintain their relative prices over long stretches of time. Wool in particular followed a unique time path, as suggested by the contrast between figures 3.1 and 3.2.

In the years around 100 BCE, the price of wool rose when the price of agricultural crops did not. There were high wool prices in several years, spaced over a few decades, although there also were some lower wool prices interspersed. These high observations affect regression trends, although they also may have represented a more short-run movement. It appears that there was some kind of wool shortage or disruption of the wool market at the end of the observed period. The statistical work reported here cannot identify the cause of this disruption; it can only identify the existence of something unusual in the wool market.

Seasonal dummies reveal a complex pattern, which I describe without reproducing the full regression results. Dates were delivered in the fall, and date prices were lower in the following half year than in the half year before the harvest. Barley was delivered in the spring, and it was more expensive in the preceding few months. But although mustard was delivered in the fall like dates, it was more expensive at the same time. The other three prices did not have seasonal patterns that can be recovered from the data with confidence. Approximately two hundred observations on the height of the Euphrates have survived, but only about one hundred of them overlapped price data on each commodity. Regressions of log prices on years and the height of the Euphrates did not reveal a significant effect of the river height on any of the six prices. The seasonal evidence therefore is ambiguous. There is some evidence that fits a model of an agricultural economy, but also seasonal evidence that does not.

Taking all these observations together, I reach two conclusions. First, careful analysis of these prices using time-series techniques confirms the conclusion in Slotsky (1997) that these prices were market prices. They moved with a great deal of randomness, and they varied over time. These agricultural prices moved like the random walk of modern prices, and they varied together in response to weather that affected all crops. These changes are understood clearly within a market framework; they are impossible to understand within an administrative one. I conclude therefore that the scribes recorded prices set in functioning markets.

Second, the pattern of prices informs us of economic conditions in Babylon before the Common Era. Prices fluctuated a lot. The return and subsequent death of Alexander led to a major shock to the supply of money and therefore to prices, sustained for a generation or more. Prices rose sharply and stayed high; normal conditions did not return for more than twenty years. This price disruption indicates how hard it was for political and economic stability to return, how hard it was to reestablish peaceful conditions where foodstuffs were available cheaply. People living in Babylon during this transition must have had a very difficult time. It appears that food was twice as expensive as usual in the city of Babylon; it is unlikely that most urban dwellers had assets that enabled them to offset the scarcity of food. Farmers by contrast may not have been affected if the prices they received for their produce rose as much as the prices of products they bought.

Prices rose in the last two centuries before the Common Era, gradually at first and then with increasing speed. This inflation suggests a gradual weakening of the political structure in Babylon in the final centuries before the Common Era since there does not appear to have been a shock to the money supply in these years. A gradual inflation does not indicate as much hardship for ordinary people as the sudden price rise of years before 300 BCE. Wool became expensive at the end of the period relative to other products, with prices that rose beyond the rise of other prices. This may have been a hardship for many people and possibly a boon for a few. Only future research can discover the cause of this price inflation and its possible effects on the lives of ordinary people.

Appendix to Chapter 3

■ ■ ■ ■ ■ ■

I employ descriptive regressions of the price of each commodity over time to examine the long- and short-run variation in prices as a whole. The results of estimating equations in the text show that contemporaries could not have predicted future prices; descriptive regressions can tell later observers what actually happened. The first such regression evaluates the long-run trend of prices. It models the relationship between each commodity's log price and the year, year squared, year cubed, and three dummy variables for different intervals:

$$\text{Log Price}_i = \alpha + \beta_1 \text{year} + \beta_2 \text{year}^2 + \beta_3 \text{year}^3 + \beta_4 \text{Dum1} + \beta_5 \text{Dum2} + \beta_6 \text{Dum3} + \varepsilon,$$

where the subscript of the log price refers to the commodity being observed. The first dummy variable, Dum1, controls for years between 323 BCE (-322) and 314 BCE (-313). This ten-year window is isolated to see if the death of Alexander had an effect on prices. The length of the window to account for any market disruptions in the wake of Alexander's death is arbitrary. To allow for a possible longer disruption to markets, two other dummy variables, Dum2 and Dum3, control for ten-year windows from 313 BCE (-312) to 304 BCE (-303) and from 303 BCE (-302) to 294 BCE (-293). These added dummy variables are included in the regression to discover whether prices returned to their level before 323 BCE or if prices continued to be higher than normal ten years and twenty years after the initial shock. The year-squared and year-cubed variables allow the path of prices to curve over the years. Any polynomial is an approximation to the arbitrary path of prices over time; a third-order polynomial allows a reasonably good characterization of the time path. Slotsky also used a cubic equation to allow for an accurate representation of the prices' patterns over four centuries.

It is hard to correct this equation for autocorrelation, and I have not done so. The problem is that the data come at irregular intervals while time is measured uniformly. Standard errors are incorrect as a result, and any significance tests need to be regarded as only approximate. I use a 1 percent confidence limit throughout to minimize the possibility of accepting an erroneous hypothesis. Results are shown in table 3.2.

In order to see if there was relative variation, that is, if the trends for the prices of different commodities differed from each other, I pooled the regressions for individual commodities to provide tests of significance for the trends of individual commodities. I expected market prices for agricultural commodities to have moved together since changes in supply and demand would have been similar for each crop. Yet wool might have moved differently from the agricultural commodities because the production of wool is quite distinct from raising a crop. To determine empirically whether the change of each price was significantly different from the change or other prices, I used a regression model of pooled commodity log prices that examines simultaneously the path of the six log prices over the years from 473 BCE to 72 BCE. The regression used is:

$$\text{Log Price} = \alpha_1 + \beta_{11} \text{ year} + \beta_{12} \text{ year}^2 + \beta_{13} \text{ year}^3 + \beta_4 \text{ Dum1} + \beta_5 \text{Dum2}$$
$$+ \beta_6 \text{Dum3} + \Sigma_i \delta_i (\alpha_i + \beta_{11} \text{ year} + \beta_{12} \text{ year}^2 + \beta_{13} \text{ year}^3) + \varepsilon,$$

where δ_i represents the dummy variable for the i-th commodity. Dates are the omitted commodity. Dum1, Dum2, and Dum3 are the dummy variables for the three ten-year windows from 323 BCE to 294 BCE. This regression determines the effect of time on each price. The extent to which trends of individual commodities differed is shown by the magnitude and significance of the α and β coefficients.

To capture seasonal variations in commodity log prices, it is necessary to model the relationship of seasons and years with log prices. Market prices could have shown consistent variation in seasons, while government determined prices would not have a clear pattern of variation. I incorporated dummy variables for winter, summer, and fall into the regressions for individual commodities. The dummy variable for spring (months I–III) is omitted. The seasonal regression is:

$$\text{Log Price}_i = \alpha + \beta_1 \text{ year} + \beta_2 \text{ year}^2 + \beta_3 \text{ year}^3 + \beta_4 \text{ Dum1} + \beta_5 \text{Dum2}$$
$$+ \beta_6 \text{Dum3} + \beta_7 \text{ winter} + \beta_8 \text{ summer} + \beta_9 \text{ fall} + \varepsilon.$$

The year and commodity dummies are defined before. The dummy variables for seasons show the relative effect that each season has on prices. The scribes collected information on the height of the Euphrates River, and it can be

TABLE 3.2.
Regressions of log prices on time

	Barley	Dates	Mustard	Cress	Sesame	Wool
Intercept	-1.71*	-0.149	-3.62*	1.25*	-0.345	2.46*
	(5.45)	(0.495)	(13.1)	(3.32)	(1.42)	(12.9)
Year	0.0316*	0.0694*	0.0328*	0.0652*	0.0269*	0.0362*
	(6.69)	(15.2)	(7.77)	(11.6)	(7.58)	(12.5)
Year^2	9.62×10^{-5}*	2.90×10^{-4}*	1.383×10^{-4}*	2.52×10^{-4}*	6.98×10^{-5}*	1.01×10^{-4}*
	(4.54)	(14.1)	(7.22)	(10.0)	(4.50)	(7.48)
Year^3	7.14×10^{-8}	3.51×10^{-7}*	1.63×10^{-7}*	2.88×10^{-7}*	3.71×10^{-8}	7.06×10^{-8}*
	(2.48)	(12.4)	(6.27)	(8.35)	(1.80)	(3.82)
Dum1	1.47*	0.980*	0.203	0.640*	1.31*	1.12*
	(6.81)	(5.83)	(1.34)	(4.60)	(12.1)	(11.7)
Dum2	2.07*	1.56*	0.173	0.191	N/A	0.515*
	(11.1)	(5.95)	(0.597)	(0.563)		(3.84)
Dum3	-0.592	0.242	1.55*	0.694	0.675*	0.704*
	(2.41)	(0.720)	(5.36)	(2.05)	(4.33)	(5.92)
Adj. R^2	0.427	0.474	0.285	0.378	0.499	0.697
Obs.	639	584	503	551	612	562

Absolute values of t-statistics are below the coefficients. * = significantly different from zero at 1% probability.
Note: Dum1 = ($-322 \leq$ year ≤ -313); Dum2 = ($-312 \leq$ year ≤ -303); Dum3 = ($-302 \leq$ year ≤ -293).

added to or substituted for seasonal dummies. I also tested for correlation of the errors in this equation to see if there were good and bad years for agriculture as a whole.

Although the seasonal dummies revealed a mixed pattern and there are not enough observations of the Euphrates River's height to yield significant results, there is a way to identify good and bad years. If these are market prices, then we expect that a good year would produce bountiful harvests of most crops and therefore lower prices. A bad year, by the same reasoning, would result in high prices. As a result the errors in the individual price regressions shown in table 3.2 would be correlated. Zellner's technique of "seemingly unrelated regressions" tests for any correlations and uses the additional information in the correlations to improve the estimates.

There are some costs to this procedure. The regression can only be done for years in which there are observations of all prices in order to calculate correlations among the residuals. The results of seemingly unrelated regressions will be more efficient, but using far fewer observations. The Breusch-Pagan test of independence of the regressions for different crops yields a chi-square with 15 degrees of freedom of 406. This is significantly different from zero at any conceivable level of significance. The errors of the equations in table 3.2 clearly are correlated; the prices behave just the way market prices of agricultural commodities in a local area are expected to act.

The resulting coefficients are almost the same as those in table 3.2. The standard errors are much larger, however, and not all coefficients are significant. This is due partly to the better estimation technique and partly to the reduced number of observations. Since the number of observations in each regression falls from over 500 to 90, the results in table 3.2 are more reliable. Of course, the trends shown in table 3.2 should be taken as purely descriptive rather than as evidence of an underlying price-formation process (Temin, 2002).

Chapter 4

■ ■ ■

Price Behavior in the Roman Empire

Returning from Babylon to Rome, I take a different approach to scarce Roman data in this chapter. The approach employs the simplification of economic models introduced in chapter 1. In this case, I summarize the complex phenomenon of Roman inflation into a simple dichotomy. Inflation was either on or off. Either there was inflation or there was not. This kind of zero-one choice is the basis of all our modern computers, and that analogy indicates that simplification can lead to complex results if handled creatively. This approach also follows the literature of ancient Rome where historians implicitly assume this binary division of experience. It enables me to ask and suggest answers to two questions in this chapter. Assuming inflation was "off" originally, what turned it "on"? Was the daily life of Romans very different under the long inflation of the late empire than it was during the stable prices of the early empire?

Despite a great scarcity of price data for the Roman Empire, ancient historians appear to have conventional opinions about Roman price movements. Prices were stable, which includes growing at only 1 or 2 percent a year, from the late republic though the second century of the empire. In fact, the onset of inflation after that time is one of the markers of the transition from the early to the late Roman Empire.

There also is a conventional view of the inflation, that it was the result of currency debasement, expressed often through graphs like figure 4.1. Howgego (1995, 123), however, argues that we should be "cautious about theories which imply a simple relationship between the coin supply and prices." There must be some relationship between the coin supply and prices; our task is to illuminate it. Lendon (1990) for example argued that we only know about inflation in Egypt and denies any relation at all between inflation and either the fineness of coins or their quantity, attributing inflation to an erosion of public

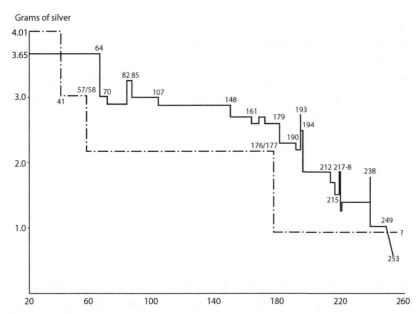

FIGURE 4.1. Currency debasement
Source: Christiansen (1988, 87)

confidence. Howgego's well-advised caution should not lead us to throw out the baby with the bathwater, and I propose an intermediate theory here.

I start by constructing indexes of inflation and political stability in the Roman Empire. I then discuss the interaction between these two indices, confronting the question of causation of complex historical events. Finally, I go behind the inflation index to propose a hypothesis about the nature of ancient inflation.

Hopkins (1980) is justifiably famous for the taxes and trade theory suggesting that the need to pay taxes may have promoted Roman trade. This work also is noteworthy for the introduction of various indices of Roman economic activity and an index of the money supply, that is, coins in circulation. I propose to avoid the hazards of estimating the ancient money supply and instead to gather the scarce price evidence that we have into an index of inflation. Given the scarcity of price data, I do not attempt to estimate the rate of inflation in the index, but only to distinguish between two states of affairs. The first state is price stability, meaning prices that change less than 2 percent a year. Stability in this sense would appear to any person living through it as price stability. The second state is inflation, meaning prices that change more rapidly. To the best of our knowledge, prices changed much more rapidly in the third century, and there is no problem of deciding which state the economy was in.

This procedure keeps us from having to estimate the rate of inflation and from deciding if the rate of inflation was constant or varying over time.

Before we examine the sparse evidence for Roman prices, we need to distinguish between market and administered prices. Market prices are the results of purchases and sales in markets. They are free to vary over time. In fact, the distinguishing characteristic of market prices is that it is not possible to predict the future variation of prices in advance. We may suspect that inflation will continue over the next decade, but it is impossible to know today if a particular price will be higher or lower tomorrow. In the jargon of economics, market prices move in a "random walk," in which the variation from this period to the next is a random variable. (If inflation is expected, prices may move in a "random walk with drift.") Administered prices, by contrast, change only infrequently. Tomorrow's price will be exactly the same as today's, except for the rare occasions when the administrative prices are changed.

There are not enough Roman prices to make a firm distinction between these two varieties of prices, but about three thousand prices survived for Hellenistic Babylon, as explained in the previous chapter. These prices were tested to see if they moved in a random walk, that is, if they were market prices. The test showed that they moved in a random walk and were market prices (Temin 2002). Babylon was not Rome, but the fortunate survival of many Babylonian prices reveals to us that market prices were widespread in the ancient world. I infer that the scarce Roman observations that resemble market prices also were market prices.

There were some administered Roman prices, such as census classes and army pay scale. These prices did not move in random walks; they stayed constant for long periods of time. When they did change, I regard the changes as responses to previous inflation. In other words, I presume that the administered prices only changed when market prices had changed enough to render the administrative prices dysfunctional. This implies that inflation *preceded* changes in administrative prices; the changes in administered prices were the result of inflation, not its cause. It is not important here if my assumption is correct. Whatever the motivation for changing prices, I only need to assume that the process stayed roughly constant.

Coinage was widespread in Roman areas by the end of the Babylonian prices series. The earliest prices we seem to have are the casual values Polybius was told about on his travels. Rickman (1980) regarded these few observations as reliable in his brief survey of wheat prices around the Mediterranean. I used these and a few other price observations in an analysis of relative prices around the Roman sea in chapter 2. The implicit assumption in that study was that prices remained sufficiently stable in the late republic and early empire that their pattern was due to the effects of location rather than inflation.

There are two ways to see that these few prices indicate price stability. Rickman compared them to a notional price of wheat in Rome. Market prices in the capital city were complicated by the annona and not easily available, and Rickman's prices need to be seen as a modern educated guesses. He said that the price of wheat was between three and four sesterces per modius around 150 BCE and between five and six sesterces two centuries later in the early empire. This is an increase of about 50 percent in two centuries. An inflation rate of 1 percent a year doubles prices in 70 years, and this assumption implies a long—approximately three century long—period of stable Roman prices. In addition, I showed in chapter 2 that prices from all over the Mediterranean fit into a coherent pattern of low prices far from Rome and higher prices in and around the metropolis. In other words, the pattern of stable prices was stable throughout the Mediterranean area for these centuries.

I therefore show no inflation for this period in table 4.1. Historians often phrase this assumption as inflation of 1 percent a year. This seems very little, but it implies more price change over these three centuries than is observed in the few prices we have. Rathbone (1997; 2007a) said that prices were stable. Hollander (2007, 153) followed Burnett's (1987) conclusion that prices doubled in three centuries. Scheidel (2009a) assumed inflation at the slow rate of 1 percent. Such a long period of price stability is not unique. Clark (2007b, 156) showed that English prices remained largely stable for five centuries from 1200 to 1700 CE, with inflation only over 1 percent during the price revolution of the sixteenth century. Even then, the rate of inflation generally stayed below 2 percent per year. Price stability in highly monetized agrarian societies may be unusual, but it is not particular to ancient Rome.

This long period of price stability came to an end at the end of the second century CE. This much is commonly accepted in the literature, although the evidence—while more abundant than for earlier years—is less direct than we would like. Many historians have reasoned that the debasement of the coinage must have led to inflation, citing evidence like the well-known graph in figure 4.1. This, of course, is only indirect evidence, and price data would be a far better indicator of inflation than the silver content of the currency.

Some market prices have survived from Egypt, which was connected to the rest of the Roman Empire in a complex way. Administered prices are known for the rest of the empire, but they pose questions about the underlying rate of inflation as discussed earlier. Harl (1996, chapter 11) described many market and administered prices both while they were stable and during the inflation, but he did not assemble them into any kind of price index.

Rathbone (2007a, 713) summarized the start of inflation in Egypt: "The price bands for other [nonwine] goods and wages display a remarkable stability from the AD 70s to the 160s, and then again from the 190s to AD 274. . . .

TABLE 4.1.
Inflationary periods in the Roman Empire

Years	Rathbo ne	Bagnall	Army Pay	Synthesis
000–025	0		0	0
026–050	0		0	0
051–075	0		0	0
076–100	0		1	1
101–125	0		0	0
126–150	0		0	0
151–175	1		1	1
176–200	1		0	1
201–225	0		1	1
226–250	0		1	1
251–275	1			1
276–300		1		1
301–325		1		1
326–350		1		1
351–375				
376–400				

Note: 1 indicates inflation.
Sources: Bagnall (1985), Rathbone (1997).

The sharp doubling of prices and wages in the later second century is best explained as a sign of temporary economic dislocation caused by the Antonine Plague." Rathbone's graph of these prices is shown here as figure 4.2. Rathbone interpreted the scarce data as the result of sharp bursts of inflation, not of a continuous process. He also noted the importance of the Antonine Plague, although the mechanism by which plague causes inflation is not clear.

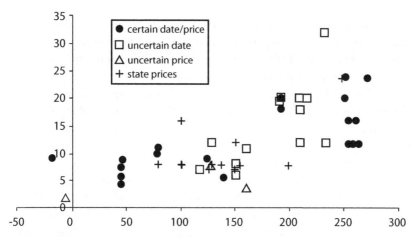

FIGURE 4.2. Egyptian wheat prices up to 270
Source: Rathbone (1997, 192)

Bagnall (1985, 64) started his survey of Egyptian prices in the fourth century. He found continuing, rapid inflation for the first two-thirds of the fourth century. The price of wheat rose from under 2,000 drachmas per artaba at the beginning of the century to almost 1,400 talents (each worth 6,000 drachmas) by 360. That is an increase of 6,000 in less than two-thirds of a century, confirmed by a few more prices for the same time period in Bagnall (1997, 226). The large number of drachmas needed to purchase a small quantity of wheat raises important questions about the nature of inflation. We do not believe that people brought more than 8 million drachmas with them to buy an artaba of wheat. Howgego (1995, 128) chided Bagnall for suggesting there might have been a myriad coin in this setting even though we lack evidence for it.

It is possible that transactions were being done in gold by 360. A far smaller weight of gold than of silver or debased silver coins would be needed to make this purchase. But this possibility only raises further questions. The *solidus* (a gold coin introduced by Diocletian) maintained its weight and purity for seven centuries (Jones 1974, 203). That makes the gold coins good money, while the debased silver ones clearly were bad money. Gresham's Law tells us that bad money drives out good, and the silver coins should have driven out the solidus. Presumably there came a time when the solidus replaced the successors of the denarius, but we cannot pin down the timing from the scarce records of transactions. Banaji (2001, 45) stated that "the most important change in the monetary system in the late empire was of course the introduction of a stable gold coinage and its progressive diffusion as a mass currency." He added (Banaji 2001, 60) that it "permeated all levels of social life." Katsari (2011) is more cautious.

This does not tell us the rate at which gold took over from the debased silver coinage or how small purchases were made, and there are very few examples of gold prices in the fourth century. Roman soldiers apparently were paid in gold, as revealed by Julian's changes in mid-century, but their pay consisted of very few solidi, exposing the issue of how they were spent (Kent 1956, 193). Whittaker (1980) and Bowman (1980) discuss the problem of stable gold prices and rising silver ones without reaching any conclusions. Were solidi functioning as real payments, that is, payments adjusted for inflation, in an inflationary world? Or were they the main currency?

Purchases may have been made by some form of credit, and silver prices were used to keep accounts rather than to indicate numbers of coins. Unless there were offsetting credit entries, coins must have been used at some point, raising questions similar to those arising from the first possibility. I take Bagnall's data at face value in the absence of answers to these questions and indicate the presence of inflation from the late second century through the third century.

These Egyptian market prices can be supplemented by some non-Egyptian administered prices for confirmation. The pay for the Roman Army is the most well-attested and long-lived of the administrative prices that have survived. Although Speidel (1992) and Alston (1994) disagree about the level of the base pay, they agree on the timing of changes, which is the important point here. Base pay was established by Augustus and was increased by Domitian (in 84 CE), Severus (197), Caracalla (212) and Maximinus Thrax (235). I assume that these prices were adjusted when the pay became dysfunctional, that is, when prices of goods and services that soldiers would buy increased so much that the pay for legionnaires no longer attracted enough of them. Inflation by this assumption preceded each of the rises in administered pay. That leads to the entries for army pay in table 4.1. The pattern echoes that of the Egyptian prices. There was price stability before the late second century with the exception of Domitian's pay hike. After that, the other increases correspond roughly with the Egyptian evidence of inflation in the third century, although they show inflation continuing during the apparent Egyptian price stability in the first half of the century.

Wheat is a good index of inflation because its quality does not vary much over time and it forms a large part of ordinary diets. Army pay is not consumed, and it is a good proxy for general inflation only if the relative price of soldiers, that is, the purchasing power of legionnaire wages, did not change. There were many wars in the third century, and the size of the Roman army probably increased. It is possible therefore that the emperors increased army pay in order to attract more workers to be soldiers, not to keep up with inflation. If so, then the Egyptian data may give a better index of inflation than army pay in the second century. This caveat illustrates one of the difficulties

with quantification in the ancient world. We know the history and its implication that army pay may have risen relative to, say, the price of wheat, but we
do not have a measure with which to calibrate how important this implication
was. Rathbone (1996, 323) cautiously suggests the dilemma is not large, stating: "I am prepared to believe in a cumulative increase [in army pay] of about
100%, which more or less compensated for the severe bout of price-inflation in
the late second century." We face the uncomfortable choice of either accepting
army pay and ignoring this complication or throwing it out as a poor proxy for
inflation. I am reluctant to discard potentially useful information, and I include
army pay as a proxy for inflation in table 4.1.

What accounts for the anomalous army pay hike by Domitian? I suggest
that it was the result of inflationary troubles under and just after Nero. The
start of these troubles may have been the fire that consumed the city of Rome
in 64 CE and the need for resources to rebuild the capital city. In any case,
he debased the currency, and it is reasonable "to assume that the reform was
intended to enable the government, either by extensive recoinage or by more
profitable use of existing bullion stocks, to achieve more with the same resources" (Griffin 1984, 198).

Nero reduced the silver content of the denarius from 3.65 grams to 3.0, a
level that was more or less maintained by his successors (Howgego 1995, 116).
Roman citizens may not have realized that the denarius contained less silver
immediately, but they would have been aware quickly that the government was
spending more. Whether because people realized the currency had been devalued or because of the extra expenditures, inflation probably increased. After
twenty years, Domitian apparently was having trouble recruiting legionnaires,
and he raised their pay. Nero's inflationary pressure must have dissipated over
time to allow the new pay scale to last for a century; it was not the start of
continuing inflation.

How rapid was the inflation once it became endemic toward the end of
the second century? The sources indicate large apparent jumps in prices, but
the period we are discussing also is long. An idea of the average rate of inflation in the third century can be obtained from Diocletian's Edict of 301 CE.
It listed the price of wheat as one hundred denarii, far higher than the prices
analyzed in chapter 2. Jones (1974, 200–201) described this contrast as follows:
"The figure of 100 denarii is therefore comparable with the low average price
of the first and second centuries, half a denarius. The price had then gone up
about 200 times in a century and a half." The silver content of the denarius had
changed dramatically in this time, and the comparison is not straight-forward
as a result. I convert Jones's statement into an inflation rate by assuming that
Roman consumers were less attentive to the silver content of the denarius than
modern numismatists.

The calculations in table 4.2 translate Jones's comparison into annual rates

TABLE 4.2.
Effects of annual inflation rates over a century and a half

Inflation rate (%)	Annual multiplier	Years	Total multiplier
1	1.010	150	4
1.5	1.015	150	9
2	1.020	150	19
2.5	1.025	150	41
3	1.030	150	84
3.5	1.035	150	174
4	1.040	150	359
4.5	1.045	150	737
5	1.050	150	1508

Sources: Author's Calculation.

of inflation. The first column lists various rates of inflation. The second column translates these rates into multipliers that can be used to convert prices in one year into those of the next year at the different rates of inflation. The third column gives the time period suggested by Jones. The final column calculates how much each rate of inflation in the first column raises prices after 150 years; it raises the multiplier in the third column to the power of the number of years in the fourth column. For example, at an inflation rate of 1 percent a year, prices only increase by a factor of four in a century and a half. But at an inflation rate of 4 percent a year, prices increase by a factor of almost 360 over a century and a half. The average rate of inflation from about 150 to 300 was just over 3.5 percent a year according to Jones. If the initial price was higher than Jones asserted or the final price lower as Duncan-Jones (1982, 66n4) suggested, then the average rate of inflation was lower. If we follow Rathbone and assert that prices began to rise later in the second century, then there was less time for them to rise to the heights of the Diocletian Edict, and the average rate of inflation was higher for a shorter time period. The precise number is not important; its order of magnitude is. This was high enough to be noticed at the time, as the European Price Revolution of the sixteenth century was noticed, but it is very far from a hyperinflation. Cagan (1956) defined a hyperinflation as more than 50 percent inflation per *month* in his classic work on modern hyperinflations—clearly a different phenomenon.

The same calculation can be used backward to understand the rate of inflation implied by Bagnall's data. For prices to rise by a factor of about four thousand in fifty-five years, the annual inflation rate must have been about 15 or 16 percent a year. There appears to have been an acceleration of inflation in the fourth century, although still nothing approaching a hyperinflation. People definitely would have noticed this kind of inflation, although it would not have prompted a flight from money like a hyperinflation. Given the limited data and questions about the relevance of silver prices, it is hard to tell if the apparent acceleration represents an intensification of long-run inflationary forces.

Instead of correlating prices with debasement, I propose an index of political instability to compare with the index of inflation. The new index counts the number of Imperial emperors in each half-century. The list is conventional, taken off the Internet, supplemented with biographical information when necessary. There are four variants of this index, all showing essentially the same picture. Two indices divide centuries; the other two start in 25 BCE to correspond more closely with the start of the empire and to make sure that using centuries does not affect the pattern. For each starting date, one index counts all emperors proclaimed by the army; the other only counts emperors confirmed by the Senate.

The four indices appear in table 4.3 and reveal a common pattern. The number of emperors in each half-century stayed in single digits until some time late in the second century, after which it stayed in double digits until 500 CE. This pattern is very similar to the pattern revealed in the index of inflation in table 4.1. As with the index of inflation, there are complications here. Turnover of emperors does not indicate political instability if they all die in their sleep. One way to see if the rising number of emperors indicates dynastic conflicts is to examine the differences between the two emperor counts. If there were more emperors recognized by their legions but not the senate, this indicates conflict and instability. The difference between the two series rises from zero in the first two centuries to two in the third century and even higher late in the fourth century, providing additional evidence of the growing instability suggested by the number of emperors in any time period.

In addition, there were coemperors starting in the late third century and separate emperors in the east and west empire starting a century later. The increase in the number of emperors therefore may indicate administrative needs rather than political instability. If so, then the fourth century was more stable than the indices suggest. This correction suggests that the indices in table 4.3 may overstate political instability in the fourth century. The large number of emperors and the growing difference between the two emperor counts indicate renewed political instability in the fifth century.

TABLE 4.3.
Numbers of Roman emperors, by date and proclamation

Years	Legion emperors	Senate emperors	Years	Legion emperors	Senate emperors
–25–25	2	2	01–50	4	4
26–75	7	7	51–100	9	9
76–125	5	5	101–150	2	2
126–175	4	4	151–200	10	8
176–225	12	10	201–250	15	13
226–275	31	29	251–300	31	28
276–325	22	20	301–350	17	16
326–375	14	13	351–400	15	15
376–425	17	13	401–450	12	4
426–475	14	9	451–500	13	13

Source: Internet emperor lists and biographies. See http://www.roman-emperors .org/impindex.htm.

The difference between the indices in table 4.3 indicate that we cannot define with precision the change from the stable political regime to the less stable regime starting in the late second century. Different definitions and time periods generate more differences in the period of transition than in more stable years. If we desire to have more precision of the timing, we will need more information to know if, for example, the auction of the empire after the murder of Pertinax in 193 was a new norm for the empire.

These indices raise two questions that must be addressed. The first question is how the Roman Empire—and the late Roman Republic before it— maintained more or less stable prices. Having lived through the inflationary twentieth century, we want to know how the Romans avoided that condition for so long without knowing any of our modern economic rules. The second question is why this long reign of stable prices came to an end in the late second century. These are very different questions that may be expected to have very different answers. Since the two questions refer to adjacent periods of the same political entity, good answers to the two questions should be compatible.

Lo Cascio (1981, 85) suggested thirty years ago that the Roman government was interested in monetary stability: "It was particularly by . . . the adjustment of the weight and fineness of an entire issue that the Roman government tried, mostly with success, to counterbalance the negative effects on the coins of a changing ratio between the metals." The desired stability extended beyond the supply of small change to include, according to Lo Cascio, army pay and "even financial relationships among the aristocracy."

The more general point is embarrassingly contemporary. "In time of crisis, lack of liquidity brings about a sharp rise in the rate of interest and a fall in land prices, and it becomes difficult to repay debt" (Lo Cascio 1981, 85). One needs only to interpret the rate of interest to mean the return on risky assets and land to mean lots with houses to see ancient crises as a distant precursor of 2008. The Tiberian response to the crisis of 33 CE, to flood the economy with liquidity, is the same as 2009 U.S. Federal Reserve System policy. Given the similarity of ancient and modern crises and policies, it is illuminating to apply modern tools to the analysis of ancient problems. I discuss the problem of bimetallic stability first and then progress to more general monetary stability.

Gresham's Law tells us that bad money drives out good money. Bad money in this phrase is coinage that is worth more as coinage than the metal contained in the coins is worth as bullion. Good money is the reverse, currency that is worth as much or more as bullion than as coins. Good money gets melted down for the metal it contains, while no one melts down bad money. The only way to keep a full bimetallic currency going is to have the relative value of coins of different metals exactly mirror the market price of the metals in the coins. If market prices change or if the ratio is set wrong, then bad money drives out good—and the economy is on a single metal standard. The United States, for example, was nominally on a bimetallic standard for much of the nineteenth century. But gold was worth more as gold than as dollars initially, and the country was on a silver standard. When gold was discovered in California in 1849, the price of gold fell and gold became bad money. The United States shifted to a gold standard, confirmed when the coinage law of 1873 omitted the silver dollar from the coins to be minted (Nussbaum 1967).

We see changes in Roman coinage, but we do not have the information on causation that we have for modern coinage changes. We therefore observe changes in coinage and use Gresham's Law to infer what must have happened on the market. In about 140 BCE, the denarius was retariffed from 10 to 16 asses. The silver denarius was raised in official value relative to the bronze as. Our modern presumption is that the relative price of silver was rising. As the relative price of silver rose, the denarius turned into good money. Denarii must have been getting scarce as they were melted down to recover the silver they contained. The retariffing was an effort to keep the currency on a silver standard and not let it go onto a copper or bronze one. The Roman government performed a number of similar revaluations designed in this case to keep the supply of small change from taking over the monetary standard and in other cases to reflect changing market prices of silver and gold (Lo Cascio 1981).

Gresham's Law depends on there being markets for the metals used for currency. We know little about the market for nonmonetary silver and infer its existence from currency changes. It is hard to believe that there was much nonmonetary silver in use, given how hard it was to mine silver in the ancient world (Rihll 2001). There were agricultural and manufactured goods whose traces we see more clearly in the records that have survived. The question is whether the Roman government intervened to keep the value of money constant, that is, to maintain the relative price of silver and, say, wheat. If the price of silver rose—that is, if there was actual or threatened deflation—did the government mint more denarii?

I do not think that the Roman government thought in these terms, but I suggest that a simple monetary rule would have produced the same effect. Assume that the government minted more denarii or debased existing denarii if it needed more resources in a hurry when it ran short. This rule does not require the emperor to think about the price level at all; he simply looked at his own demand for money. As the Pax Romana expanded and more people used currency based on the denarius, the emperor found that he was losing his currency to the provinces. He minted more money to keep up with his own demand. Nero needed money in a hurry, and he devalued the denarius instead of minting more coins to the old standard. We presume that this did not lead to a general inflation because the demand for money was rising fast enough at the time to absorb the increase in the number of denarii in circulation.

This monetary rule works well when the economy and the demand for money are expanding. What happens if the economy is declining? If the emperor needed more money quickly, like Nero, he would debase the denarius. But if the economy was not expanding, there would be more money for the same or smaller amount of goods. The result would be inflation. If emperors needed money frequently to defend their rule or if putative emperors needed money frequently to attack existing rulers, then the rule indicates successive debasements and resulting inflation.

This simple rule of thumb leads to a rule that can explain both price stability and price inflation. When the economy was expanding and the government was stable, the government's need for money was consistent with stable prices. But when the economy was not expanding and government was less stable, the demand for money at the center generated too much money to keep prices stable. The question then is why the economy and price behavior shifted from a stable to an inflationary regime.

I turn therefore to the second question about prices: why did stable prices give way to inflation at the end of the second century? To answer this question, I need to take a small detour into modern economic theory. The similarity of the two indices shown in tables 4.1 and 4.3 suggests there is a relationship between them. Economists have created methods to infer more complex interactions than just correlation. They refer to this task as the identification process, meaning the need to identify the direction of causation between the variables. There are three possibilities. It is possible that political instability led to inflation, or that inflation generated political instability, or that both inflation and political instability were caused by some third cause. With a lot of data, there are sophisticated statistical tests to identify which of these possibilities is the most plausible. These tests are hard to use with the limited data available for the Roman Empire and even more difficult to use with the simple patterns shown by the indices in tables 4.1 and 4.3.

We need instead to examine each of the possibilities in turn to see which one is the most plausible. We cannot extract from the data an estimate of plausibility for each story, but we can employ our historical understanding to identify which of the various possibilities appears most plausible. For example, it is easy to understand how political instability can cause inflation. Instability means lots of conflict and therefore demands by soldiers for pay. If the contenders have access to silver, they can issue more coins; if not, they can debase existing coins. Either way, they generate inflation. This can be seen clearly in the Hellenistic Babylonian prices described in the previous chapter. Those prices jumped dramatically after Alexander's death in 323 BCE and took several decades to return to previous levels. Given the wealth of prices that have survived for that time, we can be confident that the price rises were the result of general inflation, not changes in the demand for individual commodities.

The index of political instability in table 4.3 reveals that dynastic succession was a continuing problem in the late Roman Empire. The inflationary consequences are clear. In most contests for political power, the need for more cash was immediate. In those cases, emperors and putative emperors devalued coins instead of minting new ones. Either debasing or minting more coins is inflationary, as noted already, but debasement was the mechanism used in the late empire. This accounts for the correlation between the silver content of coins and inflation that Howgego discussed.

Unfortunately, it also is easy to construct stories of reverse causation, showing how inflation could have produced political instability. For example, if taxes were fixed in money terms, inflation would decrease government revenue. Emperors without resources would be prime suspects for replacement. Jones (1974, 193) argued that many Roman taxes were fixed in nominal terms and decreased with inflation. Bagnall (1993, 312n) argued that one third of Egyptian taxes were collected in money in the third century. Brunt (1990, 356) warned that "it is impossible to insist too strongly on the paucity of documentation for the imperial fiscal system." At the present state of knowledge, we can neither affirm nor refute this possible direction of causation.

This brings us the third possibility, that both inflation and political instability were the result of a third cause. This case can coexist with the two possibilities already described, because inflation can be both caused by and cause political instability if they both were stimulated by a third cause. If there was this kind of mutual causation, the system was unstable. Once inflation or political instability was started by the third cause, the interaction between them would have set in motion a cumulative process that would have prolonged the results of the initial impulse.

This kind of mutual causation makes the task of historians both easier and harder. Easier because we only need to find an initial cause to start the process off. The mutual causation of inflation and political instability then would have taken over to continue both processes. Harder because any event of the late second century that was not the result of either inflation or political instability is a candidate for this third cause. There are no formal tests that can help us identify the impulse that starts an unstable process; we are thrown back on our historical understanding of the time.

One big event of the late second century stands out as a possible cause of this transition: the Antonine Plague. Sallares (2007, 37) described it as follows: "The appearance of pandemics was a side-effect of the general increase in inter-regional trade and movement of people in classical times. The first pandemic was the so-called 'Antonine Plague,' which raged for about twenty years in the second half of second century AD. The causative agent responsible for the 'Antonine Plague' . . . is widely agreed to have been smallpox. . . . Later parallels make it plausible that the 'Antonine Plague' might have killed about a third of the population, at least in some areas."

This description makes it clear that the plague was what economists call *exogenous*. We believe that the variables we are trying to explain, inflation and political instability, were determined by a process I am hoping to illuminate. In the words of economists, they are *endogenous* variables. Plague, however, was not caused by either inflation or political instability. In fact, quite the reverse; according to Sallares the Antonine Plague was the result of the long period of stable political institutions and prices that preceded it. The Antonine Plague therefore is a good candidate for the third possible cause alluded to earlier.

To have this important effect, the Antonine Plague must have been large. Rathbone (2007a, 700) confirmed Sallares's view of the plague, at least for Egypt: "No one disputes that the Antonine Plague, which was carried into Egypt in AD 166/7 caused over the next decade a dramatic aggregate population loss, probably of around 20–30 percent to judge from some attested cases." This may be all the information we can gather about the magnitude of the Antonine Plague; the Justinian Plague did not leave even as much evidence as we have for the second century in the historical record (Little 2007). This evidence is sufficient for the Antonine Plague to have had a major impact.

Duncan-Jones (1996) and Scheidel (2002) analyzed the effect of the Antonine Plague on relative prices, such as a rise in wages relative to food or land due to the decline of the number of workers in the inflation. They appear to have found changes in relative prices that were consistent with the size of population declines estimated for the plague, although Bagnall (2002) was skeptical that the available evidence supported firm conclusions. Taking into account the paucity of evidence, I argue here that there is enough evidence and logic for us to take seriously the role of the Antonine Plague as an important exogenous variable.

The next step in the argument is how the plague could have affected inflation, that is, prices in the whole economy, as opposed to prices in markets peculiarly subject to disruption in a plague. Rathbone, in the passage quoted earlier about Egyptian prices, asserted that "temporary economic dislocation caused by the Antonine Plague" could have caused rising prices and wages. I described earlier how dynastic struggles induced inflation, but the Antonine Plague did not lead to a struggle over leadership of the Roman Empire, or at least did not lead to such an effect quickly or directly. Without a more specific mechanism, it is hard to evaluate whether temporary economic dislocation could have caused inflation. We must search for a more direct link.

Let me take the reasoning used by Duncan-Jones and Scheidel a bit further. Plague reduced the number of workers relative to the amount of land and therefore affected relative prices. It also reduced the number of workers and consumers relative to the supply of money in existence at the time. Plague killed people, but it did not reduce arable land, animals, or coins. Fewer people then were using the same amount of money, that is, more money per capita, to purchase goods, and prices rose. The impact on demand was increased by the plague's effect on supply. With fewer workers, grain and other agricultural production undoubtedly was lower, and the resulting products were scarcer relative to the amount of money than before. Consumers had more money than before, because there were fewer consumers, and they used this money to bid up the prices of goods.

Lo Cascio (2007, 646) added a further dimension to this argument, describing the effect of plague on the government: "The Antonine Plague drastically reduced the productive basis from which the imperial state drew its financial resources." Lower tax revenues put the government in a bind. If it responded by coining more money or debasing existing coins, then there would have been even more money chasing the reduced quantity of goods. All these arguments work in the same direction. They provide mechanisms by which the Antonine Plague could have caused inflation. Rathbone alluded to similar problems when he argued that the plague led to economic disruption. If the disruption led to political instability, this was the other element in the cumulative process. As noted earlier, there is no argument for reverse causation, for inflation or political instability causing the plague. The plague was an *exogenous* event that could have set in motion a cumulative advance of prices and political instability. More information about the Antonine Plague can be found in Lo Cascio (2012).

This argument is complicated by the simultaneous debasement of the Alexandrian tetradrachm in 176–77, during the Antonine Plague, and shown in figure 4.1. We do not know the cause of this debasement, but it does not appear to have had a large effect because subsequent issues were small and were not obtained by reminting earlier coins. And if the debasement was the result of the Antonine Plague, it would not indicate a separate cause of inflation (Rathbone 1996, 328, 334). Nevertheless, the debasement clouds the link between the plague and prices.

The cumulative process is very different from the process started by the 64 CE fire in Rome. The added demand for money led to an expansion of money and—we think—some inflation. But it did not set in motion a cumulative process of political instability. We can speculate whether this *exogenous* fire led to the dynastic struggles of 69 CE, the Year of Four Emperors, but that is a side issue. The important issue is that the political instability lasted only one year, to be followed by a century of relatively smooth transitions of power. Not all *exogenous* events generate continuing processes.

It is clear from figure 4.1 that inflation continued for a long time. But was it continuous? Rathbone (2007a, 713) summarized the start of inflation in Egypt as follows: "The price bands for other [non-wine] goods and wages display a remarkable stability from the AD 70s to the 160s, and then again from the 190s to AD 174. . . . The sharp doubling of prices and wages in the later second century is best explained as a sign of temporary economic dislocation caused by the Antonine Plague." Rathbone's graph of these prices is shown here as figure 4.2. Rathbone interpreted the scarce data as the result of sharp bursts of inflation, not of a continuous process. This deepens the question that is the prime focus of this chapter, the cause of inflation. If inflation is a series of distinct bursts, there may be separate causes for each burst. If inflation is the result of underlying factors, we need to inquire why prices moved jaggedly rather than smoothly. Rathbone also notes the importance of the Antonine Plague, although the mechanism by which plague causes inflation is not clear.

Indices summarize a lot of information. Those shown in tables 4.1 and 4.3

TABLE 4.4.
Regressions of log prices

	Model 1	Model 2	Model 3	Model 4
year	0.004* (6.260)			−0.002 (0.774)
post 190		0.781* (7.442)		
post 190 * year			0.003* (6.798)	
Constant	1.822* (14.932)	2.048* (25.800)	2.067* (24.721)	3.315* (5.251)
F	39.19	55.39	46.21	0.6
R^2	0.601	0.681	0.64	0.041
Observations	28	28	28	16

Absolute value of t-statistics are below the coefficients.
*= significantly different from zero at 1%.

have to ignore many details to show the patterns over a long period of time. Inflation never progresses smoothly, and there typically are variations over time. Bagnall showed that ancient inflation did not always advance at the same rate; Rathbone concluded that inflation paused between 190 and 270. These finer descriptions of the price data are not captured in the index in table 4.1. How do they affect the story being told here?

I used the regressions in table 4.4 to confirm Rathbone's statement quoted earlier about the spasmodic movement of Egyptian prices. Model 1 estimates the rate of inflation over the whole period of dated wheat prices in Rathbone (1997). Model 2 tests Rathbone's view that wheat prices were stable except for a discrete jump in 160–190. Model 3 tests the hypothesis that inflation began after 160–190, but progressed smoothly after then. Model 4 uses only the observations after 190 to see if there was inflation in that period alone.

Model 2, Rathbone's view, appears the most likely. It has the highest R^2, that is, it explains the highest proportion of the variance in the dated price data. The differences between the R^2 of the first three models are not large. I therefore also record F-statistics for the models. Since one can maximize the

R^2 with a separate dummy variable for each observation, the F-statistic measures how unlikely it is to observe the proposed model, given the difference between the number of variables and the number of observations. Model 2 clearly has the highest F-statistic, showing it to be the most likely representation of Rathbone's price data. This result is confirmed by Model 4, which uses only prices after 190 and shows that prices after that date exhibited no inflationary trend at all.

There is one problem that needs resolution. The Antonine Plague may have reduced the population by one-third, but prices appear to have doubled. Prices needed only have risen by about one-third to equalize the per capita money stock if that were the only cause of inflation. As noted above and shown in figure 4.1, the Alexandrian tetradrachm as devalued at the same time. If this too led to rapid inflation, then the halving of the silver content of the currency could have led to a doubling of prices. This resolves the problem of the large jump in prices at the cost of blurring the logic of the story. We do not know why the tetradrachm was debased, and we cannot assume it is exogenous. The plague was exogenous, but if the debasement is needed to explain the magnitude of the price jump, there are additional steps in the story that are not yet clear, and it is hard to maintain that the Antonine Plague was the sole cause of the change to an inflationary monetary regime.

To be consistent, we must at this point recall Howgego's caution. The preceding discussion has argued that prices stayed constant while debasement continued. In other words, while debasement had consequences for the long run, the short-run impact could be complex. It is hard in this context to say that prices doubled immediately when the tetradrachm was debased, particularly when Rathbone (1997, 188) concluded that "it will have taken a long time for tetradrachms on the new standard to have achieved dominance of the circulating coin." In other words, the debasement should have led to a slow inflation rather than the sharp jump in prices Rathbone observed. If we dismiss the debasement as a cause of the sudden price jump, then the magnitude of the jump remains problematical.

The pause in inflation after 190 complicates the story that starts from the Antonine Plague. It appears that the plague led to inflation, as explained earlier, but that the effect was temporary—like the effect of Nero's need for cash. On the other hand, army pay was increased twice in the early third century, implying that there was inflation in Europe. This raises the possibility that prices in Egypt and Europe were not correlated very closely over decades, although they moved together over long periods of time. If that is so, then it will be hard to pin down the precise interactions between the plague, prices, and politics with current data. Our price data come primarily from Egypt, while our index of political instability centers on European conditions. The two clearly are related, but as Howgego said of debasement and inflation, we must be wary of assuming simple patterns of causation.

Haklai-Rotenberg (2011) proposed an explanation for price stability in the second century. The official value of the currency stayed constant before around 270, while the silver content of the denarius fell steadily. The gap between the official value and the value of the silver in coins consequently fell until it become enormous. At that point, Haklai-Rotenberg argues that Aurelian's attempt to revise the coinage led people to switch from using the official value to the value of silver. This reduced the value of money, that is, it increased the price of goods (wheat) in terms of coins. Haklai-Rotenberg's model fleshes out Rathbone's (1996, 335–37) claim of "some link" between Aurelian's reforms and the price rise.

Economists have modeled processes like this one in the context of currency crises. Krugman (1979)—who later won the Nobel Prize—initiated an extensive literature with a model of currency crises for a country on a fixed exchange rate. If such a country has economic policies that result in declining foreign reserves (gold if the fixed exchange rate came from the gold standard), people realize at some point that the country will run out of reserves. Before that calamitous result, people will see it coming and attempt to sell the country's currency. If they overwhelm the central bank, the value of the currency (in gold or relative to other currencies) falls precipitously. This is the anatomy of a modern currency crisis.

It also describes a possible path for the value of Roman money during the long inflation. Ordinary Romans, in this view, bought and sold coins at their face value even though the silver content of the coins was falling. Any single Roman might have thought that the coins were not worth so much any more, but individual actions would not change the overall pattern. Only if there was a large-scale attack on the value of the coins precipitated by a coordinating event would the value of the coins in use fall, that is, would prices rise. Haklai-Rotenberg proposed Aurelian's coinage reform as a coordinating event, leading to a sudden decline in the value of coins and rise in prices. Other coordinating events could have caused this pattern to repeat itself at other times, making inflation into an episodic rather than a smooth process.

A letter from the early fourth century (P. Ryl. 607) gives us a window into the experience of people living through a sudden debasement. It reveals that at least some people living through sudden jumps in the value of money were aware of the episodic process I am describing and tried to cope with the change as best as possible.

> Dionysius to Apion, greeting. The divine fortune of our lords [*sic*, the emperors] has decreed that the Italian coin (*to Italikon nomisma*) be reduced to half a

nummus. Make haste, therefore, to spend all the Italian coinage (*argyrion*) that you have, and purchase on my behalf goods of every description (*eidē pantodapa*), at whatever price (*timē*) you find them. For this purpose I have dispatched an *officialis* to you. But take notice that should you intend to indulge in any mal-practices I shall not allow you to do so. I pray, my brother, that you may be long in health. (Verso): I received the letter from the *officialis* on 8 Pharmouthi.

This analysis of Egyptian inflation needs to be integrated with the story of European inflation to apply to the Roman Empire. In the absence of market prices for the third century, I used changes in army pay as a proxy. If prices in Europe rose discontinuously in the late second century as in Egypt, then the successive pay hikes for the legionnaires may have been attempts by vari-ous emperors to catch up to rising wages. Alternatively, if prices rose more smoothly in Europe—echoing the smoother Roman debasement shown in figure 4.1—then the punctuated inflation of Egypt may not extend to the whole empire. Only more price data will help resolve this choice.

The index of inflation in table 4.1 is not fine enough to pick up stable pe-riods in the course of the long inflation. It therefore does not help us discover the dynamics of price inflation in the later Roman Empire. Political instability may have led to debasement of the currency, which may have led only sporadi-cally to inflationary bursts, with the bursts of inflation coming from unknown (at this time) coordinating events. This may be an insightful view of inflation, but it will be hard to test with the available quantitative data. There may have been another period of price stability between Aurelian's and Diocletian's cur-rency reforms, supporting this idea of episodic inflation.

This chapter offers new indices of inflation and political instability for both the early and late Roman Empire. It uses these indices to suggest an explana-tion for the change from the early to the late Roman Empire. There are myriad explanations in the literature. I make no claims for originality or exclusiveness in presenting the Antonine Plague as an important event. The plague was im-portant not only because it was large, but also because it stimulated the change from a regime of stable prices to one of continuing inflation. The increase of political instability was part of the cumulative process that effected this change.

I also make no claim for the completeness of this story. The indices can-not expose the details of the inflation or the political process. This story is an abstract version of the process by which the early Roman Empire turned into the late Roman Empire. It undoubtedly is consistent with many other stories about this momentous change.

I speculate about the process of ancient inflation. We all know what stable prices are, and some of us have experienced rapid inflation. It is less clear how inflation affected the lives of ancients living through it. I suggest that what appears continuous in table 4.2 actually is episodic, that prices rose in discontinuous steps that became more frequent as the western Roman Empire dissolved. If this is an accurate representation, the lives of ordinary people may have been varied. Those living in stable periods would have not noticed, but those living through sudden drops in the value of money may have had more difficult times.

The originality in this chapter is the attempt to consider the mechanisms by which observed events interacted. While the paucity of information leaves ample room for speculation, we should restrict ourselves to speculations that are internally consistent. I have used economic theory to maintain consistency in the analysis of this epochal change. This enables us to make connections between events that are more specific than casual statements about these connections. It is easy to present hypotheses; it is much harder to find ways to discriminate among them. Careful consideration of economic interactions is one tool to use in this daunting task.

Part II

. . .

Markets in the Roman Empire

Introduction

■　■　■　■

Roman Microeconomics

This section contains most of the material that I anticipated gathering when I drew up my research plan in Roman economic history more than a decade ago. I surveyed these markets briefly in the initial research plan I took around at the Oxford conference where everyone laughed at me. That proposal grew into Temin (2001), perhaps my most widely noted paper. The chapters in this section provide a more sustained examination of Roman microeconomics, that is, the study of individual Roman markets.

Wheat was the most widely traded commodity in Roman times. I described the Mediterranean wheat market as a whole in chapter 2. I inquire into the detailed workings of the wheat market in chapter 5. The Romans made many products, from wines to pottery and glass, that are worthy of study. I hope that this inquiry into the details of the wheat market will encourage others to examine the peculiarities of other markets.

Labor is an important input into the production of wheat and other commodities. The examination of the Roman market in chapter 6 is complicated by the presence of Roman slavery. The existence of slavery was taken by a previous generation of scholars to preclude the possibility of a Roman labor market. I show in chapter 6 that this view did not take into account the unusual forms of Roman slavery—unusual in comparison with other kinds of slavery, ancient and modern. Once this institution is understood, it is clear that slaves were part of the Roman labor market.

Land, of course, is the basis of all agrarian economies. Yet land markets are different from commodity markets even today because land does not move. I therefore inquire in chapter 7 into the terms of Roman land ownership. The modern terms to describe the kind of land tenure that Romans originated in medieval times, long after classical arrangements had vanished in what would become Europe. I needed to follow the path of land tenure in European history in order to explain the terms used to describe Roman land tenure.

Capital, and particularly the mobility of capital, is the topic of chapter 8. Romans made many investments in agriculture, cities, and roads, all of which are capital. How did they amass the needed capital? I argue in chapter 8 that they were helped by Roman banks. These banks were remarkably like the first modern commercial banks in eighteenth-century London, and the comparison is illuminating. This chapter draws on work I did with Dominic Rathbone (Rathbone and Temin 2008) and consequently is more detailed and better documented than most of the other chapters.

Chapter 5

■ ■ ■

The Grain Trade

Long-distance trade in the many centuries before the telegraph was beset by information problems. There was the uncertainty present to all when ships set out and people awaited their return with little or no news in the interim. There also was the need to transact business at a distance when information traveled slowly, often by using an imperfectly controlled agent. The problem of finding good agents and providing proper incentives for them has been studied for the early modern world and even occasionally for the medieval world. I extend this exploration back into the ancient world in this chapter, analyzing how Roman merchants dealt with asymmetric information in the centuries surrounding the beginning of the Common Era.

Rome was the largest city before London at the time of the Industrial Revolution as noted earlier. The multitudinous Romans ate a great deal of grain, much of it wheat. This simple fact becomes more surprising when one considers how easily and conveniently Romans could buy that grain. Shipped from distant provinces, the grain changed hands many times before it reached Rome. This trade was organized by the state and private merchants who did not have the benefit of modern means of transportation or communication, and merchants faced high transaction costs from several sources. At times, merchants had to wait weeks to find out if their ships had sunk or if a harvest had wiped out the grain supply in a particular location. The Roman government cleared the Mediterranean of pirates in 67 BCE, completing a process reducing greatly one major source of risk for merchants.

In addition to these problems resulting from incomplete information, merchants in Rome had to rely on potentially corrupt agents—whom they could not monitor—operating in faraway provinces for months at a time. This arrangement created adverse selection and moral hazard problems from the asymmetric information available to merchants and their agents. I reconcile in this chapter the success of the Roman grain market described in chapter 2 with the apparent barriers to that success, arguing that grain merchants used a sophisticated set of institutions to mitigate their information problems.

Roman grain merchants contended with the consequences of highly limited information and of adverse selection and moral hazard, called collectively, principal-agent problems. There were large barriers of distance and time between merchants and their agents, making the coordination of buying and selling difficult to manage. Merchants could not ascertain quickly when the price of grain in Egypt, Africa, or Rome might be high or low, or even if their ship had sunk in a storm. The advent of the telegraph and then the wireless would reduce some of those problems in the nineteenth century, but merchants had dealt with these problems for several millennia before then.

Adverse selection comes about when people have choices whether to participate in an activity. If the nature of the activity attracts undesirable people, then we say there is adverse selection. For example, Adam Smith argued for usury limitations on interest rates on the grounds that only crooks and scoundrels would borrow money at high interest rates. Once people have decided to participate in an activity, they have choices in their actions. If the incentives promote choices injurious to other people, we say there is moral hazard. For example, insurance may cause people to take excessive risks because they know they are insured. Asymmetric information is shorthand for one party to a transaction knowing more than the other. An agent on the spot may know more than the merchant who sent him on a voyage, and this gives him an advantage in making choices we identify as asymmetric information. All of these concepts arise when we discuss the relations of principals who furnish resources or make rules and agents who are asked to act for the principal. They are the ordinary settings for the questions of the New Institutional Economics.

Roman grain merchants, like merchants in other times and places, had to find capable, trustworthy agents under conditions of adverse selection. As Akerlof (1970) explained in his famous "lemons" paper, when the buyer of a good or a service (the merchant in our case) has no clear way of discerning the quality of the good or service itself (the agent), the buyer typically faces an adverse selection of goods. The provider of goods and services (the agent) has an incentive to provide only lower-quality goods, and so the market for that product may even disappear entirely. Stiglitz and Spence, who shared a Nobel Prize in economics for analyzing the effects of adverse selection, both outline modern examples of the screening problems that have become particularly pertinent recently in areas such as the management of American health maintenance organizations (Altman, Cutler, and Zeckhauser 1998).

The merchant-agent relationship also established conditions for moral hazard, a problem closely related to adverse selection. Agents working in distant and therefore unobservable settings could skim profits or steal cargos from owners with little fear of reprisal. The moral hazard was exacerbated by adverse selection, since the merchants might hire agents with an inclination to cheat. This problem has been mitigated from time immemorial by using family and friends as agents whenever possible. This proclivity to use known agents is pervasive in all societies; only the details change. The Rothschilds succeeded in part because Mayer Amschel had five trustworthy sons, and president of the United States George W. Bush was helped in business by family connections (Ashton 1948; Mathias 1999; Ferguson 1998; Phillips 2004).

Many papers have demonstrated that institutions play a critical role in reducing the costs of these asymmetric and incomplete information problems when family or household connections are not enough. Akerlof (2002) suggested that business institutions such as warranties, brand names, and reputation provide means to reduce the problem of adverse selection because those types of "signaling"—proactive identification of quality or ability—increase the available information. Sixteenth- and seventeenth-century North American merchant groups hired people from within specific families or communities that were already considered trustworthy and promoted people from entry-level positions once their level of ability was clear (Carlos and Nicholas 1990; Jones and Ville 1996). Similarly, Greif argues that the Maghribi Muslim traders in early medieval times depended on a different kind of social signaling—membership in a common religious group—to mark the reputable agents. Genoese traders, on the other hand, relied on the enforcement mechanism inherent in their legal framework to ensure a selection of honest agents (Greif 1994). In general, common ways to reduce moral hazard include paying high wages to raise the costs of being fired for cheating and implementing peer-monitoring institutions (Shapiro and Stiglitz 1984; Arnott and Stiglitz 1991). Early trading companies relied on those monitoring systems and also required agents to take oaths to work solely in the best interests of the company (Carlos 1992).

These studies often take the legal environment as given, but North and others active in the New Institutional Economics have stressed the importance of a functioning legal system. The relations between merchants and agents are simplified greatly if they have contractual relations that are enforceable in a court of law. Trade itself can be done without contracts—purely for cash and only on spot markets—but the ability to write contracts facilitates the expansion of economic activity. Recent papers have questioned the relative advantages of differing legal systems, arguments that are based on the importance of this underlying institution (Beck and Levine 2005; Lamoreau and Rosenthal 2004).

One strand of the New Institutional Economics regards legal rules and other institutional aids to commerce as endogenous, that is, as designed to make the economy more efficient. We cannot ascribe this degree of rationality to the Roman economy. Some measures, those specific to maritime risks and principal-agent concerns, may have been introduced to facilitate trade. But the bulk of the formal and informal rules and practices of the early Roman Empire grew for other reasons and were adapted to aid commerce. It is this mix of "found" and created measures that makes historical description so interesting.

These information problems were not unique to the Roman merchants. They have troubled merchants throughout history. Eleventh-century Genoese and Muslim traders, joint-stock companies in England and Holland, the Hudson Bay Company, the East India Company, and colonial American traders all struggled with corrupt agents, vast distances, and poor communications (Greif 1989 and 1994; Jones and Ville 1996; Carlos and Nicholas 1990; Price 1989; Bruchey 1966). Such problems remain prominent in today's marketplace as well (Akerlof 1970; Spence 2002; Stiglitz 2002). In order to reduce the transaction costs of these information problems, merchants throughout history have turned to institutions to coordinate, disseminate, and share information. Yet few people have asked how such an institutional strategy was used in the ancient world, despite a growing interest in Roman economic activity.

Roman merchants, like later merchants, used a system of legal, social, and cultural institutions to access otherwise unavailable information, thereby mitigating the effects of potential information problems. They used a mix of specially designed and "found" institutions to help them, and they exploited the information implicit in several well-known social and cultural institutions of Rome. Merchants lessened the threat of adverse selection and moral hazard by using dependents and friends as agents, and through use of a peer-monitored information network, lawsuits, and guilds that were more trustworthy than individuals. Merchants increased their available information about the market through public institutions such as the government's office of the annona and private institutions such as merchant organizations—similar to modern companies in some ways—that shared information and worked closely with each other. Finally, a system of informal and even formal financing options helped reduce the unforeseen risks of trading.

There were many interactions between Roman economic and social structures. Roman institutions reduced transaction costs to at least the level where the grain market, based on long-distance trade, was viable; we can say little else about how much more efficient the institutions made the market. The similarities between these Roman institutions and those created by later merchants are considerable, and many Roman social structures were analogous to later ones. This Roman network of institutions may have been more elaborate and more effective than any other system that arose in the following sixteen hundred years.

The Roman Empire was more urban than most agrarian societies. There were at least half a dozen cities with populations above 100,000 in the Principate, of which Rome was far and away the largest. Roman agriculture must have been quite efficient in order to feed all these urban residents. To feed the Roman metropolis, it was necessary to have extensive food imports in addition to a prosperous local agriculture.

The population of Rome was about a million people. The diet of these residents was based on wheat, olive oil, and wine, supplemented by dry legumes and other locally grown produce. Ancient historians have inferred the average consumption of Roman residents from "subsistence levels" in less-developed countries today. A generous estimate is that each person consumed on average around 300 kg of wheat, for a total Roman consumption of approximately 300 million kilograms a year (Garnsey 1998, 239–45).

The literature about the ancient world is full of speculations about how this economic activity was organized. Modern thought has focused on the informal parts of this system, friendship and patronage, but it increasingly acknowledges that the ancient economy operated primarily on the basis of private markets. It is one thing to say that Cicero transmitted business through people he called his friends; it is quite another to specify how these agents made their decisions or how the many inhabitants of Rome who were not his friends were fed (Verboven 2002). The volume of goods being traded was too large to be dealt with informally, and the government was too small to have administered it directly (Hopkins 1980, 121). These broad generalizations do not specify how individual markets operated.

The government intervened in the wheat market when prices rose too high. The government was distributing wheat in ordinary years to keep the residents content; it also tried to moderate price rises when the supply of wheat was interrupted by harvest failures or shipping disasters. There are many instances when the Roman emperors tried to keep the price of wheat in Rome low, but these interventions were the exception rather than the rule. While we know of many instances, they are spread among even more years (Garnsey 1988, 195–222; Rickman 1980, 150–54; Höbenreich 1997). The forms of these interventions—setting maximum prices, searching for more supplies, subsidizing purchasing—show that they were attempts to control a free market. The frequent mention of grain prices in our sources reveals the existence of a market where prices were variable and important. Roman merchants were operating in relatively free markets with occasional government intervention.

Some of the risks from which the government tried to insulate consumers were risks to merchants as well. Shipping in particular was uncertain. Shipwrecks were common enough that modern historians have used their frequency to estimate the pace of economic activity (Hopkins 1980; Saller 2005). In addition to the uncertainty of knowing whether your ship would come back, merchants also had to cope with the time that even a successful voyage took. Favorable winds made the trip from Ostia to Alexandria—where much of the wheat for imperial Rome originated—a matter of a few weeks, but the return trip was going against the prevailing winds and could take far longer (Rickman 1980; Casson 1991; Erdkamp 2005). Merchants consequently had to be ready to operate at a distance in the absence of current information. Merchants employed agents for this task and faced the problems that merchants in other times and places have faced.

In order to fully explore the relationship between these merchants and agents, it is necessary to understand the social backgrounds of merchants and agents as well as how those merchants and agents were organized. The social structure and business structure closely parallel one another, and the intimate relationship between them motivates many of the institutional solutions I discuss later.

All the actors in the grain trade hailed from the upper three groups in Roman social hierarchy. The highest group, the senators, included only about six hundred politically active members with a 1,000,000 *sesterces* property qualification. Senators all came from the same homogenous, aristocratic background; they were the major landholders of the empire. In theory, law and custom openly frowned on senators who engaged in business; Cicero, *Att*, 14.12.3, even derided one entrepreneurial senator as a "business hog." Behind this façade of legal restriction many senators were active businessmen. They financed a variety of operations such as vineyards, and many senators held "unregistered" interests in numerous companies and supplied an "important part" of their capital (D'Arms 1981, 54–56). In essence, senators were the—barely—silent partners in Rome's important businesses.

The most visibly active businessmen came from the knights and wealthy freedmen. The knights were the slightly poorer relations of the senators, although some knights were wealthier than some senators. The knights had a 400,000 sesterces property qualification and were more numerous than senators, numbering about five thousand. Senators and knights formed a single class of educated, wealthy men (Jongman 1988). Since they had the leverage of high social standing without the legal and cultural constraints faced by senators, knights could become central figures in business. Below the senators and knights were the privileged freedmen, literally a first generation of educated slaves who either had been manumitted or had purchased their own freedom. Freedmen could sometimes be quite wealthy, owning such properties as mansions, villas, and farms worth more than 50,000 sesterces each (Cicero, *Att.*, 3.196.3; Cicero, *Rosc. Am.*, 133). Freedmen sometimes could reach the rank of knights, and knights could become senators if they were successful in farming, marriage, or business and interested in politics (Hopkins 1983; Alföldy 1988; Garnsey and Saller 1987).

The grain merchants responsible for supplying Rome, who might be senators, knights, or freedmen, worked in Rome and provided capital, contacts, and organization. They hired agents from among the knights or freedmen to go abroad, purchase and sell grain, and oversee its shipping. Knights themselves sometimes functioned as merchants, hiring other knights or freedmen to be their agents. Independent freedmen merchants hired other freedmen as agents. Many studies have identified the nature of these agents and commented on their long-standing ties to their merchant principals, but little attention has been paid to the need to monitor agents, even those identified as friends and relations (Kirschenbaum 1987; Aubert 1994).

While they sometimes acted alone, merchants often were organized into companies. We have few details about those companies, which were almost certainly smaller than modern corporations, but we do know that the group of merchants who had invested in the company met regularly, as do shareholders in modern corporations. Senators often were shareholders who had invested much of the necessary capital for the company. There is evidence showing that at least some Roman companies functioned similarly to the joint-stock companies of the English and the Dutch in the sixteenth and seventeenth centuries (Malmendier 2005, 2009). Those Roman companies obtained a legal identity separate from that of their investors and could exist even after the deaths of important shareholders. The most well-known companies were combinations of *publicani*, or tax farmers. Tax farming was a staple of the Roman Republic, with the auctioning of tax-collection contracts a yearly occurrence. It appears to have been phased out gradually in the early Roman Empire in favor of direct administrative tax collection.

Cato's (Plutarch, *Cato*, 21) famous statement that he would take a one-fiftieth share in a *societas* that operated fifty ships appears to be an example of such a company, but Verboven (2002, 285) insisted to the contrary that "Cato and the 50 traders simply joined hands to minimize the risks involved in the overseas merchant venture. When the journey was over and Cato's loan to finance the venture repaid, the societas would automatically be ended." This statement expands on the source. There is no way to know that this societas "automatically" would be ended, and if fifty ships were involved, many journeys would have to be completed for the societas to end. Merchants and financiers in colonial Massachusetts engaged in continuing shifting partnerships that expired after a voyage, but none of them had anywhere near fifty investors or fifty ships (Bailyn and Bailyn 1959). Unless Plutarch was exaggerating greatly, Cato was doing something far more sophisticated than financing a single merchant voyage.

In most companies, a separation existed between ownership and management. The merchants who owned the company selected executives, called *magistri*, to actually run the company. Badian suggested that companies were "hollow" in the middle, consisting mostly of capital contributors and top management as well as low-level staff. Most members were "employers" rather than "employees." Operating over extensive areas, some companies even had offices stretching from Arles to Beirut (Sirks 1991, 99). Unfortunately, there are no surviving examples of the company records and reports that must have existed in ancient times.

Individual Roman merchants dealt with problems of information in many ways. Roman law set the stage for all specific measures. Specific maritime practices increased the ability of merchants to monitor agent activity. Merchants also exploited the information derived from the group identification of agents to serve as less formal guarantees. And, finally, merchants relied on the incentives to preserve reputations in order to promote honesty and fair dealing.

If agents were afraid of being punished, they would be less likely to cheat. Rome had a sophisticated legal framework that could enforce judgments, especially fines, against agents who were found to be untrustworthy. A merchant knew that any agent he selected had a lower probability of cheating and could spend less time worrying about discerning the true "trustworthiness" of an agent. Rome had a set of courts for both public and private disputes, as well as justices, lawyers, and government officials who were in charge of enforcement.

Roman law famously lacked a law of agency; contracts in general only bound the contracting parties. Roman jurists, however, understood that provisions for agency operations were needed, and they provided a variety of legal categories in which such contracts were binding. Agents from a merchant's household such as sons and slaves could make binding commitments for a *peculium*, a sum of money designated for the purpose at hand. *Actiones institoriae* and *actiones exercitoriae* allowed ship captains to commit merchants and agents more generally to commit principals. *Actiones adiecticiae qualitatis* provided a legal basis for more complex delegation of authority and responsibility (di Porto 1984; Aubert 1994; Johnston 1999).

For a lighthearted but pertinent example of legal enforcement, we can look at an incident involving a donkey in 4 AD (Wolfe 1952). A merchant had hired an agent to carry goods using donkeys; the agent broke the contract within a year, however, by stealing the merchant's goods and killing one of the donkeys. The merchant then filed a petition for legal redress and damages. The public authority resolved the issue in a way that preserved a record of the broken contract. Any punishment meted out was made more severe by the public nature of the legal system, the proceedings in a large proportion of cases being circulated in writing afterwards.

Private judges were responsible for resolving disputes about private contracts, and Cicero's letters demonstrate that partners in a commercial venture could and did sue one another (Sirks 1991, 29). State cases were judged in more public courts, and the state had the option of suing all the guarantors of the contract consecutively, an advantage not accorded to private contracts (Meiggs 1973, 29). Thus an agent who violated a contract could expect a fine or other punishment. The public office of the annona, which acted as merchant and contracted with its own agents to import government grain, also could punish corrupt agents. That office could and did refuse to deal with whomever it wanted, denying them government accounts forever (Sirks 1991, 91).

In addition to directly refusing contracts, the office of the annona investigated merchants who attempted to defraud the government. For instance, once the Emperor Claudius introduced a plan to increase the rewards for merchants involved in the annona, merchants gained an incentive to claim that they were participating in that plan even if they were not. Some shippers simply claimed that they had built ships for the annona, but then they either used the ships for other purposes or never built them at all (Garnsey 1988, 234). The office of the Prefect employed at least one person in Ostia to investigate such claims. Identification and punishment of those "phantom shippers" provided information for agents and merchants that they might not be able to ascertain themselves.

While the courts and the government helped to protect against moral hazard, there were both public and private formal institutions that helped combat woefully incomplete information. The Prefect of the annona had the power to issue contracts for the provision of state grain, as mentioned above, and his office in Ostia was surrounded by the offices of private merchants. The Prefect appears to have engaged only a small staff, suggesting that his main tasks were to gather information about the grain trade and to coordinate with important merchants rather than to organize the entire market (Sirks 1991, 14).

The Prefect's office therefore may have functioned as an information-clearing house. Because the Prefect of the annona dealt with many merchants, he was privy to information from each of them, either through official discussion or through casual conversation. The issuing of certain public contracts could signal private merchants about expected prices and fluctuations in the market, as well as about shortages or surpluses in areas in which they did not normally deal. In essence, this information distribution is similar to speeches given today by individuals like the chairman of the U.S. Federal Reserve Board, who, with a massive amount of economic information, take actions that signal market conditions to private businessmen. Industry associations perform similar functions.

Although merchants could not collectively concentrate their information in one place, as did the Prefect's office, they could still develop private, formal networks to share that information. The Roman "company" was a sophisticated information-sharing institution. Companies kept copies (or originals) of letters sent by their agents, so they presumably had the ability to trace pricing and quantity trends over time, as well as to compare older contracts with newer ones (Badian 1983, 78). Some companies had physical offices in multiple provinces, an arrangement that suggests further information-gathering capabilities. The group of top managers could pass information easily among themselves, since different companies were owned or controlled by men from the same social circles. They might have discussed minutiae like the spot price of wheat in this farm versus that one, and more important, it does not seem unreasonable to imagine them sharing information about employees, profits, and ships through their many social interactions.

Another way grain merchants limited risk was through private financing, just as more recent long-distance traders do (see chapter 8; Rathbone 2001, 2003b). Athenian merchants in the fourth century BCE used loans to finance maritime trade that did not have to be repaid if a ship was wrecked (Cohen 1992). Roman financing followed the same model, and merchants and shippers were able to borrow conditional on a safe return. The interest rate charged was higher than usual and not subject to the normal limitation of 1 percent per month in an explicit acknowledgement that the payment included both interest and insurance: "Money lent on maritime loans (*traiecticia pecunia*) can bear interest at any rate because it is at the risk of the lender as long as the voyage lasts" (de Ste. Croix 1974, quoting Paulus, *Sent.* II, xiv, 3; Johnston 1999). Rathbone (2001) argued that maritime loans were common enough to warrant a standard loan contract, and contemporary Roman commentators discussed market interest rates for such loans (see chapter 8). Rathbone concluded that a particularly large amount of financing occurred during the first and second centuries CE, precisely the time period in which the operations of these grain merchants were at their height. The existence of this financing is particularly substantial if there was little or no government control over the grain trade. Merchants had to bear the risks privately.

While formal, legal institutions like the court system and Roman companies helped combat both asymmetric and incomplete information, other formal institutions, while not codified under law, increased the ability of merchants to monitor agent activity. Just as the legal enforcement of contracts raised the cost to an agent of being caught, a complicated system of documentation increased the agent's risk of being caught. These documents all provided information about the owner, amount, and quality of grain to third parties, either another agent purchasing the grain from an agent or a port official. This elaborate peer-monitoring system helped to ensure that, though an agent could cheat or steal on a long voyage or in a distant land, he would be exposed once he returned.

The problems of agency arose in gathering both public and private supplies of wheat. The public administration used a system of receipts to record important information about grain cargoes that were available for merchants buying grain or by other third parties. The following receipt, issued in 211 CE, is representative (Rickman 1980, 121–22):

> Given to Didymus, strategos of the Oxyrhynchite nome, by Posidonius also called Triadelphus, master of eight boats carrying 40,000 artabae in the Neapolis administration, I have received and had measured out to me the amount ordered by you the strategos and by basilicogrammateus of the same nome, from the sitologoi of the Psobthis district, in accordance with the order of his excellency the procurator Neaspoleos, from the public granaries of the said village at river Tomis, [a specified amount of] wheat, produce of the [year] specified, unadulterated, with no admixture of earth or barley, untrodden and sifted, which I will carry to Alexandria and deliver to the officials of the administration safely, free of all risk, and damage by ship. This receipt is valid, there being three copies of it, which I have issued two to you the strategos and one to the sitologoi.

The receipt identified to whom the cargo belonged and to whom it was being shipped. It also explained specific attributes of the grain, such as the year of harvest and the quality of the product. By identifying its attributes, the receipt made the grain more difficult to steal.

This receipt also suggests the complexity of the system of documentation that Roman officials and merchants used. Receipts existed in triplicate and were sent to different offices providing evidence for a system of quasi-permanent record-keeping. Sending two copies of the receipt to the same person is even stronger evidence for permanent records, since there could be few other reasons for duplicates. The statement "this receipt is valid" implies that there was some legal or understood code of conduct in which three receipts were required in order to make a transaction valid. Since no record exists in documents concerning Roman trade law about such a requirement, merchants may have taken it upon themselves to create such a system of receipts. Not surprisingly, there are even reports that businesses kept archives with letters and other documents, although no records remain of the archived documents (Badian 1983, 72–73). Other evidence stresses the critical importance of receipts to merchants.

Several documents tell of ship crews who waited for as long as fifteen days, often in the middle of prime sailing season, for a receipt of the cargo to be issued in Ostia (Sirks 1991, 43, 156). It is unlikely that the crews would have waited for a receipt if it were not an indispensable part of conducting business. The captain of each ship involved in government shipping also was given a document attesting to the quality of that grain; he had to surrender that receipt to the Prefect of the annona at Ostia on his arrival. Ship captains must have carried additional information, since a ship arriving at Ostia or Portus had to present identification papers to be assigned a berth by the harbormaster (Casson 1965).

In addition to the straightforward receipts discussed above, merchants used even more clever alternatives, such as the labeling of cargo, to assist them in controlling the behavior of agents. A particularly ingenious form of "receipt" involved separate sample containers. Throughout the late republic and early empire, grain merchants sent sealed pots or pouches containing a sample of the grain cargo on trading ships. When the cargo arrived at its destination, the recipient could open the sealed container and test the grain held in it against the grain in the ship's main hold; any difference suggested that the bulk of the grain had been doctored in some way. These seals were signed by the granary official and a merchant, with an additional signature from a witness (Rickman 1980, 122). Such a safeguard against fraud made it extremely difficult for an agent to "cut" his grain with barley or dirt in order to increase the size of his sale. This procedure was doubly valuable, ensuring that the merchant who was ultimately selling the grain would not be embarrassed by a wayward agent and that the merchant ultimately purchasing the grain would not be defrauded. The Bank of England mandated roughly seventeen hundred years later "that every Teller receiving money shall immediately weigh the same, and put a Ticket on the Mouth of the Bag importing the weight and contents thereof, and the like Ticket also within the Bag."

Other simple tricks helped raise the cost of moral hazard. For instance, when grain was poured directly into a hold rather than into sacks, merchants could draw a line on the inside of the hold to mark the height of the grain when it was loaded (Sirks 1991, 100). Indirect, comparative evidence of other product labeling bolstered the practices's viability. Wine merchants labeled their *amphorae* to identify both the contents of the jug and its owner and sometimes a great deal more. One intact pot contained the following label (Frank 1933–40, 72):

> Received; Hispalis; value 20 sest.; weight 215 lbs.; from estate of Capito; export duty: 2 asses; name of clerk; consular date. (AD 179)

Grain was carried in sacks, not in amphorae, and, though no sacks have survived, it would not have been difficult to label sacks with paint, or even colored thread to signal the merchants, the quality of grain, or other pertinent information.

The guild system, especially in Ostia, provided another institutional barrier against moral hazard. Since each transaction involving grain increased an agent's opportunities to cheat, merchants sought to limit the amount of exposure their agents had to the grain with which they were entrusted. The existence of a developed guild system in Ostia and other ports made it unnecessary for agents to perform certain functions, such as unloading the ships, storing the grain, and bringing it from Ostia to Rome. Merchants preferred that guilds perform these tasks, because the guilds already had internal checks against moral hazard—guild members came prescreened.

There were at least four Ostian guilds that directly concerned the grain merchants: the sack-carriers, similar to longshoremen, unloaded grain from ships; the grain measurers weighed the government's grain upon arrival and departure; the shippers who owned small boats that they used to carry grain to Rome, and they may also have checked an incoming ship's documentation; the barge-men guided barges full of grain that were pulled by oxen to Rome. There was even a guild of divers who recovered cargo that fell into the water (Sirks 1991; Meiggs 1973).

To understand how guilds could be tightly controlled, it is useful to review the inner workings of the guilds. While guilds were formal organizations of men tied together by a common occupation, they differed from the European craft guilds of the Middle Ages and early modern period. Many Roman guilds, such as the sack-carriers, or longshoremen, did not require mastery of a specific artisanal skill; their work was unskilled. The guilds of skilled workers focused more on cerebral tasks like piloting ships. All guilds allowed their members to compete freely with each other, and nonguild workers could also find employment in tasks normally performed by guild members. There were significant benefits to membership, as we shall see, although there is no evidence that guilds acted as unions to control wages.

Guilds could prevent crime because they functioned as self-enforcing cartels; a guild could easily refuse membership and its benefits to an outsider or punish active members who stole or behaved corruptly. Elections ultimately determined guild membership, although some guilds required an entry fee in addition. Some guilds, such as the public grain-measurers, forced new members to "take a valid oath to do honest work" (Frank 1933–40, V, 247–49). The guild members collectively elected officers and managed business operations. Those officers held terms of between two and five years, depending on the guild. While membership was not a hereditary right, sons often followed fathers into the same guilds, and freedmen similarly followed the families from which they had won their freedom and now considered their patrons (Meiggs 1973, 316–23). It is unclear how many members each guild had; Casson (1954) reports that sizes ranged from 19 to 250.

The strong organization of the guild and its ability to exert collective action made guild membership desirable. Guilds often pooled resources, and most guilds had guild houses stocked with gifts and decorations given by members. Many also had their own temples, while others used their resources to engage in civic life. The measurers, for instance, were one of the guilds who erected statues to the Prefects of the annona. Guilds also elected "patrons," men of varying influence and wealth, giving members access to those men. Less powerful guilds invited reputable local men to be their patrons; more significant guilds, like the shippers, included a handful of senators on their list of patrons. A guild member would not lightly throw away such positive social benefits (Meiggs 1973, 316, 324; Sirks 1991, 261).

Guilds must have monitored their members' behavior closely. The common treasury would have produced a strong interest in members to monitor one another. More important, the reputation of the entire guild could have suffered from the bad acts of one of its members. Even if corrupt members were not expelled, it is unlikely that they would ever have been voted into officer status or given special honors by their peers.

Legal systems, and other formal organizations do not exist in a vacuum; it is often informal social custom that proves even more effective than official sanctions (Milgrom, North, and Weingast 1997). Merchants relied on informal institutions to promote honesty and trustworthiness. The guarantee of reputation is the most likely candidate for the unofficial enforcement mechanism in Rome. This *ex-ante* solution would have prescreened the agents available to the merchants.

If the Romans used a reputation mechanism, what was the signal that established trustworthiness? Roman religion did not involve an ethical code, as is present in Judaism, Christianity, and Islam, so an appeal to religious values could not ensure trustworthiness. Instead, it seems plausible that the criterion for establishing trustworthiness was the recommendation of another merchant knight or senator, especially given the homogeneity of the two primary classes of senators and knights and the close proximity in which merchants worked in Ostia, as we shall see later. In addition, honor and probity were important secular values among the Roman aristocracy; men of these higher ranks were considered to be de facto trustworthy and could explicitly lend that trustworthiness to others. Naturally, not all members of these classes were trustworthy, but the small, close-knit community ensured that a deviant individual could not hide behind his rank indefinitely.

A letter from Cicero (*Fam.*, 13.75) provides evidence of this reputation mechanism. In the letter, Cicero, a wealthy senator, writes to a merchant principal, Titus, about an agent, Avianius. Avianius worked for Pompey, one of Cicero's friends and also a merchant principal:

> What I beg of you is this—that you would accommodate Avianius as to the place and time for landing his corn: for which he obtained by my influence a three years' license whilst Pompey was at the head of that business.

This letter contains two instances of the reputation mechanism. First, Cicero clearly used his social ties to Pompey, another merchant principal and member of the senatorial circle, to secure Avianius a contract in the first place. Second, Cicero, with his personal reputation, persuades Titus to give Avianius a favorable reception. Cicero's letter "brands" Avianius as a trustworthy agent, just as a personal endorsement from a standing president might brand a candidate "honest" or "trustworthy."

The use of the same agent by multiple senators strengthened the reputation mechanism. Since some agents worked for several wealthy families, information about their reputations could travel particularly rapidly. Cicero (*Cornelius Nepos*, 25.15) gives an example of this phenomenon by writing about Atticus, his own agent as well as the agent for four other aristocratic families, including that of Marc Antony.

While the aristocratic ownership of Roman companies bolstered the reputation mechanism through their personal communications, the companies themselves helped minimize the damage a dishonest agent could cause. At least some merchant groups offered to replace a failing agent with another one. Associations even used their own property as collateral to guarantee fulfillment of a contract and threatened their own criminal members with fines or prosecution for criminal activity (Garnsey 1998, 77). These pledges were not legally binding, but they did control anyone who wished to remain part of an association.

If an agent were caught cheating, the costs could be high. Through a straightforward procedure, a private merchant could simply end his contract with an agent who cheated. The government could also refuse to work with cheating agents in the future. The reputation-based enforcement mechanism would ensure that any agent who had been fired would be unlikely to find any work whatsoever. The legal framework that helped create more trustworthy agents also increased the chance that cheating agents would be punished if caught.

Informal Roman institutions also proved useful in addressing problems of incomplete information. Merchants typically came from the same elite social groups, and their informal relations supported and aided their commercial transactions. Various authors have presented an economy of friends as a substitute for a more formal market, but in fact they are complements. As noted earlier, families, extended households of slaves and freedmen, and friends were used to reduce the extent of adverse selection. They also conveyed information that reduced the opportunity for moral hazard. Kirschenbaum (1987, 180) concluded, "These were relations that never reached the inside of a courtroom. Their entire tone precludes contract and suit, action and liability; yet they were most effective in fulfilling the roles and needs lawyers associate with agency."

Verboven (2002, 351) added, "Little of what we have found can be considered unique for the Roman Economy."

Given the level of communications technology, no one had access to all the information about the grain trade. Because numerous people had access to different pieces of information, merchants participated in institutions that helped share or diffuse information. This information sharing evolved in two ways: merchants collectively sought information from a public source, the government's Prefect of the annona; merchants could also acquire information privately from other merchants. In addition, those private merchants could also reduce the risks of incomplete information through a system of financing that was surprisingly modern in several ways.

A second way for merchants to more efficiently spread information was to work physically near each other. Knowing each other, seeing each other each day, and gossiping together would undoubtedly increase the information flow between the merchants. The Piazzale delle Corporazioni was the primary physical institution for grain information exchange in Ostia (Meiggs 1973, 284–88). The building, decorated with mosaics including many depicting grain ships, is located near the harbor and housed numerous types of merchants in a colonnade surrounded by many small offices. Such a space lent itself to the casual communication between merchants.

With no indication that the Prefect of the annona ordered any of these merchants to establish their offices in the Piazzale, it appears that merchants came there deliberately to coordinate among themselves (Meiggs 1973, 283). There were no offices in the Piazzale large enough to hold goods, further suggesting that these offices existed so that representatives could place orders and negotiate. Larger shippers certainly had agents who either had an office in the Piazzale or frequented the space at a minimum. Wine merchants enjoyed a similar arrangement in the Forum Vinarium, where wine merchants from Rome and from Ostia worked side-by-side. This open-air, public coordination could also be found among the Maghribi traders. Greif (1994, 923–24) reports that their "important business dealings were conducted in public."

Merchants could use both public and private institutions to overcome problems of inadequate information. The Prefect of the annona may have served as an information clearinghouse about the grain market, while private merchants shared information through their company ties and the proximity of their offices.

While asymmetric information remains a major problem in the modern economy, lack of information has become a decreasing concern as improvements in technology have built stronger communication networks. Incomplete information posed a serious problem for merchants until the nineteenth century. One strategy earlier merchants used to reduce the effect of their poor information was to place total control for an operation in the hands of agents. For instance, some traders in the colonial America gave their agents a broad set of general orders and hoped they would be followed. In November 1736, Captain James Brown wrote the following to one of his agents (Bruchey 1966, 176):

> If you can Sell your pitch, rice, & Turpentine for a good price in money Sell it all but Twenty barrels of pitch and two barrels of Rice and two ditto of Turpentine, which I Shall want for my own Youse [*sic*]. And if you Cannot Sell it to your Satisfaction Schooner and all together if you can find any room take a hundred bushels of Salt of Capt. Whipple or any body else that you can get it Cheapest off, and make what dispatch possible you can home.

Rather than attempt to increase the information available to the merchants, the strategy exemplified by this letter works by placing complete responsibility for the operation in the agent's hands. This is an extreme example in which the merchant acknowledged that he could not control his agent and hoped for the best. Roman merchants, facing similar asymmetric and incomplete information problems, employed all sorts of formal and informal institutions to avoid being forced to rely solely on the good offices of their agents.

Roman grain merchants faced asymmetric and incomplete information concerns, contending with the selection and monitoring of agents, as well as incomplete information about price shocks, shipwrecks, and other conditions. Merchants used economic and social institutions to reduce the transaction costs resulting from their uncertainty. Those institutions increased the amount of available information and reduced its cost. Some institutions, such as early banks, could help reduce the risks of incomplete information, even if they did not create or provide additional information themselves. This analysis suggests that the Roman market rivaled early modern European and colonial American markets in terms of institutional complexity and, perhaps, efficiency. Greif assumed that medieval merchant groups had to choose between two types of institutions to increase information about agents: they could develop either an enforcement-based mechanism or a reputation-based mechanism, depending on the institutions that already existed in their society. Unlike the groups of traders in Greif's paper about eleventh-century merchants, the Romans utilized both methods. Even without systematic comparisons to other informational systems, it is apparent that Roman merchants in the early Roman Empire had a system that was as good as any existing before industrialization and perhaps not equaled for another millennium and a half.

Chapter 6

• • •

The Labor Market

It often is said that ancient Rome was a slave society. Hopkins (1978) was the first to assert that Rome was one of only five slave societies in recorded history, a view adopted quickly by Finley (1980). This characterization is important because slavery is used as a sign of a nonmarket economy. Polanyi (1944) located the center of the transition to an industrial economy in the labor market. He argued that labor markets in the modern sense did not exist before the Industrial Revolution and the Poor Laws that accompanied it in England. This view is consonant with Weber's (1930) judgment that a critical component of capitalism was free labor.

Finley, and others following his lead, argued that ancient economies were not market economies, but an alternate, even primitive, form of organization. Finley (1980, 68) stated, "In early societies, free hired labour (though widely documented) was spasmodic, casual, marginal." According to Hopkins (1978, 23), "There was no effective labour market of mobile, landless labourers," in the early Roman Republic. Hopkins (1978, 109) argued that this condition continued into the early Roman Empire: "Slaves were . . . a means of organizing labour in an economy without a labour market."

In his "Further Thoughts" to his Sather Lectures, Finley (1999, 185) reaffirmed his positions that "free hired labor was casual and seasonal" and that "there was no genuine competition . . . between slave and free laborers." He said these positions were "still valid" although needing "nuancing." Following Brunt (1980), Finley acknowledged abundant free laborers in the largest cities, but he insisted that their employment was "strictly speaking casual."

This view is mistaken. A variety of evidence indicates that Rome had a functioning labor market and a unified labor force. Wage dispersion in the early Roman Empire, to the extent that we know it, is indistinguishable from that in preindustrial Europe. Roman labor contracts have a distinctly modern allocation of risks and rewards. In addition, Roman slavery was so different from modern slavery that it did not indicate the presence of nonmarket, traditional actions. Instead, ancient Roman slavery was an integral part of a labor force that shares many characteristics with labor forces in other advanced agricultural societies. Contrary to Finley (1980, 127), who asserted, "Ancient slavery . . . co-existed with other forms of dependent labour, not with free wage-labour," and Schiavone (2000, 156), who added that "slavery . . . led to the eventual stagnation of the [Roman economic] system, blocking off other paths," the analysis in this chapter finds that free hired labor was widespread and that ancient slavery was a part of a unified labor force in the early Roman Empire, not a barrier to economic progress.

A functioning labor market couples a labor demand with a labor supply. Two conditions must be filled, at least partially: workers must be free to change their economic activity and/or their location, and they must be paid something commensurate with their labor productivity to indicate to them which kind of work to choose. Labor productivity here means the output of goods or services that results from the employment of this worker. It is not the average labor productivity of all workers, but the productivity of the worker in question. In economics jargon, it is the marginal product of labor. Contemporary studies maintain that labor needs to be mobile enough to bring wages for work of equal skill near equality. Though this stipulation does not mean that everyone has to change jobs with great frequency, enough people must be able and willing to do so to keep payments to labor from being excessively higher or lower than the wages of comparable work in other locations or activities. Even in the United States today, which contains the most flexible labor market in history, wages for comparable jobs are not completely equalized: "There exist sizable wage differences across regions or states in the United States, even for workers with particular skills looking for similar jobs" (Borjas 2001, 71).

When these conditions are not fulfilled, there is no labor market, or perhaps only local, isolated labor markets. People might not be able to change their economic activities due to hereditary or guild restrictions. They might be restricted in what they can earn or be entitled to income for reasons unrelated to their work. Wages, in the sense of a return for labor services might be "spasmodic, casual, marginal." The choice between these two alternatives is important because the nature of the labor market is an important component to the nature of the economy as a whole. With a functioning labor market, an economy can respond to external influences like market economies do today. Labor can move to take an advantage of a technical change that makes an activity more profitable or a discovery that provides an economic opportunity in a new place. In a local, nonlabor market, labor would not be able to respond to changes in the external environment. The economy instead would continue to act in traditional ways, perhaps with a small gesture toward the new opportunities.

The task of distinguishing these two conditions in the early Roman Empire is rendered difficult, as always, by the absence of comprehensive evidence. The chief evidence for the absence of a labor market in the early Roman Empire has been the presence of slaves. The question is not how many slaves were present, but rather how slavery operated. Slaves in the American South before the Civil War were not part of a unified American labor market because their activities and incomes were so restricted that they had no incentive to seek better working conditions. Slaves in the early Roman Empire did not suffer under the same restrictions, but despite Rome's use of slavery, free hired labor was the rule, not the exception, in the rest of the early Roman Empire.

The abstract conditions that define a labor market typically are related to labor markets in industrial economies; they need modification to apply to labor markets in agricultural economies. Most of the workers in such an economy are rural, working either in agriculture or in associated crafts and services; they rarely change occupations or residences without strong pressure. A rural labor market exists when enough of them are free to move in response to economic stimuli, thereby keeping rural wages at a moderately uniform level but also allowing for substantial geographical variation in both the level and the rate of change of rural wages. For example, migration and wages interacted in early modern Britain to keep wages similar, but by no means equal.

One possible move for a substantial fraction of rural workers in advanced agricultural economies is to a city. It is rare, both in past and current agricultural economies, for rural and urban wages to be equalized by migration. Economists do not regard this discrepancy as negating the existence of a unified labor market; they explain the difference by noting that new urban workers often are unemployed and that only the expected wage (that is, the wage times the probability of earning it) should be equalized by migration. Living costs also typically are higher in cities; urban wages can exceed rural wages for this reason alone. Urban wages that are double rural wages do not strain the ability of these factors to account for the discrepancy (Harris and Todaro 1970).

Wages vary in a labor market by skill as well as by location. Almost all workers have skills, basic skills of agriculture and often more advanced skills as well. Economists call these skills human capital. Most ancient workers had few skills, including the ability to read, that is, little human capital. Craftsmen and some agricultural workers had competencies that did not depend on literacy and would receive a higher wage in a rural labor market for them. But these skills would not earn much, if anything, in urban areas. Although we tend to know more about literate workers—despite the relative paucity of them—than about less-skilled workers because of the literary bias of our sources, the great mass of workers in the early Roman Empire were illiterate and—by modern standards—unskilled (Harris 1989a).

Recent scholarship has revealed the existence of many market prices and wages in ancient Rome, suggesting that the Roman economy was not substantially different from more recent agrarian economies. Yet the abstract conditions that define a labor market in modern analyses need modification to apply to labor markets in agricultural economies. Steinfeld (1991) demonstrated that workers were not free to change jobs at will until near the end of the nineteenth century. Even in the United States and Britain, two of the most market-oriented countries that the world has ever known, the rights of workers were sharply restricted. Both urban and rural workers were subject to prosecution if they left a job without their employers' permission. Steinfeld (1991, 26) argued that work in these advanced economies was directed by a mixture of monetary and other incentives. This context permits no sharp distinction between free and unfree labor, only a continuum along which various economies, or even activities within an economy, can be placed. In his words, "Practically all labor is elicited by confronting workers with a choice between work and a set of more or less disagreeable alternatives to work."

Steinfeld (2001, 8–9) elaborated this framework in a subsequent book:

> We should recognize that employers of all forms of labor confronted certain basic problems that derived from the ability of workers to thwart their economic objectives and that employers of all forms of labor, *including wage labor*, found nonpecuniary pressures useful in trying to deal with these problems. What was different about the different forms of labor was the harshness and comprehensiveness the state permitted employers to bring to dear. . . . As vast as these differences undoubtedly were, they should be understood as establishing the terms of labor along a very broad continuum rather than a binary opposition. . . . English wage workers [before 1875] could be imprisoned at hard labor for failing or refusing to perform their labor agreements.

Steinfeld's analysis of English-speaking workers in the process of industrialization provides a standard against which to evaluate Roman labor markets. Wages were an important tool for the allocation of labor in eighteenth-century England, but their use was limited by the restrictions on labor mobility. Wages in such a system would not reach equality for similar skills, and most workers would not feel free to look around for more lucrative activity. Slaves were part of this continuum of flexibility and restraint, as will be demonstrated shortly.

Free urban workers in the early Roman Empire were paid for their work and were able to change their economic activities. Hereditary barriers were nonexistent, and Roman guilds do not appear to have been restrictive (see chapter 5). Workers in large enterprises, like mines and galleys, were paid wages, as in more modern labor markets. Workers engaged in more skilled and complex tasks received more elaborate compensation, probably for long units of time than those doing wage labor, again as in more modern labor markets, even though explicit long-term contracts were not yet established. The force of competition under those circumstances probably brought wages and labor productivity into the same ballpark (Frank 1933–40, V, 248–52; Meiggs 1973, 314).

Some of the work in the early Roman Empire was done for wages and some under the duress of slavery. The early Roman Empire even had salaried long-term free workers in Egypt. Craftsmen sold their wares in cities and also supplied them to rural and urban patrons in return for long-term economic and social support. Similarly, people who worked for, or supplied, senators and equestrians often worked for long-term rewards and advancement. The episodic nature of monumental building in Rome, accomplished largely by free laborers, gives evidence of a mobile labor force that could be diverted from one activity to another. Free workers, freedmen, and slaves worked in all kinds of activities; contemporaries saw the ranges of jobs and of freedom as separate—even orthogonal. In particular, rural slaves hardly comprised an undifferentiated gang of laborers; lists of rural slave jobs are as varied as the known range of urban or household "slave" jobs. Some rural laborers received piece rates and others, daily wages. Cicero, anticipating Marx, conflated legal and economic relations by equating wages and servitude (Rathbone 1991, 91–147, 166; Brunt 1980; Cicero, *de Officiis*, XXI, 1.150–51).

A labor market in the early Roman Empire would have tended to equalize real wages in different parts of the empire. Suggestively, Cuvigny (1996) found equal wages of miners in Egypt and Dacia in Eastern Europe. Either an administrator imposed uniform wages across the empire or scraps of data like this provide evidence of a well-functioning labor market. The combination, perhaps even their interaction, may have integrated conditions across the broad Mediterranean area described in chapter 2.

In a functioning labor market, wages increase as the number of laborers decreases because of the competition to hire them; workers are more productive when fewer of them are available to work. It is hard to know of small changes in Roman labor supplies, but plagues led to rapid, large falls in the pool of available labor. Egyptian wages doubled after the major Antonine Plague of 165–175 CE. This clearly is the standard labor-market response to a sharp decrease in the supply of labor. It demonstrates that wages in the early Roman Empire moved to clear markets, in this case to allocate newly scarce labor (Duncan-Jones 1996; Scheidel 2002).

Employment contracts also give evidence of labor-market activity in which workers could choose their jobs. The modern division between wages and salaries finds it analog in Roman Egypt: "As a general rule permanent employees of the Appianus and related estates can be distinguished by their receipt of *opsonion* (salary), a fixed monthly allowance of cash and wheat and sometimes vegetable oil, whereas occasional employees received *misthos*, that is 'wages.'" Some of these "free" workers were tied to the estate for life, like those subject to the more modern worker contracts studied by Steinfeld, but others were free to leave when their jobs were done (Rathbone 1991, 91–92).

Miners and apprentices had employment contracts. One dating from 164 CE shows that workers were paid only for work done and that they had more right to quit than the nineteenth-century workers described by Steinfeld:

> In the consulship of Macrinus and Celsus, May 20. I, Flavius Secundinus, at the request of Memmius, son of Asceplius, have here recorded the fact that he declared that he had let, and he did in fact let, his labor in the gold mine to Aurelius Adjutor from this day to November 13 next for seventy denarii and board. He shall be entitled to receive his wages in installments. He shall be required to render healthy and vigorous labor to the above-mentioned employer. If he wants to quit or stop working against the employer's wishes, he shall have to pay five sesterces for each day, deducted from his total wages. If a flood hinders operations, he shall be required to prorate accordingly. If the employer delays payment of the wage when the time is up, he shall be subject to the same penalty after three days of grace. (CIL III, p. 948 no. 10, translated in Lewis and Reinhold, 1990, 2, 106–7)

Most free workers were farmers, many of them tenant farmers, although employment categories in the countryside were fluid (Garnsey 1998, 139; Kehoe 1997). Roman tenancy contracts allocated risks between landowners and tenants in much the same way as analogous contracts did in eighteenth- and nineteenth-century Britain. Major risks were borne by the landowners as events beyond the tenants' control, whereas minor risks were borne by tenants in return for the opportunity to earn more and keep their earnings: "Force majeure ought not cause loss to the tenant, if the crops have been damaged beyond what is sustainable. But the tenant ought to bear loss which is moderate with equanimity, just as he does not have to give up profits which are immoderate. It will be obvious that we are speaking here of the tenant who pays rent in money; for a share-cropper (*partiarus colonus*) shares loss and profit with the landlord, as it were by law of partnership" (Gaius, *D.* 19.2.25.6, quoted in David Johnston 1999, 64).

We know a lot more about wages in England before industrialization than in the Roman Empire. Wages for comparable work were similar throughout England, but they were not uniform. Agriculture was more prosperous in the South than in the North, and wages were higher in the eighteenth century. (This pattern was reversed in the nineteenth century when the North industrialized.) Substantial variation was evident within regions, due to the immobility of the population. A recent summary of the English data shows daily winter wages in the North to be only half of what they were in the South in 1700. They approached each other gradually during the next century and a half (Woodward 1995; Clark 2001, 485).

England is much smaller than the Roman Empire was. If we use Roman data from Egypt and Davia, a more suitable comparison is preindustrial Europe. Clearly, labor had even less mobility between countries than within England, and wages varied more, though they did remain at the same general level. Allen (2001) demonstrated that wages within Europe began to diverge in the sixteenth and seventeenth centuries. By 1700, the real wages of masons in London and Antwerp were more than double those in other European cities.

Based on this more modern evidence, we do not expect to find wages that are equal in distant places except by coincidence, but we expect wages to be similar. If the early Roman Empire had a labor market that functioned about as well as the labor market in preindustrial Europe, then wages in the early Roman Empire would have been approximately equal. Real wages for similar tasks might have varied by a factor of two or three, as real wages did in eighteenth-century Europe, but they were not different orders of magnitude. As just described, this presumption is consistent with the fragmentary evidence about wages in the Principate.

The army must be distinguished from the private sphere, as in modern economies. Peacetime armies are often voluntary, recruited via the standard organizational lures—favorable wages and working conditions. Wartime armies, by contrast, often rely on conscription, which is a nonmarket process. Actions within armies are directed by commands, not by market transactions. Armies therefore represent at best a partial approximation to a free labor market and typically an exception to it. Since armies, unhappily, are present in almost all societies, we place this exception to the general rule to one side.

The wages of the Roman army, which was staffed by a mixture of attraction and conscription, stayed constant for many decades at a time. When the army was not fighting, which was most of the time, soldiers had to be set tasks to keep them fit and out of trouble, like building roads and public monuments. This construction work did not interfere with the labor market in Rome or elsewhere in the center of the empire since the army was stationed at the frontiers (Brunt 1974; Watson 1969, 45).

Slaves appear to be like soldiers in that they are subject to command, but such was not necessarily the case in the early Roman Empire, especially in cities. Unlike American slaves, Roman slaves were able to participate in the labor market in almost the same way as free laborers. Although they often started at a low point, particularly those who were uneducated, many were able to advance by merit. Freedmen started from a better position, and their ability to progress was almost limitless, despite some prominent restrictions. These conditions created powerful positive work incentives for slaves in the early Roman Empire.

The prevalence of slavery in ancient Rome has stood in the way of comparisons with more recent labor markets since it seemed to indicate that a large segment of the Roman labor force was outside the market. Classicists have used evidence of modern American slavery to illuminate conditions in ancient Rome. Bradley (1989) on slave rebellions opens with a chapter on slavery in the New World. Although Bradley and Hopkins emphasized the complexity of Roman slavery, their use of modern evidence implicitly assumed that slave economies separated by two millennia were essentially the same. Slavery, however, is not always and everywhere the same. Roman slavery was at the opposite extreme from slavery in the southern United States; many Roman slaves—like free workers—responded to market incentives.

Historical slave systems have differed between polities and across time. There is no reason to think that the choices for all slaves at all times were close to completely divested of freedom. In order to understand the role of slavery in ancient economies, we need to inquire about the choices open to slaves in the ancient world. Our interest here is in differences between conditions of slavery in different times and places. For example, George Washington wrote in 1775 that the "plains of America are either to be drenched with blood, or Inhabited by Slaves" (Fischer 2004, 16). He believed that only people of independent means could be truly free, and he saw the boundary between slaves and free people as being both economic and political. The Marxian term, wage slavery, emphasizes how hard it is to represent labor conditions by a simple binary comparison, since the term, slavery, was used to express the limitations of choice by "free" workers: "The worker of today [mid-nineteenth century England] seems to be free because he is not sold once for all, but piecemeal by the day, the week, the year, and because no owner sells him to another, but he is forced to sell himself in this way instead, being the slave of no particular person, but of the whole property-holding class" (Engels 1993, 91).

Few people chose to be a slave; almost all Roman slaves were forced into slavery as captives, children of slaves, abandoned children, or debt bondage. It was bad to be a slave in the early Roman Empire, as it has been bad to be a slave throughout history. A Roman slave was subject to the cruelty endemic in the early Roman Empire with less protection than free people; a person who found himself or herself in slavery had drawn a poor hand from the deck of life. But even if slaves were at or near the bottom of society and the economy, it makes sense to ask how hopeless their position was. Slaves were unfortunate people, but they were still people.

All people, even slaves, need to have incentives to do their work. Free people may work to increase their income. If slaves cannot legally lay claim to the fruits of their labor, other incentives must be constructed. These incentives may be classified as positive (rewards for hard or good work), or carrots, and negative (punishment for slacking off or not cooperating), or sticks. There is a large literature on the incentive structures of modern American slavery, possibly because the high emotional content of this literature makes consensus elusive (Wright 2006). But while disagreements remain on many points, there is agreement that negative incentives, that is, punishments and sanctions, dominated the lives of modern slaves in the Americas (David et al. 1976; Patterson 1982).

By contrast, positive incentives were more important than negative in motivating Roman slaves. Sticks can get people to work, but generally not to do skilled tasks that require independent work (Fenoaltea 1984). If it is hard to distinguish poor performance from bad luck when work is complex, carrots are far more effective than sticks in motivating hard work. Consider a managerial job, like a *vilicus*. A slave in such a position motivated by negative incentives could claim that any adverse outcomes were the result of bad luck, not his actions. Beating him or exacting worse punishment would lead to resentment rather than cooperation and—one confidently could expect—more "bad luck." A vilicus motivated by positive incentives would anticipate sharing in any good luck; he would work to make it happen. Contrast this example with that of an ordinary field hand. His effort could be observed directly and easily; slackers could be punished straight away. And since field hands typically work in groups, positive incentives that motivate individuals to better efforts are hard to design (Dari-Mattiacci 2011).

There was cruelty in ancient slavery, as there was in early modern indenture. It has been described often because it contrasts sharply with our modern sense of individual autonomy. But cruelty was a hallmark of the early Roman Empire as it has been of most nonindustrial societies. Imperial Rome appeared to celebrate cruelty more than usual as an offshoot of its military orientation; ancient cruelty was by no means reserved for slaves. Wickham (2009, 21) opens with a graphic description of cruelty in legal proceedings and the assertion that "the Roman world was habituated to violence and injustice." The vivid examples of violence toward slaves do not make the case that cruelty dominated the lives of slaves more than free men since we also have many competing stories of more benevolent slave conditions. Slave revolts also do not give evidence of predominantly negative incentives. Most attested slave revolts were concentrated in a short span of time in the late republic, a time of great social upheaval (Bradley 1989; Roth 2007; Urbainczyk 2008).

For example, the miserable condition of slaves working in the bakery overseen by Apuleius's golden ass (*Golden Ass*, 9.2) do not illustrate the harsh conditions of Roman slavery, but rather the dismal conditions of ordinary labor in preindustrial economies. In these Malthusian economies, greater productivity resulted in larger populations rather than gains in working conditions or real wages. Almost all workers before the Industrial Revolution and the demographic transition lived near what economists call subsistence. This does not necessarily mean the edge of starvation, but it often means people working to the limit of their endurance. And work in a small bakery was and is very hard, long, and hot, even today.

It is necessary to distinguish between rural and urban conditions when evaluating the balance between positive and negative incentives. Rural slaves in antiquity were those slaves most like modern slaves; they performed work that was easily supervised and were subject to negative and even cruel incentives. Urban slaves in the early Roman Empire, which have no modern counterpart, were in a different position. Rio de Janeiro in the early nineteenth century provides a partial parallel. But this modern example exposes the uniqueness of ancient Rome (and perhaps other ancient cities as well) because the prevalence of slaves in Rio was very short-lived, the slaves there were almost all unskilled, and Rio was a city at the fringe of market activity (Karasch 1987; Frank 2004). Urban Roman slaves are the main focus of this discussion, since their conditions have not been understood. We do not know how large a share of Roman slaves were urban. It was a substantial fraction, even possibly reaching half of all slaves at some times.

To understand the differences between slave systems, it is necessary to differentiate slavery in two dimensions. The first dimension comes from anthropologists, who distinguish between open and closed models of slavery. Open slavery is a system in which slaves can be freed and accepted fully into general society. In anthropological terms, freedmen and women are accepted into kinship groups and intermarry freely with other free persons. Closed slavery is a system in which slaves are a separate group, not accepted into general society, and not allowed to marry among the general population even when freed. Roman slavery conformed to the open model; freedmen were Roman citizens, and marriages of widows with freedmen were common. By contrast, "American slavery [was] perhaps the most closed and caste-like of any [slave] system known" (Watson 1980, 7). (The anthropological classification is different from that used in Harris [1999], where a slave system was open if slaves

TABLE 6.1.
Varieties of slavery in the five slave societies

	Frequent manumission	*Only exceptional manumission*
Open systems	Early Roman Empire	
Closed systems	Classical Greece, 19th century Brazil	Southern United States, the Caribbean

Source: Temin (2004b).

were being imported; closed, if not.) This difference placed Roman slaves in a very different position relative to other workers than that occupied by modern American slaves.

In addition, manumission into Roman citizenship offered an important incentive for urban and perhaps also for some rural slaves. It is the key element that defined slavery in the early Roman Empire, and it reveals the open nature of Roman slavery. Manumission was common, but not universal. There were no rules determining who would be freed, but more cooperative and productive slaves had the best chance for manumission by their owners.

Slaves often were able to purchase freedom if they could earn the necessary funds in a peculium, which served as a tangible measure of slave productivity. The right of slaves to accumulate and retain assets was an important part of the incentive structure of slaves that brings their conditions closer to free men. If a slave was sold or freed, he kept his peculium, even though slaves technically could not own property (Crook 1967, 187–91). Of course, if a slave used his peculium to purchase his freedom, his former owner acquired possession of the slave's earnings. Slaves even owned slaves.

There was nothing like the peculium in modern American slavery. Brazil offers a partial modern exception, where some slaves could earn enough to purchase their freedom (Schwartz 1974; Pinto Vallejos 1985; Karasch 1987). Brazilian slaves even could earn a *pecúlio*, a right made official by reference to Roman law in 1871 (Childs 2002).

I summarized these observations in table 6.1. Fenoaltea presented an abstract model that cannot cover all bases; its advantage was to isolate important characteristics of labor systems. It resembles the simple models explained in chapter 1. In this vein, I proposed a simple classification of slave systems to show how unusual Roman slavery was. Scheidel (2008) expanded this matrix as shown in table 6.2 to allow for intermediate cases and for variations within each system. Rome, Athens, and Brazil each appear twice in Scheidel's table

TABLE 6.2.

Varieties of slavery in the five slave societies

	Frequent manumission		Only exceptional manumission
Open systems	Rome (household?)		Rome (agricultural?)
		Brazil, Athens	Brazil, Athens
Closed systems			Southern United States, Caribbean

Source: Scheidel (2008).

to represent complexity within the slave conditions in these three places. Even in the expanded table, Rome stands out as having had the most open slavery, revealing that manumission was uniquely attractive when available. It is possible, although there is little evidence, that manumission was more prevalent in Roman cities than in the Roman countryside.

In the expanded table also, Roman and modern American slavery are differentiated; there is no overlap in the conditions of these two slave systems. In fact, Roman slavery is the only slave system that seems to have had frequent manumission, and therefore the only system in which freed slaves fully entered free society—albeit only in a generation or so to hold political office. Trimalchio, the lavishly ostentatious freedman portrayed in Petronius's *Satyricon*, is a uniquely Roman figure. Comparisons between American and Roman slavery may be an inevitable result of the scarcity of Roman data, but they should be used only to pose questions, not to imply similarity.

Modern American slavery was a closed system. The New World slaves did not enter Eurocentric American society on easy terms; their opportunities were severely limited. Their descendants in the United States are still awaiting complete integration into society. The descendants of former African slaves have fared much better in Brazil, where manumission was more frequent. Even in Brazil slaves only began to be freed with any regularity in the nineteenth century when pressure for the abolition of slavery rose. Yet, since freed slaves were still excluded from respectable society by former Europeans, few positive incentives were available to them.

Roman slavery had some attributes of another modern institution, indentured service. Poor Englishmen who wanted to immigrate to North America in the eighteenth century would indenture themselves to pay for their passage across the Atlantic. Not being able to pay up front, they mortgaged their future labor to pay for their passage. Indentures were for a fixed number of years, often fewer than five, and immigrants were able to resume life without stigma after their indenture was over. While indentured, the immigrants had their freedom to move, to choose occupations, or even to determine the particulars of their life severely circumscribed. They were, in a descriptive oxymoron, short-term slaves (Galenson 1981).

The frequency with which Greek slaves were set free is unknown, but freed slaves in Athens did not become members of Greek society. They inhabited "a limbo world in which full political and economic membership of the community was denied them." Unlike Athenian citizenship, Roman citizenship was inclusive. This fundamental difference between the two may have determined how each society interpreted slavery. In any case, the prevalence and visibility of manumission among Roman slaves made Roman slavery far different than slavery in Athens (Garnsey 1996, 7).

By the time of the Principate most slaves were probably slaves from infancy, either as the children of slaves or unwanted children of free parents, since captives were few by then. A debate about whether slaves were replenished through reproduction or maintained through foundlings and the slave trade persists, but most scholars agree that the supply of captives had dwindled. Rules for manumission became explicit. Augustus enacted a law (*lex Fufia Caninia*) restricting the proportion of slaves that a slave owner could manumit at his death but also preserving the structure of incentives by forcing owners to decide which of their slaves to set free. Rights of freedmen were expanded. The incentive for slaves to act well became clear. Freedmen moved into skilled and well-rewarded trades and other activities, and their children born after manumission entered society with all of their rights (Scheidel 1997; Harris 1999).

Manumission was common and well known in the early Roman Empire. Livy recounted a legend about a slave who was freed in 509 BCE, the first year of the republic, as a reward for faithful service, albeit of a political rather than an economic nature. Although Livy could not have known whether the story was true, he thereby revealed attitudes in his own time. A legal principle of the era dealt with the status of a child born to a woman who conceived while a slave, was freed, and then enslaved again before giving birth. For this to have been an interesting question, the boundary between slavery and freedom must have been permeable (Livius, *History*, I, 2.3–5; *Pauli Sententiae*, 2.24.3).

No counts of Roman manumission exist, but the myriad references to manumission and freedmen in the surviving records attest to its frequency. Scheidel (1997, 160) assumed that 10 percent of slaves in the early Roman Empire were freed every five years, starting at age twenty-five in a demographic exercise. Some of Scheidel's assumptions have attracted vigorous rebuttal, but not this one (Harris 1999). These estimates and opinions apply to the totality of urban and rural Roman slaves. In the judgment of a modern observer, "Most urban slaves of average intelligence and application had a reasonable expectation of early manumission and often of continued association with their patron" (Weaver 1972, 1). In the judgment of another, "Roman slavery, viewed as legal institution, makes sense on the assumption that slaves could reasonably aspire to being freed, and hence to becoming Roman citizens" (Watson 1987, 23).

The Egyptian census listed no male slaves older than thirty-two. Since the census counted household slaves only, this age truncation suggests widespread manumission rather than exceptionally high slave mortality. Female slaves generally were freed if they had more than three children, which may not have been uncommon in an age without family planning. Manumission on this scale must have been apparent to all slaves, certainly to all urban slaves, and a powerful incentive for them to cooperate with their owners and to excel at their work (Bagnall and Frier 1994, 71, 342–43; Columella, 1.8.19). Apparently, slave women had to have undergone either three live births or had to have three living children at the time of the next birth. The stipulation is clearer in a will cited in Justinian's *Digestum* (1.5.15), which deals with the disposition of triplets under a will that freed the mother at the birth of the third child

Slave conditions in the southern United States were completely different. Manumission was the exception rather than the rule; American slaves could not anticipate freedom with any confidence. Manumission required court action in Louisiana, an onerous process that left traces in the historical record. An exhaustive count of Louisiana's manumission showed that the rate in the early nineteenth century was about 1 percent in each five-year period, an order of magnitude less than Scheidel assumed for the early Roman Empire (Whitman 1995; Hall 2000; Cole 2005). Many of those freed were children under ten, and the majority of the adults freed were women—presumably the children's mothers. Fogel and Engerman (1974, I, 150), champions of positive incentives in American slavery, reported even lower manumission rates at mid-century: "Census data indicate that in 1850 the rate of manumission was just 0.45 per thousand slaves." That is, .045 per 100 slaves or 0.2 percent in a five-year period, two orders of magnitude lower than Scheidel's reasonable guess for Rome. American slaves, and particularly male slaves, had little anticipation of freedom and little incentive to cooperate in the hope of freedom.

In Brazil, manumission began roughly at the outset of slavery, although many legal and circumstantial barriers prevented it from becoming a matter of course. Its pace was slow before the nineteenth century, but it accelerated rapidly during the last decades of Brazilian slavery. Rio de Janeiro contained 80,000 freed slaves in a total urban population of 200,000 in 1849. Brazil as a whole contained 1.1 million slaves and 2.8 million "freemen" in 1823 and 1.5

million slaves and 8.4 "freemen" in 1872. Nonwhite free persons had become a majority of the population in Salvador by 1872. Brazilian slaves often could earn enough to purchase their wives' freedom, although they frequently did not have enough to obtain their own. As in Louisiana, two-thirds of the freed slaves in Brazil and in Rio de Janeiro were women. A recent study of early nineteenth-century censuses in São Paulo confirmed the Brazilian predilection to manumit women rather than men—125 men for each 100 women among Brazilian slaves in 1836, but only 87 men for each 100 women among free coloreds. Any effect that manumission might have had on Brazilian slave workers as an incentive was diminished by the clear Brazilian pattern of freeing slave women rather than slave men (Schwartz 1974; Mattoso 1968, 50, 164; Nishida 1993, 365, 376; Luna and Klein 2003, 162–63).

Successful freedmen intensify the incentive for manumission that merges the work of slaves and free workers. Even freedmen living a marginal existence can serve as models for slaves, since freedom is desirable, whatever the economic cost. But its attraction undoubtedly increases to the extent that freedmen are accepted, even prominent, in free society. Unlike in other slave societies, freedmen in the early Roman Empire were citizens (Duff 1928; Treggiari 1969). In fact, they were ubiquitous in the late republic and early empire, engaged in all kinds of activities, including administration and economic enterprise. The number of men who identified themselves as freed on the tombstones during this period is astonishing. They may not have ascended to high Roman society, but their children bore little or no stigma. Their success was common knowledge. Seneca (*Epistulae Morales*, 27, 5) ridiculed a rich man by remarking that he had the bank account and brains of a freedman. In Finley's (1980, 98) words, "The contrast with the modern free Negro is evident."

Why were freedmen so prominent? The process of manumission separated the more able from the others. The prospect of manumission was an incentive for all slaves, but the most active, ambitious, and educated slaves were more likely to gain their freedom as a reward for good behavior or by purchase. The system did not work perfectly; many slaves were freed for eleemosynary motives or at their owner's death. But, for the most part, freedmen were accomplished individuals. It was good policy to deal with and hire them, and it makes sense to say so only because Rome had a functioning labor market. Contrast this scenario with that of freed slaves in the antebellum United States, where the infamous Dred Scott decision of the Supreme Court (60 U.S. 393, 407, 1857) decreed in 1857 that freed slaves could not be citizens and "had no rights which the white man was bound to respect."

Freed slaves in Brazil lived a similarly marginal existence, not bound but not fully free either. Known as *libertos*, they and their children were clearly isolated from the main society and were not prosperous. Census material and related data always indicated to which group a free person belonged. Even though freed slaves were Brazilian citizens, their legal rights were "quite limited." Libertos "continued to owe obedience, humility, and loyalty to the powerful." The physical appearance of freed slaves in Brazil made them easy to distinguish. The marginalization of freed persons in North and South America demonstrates that slavery in these areas was a largely closed system—although Brazil was not as closed as the United States—in contrast to the open system of the early Roman Empire (Mattoso 1986, 179–83; Schwartz 1974; Karasch 1987, 362; Chalhoub 1989; Nishida 1993; Libby and Paiva 2000; Luna and Klein 2003, 172).

Education is a key to the nature of Roman servitude. American slave owners relied on negative incentives and discouraged the education of slaves because they were afraid of slave revolts led by educated slaves. Roman slave owners used positive incentives, allowing, and even encouraging, slaves to be educated and perform responsible economic roles. Education increased the value of slave labor to the owner, and it increased the probability that a slave's children would be freed. Educated slaves had the skills to accumulate a peculium, and they would be good business associates of their former owners. Most freedmen worked in commercial centers, which provided an opportunity for advancement.

Educated slaves are markedly associated with positive incentives and uneducated slaves with negative incentives. Many educated Roman slaves were administrators, agents, and authors—for example, Q. Remmius Palaemon, who was educated in the first century C.E. ostensibly "as a result of escorting his owner's son to and from school (Bradley 1994, 35)," who probably had more direct exposure than simply acting as a *paedagogus*. In the republic, Cato educated slaves for a year, in a sort of primitive business school, and then sold them (Plutarch, *Cato the Elder*, 21). Anyone enacting such a plan with American slaves would not have been celebrated; he would have been ostracized, jailed, and fined. The Virginia Code of 1848 (747–48) extended to freedmen as well as slaves: "Every assemblage of Negroes for the purpose of instruction in reading or writing shall be an unlawful assembly. . . . If a white person assemble with Negroes for the purpose of instructing them to read or write, he shall be confined to jail not exceeding six months and fined not exceeding one hundred dollars." Education does not even appear in the index to Fogel and Engerman (1974). So few Brazilians of any sort were educated that no contrast between slave and free workers in this context is possible.

Many Roman slaves, educated or not, competed with freedmen and other free workers in a unified labor market. Various occupations emerged to meet the demands of urban residents, particularly rich ones. Skilled slaves were valuable to merchants and wealthy citizens because they could serve as their agents, in much the same way was their sons could: "Whatever children in our power and slaves in our possession receive by *manicipatio* or obtain by delivery, and whatever rights they stipulate for or acquire by any other title, they acquire for us" (Gaius, *Inst.* 2.87). Watson (1987, 107) expressed surprise that the Romans did not develop a law of agency, but the Romans did have a law of agency—the law of slavery (and sons). Slaves were more valuable than free men in that respect. Witness the frequent references to literate, skilled slave agents in the surviving sources (Lintott 2002; Jones 1956).

Columella (1.8-1-2) aptly exposed the difference between ancient and modern slavery: "So my advice at the start is not to appoint an overseer from that sort of slaves who are physically attractive and certainly not from that class which has busied itself with the voluptuous occupations of the city." This warning would not, and could not, apply to modern slavery, both because modern slaves could not indulge in "voluptuous occupations" like Columella's list of theater, gambling, restaurants, etc., and because a modern slave could not have been appointed as manager of a substantial estate.

Implicit in Columella's advice is the ease with which slaves could change jobs. For example, when Horace was given an estate on which he employed five free tenants and nine household slaves, he chose a vilicus from an urban household with no apparent training in agriculture. The mobility of labor must have been even more pronounced for free labor. The demand for unskilled and semiskilled labor for particular tasks varied widely over time in both the country and the city. Agricultural demand varied seasonally; in the late republic and undoubtedly at other times, the peak rural demand for labor was satisfied by the temporary employment of free workers. Urban labor demand varied less frequently, but possibly more widely. Public building activity in the Principate was sporadic; workers must have been attracted to these projects in one way or another. The presumption among classicists is that free workers were hired for them, lured by the wages offered. If so, they also must have had ways to support themselves and their families when public building activity was low (Aubert 1994, 133; Garnsey 1998, 143–45; Brunt 1980; Thornton and Thornton 1989).

Slave wages are not widely documented, despite the fact that some slaves must have earned wages to accumulate a peculium. The preceding discussion indicates that slaves were interchangeable with free wage laborers in many situations. Although the evidence for monthly and annual wages comes largely from Egypt, and the information about slaves comes mostly from Italy, Roman slaves appear to be like long-term employees. The analysis of slave motivation and the wide distribution of slave occupations suggest that slaves were part of an integrated labor force in the early Roman Empire.

How did the Romans create such an integrated labor system? Why is Roman slavery an outlier in figures 6.1 and 6.2? There are two reasons. Roman slavery expanded and developed into the form in which we know it during the conquests of the Roman Republic in the third and second centuries BCE. The Roman conquests were centered on the Mediterranean Sea, and the war captives looked like Romans. This made it easier to have an open slave system, contrasting with modern slavery composed of captives brought across the Atlantic from Africa to America. In addition, the Romans conquered the Greeks, taking educated captives into slavery. It was natural for the Roman slaveowners to employ these captives in activities that would benefit from their knoweldge and skills. These activities were harder to monitor than simple physical labor, and carrots worked better than sticks. Manumission is the ultimate carrot for a slave (Dari-Mattiacci 2011).

The observation that educated people became slaves reverses the causation noted earlier in this chapter that open systems of slavery with manumission promoted education. The earlier statement was that manumission led to education; the previous paragraph asserts that educated slaves led to manumission. Which is correct?

This is an identification problem, just like the one considered in chapter 4. There I asked whether inflation was the cause or effect of political instability. Here I ask whether frequent manumission was the cause or effect of educated slaves. The resolution of this problem is the same in both cases; the two phenomena emerged simultaneously and were jointly caused by another, separate event. In this case the independent event was the Roman conquest of the Mediterranean, which led to both educated slaves and frequent manumission. The uniqueness of Roman history generated a unique form of slavery.

Hopkins (1978, 115–32) asked, "Why did Roman masters free so many slaves?" His answer was complex. On one hand, he noted that the promise of freedom was a powerful incentive: "The slave's desire to buy his freedom was the master's protection against laziness and shoddy work." He distinguished Roman slavery from that in the southern United States. On the other hand, he emphasized the similarity of these two types of slavery and emphasized the role of cruelty and negative incentives. He devoted more space to slave resistance and rebellions than to slave achievement and cooperation. He argued that the apparent sharp line between slavery and freedom was part of a continuum of labor conditions, but he failed to break away from the view of American slavery being formulated at the time he wrote. This imperfect analogy still dominates the field (Bradley 1994).

Garnsey (1996, 87) argued that ancient slavery was less harsh than slavery in the southern United States. This judgment was placed late in a book of intellectual history that stretched from Greeks to Christians, and Roman slavery as a distinct labor system was not emphasized. Garnsey (1996, 97) noted that "the prospect of manumission gave [Roman] slaves an incentive to work and behave well." He drew out the implications of this proposition for the idea of slavery, particularly among Christians. I draw implications for the economic role of Roman slavery in the Roman labor force.

Bradley (1987) devoted a chapter in his study of Roman slavery to manumission, but he minimized its role as an incentive. He described manumission as bribery and as social manipulation, confirming his overall judgment that "the Roman slavery system was by nature oppressive and was maintained for the benefit of the privileged only" (Bradley 1987, 19–20). He seemed to view Roman slavery as a closed system where slaves and freedmen remained socially distinct from the free population, a presumption made explicit in his later book comparing ancient and modern slavery (Bradley 1994).

In addition to buying freedom, some valuable Roman slaves were freed without payment. This might be a reward for more complex achievement, or it could be for noneconomic reasons. This incentive mechanism therefore operated with considerable uncertainty. That made manumission in the early Roman Empire a bit like speculating with a new company today. Success is a product of both skill and luck, and the latter can be the more important. Success only comes to those that try, that is, those people who are willing to take the risks present in any start-up company. And there does not seem to be a shortage of people willing to take such risks today. Manumission represented the same kind of opportunity for Roman slaves. If a slave tried, both skill and luck would play a part in his eventual success or failure, but we should not think that the risks of the process discouraged many slaves.

One way to see this argument is as an expansion of remarks in *A Theory of Economic History* by J. R. Hicks, a Nobel laureate in economics who was interested in history as well as theory. Hicks argued, "There are two ways in which labour may be an article of trade. Either the labourer may be sold outright, which is slavery; or his services only may be hired, which is wage-payment" (Hicks 1969, 123). Hicks acknowledged that slavery typically is a cruel, brutal institution, but he softened this indictment when slaves have personal relations with their owners and can take economic actions on their own, as he said they did in the early Roman Empire. Hicks remarked, "Perhaps it should be said when this point is reached, the slave is only a semi-slave" (Hicks 1969, 126n).

For some poor people, the life of a slave appeared better than that of a free man. Ambitious poor people sold themselves into Roman slavery in a concrete realization of Hicks's long-term employment contract that promised, however uncertainly, more advancement than the life of the free poor (Ramin and Veyne 1981). This action, however rare in the early Roman Empire, would have been inconceivable in a closed system of slavery system built on negative incentives. Saller (2000, 835) explained how it came to be in Rome: "The disproportionately high representation of freedmen among the funerary inscriptions from Italian cities reflects the fact that ex-slaves were better placed to make a success of themselves in the urban economy than the freeborn poor: upon manumission many of the ex-slaves started with skills and a business."

Some Roman slaves were educated, and even educated people sometimes had the bad luck to be enslaved. Hereditary slaves in cities often received education as well. There was no prohibition against educating slaves as there was in modern slavery. Modern slave owners relied on negative incentives and were afraid of slave revolts led by educated slaves. Ancient slave owners used positive incentives and allowed and even encouraged slaves to be educated and perform responsible economic roles.

Freedmen were accepted into free society on an almost equal basis, that is, they were granted Roman citizenship. The well-known association of freedmen with former masters worked to their mutual benefit. Information was scarce in the early Roman Empire. When people engaged in trade or made arrangements for production, they needed to know with whom they were dealing. Roman society was divided into families, which provided some identification for individuals to minimize moral hazard and adverse selection. Slaves retained the names of and connections with their former owners and therefore could be identified as members of their owners' family (Garnsey 1998, 30–37). This identification helped the former slave to operate in the economy, and a productive freedman returned the favor by increasing the reputation of his former owner and his family. Freedmen could marry other Roman citizens, and children of freedmen (who were free) were accepted fully into Roman society. Findlay (1975) derived the optimal timing of manumission for a profit-maximizing owner.

Why did so many freedmen identify themselves as such on their tombstones (Taylor 1961)? It does not seem like something to be proud of in the traditional view of Roman slavery. But if manumission was an incentive and freedmen were the people who had responded most ably to that incentive, then there is something to be proud of. A freedman was attractive to deal with or hire because he had shown ambition and ability to get freed. These qualities were something to be proud of, and freedmen should have been proclaiming them when they could. To identify yourself as a freedman was to show you had been, in modern parlance, a self-made man, not the recipient of inherited wealth. This opportunity is the hallmark of open slavery.

Following Steinfeld (2001), we can think about a continuum of incentives, from almost all negative, as in a Nazi concentration camp or the Soviet gulag, to virtually all positive, as in a progressive school where no child is criticized and all children are winners. Most working conditions fall somewhere between these two extremes. Modern jobs clearly are near, but not at, the positive end; one can be fired or demoted for nonperformance. American slavery was near the opposite end; the threat of punishment was ubiquitous, while rewards for good service were rare. Roman slavery, by contrast, was far closer to the positive end than this, although hardly as close as modern jobs. Rural, illiterate, and unskilled slaves in the early Roman Empire may have experienced something like American slavery. Educated urban slaves experienced something close to the working conditions of free men.

Scheidel (2005b; 2008) and Harper (2010) argued that the choice of labor system was affected by the relative prices of free and slave labor. They accept in this view Hicks's and Steinfeld's points that slave labor was not too different from free labor. Slaves and free workers might be used for different purposes when free laborers could not be attracted to specific jobs or where they could not be contracted to stay for a long time, but there was enough overlap of slaves and free workers that relative prices were important in the choice of labor systems. Wickham (2009, 36) argued that this interchangeability continued into the late Roman Empire where free and unfree (in Wickham's term) workers lived alike.

Slaves were able to participate in the labor market of the early Roman Empire in almost the same way as free laborers, although their starting point often was considerably less favorable. The example of shackled slaves on Cato's estate has been taken as typical of Roman slavery, making it even harsher than the army. This assumes that the few cases of large slave holdings were typical of Roman slave holdings. It seems more likely that the few shackles that have survived until today are representative of only the extreme upper tail of the distribution of slave holdings. Most slaves probably were held in small numbers by farmers and households. Senators may well have held slaves in large units and under stressful conditions, but they were the exception to the lives of most Roman slaves (Roth 2007).

In other words, slaves started from a low place—the bottom only if they lacked education—but they did not need to remain there. Freedmen started from a better position, and their ability to progress was almost limitless, despite the existence of some prominent restrictions. These conditions created powerful positive incentives for slaves in the early Roman Empire. As Gibbon magisterially pronounced early in *The Decline and Fall of the Roman Empire*: "Hope, the best comfort of our imperfect condition, was not denied to the Roman slave; and if he had any opportunity of rendering himself either useful or agreeable, he might very naturally expect that the diligence and fidelity of a few years would be rewarded with the inestimable gift of freedom" (Gibbon 1961, 36).

Newly published documentary texts are constantly revealing more cases of slaves who clearly are well above the margin Gibbons described, such as Phosphorus Lepidianus, slave of the emperor Claudius, lending the bank of the Sulpicii the substantial sum of HS 94,000, equivalent to the gross annual salaries of over one hundred legionaries, for just over a month in 51 CE. In some cases these freedmen and slaves were clearly acting as agents of the emperor's *patrimonium* (privy purse), and at a local level they, like the managers of any large private estate, must have been involved in all kinds of credit arrangements. However, no source even hints that the patrimonium was a regular source of credit for individuals. In other cases, as with Phosphorus, it seems that imperial freedmen and slaves were acting on their own account, which raises the question of the source of their finances. They may have been temporarily diverting public or patrimonial resources which they were handling to make short-term private investments (*TPSulp.* 69; Plinius, *Nat.* VII,129).

Having shown how Roman slaves fit into the economy, we need to ask where they came from, as well as how numerous and valuable they were. The Romans engaged in many wars during the late republic, and the Roman Empire was the result of all the military successes of the republic. Why did the Romans engage in these expansionist campaigns? There must have been multiple motives, but one of them surely was economic gain (Harris 1979). Having conquered another group, the Romans were entitled to take all the booty they could carry and to tax the surplus from the defeated people on a continuing basis thereafter. It is clear that the Romans found many valuable objects to take away with them. They were exhibited in victory parades in Rome, and we can see the remains of one campaign in the triumphal Arch of Titus in the Roman Forum.

Defeated people posed a difficult issue. The victorious Romans could get immediate gain from bringing them back as slaves, or they could leave them in place and collect taxes from them. If the Romans were modern economists, they would make this choice according to the expected future value of the gains from slaves in Rome and in the conquered provinces. We know that immigrants from less-developed countries to Europe and the United States earn more than their friends back home (Borjas 1987). The same probably was true of slaves in Roman Italy relative to taxable people in the provinces. If the Romans figured this out, then it made sense for them to bring as many defeated people back with them as slaves as they could. We do not know why they brought so many slaves back to Roman Italy, but it may have been the results of thoughts like these.

The result was that slavery was most common in Roman Italy, although smaller concentrations of slaves were spread around the empire. Hopkins (1978) guessed that slaves represented about one-third of the Italian population at the start of the Principate, but more recent scholarship has reduced this percentage. The most recent survey of Roman slave demography explains in detail why all demographic estimates are the result of assumptions and concludes:

"According to my reconstruction, the total number of slaves in Roman Italy never exceeded one or at most one-and-a-half million. The population had been created by the influx of anywhere between two and four million slaves during the last two centuries B.C." (Scheidel 2005a, 64).

The free population of Roman Italy is not known with any confidence. The low estimate is about 6 million, while the high estimate is about twice that (Scheidel 2004). Even with the low estimate, the proportion of slaves was smaller than Hopkins asserted. The stock of slaves in Roman Italy was lower than the inflow because of a large outflow of slaves through death and manumission. Urban slaves—like urban citizens—had high mortality, and manumission was frequent. The result is that the proportion of slaves in Roman Italy probably reached its peak around the start of the Roman Empire and declined slowly after that. There were fewer slaves in the Roman provinces, and slaves were a smaller proportion of the population in the rest of the Roman Empire. If the high estimate of the total Roman population is adopted, the proportion of slaves is even smaller.

Slaves therefore were not the dominant labor force either in the city or the Italian countryside of the early Roman Empire. Slaves were less than one-fifth of the Italian population and fewer than that elsewhere in the empire during the Principate. The number of slaves was around 10 percent of the population by the fourth century, and Italy had lost its unique concentration of slaves (Harper 2011). Slaves in Egypt appear from surviving census returns to have composed about 10 percent of the population, spread among households that each held very few slaves. As two-thirds of the listed slaves were women, they appear to have been household rather than agricultural workers (Bagnall and Frier 1994, 48–49, 71).

Roth (2007) argued that the description of slaves in the agricultural manuals of Cato, Varro, and Columella conforms to Roman literary styles. They described how to grow crops, and they discussed the labor force for this activity. They were not describing the labor requirements of large plantations or villas, because the art form of their essays did not focus on this question. In particular, Roth pointed to evidence of weaving activity for clothes and other textiles that was done traditionally by women. And there were other household activities to be done that were best done by women. Only if there were women and families on large plantations would the slave population been able to remain relatively constant over time.

Slavery endured as long as the Roman Empire itself lasted. Wickham (2009, 36) asserts that the western empire "was not at risk" in 400. The apparent prosperity of the fourth century may not have equaled the abundance of the early empire, but it supported "middling consumption on a mass scale . . . that fueled strong demand for farm labor" (Harper 2011, chapter 1). The people we call slaves were still called *servi*, who lived side by side and similarly to *coloni*, as free tenants were known. The eastern empire fared better after the fourth century, and slavery consequently endured there longer.

Slaves were not restricted to the countryside. By the fourth century Rome was only half as large as it had been earlier, but cities still were substantial. John Chrysostom (*In epistulam ad Ephesios, homilia* 22.2. PG 62, col. 158) said in the late fourth century, "I say that even the household of the poor man is like a city. For in it there are also rulers. For instance, the man rules his wife, the wife rules the slaves, the slaves rule their own wives, and again the men and women rule the children." This proclamation and similar ones from Augustine Enarrationes in Psalm 124.7 (CC 40: 1840–41) and Synesius of Cyrene (Syn. Regn. 20 [Terzaghi: 46–48]) suggest that slaves were prevalent in cities as well as in the country, although Roman Italy may no longer have had the highest concentration of slaves. In the absence of any reasonable numbers, it may be best to assume that the prevalence of slavery may have been around 10 percent of the population throughout the late empire.

In other words, there was no gradual transition from slavery to serfdom in late antiquity. Instead, many institutions of the early Roman Empire remained more or less intact until the destruction of the western empire in the fifth century. Among these institutions was Roman slavery with its strong aspects of organized manumission and the open nature of slavery. While the empire had become more bureaucratic and the role of the central administration was stronger, there was no more separation between slave and free labor than before. Violence was still endemic, but there is little evidence that it was markedly worse for slaves than for comparable free persons. We can talk about the supply and demand of slave labor in the same way we think of the supply and demand of agricultural labor (Harper 2011).

We have slightly more data on the price of slaves than we do on their quantity. We must remember that these prices only make sense in the context of a Roman labor market as described earlier. Only if there was a functioning labor market can we assume that the isolated price observations that have survived are representative of prices in a particular place and time. And only if slaves and free workers were substitutes in many jobs can we compare slave prices and wages.

Scheidel (2005b, 2008) contrasted the price of slaves with the wages of free workers in Athens and Rome. He found that slave prices were low relative to wages in Athens and high in Rome. Scheidel explained this apparent contrast by differences in the *quantities* of slaves available in the two places and times. It is more likely that the price difference comes from the different *qualities* of slaves in the two systems than the different *quantities*. Since we are talking about long time periods, there was plenty of time for quantities to adjust, but the quality of slaves stayed constant because the institutions of slavery endured. The arrays in tables 6.1 and 6.2 show that Roman slaves were alone in being in an open slave system and alone in having a good chance of manumission. As noted already, this unique combination—in all the slave systems shown in the table—created conditions for educated and valuable slaves. Just as the wages of educated and skilled free workers were high, the prices of educated and skilled slaves were high. This is a more likely source of the contrast between Athens and Rome than the appeal to slave quantities. Even in table 6.2, Athenian slavery differed from Roman.

Harper (2010) extended the price series for Roman slaves into Late Antiquity. He found that the pattern of relatively high slave prices extended into the fourth and possibly the fifth century. It would be extraordinary if the conditions of slave quantities remained unchanged from the late republic to the late empire. It is more likely that the nature of Roman slavery remained unchanged, as Harper (2011) argues. He documents from a variety of literary sources that the institutions of slavery remained quite stable until the early fifth century. The stable relative prices lend additional support to his interpretation.

Workers in the unified labor market of the early Roman Empire could change jobs in response to market-driven rewards. As in all agricultural econo- mies, the labor market worked better in cities than in the countryside. Slaves participated in this system to a large extent. The restrictions on labor mobility may have been no more severe than the restrictions on labor mobility in early modern Europe. Education was the key to the good life in the early Roman Empire, as it is today. Roman workers appear to have received wages and other payments commensurate with their productivity, and they were able to re- spond, at least as fully as in more modern agrarian societies, to the incentives created by these payments.

"The Roman lawyer Gaius wrote that the fundamental social division was that between Slave and Free" (Garnsey 1998, 134, citing Gaius, *Institutiones*, 1.9). The fundamental economic division in the early Roman Empire, however, was between educated and uneducated—skilled and unskilled—not between slave and free. Saller (2000, 835) summarized this view succinctly: "The dispro- portionately high representation of freedmen among the funerary inscriptions from Italian cities reflects the fact that ex-slaves were better placed to make a success of themselves in the urban economy than the freeborn poor: upon manumission many of the ex-slaves started with skills and a business."

Chapter 7

■   ■   ■

Land Ownership

The market for land in the Roman Empire worked approximately like the land market today. We buy and sell land today with few impediments and use it as we wish; we own land as a *freehold*. The Oxford English Dictionary defines a freehold as "permanent and absolute tenure of land or property with freedom to dispose of it at will." The dictionary continues that the term originated in the fifteenth century and "was originally used to denote the holding of an estate in land with the rights of a free man, as opposed to a villein, and was taken to include the holding of an estate or interest in fee simple, in fee tail, or for term of life." These terms—villein, fee simple, fee tail—postdate the Roman Empire, and the use of these terms to indicate current conditions illustrates how hard it is to understand the distant past. In the United States, land legally is still held in fee simple.

Nothing about land is quite what it seems, and land owned in fee simple or a freehold is subject to many constraints. There are zoning laws in most parts of the United States that determine what you can build on land and for what purpose. There are building codes that determine many of the details of any structure you construct on your land. And governments reserve the right of eminent domain, that is, the right to confiscate your land if they choose to do so. In the complex federal system of the United States, these restrictions on land ownership are imposed by localities, state governments, and the federal government (Lamoreaux 2011).

The problem is that land is immobile. As the old saw goes, the properties that determine the value of land are location, location, location. If your neighbor is doing something you don't like, you can move away but you cannot take your land with you. Many of these neighborly impacts do not go through markets and therefore are called *externalities* by economists. The presence of so many externalities complicates the functioning of any land market from Roman times to today.

Even today, there are large transactions costs in conveying ownership of land and houses from one person to another. Since land does not move, brokers need to be hired to arrange for putative buyers to come to the land. The title of the land must be searched to make sure that the seller has the right to sell the property to the buyer. Then the buyer has to register his or her ownership of the property in a government register to be taxed and in order to be able to sell it again at some future time. The cost of these operations can be considerable. These transaction costs often are close to 10 percent of the price and more than 10 percent for cheaper properties.

These problems indicate that the land or housing market can never work as well as the market for grain or even for labor. Three attributes of land ownership can indicate a functioning market for land. First, there is a price for land that can change freely when conditions change. Second, people can buy and sell land at this price without reference to many outside authorities, that is, they can make their own decisions rather than reflecting the decisions of people not directly involved in the land sale. And third, there are few restrictions on or obligations from most landholdings and land transfers other than the payment of taxes.

Direct evidence of the latter two attributes, that land can be sold without too many strings attached, has been compiled by Myrto Malouta (in progress, 2011). There are papyrus records of many land sales in Roman Egypt during the first century of the Principate. The properties were both rural, often vineyards, and urban, including houses and land. Many sales were listed with accompanying mortgages, typically at 12 percent. A few examples suggest the nature of these transactions. One third of one fourth of a three-story house was sold in 30 CE; three-quarters of an old house and courtyard were sold in 40 with a mortgage of 72 drachms of minted silver, at 1 drch/mna interest a month (P. Mich. V 257, 329).

These records indicate a thriving land market, since land served as collateral for mortgage loans. If the purchaser defaulted on the loan, the lender needed to be able to sell the land to make it reasonable collateral. The records cannot demonstrate that prices moved because they are isolated observations lacking price information. They consequently need to be supplemented by anecdotal evidence that indicates land prices were flexible in the late republic and early empire. For example, Columella (*On Agriculture*, I. 2. 1) said, "I am of the opinion, therefore, that land should be purchased nearby." This is the kind of advice that one gives quite naturally in modern surroundings and seems no more remarkable to Columella then. Varro (*On Agriculture*, I. 4. 2–3) was even more explicit: "For any man would rather pay more for a piece of land which is attractive than for one of the same value which, though profitable, is unsightly. Further, land which is more wholesome is more valuable, because on it the profit is certain." He not only revealed that land could be purchased freely but that land values reflected aspects of the land that ordinary people find attractive, ranging from attractiveness—that is, favorable externalities—to productivity.

The well-known biography of Marcus Crassus by Plutarch describes the ease in buying and selling urban land and buildings that echoes the agricultural writers:

> Marcus Crassus, observing how extremely subject the city was to fire and falling down of houses, by reason of their height and their standing so near together, he bought slaves that were builders and architects, and when he had collected these to the number of more than five hundred, he made it his practice to buy houses that were on fire, and those in the neighborhood, which, in the immediate danger and uncertainty the proprietors were willing to part with for little or nothing, so that the greatest part of Rome, at one time or other, came into his hands.
>
> Later in life he was suspected to have been too familiar with one of the vestal virgins, named Licinia, who was, nevertheless, acquitted, upon an impeachment brought against her by one Plotinus. Licinia stood possessed of a beautiful property in the suburbs, which Crassus desiring to purchase at a low price, for this reason was frequent in his attentions to her, which gave occasion to the scandal, and his avarice, so to say, serving to clear him of the crime, he was acquitted. Nor did he leave the lady till he had got the estate.

These are anecdotes, but their uniformity indicates that the process of purchasing and selling Roman land was not particularly difficult. Even in only a few examples, we have reference to rural, urban and suburban land being sold freely at prices agreed on by the buyer and seller. A final anecdote reveals how flexible Roman land prices were. There was a credit crisis in 33 CE in which land prices apparently fell rapidly, like stocks and houses in a modern crisis.

According to Tacitus (*Ann.* 6.16–17), the crisis originated with a conflict among the ruling class. One group accused the other of violating old usury laws that limited the interest rate to 1 percent a month or 12 percent a year or perhaps of having more loans than the law allowed. The Senate was divided, as most senators apparently were extending credit to others in some form, and the emperor, Tiberius, gave the senators eighteen months bring their affairs into conformity with the law.

Tacitus describes the implications of these events as follows.

> Hence followed a scarcity of money, a great shock being given to all credit, the current coin too, in consequence of the conviction of so many persons and the sale of their property, being locked up in the imperial treasury or the public

exchequer. To meet this, the Senate had directed that every creditor should have two-thirds of his capital secured on estates in Italy. Yet creditors were suing for payment in full, and it was not respectable for persons when sued to break faith. So, at first, there were clamorous meetings and importunate entreaties; then noisy applications to the praetor's court. And the very device intended as a remedy, the sale and purchase of estates, proved the contrary, as the usurers had hoarded up all their money for buying land. The facilities for selling were followed by a fall of prices, and the deeper a man was in debt, the more reluctantly did he part with his property, and many were utterly ruined. The destruction of private wealth precipitated the fall of rank and reputation, till at last the emperor interposed his aid by distributing throughout the banks a hundred million sesterces, and allowing freedom to borrow without interest for three years, provided the borrower gave security to the State in land to double the amount. Credit was thus restored, and gradually private lenders were found. The purchase too of estates was not carried out according to the letter of the Senate's decree, rigor at the outset, as usual with such matters, becoming negligence in the end.

In these turbulent times of 2012, we can translate Tacitus's statements into our current framework. The crisis may have originated in the deflation of a housing boom (Frank 1937). Creditors were suing for relief, and senators were selling land to raise money. This led land prices to fall, and the fall was intensified by two processes familiar from the Great Depression. First, many senators hoarded their money to remain safe in these troubled times, reducing the purchasing power to buy land. Second, as land prices fell, the burden of senators' debt rose in relation to the value of their property and reduced spending even more. The first of these was called the Paradox of Thrift by Keynes (1936); the second, the Debt-Deflation theory of the Great Depression by Fisher (1933).

In addition, the fall in land prices was sufficiently rapid to lead to a potentially dangerous destruction of private wealth, causing Tiberius to step in to stop the panic. Again, he used a technique that we still use two millennia later, known since 2000 as the "Greenspan put." (The chairman of the American Federal Reserve flooded the market with money after crises to help maintain the value of financial assets—similar to land in Roman times.) The important point here is not the panic, but rather that land prices were uncontrolled and capable of changing rapidly. This is consistent with Crassus sweet-talking Licinia to get a good price for her land. While we cannot observe actual land prices directly, we see the process of land price changes in these stories. The financial dimensions of this crisis are explored further in chapter 8.

Hopkins (1978) generalized these descriptions to propose a wholesale transfer of Italian land from small to large landowners by the same kind of purchases as recorded for Crassus. The operative change was not the immediate crisis of an urban fire, but rather the newfound wealth of high-ranking Roman military men. Hopkins thought of the relationship between land ownership and conquest as interactive where each affected the other. My interest here is with the land market, and I do not need to evaluate or even explore the whole model. Let me therefore describe the one-way process that is at the key of Hopkins's synthesis. Rome expanded greatly in the last two centuries of the republic, the last two centuries before the current era. This expansion was made possible by Roman military prowess which overcame all opponents. (The organization of the Roman army may have been the independent event that started the interactive system in motion. To understand why an independent change is needed to start such a process, recall the discussion of inflation in chapter 4 and of slavery in chapter 6.) The result was a great inflow of booty into Rome in the form of both precious objects and slaves.

The objects must have been for sale, and returnees found that they had money in hand. They used this money to buy land in Italy, land being the only large asset that could be held by rich Romans. The purchasing of land does not seem to be a problem for Hopkins, and it forms a critical part of his interpretation of late republican Rome. If he is right, the inflow of cash into the Italian land market must have inflated the price of land. The countryside at this time therefore must have looked different from the variety of points of view we can imagine. From the point of view of the wealthy, land must have gone from being cheap to being expensive. From the point of view of the small landowners, the rise in price must have been a windfall. Hopkins ignored this aspect of the land sales and assumed that many small farmers went into the army.

It is reasonable to divide the common farmers into two groups. Some of them owned small farms while others were farm laborers without owning any land. Landowners must have gained from the sale of their land—otherwise why did they sell—and most probably went to towns (Geraghty 2007). Landless farm workers were displaced in this model by the slaves that were the other part of wartime booty. They enhanced the army and allowed more conquests to take place. They did not benefit from the riches brought back from conquest; they probably lost as the addition of more slaves increased the Italian labor force and decreased their incomes and wages.

This is the result if there was a Roman labor market as I have argued in chapter 6. The booty increased inequality in Rome by increasing the riches of those who had a claim on wartime booty and by decreasing the incomes of those who did not and suffered from greater competition as a result of the imports of slaves. This according to some was the beginning of the end of the republic (Tainter 1988).

We need to be cautious about Hopkins's views since he asserted that "slavery also allowed the rich to recruit labor to work their estates in a society which had no labor market" (Hopkins 1978, 14). A labor market, however, is not necessary for the analysis of land ownership, as opposed to large questions about the fortunes of Rome. Duncan-Jones (1990, 126) argued that "the usual processes of transfer of wealth appear to have been by inheritance, by bequest and by marriage." He added that the comments of Columella and Varro do not indicate that most property was acquired by purchase, but he argued in the context of the Tiberian crisis of 33 that the preference of the upper classes "for land rather than cash was probably a deliberate economic choice" (Duncan-Jones 1994, 24).

These comments appear confused. It is not necessary that all land or even most land be bought and sold in some time period to make a market. It is only needed that enough land be bought and sold that we can speak of the price of land in general, as Tacitus did. If Duncan-Jones is right that wealthy Romans made an economic decision about the assets in which to hold their wealth, they must have considered the price of these assets. That is the essence of economic decisions.

The law of 111 BCE converted much the public land in Italy into private. In other words, the law made more land available for purchase and sale. Both public and private land was available after the legislation, but the Italian and civil wars made it made it "easy to acquire, either by unauthorized occupation or by legal purchase, large quantities of private land, especially land seized from the Italian enemies of Rome or proscribed Romans" (Lintott 1992, 58). Lintott, differing with Hopkins, argued that the growth of large Italian estates was due more to civil wars rather than the conquest of new territories.

The Roman Republic financed its army from captured booty and from operating silver and other mines during its period of expansion. The Romans instituted a poll tax to mark personal subjection to Rome and a land tax to indicate Roman control of land. Without a large bureaucracy to assess these taxes, the republic farmed the taxes to people known to us as *publicani*. We know a lot about the operations of publicani, but less about which taxes were most important for revenue (Badian 1983; Malmendier 2009). Revenue from the mines and tax farmers apparently was sufficient to maintain the highly effective Roman army.

Augustus reorganized this system to account for both the advent of the new empire and the cessation of major territorial expansion. He split the revenue into two streams, the traditional taxes controlled by provincial governors as in the republic and a new stream of revenue controlled by the emperor, the *fiscus Caesaris*. "Uniform, if not universal, criteria for counting subjects and assessing their wealth were extended first of all to the *provinciae Caesaris*, the provinces under the direct control of the emperor, and later to the *provinciae populi* as well" (Lo Cascio 2007, 631). It is necessary to unpack this summary statement to understand the complexity of this change.

Wealth in this context was land. The Romans adopted a scheme for surveying land that indicated its extent, starting from a central point. The process of *centuriation* imposed a grid onto land that did not appear to take much account of natural features like streams and hills. Land surveys were incised on a bronze map, one copy of which was kept locally and another in Rome. One surviving example from *colonia Arausio* suggests strongly that these maps were used as a basis for tax collection, as the tenants of taxable land, *ager vectigalis*, were listed individually. Private land was not allocated to owners either because this map was only about tenants or because owners were tax exempt due to the nature of the colony (Crook 1967, 148). Given the tiny bureaucracy in Rome until the end of the fourth century, it is not clear who kept track of what must have been a large number of bronze land maps in Rome. Land centuriation was slated to be done by censors every five years, but we have too few surviving maps and surveys to know if this schedule was binding.

The survey process was set out by Ulpian (Dig. 50.15.4) in the early Roman Empire, although written down centuries later: "It is laid down in the list of rules for the census that land must be entered in the census in this way: . . . how many *jugera* of land have been sown for the last ten years, how many vines vineyards have, how many jugera are olive plantations and with how many trees," as well as how much land was devoted to hay, pasture and wood. After all this detail, Ulpian said, "Omnia ipse qui defert aestimet: The man who declares anything must value it" (Watson 1985, IV, 932).

Lo Cascio stated that the land tax was related to "the monetary value of estates" (ibid.), which must mean the estimated value. In Italy, the value of estates was used as a basis for mortgages to the emperor, which paid for the support of children (CIL, IX, 1,455; CIL, XI, 1,147). The mortgages were made at 5 percent, far lower than the Egyptian mortgages noted earlier and possibly below the usual rate in Italy (Lewis and Reinhold 1990, II, 256). The value was based on the revenue, according to judicial rules on prices—"If [someone] bought a farm . . . at a price settled according to the revenue" (Dig. 30.92 pr)—and was checked by the administrators of the alimentary activity. The presumption is that this system worked similarly outside Italy where land was subject to taxation instead of mortgages to finance child support, but there is essentially no evidence for the administration of this process in the provinces. Goffart (1974) suggested that taxes were levied on total wealth and only transformed into a true land tax in the fourth century.

It seems odd for the emperor to be loaning money to landowners. We expect the borrower to take the initiative in getting a mortgage, but the surviving documents imply that the emperor wanted to make loans. Perhaps this was the way to make social expenditures the responsibility of the central rather than the local authorities. If so, then the existence of these loans raises a further question: what did landowners do with their loans? They might have increased their consumption, improved their land, or found some other use for the loan. In any case, the low rate of interest suggests that the emperor was subsidizing the landowners to help with poor relief. This arrangement—where the emperor gives money to landowners—is documented where land taxes were abated. In the rest of the empire where landowners and lessees paid taxes to the emperor, some other arrangement must have been used.

The tax rate appears to have been about 1 percent of the value which amounted to about 10 percent of the revenue. If the tax was indeed leveled on the value of the property, there must have been land sales to indicate this value. If it was leveled on the value of the produce, some person or agency must have been observing it. If it was levied on the quantity of produce, again someone must have been observing this sharecropping (Crook 1967, 148; Lo Cascio 2007, 640). In any case, there must have been a lot of market activity for land and grain underlying the assessment of the land tax.

As Hopkins (1980) famously argued, this process spurred the monetization of the Roman Empire as well as trade within it. He imagined that taxes were levied in the provinces and spent in Rome, but much of the revenue went to the army that was billeted in the provinces. Since soldiers ate the products of farms, much of the tax collection and disbursement could have been made locally and in kind. The sources do not indicate a kind of sharecropping on land owned by the emperor rather than a monetary tax on the value of privately held land.

The army may have consumed up to three-quarters of the tax revenue, and the remainder was used for various expenses in Rome. The emperor had to maintain his household, which was extensive even if not a bureaucracy. He had to support continued construction in and around Rome for urban and religious purposes as well as to maintain the city. Nero received a bad press for his extravagant expenditures, but the bulk of them were to rebuild Rome after the disastrous fire of 64 (Griffin 1984). And emperors distributed coin and food to the urban poor in Rome and later smaller towns as well to keep the peace. We know that a large amount of grain was shipped from Africa and Egypt to Rome to feed the population, but it is hard to know if this was taxation in kind or monetary taxation and purchased grain (Erdkamp 2005).

Lo Cascio asserted that the assessments underlying the land tax were uniform, but even this cursory survey of Roman tax administration casts doubt on that conclusion. The rules for assessing land may have been uniform, but their administration must have varied provincially and as personnel changed. There is little evidence of resistance to paying the land tax; there is much more evidence of corrupt provincial governors—of which Verres was the exemplar according to Cicero—than of hostile taxpayers. This suggests that the tax rate was low and its administration uniform enough for Roman times.

The argument so far has developed two points. There was a market for land in Rome that allowed there to be market prices and assessed values for tax purposes. Prices could vary. Land could be sold quickly and easily, although the intrinsic imperfections of land markets noted earlier may have precluded frequent land sales. In addition, land taxes in some form sustained the Roman Empire. These points in turn raise two questions that now need to be answered. Who actually owned Roman land, individuals or the emperor? And what happened to this land and tax system under later emperors?

The jurists and legal commentators described a complex two-part law of land tenure. There were two sets of rules, one for what has been labeled ownership and one on possession. The line between these categories is not clear, and one puzzle for modern observers is to know which set of rules was applicable in any particular case.

Ownership in ancient Rome was a concept distinct from possession of an object. Called *dominium*, ownership conveyed certain rights; namely the right to receive damages from a theft, and most importantly *vindicatio*, which was a legal action taken by the rightful owner of a piece of property to recover his property from the current possessor. The difficulty here lay in actually proving oneself to be the true owner, and something like a modern title search often was used in the process of a vindicatio (Johnston 1999, 53–60.)

Ownership could be acquired in two ways, *ab initio* and *usucapio*. Ab initio is the claiming of an unowned place or thing or the creation of one. Usucapio, by far the most important method, was the acquisition of ownership through possession for a period of time (two years for land) as long as it was not acquired illegally. Ownership extended to buildings on the land; there was no modern distinction between the structure and the land itself. Only land in Italy could be privately owned, although exceptions were made for some larger *coloniae*, communities of colonial status. They had an "Italian right" (*ius Italicum*) that created the legal fiction that their land was Italian, that they had full *dominium* over it, and they were exempt from taxes (Crook 1967, 140). And land could be leased. Much of agricultural land must have been leased to tenant farmers, possibly in the form of sharecroppers, in which the tenants paid the landlord with a predetermined share of their crops. "Although it is not possible to quantify this, it seems clear that farm tenancy was an important form of land tenure throughout Roman antiquity" (Kehoe 1997, 5). "As a general rule, the imperial administration exploited these [African and Egyptian] properties by leasing them out, in various forms, to individual small-scale cultivators" (Frier and Kehoe 2007, 139).

Turning to possession, tenants appear to have had durable tenure on their land even if they did not own it. Taxes appear to have been levied on tenants rather than landowners. Land ownership appears to be special to Italy and public land elsewhere that did not pay taxes. Provincial land was largely ager vectigalis that owed taxes. Tax liability went with sales of land even though most taxed land was leased rather than owned. Tenancies could be inherited as long as the taxes were paid, and their transfers were spoken of as buying and selling as commonly as letting and hiring (Crook 1967, 148, 158). It must have been possible to buy and sell leases, possibly using simpler rules than the cumbersome legal processes for owned land.

Tenants also had rights relative to their landlords that appear to have been supported by the courts. These rights appear to be like common-law rights in the modern world, although there was no common law at the time. Roman courts were consistent in their support of tenant rights when the tenants argued that landowners were encroaching on their rights. "Rather, the state used the law to establish a more even playing field to facilitate the type of investment and cooperation that could lead to economic growth" (Kehoe 2007, 194).

Egyptian taxes were an exception to the general rule of tax liability since landowners appear to have paid taxes in Egypt. Modern scholars refer to surviving Egyptian land surveys as landholdings, leaving ambiguous whether the surveys recorded ownership as opposed to tenancy. The surveys clearly were compiled for tax purposes even if not all the land parcels paid tax at the same rate. Bowman referred to landowning and compared the concentration of ownership in fourth-century Egypt with nineteenth-century Britain, implying Roman Egyptian ownership rather than tenancy (Bowman 1985; Bagnall 1992).

While the forms of land tenure clearly were varied, we can attempt an abstract statement of Roman land tenure arrangements. Land was private or public, owned either by individuals or the emperor. Public land was leased, and tenants had the right to buy and sell leases. They paid taxes on their land, probably a share of their crop. Private land also could be bought and sold; most of it was leased, and tenants paid rent to the owners. Owners did not pay taxes, and it is reasonable to assume that rents on private land were similar to taxes on public land. There may also have been local taxes to support municipalities, and the incidence of these taxes is unknown. "By the third century, royal [Egyptian] land had become largely assimilated with private land, the one significant difference being a separate rate of taxation" (Frier and Kehoe 2007, 141).

A new census of people and land was made at the end of the third century to provide a new basis for taxation. In Syria, one *iugera* of good land was considered equal to two of average land and three of poor land. Cropland was distinguished from vineyards as well. This was the most elaborate of land rankings, and there were many regional variations. While the census was extensive, there was little uniformity. Jones (1964, 64) observed that "under Diocletian the annona, the requisition in kind, seemed to have been assessed on land only, while the *capitatio*, the poll tax, was paid in money." If so, the annona may have been sharecropping in practice.

These rules stayed in place for at least four centuries. During that period, the Roman Empire preserved peace around the Mediterranean basin and allowed the system of land ownership and taxation to continue. Starting in the fifth century, the ability of the western Empire to preserve peace began to erode. Rome was sacked early in the fifth century, a traumatic event that led Augustine to write the *City of God* distinguishing belief in the Catholic Church from the defense of any earthly city. More important if less visible to most people living through it was the capture of Africa by the Vandals in 439. This loss deprived the central government of an important component of its tax base and made it impossible for the government to mount effective counterattacks against the various invaders of the Roman Empire. This clearly set up a cumulative process that led in a few decades to the demise of the western Empire (Heather 2005; Wickham 2009).

What was the effect of this cataclysmic change on Roman property owners? I suggest that many landowners were unaffected as the decline of central authority began. Most of their activities were local, and local authorities continued to guide local economies. Invasions were sporadic and affected only swaths through the vast empire. Landowners in the path of the invaders must have experienced problems with their land ownership, but landowners in other areas probably carried on as they and their fathers had done before. Imported goods to any area became more rare and expensive as travel became more dangerous. "Across the sixth and seventh centuries African goods are less and less visible in the northern Mediterranean; they vanish first from inland sites, and then from minor coastal centres" (Wickham 2009, 218).

The process of Roman decline was not one of uniform decline that affected everyone alike. Instead it was a selective process that involved more and more people over time. The spread of violence was sporadic and uneven. As more and more areas were affected, land ownership under Roman rules became more and more localized. Land ownership in the form described earlier was confined to Roman islands in a barbaric sea (with apologies to Pirenne 1956). These islands shrank over time as the violence overspread the declining empire until most of them disappeared at some undetermined time (McCormick 2001).

We see remnants of the Roman land system in an account of taxes due from tenants to the Abbey of St. Martin de Tours around 700 listing fourteen hundred tenants and the modii of wheat, rye, barley, oats and spelt due (Gasnault 1975, 95ff). There is more detail in a list of tenants of the Abbey of St. Germain-des-Pres a century later. There is a list of more than fifteen hundred farms with "at least" ten thousand residents. Almost all of these farms were were "ingénuilles", but some were "lidiles" and "serviles." Most of islands of Roman land tenures must have clustered around abbeys, the most stable landholders in Merovingian and Carolingian times (Longon 1978, Tome I, 243).

The eastern Empire did not collapse, although it lost control of Egypt in 698. The Byzantine state remained strong and land taxation continued to provide a fiscal base to the state. "Indeed, payment of the [land] tax was itself proof of ownership. Since the early eighth century, perhaps earlier, the tax was estimated on the value of the land" (Laiou and Morrisson 2007, 50). High-quality land was worth the most; second-quality land, less; and pasture, even less. The tax rate, which appears to have endured into the twelfth century, was about one quarter of cereal production. Although there appeared to be land consolidation later in this period, the tax rate remained level for landowners and was higher only for the increasing proportion of tenant farmers (Laiou and Morrisson 2007, 107).

Agricultural production was divided between what can be called estates and village. Estates were the successors to Roman *latifundia*, and villages were composed of independent proprietors. The latter paid taxes to the state as in Roman times, and their tax rate was only half the dues paid by tenant farmers. This major difference was due partly to the protection offered by the estate and partly to services and capital provided by the lord of the estate. "*Paroikoi* [tenants] were considered by Byzantine jurists as the heirs of the proto-Byzantine *coloni*" (Lefort 2002, 238). Wage laborers were scarce, and labor services on estates were small to the extent we can judge. It looks as if Byzantine independent proprietors were the analog of what I have called Roman islands in the West. Since the state was stronger and more continuous in the East, these Roman remnants were a more important part of the rural landscape (Lefort 2002).

The Byzantine system of land tenure was taken over by the Ottoman Empire and continued into modern times. In fact, the land tax in modern Israel is known as the *arnona*, a Hebrew term that goes back to the Talmud, where it denoted a tax on livestock and grain. It is most likely derived from the Latin word, annona, the Roman land tax to finance food distribution in the city of Rome.

In contrast, invasions of Western Europe multiplied and violence spread after the western Empire collapsed, and the Roman organization of society broke down entirely. We know little about the terms of land tenure in the Carolingian period as the terms used disappeared in later centuries. Archaeology has uncovered some holdovers in early medieval fields of the Roman *centuriatio* (Verhulst 2002, 18–19). After the Carolingians came the Northmen and further disintegration of landholdings.

Marc Bloch (1961) described how feudalism gradually created order out of chaos, and I follow his lead in this discussion of land tenure. There was no land tenure in the period of chaos when you only had authority over a plot of land if you were physically present and could fight off other claimants. It was hard even to grow a crop in such a situation as there was no way to ensure you could reap the harvest from seeds you had sown. Population consequently was very small, declining sharply to the extent we know it after the western Roman Empire collapsed.

Travel was so hazardous that it was easier to bring people to food than food to people. "The nobleman with his entourage moved round constantly from one of his estates to another; and not only in order to supervise them more effectively. It was necessary for him to consume the produce on the spot, for to transport it to a common center would have been both inconvenient and expensive" (Bloch 1961, 63). Land ownership was exceedingly tenuous.

This chaotic period when central authority disappeared was traumatic in European history. Shakespeare employed the memory of this period many centuries later to set the stage for the tragedy of King Lear, based on a twelfth-century play. In the first scene Lear divides his kingdom between his two faithful daughters—as he sees them at the time—and adds, "Ourself, by monthly course, / With reservation of an hundred knights / By you to be sustain'd, shall our abode / Make with you by due turns." In modern prose, the king says he will travel with a large armed escort from place to place to consume the local produce. The many knights were to protect him; the traveling was to take him to the food instead of vice versa. It is extraordinary that in the well-ordered England of several centuries later that this memory of the hard times should be used as the entry to a searing play of morals.

There was no ownership of land in this situation, as control could not be exerted at a distance. There was instead possession by people on the land who could and would defend it. This kind of possession was called a fief, an adaption of the Carolingian Latin *feodum*. "By fief was meant a property granted not against an obligation to pay something . . . but against an obligation to do something" (Bloch 1961, 167). A fief lasted only as long as the person possessing the land gave service; it was not inherited. It was far different and less stable than land ownership or possession in Rome.

Wickham (2009) described this transition in great detail in his account of Europe from 400 to 1000. But while his account is rich in detail, the transition of land tenure arrangements is obscured by his language. Wickham wrote of a change from a society based on taxes to one based on ownership: "Tax was, that is to say, no longer the basis of the state. For kings as well as armies, land-owning was the major source of wealth from now on." He refers to this process as "the shift from taxation to landowning" (Wickham 2009, 103–4). As I have discussed and Wickham acknowledged in his book, land taxation has to be based on land ownership or possession. There can be no taxation without some way of knowing who to tax. The decline of the Roman Empire led to a decline of both land taxes and land ownership. The growing chaos Wickham described precluded both activities. A better frame would have been to say that the society changed from one based on taxes to one based on personal service. What does it mean to own land if taxes on the land no longer sustain a government?

Feudalism was the way out of this chaos. It is best seen as a way to organize defense in a violent world. There was not enough security for a central government to collect taxes and field a military force, and all action had to be local. Subject to this constraint, it was natural for families and then close acquaintances to band together for their mutual defense. Adam Smith told us that labor specialization is limited by the extent of the market. Markets in these conditions were local and small, and the labor differential was limited to two classes of people, those who fought and those who farmed—knights and farmers.

A fief allowed a knight to fight for the defense of the farmers in the fief, but isolated knights were not much use against concerted attack. Feudalism was a way for knights to come together through lord and vassal arrangements that constructed a hierarchy of vassals under a lord who could field a group of knights. Vassals then used the resources of their fiefs to support their military activities, which were used in the service of their lords. The farming that underlay all this was done by the lords' villeins and other serfs. The lords in return for the vassals' support used their military resources to preserve the vassals' fiefs. Fiefs were retained as long as vassals fulfilled their part of the bargain, giving rise to elaborate rituals to assure lords that vassals would come forth when needed.

The feudal system succeeded in bringing more peaceful conditions to Western Europe, and problems changed from defending from invaders to defending against neighbors. There developed a small arms race in armaments for knights and their horses. The small economies of scale in this arms race accentuated the need to have substantial fiefs for knights. Since there was no market for fiefs, the issue of size only came when a vassal's service ended and the fief reverted to the lord, typically when the vassal died.

The nonhereditary fief eventually was supplanted by a hereditary model as lords needed a reliable source from which to obtain vassals. The most convenient way to obtain future vassals was by making new acts of homage with the children of current vassals. Once this practice started, the converse situation where children of vassals were denied the fiefs of their fathers made it harder to add more vassals. Fiefs consequently took on a hereditary character as feudalism evolved, and eventually this characteristic of the fief became law in several regions of Europe. This heritable land could be sold, but the lord clearly had a large influence on who could buy it. "The medieval arrangement of property rights to land, with all kinds of overlapping claims and rights, served other needs than purely economic ones aimed at market exchange" (Van Bavel 2008, 16).

Society thus was divided into two parts. Knights and clerics did not work and paid no taxes. Peasants worked and paid for the consumption of the upper class as well as their own, a division of society that lasted into the eighteenth century. A major problem for the new aristocracy was how to avoid the dissolution of their position by partible inheritance, which was widespread among Germanic cultures. And as fiefs became hereditary, some way needed to be found to keep them intact to preserve the size needed to support knights (Duby 1974, 168–74; Hay and Rogers 1982).

One way to preserve fiefs was for polities to adopt a rule of primogenitor, where only the oldest son inherited the fief. Another way was to entail a landholding, that is, to impose rules on the deed that limited inheritance to members of a family. A fee tail is a type of entail that fixed the rule of inheritance within a family and can be traced to another land tenure mechanism known as the *maritagium*, when a grant was made by a woman's relative, usually the father, to her husband. This kind of grant served as the woman's inheritance, provided material support, and encouraged an alliance between the families through marriage. Under maritagium land could only be inherited by the woman's children and would revert back to the original donor in the case where there were no heirs.

There were many restrictions on land and land transfers as the need for service and the desire for inherited land got in each other's way. There must have been an evolution of these restrictions, but many different approaches appear to have been in use at the same time. This appearance may reflect the scarcity of historical evidence, but it more probably reflects a combination of regional differences in customs and uneven evolution even in local areas. Travel was difficult and transport was expensive; regions were far more isolated than in Roman times. "Regional differences were sharp, even between neighboring regions" (Van Bavel 2008, 14).

An "unusually perfect feudal structure was imposed after the Norman Conquest. . . . The whole social structure was based on landholding in return for service." Knight's service or other personal services known as grand sergeanty were the basis of land tenure, which was granted by the Crown. In addition to tenures, landed estates held by subjects of the king were held for life, in fee tail (inheritable by lineal descendants) or in fee simple (inheritable by heirs more broadly). Most agricultural labor was done by villain tenants (Megarry and Wade 1975, 13–15, 24, 42).

Feoffment is the English term for the action of investing a person with a fief or fee, the two terms used for land possession in medieval England. Normally, as noted already, acquiring a fief or fee obligated an individual to render military service for a lord. Missing is any mention of land sales, taxes, or prices. In addition, tenants, that is, villeins, had no bargaining power as they had no mobility; they were serfs. There are no court records of tenant appeals, as there was no central state to oppose the lords (Kaye 2009). This is what it means to lack both a land and labor market.

Not all land was contained in fiefs or held in fee. Independent plots of land were known as allods, and they were at risk from lords and knights supported by fiefs. A recent survey of land ownership in the eleventh and twelfth centuries in the north of France revealed the presence of many small landowners that contrasted with the nearby holdings of the Count of Ponthieu. The allods lasted until the expansion of royal power in the late thirteenth century (Van der Beek 2010a, b). We tend to know of their existence largely by records of their incorporation into fiefdoms, which creates a presumption that they were disappearing. As population increased in the increasingly peaceful feudal age, it became harder for allods to escape notice, and they were at increasing risk from armed lords and vassals.

The burden of rents and feudal dues on peasants has been calculated as about 40 percent of their production, although it varied quite a bit between manors (Allen 2005, 36; Van der Beek, 2010a). This is higher than the commonly accepted levels of taxation in the early Roman Empire, which hover around 10 percent of production. If these estimates are even approximately accurate, then one of two things must have happened in the first millennium. Either farming must have become vastly more efficient, or the after-tax income of farmers must have shrunk dramatically. The latter choice appears more likely at our current state of knowledge.

Feudal warfare relied on direct hand-to-hand combat, which established the knight as the primary military unit. Over time, military armies employed greater use of archers, which provided key advantages over knights in battle, and the knight as a military unit decreased in importance and gradually disappeared. With the introduction of firepower, archers made way for musketeers who used muskets as a means of offense. Although early firearms were less accurate and efficient than the bow and arrow, continual technological improvements in guns eventually rendered archers obsolete. Considering that it usually took many years of training to make an archer, while only days were required to train and field a musketeer, it became more efficient to employ musketeers as a military unit. The lower costs and faster production associated with training and fielding musketeers allowed for significant increases in army sizes.

In economic terms, the process was determined by economies of scale. In the feudal age, when chaos was the issue, there were economies of scale for individual fighters, that is, knights. There were few economies of scale after this limited scope. As security increased and warfare changed, archers and musketeers provided economies of scale that extended to larger numbers of soldiers. Economies of scale near the origin were reduced as archers and then musketeers needed less equipment and training than knights, while economies of scale for groups of soldiers increased as the power of firing in volleys became apparent. The new economies of scale came more from military organization than individual training. The new system was clear enough to be described clearly around 1600. "Maurice of Nassau and Gustavus Adolphus developed a system of organization, tactics, and drill that harked back to the Roman legions" (Boot 2006, 103). The economics of warfare had come full circle.

Land tenures had been advancing as military technology improved, at least in the most urbanized parts of Europe in northern Italy and the Low Countries. Land sales by peasants are recorded as early as the eighth and ninth centuries when northern Europe was in chaos. The clarification of property rights and the introduction of civil courts stimulated land markets in the later twelfth century. The Low Countries caught up by the fourteenth century when voluntary registration of private land transfers by public courts became common. Although these two regions developed differently, the growth of private land ownership and transfer increased in both during the medieval period (Van Bavel 2011).

Tilly (1985) argued that coercive exploitation played an important role in the creation of European nation-states. He used the concept of a protection racket to describe European developments into state-making, where a strong individual or group forces weaker individuals to pay tribute in some form in exchange for protection or avoidance of damage. Tilly argued that states achieved a monopoly of violence and carried out varied activities of organized violence: making war, creating states, protection, and extraction of resources through taxes.

Independent lords became like allods in the feudal era; they could not defend themselves from the new states and were subject to capture or submission. Lords stopped being vassals and turned into landowners. The land that they owned, however, had the restrictions that had been imposed when the land had been a fief, when fee tails had evolved into entails. These impediments to market activity were retained by the aristocracy to preserve the integrity of the

family estate. Lord Peter Wimsey is a fictional character of the early twentieth century, but his role as the landless younger son of the mythical Duke of
Denver was a staple of British aristocracy for many centuries.

This restricted survey of European history brings us to the present. Some
land is still entailed or subject to other restrictions, and the way to indicate
that there are no such restrictions on a property is to hold them in fee simple.
That term means that they are remnants of fiefs but lack all the obligations that
made fiefs what they were. This curious way of designating land that can be
bought and sold freely like many other marketable assets is the product of the
a millennium of European history and expresses our freedom from the constraints of feudal forms of land tenure.

The familiarity of more recent history makes it hard to understand the
terms of land ownership in antiquity. We are used to a monotonic history,
typically starting from the agricultural revolution and continuing through the
industrial revolution. But the modern history of land tenure comes from the
violence that followed the end of the Roman Empire; it says nothing about
the conditions that obtained while the Roman Empire was intact. It is hard to
visualize a modern type of landholding in the ancient world, but the evidence
suggests that the intervening impediments to land usage and sale are not relevant to the history of ancient Rome. Land, then as now, typically was held in
fee simple.

Chapter 8

．　．　．

Financial Intermediation

In order to evaluate the sophistication of the Roman financial market, we need to know if there were credit intermediaries, that is, institutions that mediated between borrowers and lenders, obviating direct contact between them. The most popular credit intermediaries in many societies are banks, and it is fortunate that ancient historians and modern economists employ the same definition of a bank. Cohen (1992, 9) opened his discussion of Athenian banking by quoting the legal definition in use in the United States today. This same definition can be found in a recent textbook on financial markets and institutions, which states: "Banks are financial institutions that accept deposits and make loans" (Mishkin 2010, 7). The text explains that, "banks obtain funds by borrowing and by issuing other liabilities such as deposits. They then use these funds to acquire assets such as securities and loans" (Mishkin 2010, 225). Deposits are bank borrowing for which banks furnish services in place of paying interest, either in part or in full. Demand deposits, which are totally liquid, typically do not pay any interest today. Savings deposits, which are available only with a delay, pay a low interest rate, and time deposits, available at a predetermined time, typically pay more.

This definition has been used by ancient historians investigating the financial markets. Bogaert (1968) defined banks, typically individual bankers identified as *trapezitai* or *argentarii*, as accepting deposits and making loans. Andreau (1987a, 17) expanded this definition slightly by adding a third function: "Banking is a commercial business involving receiving deposits from clients to whom the banker provides cashier services and lends available funds to third parties with whom the bank acts as a creditor." By adding cashier services, Andreau appears to be saying that ancient banks must have dealt with the day-to-day needs of their clients for cash even if most deposits were not available on demand, that there were financial arrangements like demand deposits in addition to other, less available, deposits.

Andreau in *The Cambridge Ancient History* minimized the role of ancient banks, asking and answering, "Should the ancient bank be compared to that of the nineteenth century, or even to that of the eighteenth? If the question is put this way, then the reply is clearly negative" (Andreau 2000, 775–76). A more accurate reply to Andreau's question, rephrased to focus on the eighteenth century, should be a qualified yes. Andreau contrasted the agrarian economy of Rome against the industrial economy of the nineteenth century. He also noted the variety of financial conditions around the Roman Empire, but he implicitly assumed that all of modern Europe was the same. In this chapter, I compare the early Roman Empire with preindustrial Europe and stress the range of financial structures that existed even among even the most advanced agrarian economies of the eighteenth century.

Loans between individuals are an important part of any financial system, but they do not by themselves show the existence of a sophisticated web of financial transactions. For example, the presence of interest-bearing loans informs us only about one way of raising funds for someone seeking to start or expand a business activity. Money from family and friends has been a resource throughout the ages, while selling equities (stocks) has become frequent only in the twentieth century. Financial analysts organize the variety of ways to raise money by recognizing a hierarchy of financial sources of business activities.

I present a theory of financial intermediation in this chapter to describe the hierarchy of financial sources and its relation to the functioning of the economy as a whole. This facilitates an abstract evaluation of the Roman evidence, but not a historical one. I survey briefly the history of financial intermediation in preindustrial Western Europe to provide a standard against which to evaluate the Roman evidence. I then describe the nature of financial arrangements in the early Roman Empire in terms of this hierarchy. The issue turns out to be not whether financial markets in Rome resembled those in other advanced agricultural economies, but rather which eighteenth-century European economy did it resemble most closely.

The opening sentence of an essay in a Harvard Business School volume about the functions of a financial system today sets the stage: "Financial systems facilitate *pooling*, or the aggregation of household wealth to fund indivisible or efficient-scale enterprises" (Sirri and Tufano 1995, 81). The authors go on to explain, "Without pooling aggregate wealth to fund enterprises, firm size would be constrained by the wealth under the control of a single household. Pooling relieves society of this limitation, bridging firms' capital needs and households' investing needs" (Sirri and Tufano 1995, 88).

The economic problem of funding economic activity was raised to prominence by John Maynard Keynes when he observed that in industrial systems, savers were not necessarily investors. One group of people had accumulated resources by not consuming all their income, or by being the children of people who had been abstemious. Another group had ideas, projects, or business enterprises for which they needed resources. The problem of a capitalist system was to bring them together. In Keynesian economics, mass unemployment is the result of an aggregate mismatch between the amount that savers want to save and investors want to invest. While macroeconomics has progressed speedily since Keynes wrote in the 1930s, this insight has remained central to policy planning in industrial societies.

Keynesian unemployment does not exist in mostly agricultural societies because large savers typically are large investors. Large landowners often have incomes that exceed even their large consumption, and they have projects of land improvement or transport enhancement that can absorb the extra resources. There is no need for financial intermediation in such a system because there is no need to intermediate between distinct savers and investors. Of course, there may be mismatches between savers and investors in such an economy, if a landlord is particularly profligate in his consumption or if a poor landowner sits on a bend in the river where canalization would make transport easier. These mismatches would not lead to Keynesian unemployment; they would make the economy function less efficiently than if a financial system could eliminate or reduce the mismatches.

Most economic organizations in history operated somewhere between the conditions of modern life and this purely agrarian case. In order to assess the financial systems of historical economies, we need an index of financial sophistication that can be used to evaluate any specific society. A suitable measure can be constructed from modern discussions of the sources of capital for modern businesses summarized in table 8.1. The table lists a hierarchy of sources of capital for investment in the first column. The second and third columns distinguish sources by the type of the obligations between the parties involved. Debt capital consists of loans, where the lender gets the assurance of a known rate of return, and the borrower has the right to keep any earnings over the cost of his loans. Equity capital participates in the ownership of the investment. The investor shares the risk of the operator who is doing the work, and he has the possibility of earning far more than a lender—and also of earning less. The operator shares his risk with the investor, and the extent to which the risk is shared depends on the legal context in which this transaction takes place. This distinction corresponds to the difference between bonds and stocks today.

The entries in the first row of table 8.1 list the sources of capital for autarkic farms or businesses. They find their resources within the organization, that is, from internal sources. The owners of the farm or business can loan money among themselves for individual projects or they can share the results of their joint earnings from old investments to take shares in new projects. In each

Table 8.1.
Sources of capital for private investments

Type	Debt Capital	Equity Capital
Internal sources	Loans from owners	Retained earnings
Informal external sources	Loans from family and friends; trade credit, brokers	Investments by informed participants
Financial intermediaries	Lending by financial institutions (banks)	Some joint-stock companies
Public markets	Bond issues	Stock issues

Source: Adapted from Sirri and Tufano (1995), 98.

case resources are found within the enterprise to make an investment; the difference is in the allocation of risk and reward among the people involved. This source of capital is still used today, even in our sophisticated economy. Businesses today are hardly autarkic, but they often find that internally generated resources are cheaper than those obtained through one of the other types. Retained earnings are an important source of capital even for very large firms.

The informal external sources of capital described in the second row are those used in societies without highly developed financial systems, although they also are used today as components of a finely tuned and articulated financial system. This source anticipates getting capital from outside the farm or firm desiring to make an investment, but still within the circle of family and friends of the owners. Owners can borrow from their relatives and friends because they are known to their relatives and friends. If a person borrows from a member of his local or religious community, he is far more likely to repay the loan than he would be to a stranger, particularly if the legal system is not very good at finding and punishing people who renege on their financial obligations (Mathias 1999). Potential investors who lack rich relatives or associates who know them are forced to go out into the wider world and attempt to borrow from strangers. This in general will be almost impossible, for strangers will not be able to judge whether the aspiring investor is creditworthy or a con man. In some contexts, lenders may be so suspicious of aspiring borrowers that even a creditworthy borrower will be unable to distinguish himself from con men, and there will be no loans at all. In the language of economics, the investor has asymmetric knowledge. He knows if the investment is good, but the putative lender does not. This is an example of the asymmetric information described in chapter 5.

There are two institutions in which this problem of asymmetric information can be attenuated. Merchants are engaged in many repetitive transactions with each other, during which they are able to gather information about each other. The merchant who pays his bills on time quite possibly is the one who will repay a loan on time. A responsible merchant gains a reputation for honoring his obligations, and a good reputation may substitute for a family connection or personal friendship in providing enough assurance to a lender to justify making a loan (Greif 1994). In addition, brokers who bring lenders and borrowers together solve a variety of information problems. They find people who want to borrow and bring them into contact with people who want to lend. They also may investigate aspiring borrowers to make sure that they are responsible and to reduce the extent of asymmetric information.

The same problems of information arise when investors contemplate sharing the risk with strangers, that is, raising equity capital instead of debt capital. The problems are more severe for equity than for debt because the equity purchaser assumes more risk than the lender. People therefore typically only make equity investments with people that they know. Neither reputations nor brokers are strong enough to overcome the problems of asymmetric information when equity investment is involved. In economies with few financial intermediaries, there is more loan activity than equity investments.

The entries in the third row of table 8.1 introduce financial intermediaries and pooling institutions for the first time. Financial intermediaries collect funds from people with resources they have saved, pool them together into a single fund, and then make loans from this pooled fund of resources. Individuals lend money to banks by depositing money in them, and the banks then lend their accumulated funds to other individuals. There is no direct connection between the final borrowers and lenders; they communicate only with the financial intermediary. The presence of this intermediary, which we can call a bank for its simplest manifestation, solves a lot of the information problems present in the conditions of the preceding row. The bank solves the problem of finding borrowers and lenders because they each know to go to the bank to place their excess purchasing power or to borrow. It also assumes the risk of not being paid back by a borrower. The lender need not worry, unless the bank operates with such bad judgment that it has so many failed loans that it fails itself. The bank has the responsibility for evaluating potential borrowers, and banks typically develop expertise or staffs to make these kinds of decisions.

Banks reduce the risks from asymmetric information, but they cannot eliminate them entirely. The same restriction to known groups seen in informal lending appears among banks. Merchant banks, to cite an important example, loaned to the merchant community. They relied on the expectation of continued patronage and the ease of communication within the merchant community the same way informal lenders did (Neal 1990). Banks in rural New England in the early nineteenth century loaned within their local communities, and even their own families, for similar reasons (Lamoreaux 1994).

Financial intermediaries that provide equity investments are harder to characterize than banks. In the modern world, intermediaries that provide equity capital on an individual basis are known as venture capitalists. In earlier economies, some joint-stock companies acted in this way. They served as financial intermediaries if they engaged in varied activities, that is, if they used their resources to fund several activities and groups. Savers bought shares of these companies to participate in the average fortunes of these ventures. They were not making a bank deposit with its sure, albeit limited, return; they were participating in the equity of the joint-stock company to grow rich or poor as the company's investments did. Joint-stock companies that sent out expeditions and made other investments from the pool of resources raised by selling shares were financial intermediaries. (Joint-stock companies that used their resources to fund a single group performing a single activity used stocks to pool resources, but they were not financial intermediaries.) We think of early joint-stock companies in terms of their activities in various parts of the world, but some of them were financial intermediaries and precursors of modern conglomerate firms.

The modern type of capital raised in public markets by large companies today is shown in the final row of table 8.1. These companies are large enough and the information about them is plentiful enough that there are public markets in which people can loan to them by purchasing their bonds or participate in their activities by purchasing stocks. There is no need for financial intermediaries at this stage. Unrelated individuals can choose which companies they want to lend to or invest in, and they can make their purchases of bonds or stocks at reasonable cost. New financial intermediaries have grown up to solve some of the information problems facing savers who do not have the time or interest to gather the information needed to choose which company to buy or sell or do not have enough resources to diversify their investments easily by themselves. Mutual funds are the modern analogue of the older joint-stock companies that financed varied projects. This analogy allows us to describe some joint-stock companies as early mutual funds and illuminates the differences between those companies that acted like a mutual fund and those that conducted a single business.

Even today most companies are too small to go to the open market for their capital. They start with internal and informal external sources of capital; they progress to the use of public markets only if they are very successful. They may have the form of joint-stock companies early in their history, but only after they are known outside a small circle can they "go public" and sell shares on the open market. The types of capital sources shown in the rows in table 8.1 can be seen as a progression of funding sources for a modern enterprise that starts with capital from an individual or a family and progresses through the types of sources shown in the table to arrive finally at the New York Stock Exchange or the Nasdaq Market. While it is not necessary for all companies to go through all these stages, the progression shows an idealized history of modern firms. In the modern world, we expect to see all types of capital coexisting (Calomiris 1995).

We can use the same progression as a measure of financial sophistication of economies from the past. If only the first type of capital, internal sources, is available to people who want to engage in economic activity, then that economy should be described as lacking a financial system at all. If informal external sources also are available, then the economy has a limited financial system. If financial intermediation is available, an economy has a very good financial system, adequate to finance many activities, certainly any activity of the preindustrial world. And the presence of public capital markets indicates the kind of modern financial system that we find in advanced industrial countries. If we compare financial markets in ancient Rome and in early modern Europe, then it is likely that we will be looking at the differences between informal external sources of capital and financial intermediation. Were there financial intermediaries such as banks, or only brokers? Were the trade credits that arose among merchants accessible to other people? Were joint-stock companies prevalent? These are the kind of questions we need to pose.

To provide a standard of comparison with which to evaluate the capital markets of Rome, I briefly survey the capital markets of early modern Europe. The most advanced capital markets were in Amsterdam and London, and the most common way that credit was extended there was by book credit on the part of a merchant. The merchant loaned money to his purchasers by not requiring payment immediately. He loaned money to his suppliers by paying them quickly or in advance for goods he received. There was no intermediation; the merchant had excess resources that he loaned to others. The bill obligatory or promissory note was a more formal form of credit. This was a way for prominent merchants and individuals to borrow on their good names. A bill obligatory could be sold to a third person in England, but it did not travel far because it had to come back to the borrower for payment. The original bill obligatory did not need intermediation; it was a simple loan. If a third party bought a bill, there was simple intermediation but still individual placement of loans.

More extensive credit intermediation was accomplished through bills of exchange in the course of international trade. Bills of exchange were a way of financing trade by arranging for payment at a distance and a later time. Sellers like to be paid when and where the goods are shipped from, while buyers like to pay when the goods are sold and at their eventual destination. The bill of exchange was a way to deal with the ownership of the goods in the gap between these two events, which could easily be three months or more in time and across an ocean in space. A seller drew a bill on a buyer who accepted the obligation in the bill. The accepted bill could be sold to a third party.

The sale of accepted bills was a form of financial intermediation; merchants or others who bought bills were extending credit indirectly. The presence of a uniform credit instrument allowed people who had resources to lend to find people who wanted to borrow. The use of multiple signatures on the accepted bills reduced the need for the lender to know all about the credit-worthiness of the borrower. The drawer and the acceptor both stood behind the bill, as did other people who had purchased it on its way to the eventual holder. Because bills could be bought and sold, because they were assignable, they facilitated credit intermediation (Neal 1990; 1994).

Inland bills of exchange were used to finance trade within England. They were given the same legal standing as foreign bills at the start of the eighteenth century. An inland bill could be drawn and made payable in the same place, making the provision of credit much simpler. It could circulate in a local area where potential purchasers of the bill knew the people involved in its origins. After 1765, it could even be made payable to bearer, making it suitable for use as money.

These are all short-term debt instruments, typically for three months. Longer loans could be secured by rolling over these bills, and often was. The English and French governments both found themselves with a lot of existing debt at the start of the eighteenth century from their wars in the previous century. They experimented with schemes to reduce the burden of these debts under the influence of the notorious John Law, and they experienced financial panics around 1720. The English government retreated into offering 3 percent perpetual bonds, that is, loans that never came due. These bonds were collected into the Three Percent Consol—for consolidated annuity—in 1751. Consols became in time the safest and most liquid (that is, saleable on short notice) financial assets available for potential lenders.

There were several kinds of financial institutions in eighteenth-century England, mostly specialized to a particular kind of credit. Goldsmiths and scriveners, who performed research into land titles, had begun to accept deposits in the seventeenth century on which they paid interest, suggesting that the funds were loaned out. Merchant banks, which loaned both to the government and to merchants, grew during the eighteenth century. They "accepted from merchants and large landowners deposits on both current account and on term; they lent money at interest by opening credit on current account or by advances, and discounted inland or outland bills and various official securities" (Van der Wee 1977, 351). They built on Dutch models, but the common law allowed private and then joint-stock banking to flourish in Britain.

Private banking began slowly in the early years of the eighteenth century, and their numbers grew over the century. These banks, located in the west end of London, were quite distinct from bankers loaning to the tight community of merchants, and they had to learn the craft of banking anew. They loaned to a wider class of people, but they also retained some archaic practices, for example, charging simple interest for their loans (Joslin 1954; Capie 2001, 46; Quinn 2001; Temin and Voth 2006). The reform of government finance and the creation of Bank of England further stimulated the growth of English banking and the use of its bank notes as currency.

England in the eighteenth century therefore had a variety of financial intermediaries from which aspiring borrowers could choose. Borrowers also had a means of payment that derived from the actions of these intermediaries, namely their obligations. The most useful obligation was Bank of England notes, which became paper money. This further facilitated the pooling of resources for business by making it easier to transfer money from place to place. There had been some use of short-term loans as money in the seventeenth century, but the success of the Bank of England in the eighteenth provided England with a new and better form of money. The widespread use of bank notes increased the supply of money beyond what the use of coin would have permitted.

Joint-stock companies multiplied and grew during the seventeenth century. The financial bubble and collapse in 1720 led to restrictions on these companies, and they did not grow much if at all in the eighteenth century. Joint-stock companies clearly pooled resources, and they facilitated equity investments by informed participants, as described in the second row of table 8.1. Some joint-stock companies engaged in a variety of activities, subcontracting their operations to many smaller operations. They were financial intermediaries, as described in the third row of table 8.1. But it is hard to see in the surviving records how these companies were administered. Modern accounts discuss the operations of the companies as if they were administering their activities from London, implying that they were pooling funds but not acting as financial intermediaries (Scott 1995).

Joint-stock companies played another, possibly even more important, part in credit intermediation as well. Their shares could be used as collateral for bank loans. This began in Holland in the early seventeenth century with shares from the Dutch East India Company (VOC) and spread to England (Gelderblom and Jonker 2004). By the time of the South Sea bubble in 1720, it was common for borrowers to pledge stocks as securities for bank loans (Temin and Voth 2006). After the English government straightened out its finances and introduced consols, government bonds became good collateral, but the practice of using shares to secure credit intermediation began with shares of private joint-stock companies.

The Dutch financial market was more developed in the seventeenth century than the English, and the English borrowed institutions and practices from them at the end of the century. Dutch financial institutions did not develop as fast as the English ones in the eighteenth century, but they already had achieved an impressive level. There were extensive merchant banks, dealing primarily with trade, as well as abundant private shares and government debt that changed during the eighteenth century from named to bearer bonds. There were many loans among individuals secured by public and private stocks, but few institutions like banks that pooled funds. Cashiers, or *kassiers*, provided transfers of funds, but never developed into banking institutions (Riley 1980, 31; de Vries and van der Woude 1997, 132). The Bank of Amsterdam held deposits and transferred money between accounts by a giro system, but it provided loans only to major companies. These large companies in turn appear to have acted as credit intermediaries by reloaning to smaller businesses (Dehing and Hart 1997, 47). There were a variety of institutions facilitating payments both internally and externally, but only a few institutions that provided banking services to the domestic economy.

The French credit market in the eighteenth century appears to have been more limited than the English or Dutch. Inland bills never became legal instruments and could not circulate. Bills of exchange were allowed only when currency exchange was involved, and the credit market for merchants could not spill over into more general credit provision as it did in England. Interest rates were fixed by law and did not vary. Joint-stock companies were exceedingly rare. Payments typically were made in coin; there was little paper money. The French fiscal system was based on farmed taxes that did not raise enough revenue to make government debt secure. Frequent defaults by the French government did not encourage the growth of private finance (North and Weingast 1989).

Short-term domestic loans were made with the French version of the bill obligatory, an unsecured note backed by the reputation of the borrower. Longer credits were arranged through notaries who recorded them for legal reasons and preserved the records in order to provide credit histories of borrowers. There were 113 notaries in Paris throughout the eighteenth century. This number is more than sufficient to create a credit market, but probably not enough to make credit available throughout the economy. They were not banks that separated the acquisition and disbursement of funds in deposits and loans, providing intermediation where borrowers need not borrow for the same period that lenders want to lend. Notaries were brokers who brought borrowers and lenders together. Some Parisian notaries attempted to pool the funds invested with them and act as banks around 1750, but they returned to being brokers in the 1760s after a wave of bankruptcies among the notaries (Hoffman et al. 2000, 136–45). There also were other banks in Paris, but they do not appear to have offered much competition to the notaries. The literatures on the notaries and the banks, however, have not yet been connected (White 2003).

The rate of interest on loans in France did not vary. Usury laws restricted the maximum rate of interest that could be charged to 5 percent for the entire century (with a few short suspensions). This maximum rate was binding, and almost all loans arranged by Paris notaries were at this rate. Loans to the general public in London also were at their legal maximum in the early eighteenth century, contrasting with the more sophisticated practice among merchants (Temin and Voth 2006). A recent study of the Paris notaries describes the French credit market as a priceless market—meaning without variable prices rather than very expensive (Hoffman et al. 2000). A financial market with a fixed interest rate provided credit, but the absence of price flexibility restricted its range of operations. Faced with a risky prospective borrower, the French notary could only decide to arrange a loan or not; he could not raise the interest rate in response to the added risk. Credit was far harder to obtain for moderate risks in Paris than in London in the eighteenth century (Kindleberger 1984).

One view of the French financial market comes through the eyes of Voltaire, who mentioned his financial dealings in his letters. The primitive state of the French financial markets can be seen in a 1737 letter from Voltaire to his agent in Paris, monsieur l'abbé Moussinot: "You can very safely place the 300 L. well packed into the stage coach without declaring them and without paying anything as long as the crate is correctly and duly registered to the address of Madame la Marquise, as precious furniture" (Voltaire 1977-, vol. 1, lettre 872, 1004). A few days later, Voltaire asked for a promissory note of 2,400 livres tournois, showing that smuggling cash was not the only way to move credit around the country.

In fact, Voltaire was engaged in both lending and borrowing money, apparently making all the arrangements himself. He worked through a notary from time to time, but there is no sense that he could deposit money with the notary without specifying a specific use for it. This can be seen in his own summary of a complex set of instructions to his agent in January 1738, "The result of all this verbiage is that you would place twenty-five thousand livres in life annuities at 5 percent and that you would try at your leisure to assure towards the month of April a loan of around 20 to 30 thousand livres to place by privilege on a land of 3000 livres tournois of rent. That would not, I think, be difficult" (Ibid., lettre

911, 1063). Voltaire appears to have been lending half of a sum of money to the government at the legal limit in return for an annuity and seeking to place a loan himself with the other half that would yield between 10 and 15 percent. There is no evidence of credit intermediation. Voltaire expressed the interest rate on the annuity as *au denier 20*, literally "at one penny [interest for a loan of] 20," not very different from the Roman shorthand for interest.

Credit markets elsewhere in Europe were in the range of England and France. The Dutch credit market was the most sophisticated in the seventeenth century, but it lagged behind the English market in the eighteenth. Merchants in what would become Germany and Italy had access to ample credit intermediation, but ordinary residents probably had more trouble than Voltaire moving and lending money. Joint-stock companies and stable government securities also were confined to England, France, and Holland. Adventurous people who wanted to engage in economic activity had a hard time accumulating the needed resources; there were few opportunities for pooling wealth. Economic activity therefore had an accidental quality, happening only if an entrepreneur happened to be rich or related to rich people. There is less information about credit markets outside England, Holland, and France because they did not exist in any real sense.

These historical observations can be summarized with the aid of table 8.1. Investors in England in the eighteenth century could make use of internal sources, informal external sources, and financial intermediation, that is, the sources of capital in the first three rows of the table. There were banks, at least in London, and a few joint-stock companies. Some investors in Holland had the same opportunities, but not all. French investors by and large were restricted to the sources listed in the top two rows; they did not have access to financial intermediaries. Potential investors in other countries were like France, although perhaps even more dependent on the internal sources listed in the first row. Only England had a good all-purpose financial system; other countries had only limited ones.

Returning to the topic of this chapter, it is clear that wealthy Romans frequently provided each other with cash on a one-to-one basis normally at interest, sometimes without. These arrangements, which created or reinforced social obligations alongside the financial ones, are the ones best attested in the literature of the elite. The classic case-study for the financial behavior of the elite from the late republic is Marcus Tullius Cicero and his brother Quintus (Pittia 2004). The legal sources also focus on lending and borrowing by the elite.

Roman contracts traditionally were oral, but there was a trend in the Principate to record them in a *chirographum* ("handwritten record," a Greek word) and to treat the document as primary evidence of the terms. In Italy and the western provinces this was usually done in the traditional Roman format of a sandwich of two, later three, waxed tablets (*tabulae*), with one inner and one outer copy of the text, tied together and sealed by the witnesses (Meyer 2004). A loan could be arranged informally and recorded as an entry (*nomen*) under outgoings by the creditor in his accounts; the borrower was expected but not obliged to make a corresponding entry under receipts in his own accounts, or he might take a witnessed statement (*testatio*) of the transaction, itself recorded in a diptych, later triptych, of waxed tablets. The accounts or testatio could be produced as evidence in court. The jurists envisaged structured chronological accounts, called (with variants) *rationes accepti et expensi*, "accounts of receipts and outgoings," but individual formats must have varied considerably. From the mid-first century CE it seems to have been common practice for frequent lenders to keep a *kalendarium*, a special ledger of loans made, perhaps with details of their terms, which was so called because interest was calculated monthly to the Kalends (day 1) of the next month. Already in the mid-republic the Romans had recognized that in practice loans could be contracted without money changing hands, purely as a paper transaction (*litteris obligatio*, literally an obligation through writing), through the simple writing of a transfer entry (*nomen transscripticium*) by the lender in his accounts (Gaius III, 128–34). In theory Roman contractual forms could only be used by Roman citizens, which excluded most of Rome's provincial subjects, but the tablets of the Sulpicii and papyri of Egypt reveal that actual practice was fairly indiscriminate in business agreements involving non-Romans and many contracts were hybrids of Roman and Greek usages.

It is generally assumed that a Roman gentleman in need of cash would look first to family and friends, as indicated in the first two rows of table 8.1. The younger Pliny, with purchase of an adjacent farm in mind, is commonly cited: "and borrowing will be no problem; I can get money from my mother-in-law whose strongbox I use just like my own" (Plinius, *Ep.* III,19,8). Romans also used their social networks to obtain cash in an emergency or when they were away from home. When Cicero's son Marcus was studying in Athens, Cicero provided him with cash by assigning the rents of some of his properties in Rome to his friend Atticus who had a debtor of his in Athens advance cash to Marcus (Andreau 1999, p. 20–21). The Cicero brothers apparently never lent to each other, even though they both had extensive credit dealings with unrelated parties (Pittia 2004, 36–37). Wealthy Romans with surplus cash could make loans through their freedmen, as is attested in the *Digest* and exemplified by Crassus in the late republic and the fictional Trimalchio, by making the freedman their legal agent (*institor*), perhaps in some cases by forming a legal partnership (societas) with him (*Dig.* XIV,3,19,3; Cicero, *Parad.* VI,4,6; Petronius

76). This situation only made sense if the freedman was given considerable latitude to choose creditors on his own initiative. The freedman's business in all these cases was restricted to making loans; he was not set up as a banker.

Loans were numerous enough for commentators to speak of a market rate of interest. They spoke or wrote of the rate of interest separate from the rate on any particular loan, which has meaning only if it was possible for people to borrow at this rate more or less on demand. Cicero (*Att.*, 4, 15, 7) commented that "interest [rates] went up on the Ides of July from 1/3 to 1/2 percent [per month]." There was "a 60 per cent drop in interest-rates after Augustus brought back treasure from Egypt" (Duncan-Jones 1982, 21). Providing a possible earlier example, Livy (7, 27, 3–4) reported that in the peaceful consulship of Titus Manlius Torquatus and Gaius Plautius in the fourth century BCE, "the rate of interest was reduced [by the city] from one percent to one-half per cent [per month]."

More often we see loans at 1 percent a month or 12 percent per year. This was the official maximum, and it appears to be the default rate on many loans. Bogaert (2000) catalogued dozens of loans in Roman Egypt for 12 percent. The presence of so many loans at this fixed rate indicates that this market probably was not a totally free market rate, for the random movement of a market rate would not return to any given value so often. It also does not mean the opposite, that interest rates could not vary. As just noted, we find many comments that interest rates were below 12 percent and variable. We also have examples of rates above 12 percent. Livy (35, 7) reported that prohibitions against higher rates were evaded in the late republic by transferring the loans to foreigners who were not subject to rate restrictions. This has a modern ring to it both because of the picture of financiers evading regulations by going "offshore" and because it appears to have been easy to transfer ownership of commercial loans among interested parties.

The inscription of a second-century Dacian loan says that the borrower will repay whomever is holding the loan when it comes due:

> Julius Alexander, the lender, required a promise in good faith that the loan of 60 denarii of genuine and sound coin would be duly settled on the day he requested it. Alexander, son of Cariccius, the borrower, promised in good faith that it would be so settled, and declared that he had received the sixty denarii mentioned above, in cash, as a loan, and that he owed them. Julius Alexander required a promise in good faith that the interest on this principal from this day would be one percent per thirty days and would be paid to Julius Alexander or to whomever it might in the future concern. Alexander, son of Cariccius, promised in good faith that it would be so paid. Titius Primitius stood surety for the due and proper payment of the principal mentioned above and of the interest.

Transacted at Alburnus Maior, October 20, in the consulship of Rusticus (his second consulship) and Aquilinus. (*CIL* 3.934–35; reproduced in Shelton 1998, 136–37)

This contract exemplifies the assignability of loans assumed by Livy, although the assignment referred to here normally was done only if the lender was deceased or otherwise indisposed. This kind of loan sets up the possibility of wider negotiability, but we do not have any evidence that it happened.

One cause of the land crisis of 33 CE described in chapter 7 probably was that most senators were in breach of Julius Caesar's law that no more than a third of their *census* (property) in Italy should be in loans rather than land. Seneca's (*Ep.* 41,7; 87) generalized fortunate man "sows a lot and lends a lot," his rich man has "a large kalendarium ledger"; he himself was known for "his spreading estates and equally extensive lending" (Tacitus, *Ann.* XIV,53). "I am almost all in property," said the younger Pliny (possibly thinking of Caesar's law), "but I have some money on loan" (Plinius, *Ep.* III,19,8).

There is little evidence to tell us how far straight one-to-one lending went down the socioeconomic scale in Rome and Italy. Borrowing from banks reached down to the level of the small shippers and petty businessmen who appear in the tablets of the Sulpicii. In Egypt of the same period the broader range of discarded documents which survive shows that one-to-one lending was common down to village level, although unsurprisingly, most creditors were those with metropolitan (urban) status (Tenger 1993). Romans from top to bottom of the social scale lent out and borrowed money in one-to-one arrangements in the first century CE.

Some financial intermediation was integrated with commercial activity when credit was granted for purchases or sales. In Italy credit attached to dealings of the elite is best attested. When a friend bought some Greek statues on Cicero's behalf from a dealer in Campania, the dealer told Cicero he would defer making the entry (of debt) in his accounts until the day Cicero (*Fam.* VII, 23,1) chose to receive him in Rome. This is an example of a *nomen transscripticium*, a debt created by an account entry to replace the price due from a sale. Men who purchased at auction wine or oil "on the tree," that is who contracted to arrange and pay for the harvesting and processing, were allowed a long period to pay the sum they had bid (Cato, *Agr.* 146–47; Plinius, *Ep.* VIII,2). However, credit at auctions of goods with immediate delivery normally was provided by a banker.

In Roman Egypt peasants in need of cash to pay taxes or pay off a cash loan might sell their crop to a dealer in advance of the harvest, and if we had documentary evidence from the Italian countryside, we would undoubtedly find similar transactions. Bagnall (1977; *P.Oslo* II,63) hints at large-scale speculative forward selling of produce in the third century CE, and Varro (*R.* II,6,5) reveals that itinerant dealers bought up the crops of smallholders in Italy. Because there was a chronic undersupply of small change, retailing and related businesses must have depended heavily on ad hoc credit arrangements.

While some of these loans surely were to finance consumption, many more may well have been for production. Columella (3, 3, 7–11) advised people setting up vineyards to include the interest on borrowed money among their costs as a matter of course: "[And] if the husbandman would like to assess his debt according to the vineyards like the moneylender does with the debtor, the owner may [consider] the preceding 1/2 percent per month on that total as a perpetual annuity; he should take in 1950 sesterces every year by this calculation, [since] the return on seven *iugerum*, following from the opinion of Graecinus, exceeds the interest on 32,480 sesterces." Columella clearly understood that investors needed to think about the opportunity cost of invested funds, whether borrowed or not. His advice shows financial sophistication in addition to suggesting that loans may have been used to promote productive investments. Columella also based his calculation on a 6 percent loan—half the legal limit often seen in Roman Egypt.

We know of many loans made to finance trade. Merchants typically were at the center of European capital markets before the Industrial Revolution, and they appear to have been in antiquity as well. Cohen (1992) documented the extensive use of loans to finance maritime trade in classical Athens. Andreau (1999, 54–56) argued that maritime loans were as extensive in Rome, albeit not as well documented. Rathbone (2000) identified the Muziris papyrus as the "master contract" for a standard maritime loan of the early Roman Empire. The careless grammar and syntax and the general sloppiness of the document suggest a scribe copying the boilerplate of a standard contract. In other words, maritime loans were common enough in the early Roman Empire to have a standard form known to all the merchants and their clerks. This particular loan was for a shipment worth 6,926,852 sesterces, twenty times the size of Columella's hypothetical agricultural investment and seven times the property requirement to be a Roman senator.

Finance for a commercial activity could be organized through a societas, a legal form of partnership that the Romans had developed by the later third century BCE (Crook 1967, 236–43; Zimmermann 1990, 451–71; Johnston 1999, 106–7; France 2003). A societas was a contractual arrangement between two or more associates to pool resources for a particular venture and share the resulting profits or losses. Some societates, including the earliest known, were formed to bid for state contracts for military supplies, to collect taxes, and to provide other government services, and their active members were called *publicani* (public contractors). The tax-collecting societates were particularly large, with hierarchies of *magistri* (executive officers) and agents, and complex record-keeping procedures, but we also hear of a private trading societas in the earlier second century BCE of fifty or so members (Cicero, *Verr.* II, 167, 171, 182, 186–87; Plutarchus, *Cato Maior* 21,6). Toward the end of the republic the state reverted to collecting direct provincial taxes through its own officials, but societates still collected indirect taxes like the imperial customs dues (*portoria*) and were involved in military and civilian supplies (the annona), building projects, and other urban services, including the disposal of waste and corpses. In the private sphere societates flourished in all areas of enterprise, including large-scale maritime commerce (Rathbone 2003a, 211–13). A moneylending societas in attested in the province of Dacia, and some banks were set up as societates (*CIL* III, 950–51 (no. 13) = *FIRA* III, no. 157, 481).

Although the societas had originally been envisaged as a short-term arrangement between equal partners for a specific venture, its scope soon expanded. Contracts were easy to renew with changing partners while leaving the employed agents and stock of the societas in place. An asymmetric societas was probably common, that is, a societas dominated by one or more rich investors with one or more resourceless partners who did the donkey work. Yet a societas was not like a modern company with shares, dividends, and public reports. If a partner wanted out, he took his current share of profit or loss and left; a new partner simply added his investment to the pot and would be rewarded proportionately. In theory the partners had to agree individually to any new venture, but actual practice was probably less rigid. Societates provide a rare example in an agrarian economy of pooled equity capital. Although they fall in the right-hand column of table 8.1, they were not quite joint-stock companies (Malmendier 2009).

Most societates had no corporate legal persona (*corpus*), apart from some large societates of public contractors which it suited the state to recognize officially as *corpora*. Thus in legal theory third parties could only deal with *socii* as individuals, but the potential awkwardness of this is exaggerated by modern scholars. Roman courts came to concede that third-party claims extended to all the members of a banking societas, and perhaps all societates were increasingly treated as though, like the principal publicani, they formed corpora. Socii, and hence societates, could themselves borrow from or lend to individuals, moneylenders, other societates, and banks (Malmendier 2009).

The central Roman state of the Principate, as that of the republic, almost never lent or borrowed money. In the critical years 215–210 BCE of the Hannibalic War the state had deferred several payments due to individual citizens and had solicited contributions in bullion and coin, which it later decided to repay (Livius XXIII, 48, 4–49, 4; XXIV,18, 10–15; XXVI, 35–36). In the civil wars of the 40s–30s BCE at the end of the republic some generals had raised loans in the provinces, mostly with senatorial authorization (Caesar, *BC* III, 32; Dio XLII, 50–51; Cicero, *Phil.* X, 26; *Brut.* II, 4,4; *Fam.* XII, 28,1). In 69 CE Vespasian and his supporters probably borrowed cash in the eastern provinces, as well as levying it, to finance his bid for power, and in 70 CE, after two years of civil wars the senate voted to borrow HS 60 million from individuals, the one known Roman plan to raise a state loan, although it was not carried out or needed (Tacitus, *Hist.* II, 84; IV, 47; Suetonius, *Ves.* 16,3).

Civic administrations, on the other hand, especially in the eastern provinces, could and did borrow, sometimes substantial sums, typically for building projects, and newly annexed areas tended to borrow from Romans to pay Roman cash taxes. The central imperial government was constantly worried by the problems civic bankruptcy would cause and banned borrowing against future revenues.

The Hellenic cities of the Roman Empire were also lenders. An exchange of letters between Pliny the Younger and Trajan in 109 or 110 CE, when the emperor sent Pliny to Bithynia in Asia Minor to straighten out the local government finances, reveals some details. Pliny wrote that tax revenues were accumulating at the local government, but that they might lie idle because no one wanted to borrow at the offered rate of 9 percent (Pliny, *Letters*, 10, 54). (The interest rate is unclear from the Latin, *duodenis assibus*, which could refer to 12 out of 16 asses to a denarius, meaning ¾ percent a month or 9 percent annually for a loan of 100 denarii, or might mean 12 asses, one a month, indicating the maximum legal rate of 12 percent for a loan of 100 asses. The lower rate appears more likely because it fits with the normal practice of quoting rates on a monthly basis (Billeter 1898, 105).) Pliny asked the emperor if he should allocate the funds to town councilors by fiat. Trajan responded, "I see no other method of facilitating the placing out of the public money, than by lowering the interest. . . . But to compel persons to receive it, who are not disposed to do so, when possibly they themselves may have no opportunity of employing it, is by no means consistent with the justice of my government" (Pliny, *Letters*, 10, 55).

This interchange reveals that local governments holding government revenues for some future use loaned out this money as a matter of course. The whole reason for Pliny to write was to avoid having the funds sit idle in some strong box. Trajan's response was to choose a market solution over an administrative one, and his imperial directive had the force of law. His realization that a financial institution could loan more by reducing the interest rate shows further that Romans up to and including the emperor conceptualized a demand curve (like those described in chapter 1) for loans.

An important element of civic finances was capital donated by benefactors to the city or a civic cult (temple) to fund some activity, or accumulated as surplus civic income, which was lent out to members of the local elite, normally at a favorable rate of interest (Plinius, *Ep.* X, 54–55; *BGU* II, 362; *lex Irnitana* ch. 79; Liebenam 1900, 330–40). To some extent this practice spread to the municipalities of Italy and the Latin-speaking provinces, above all Africa, in the later Principate, but western benefactors preferred to donate agricultural property whose rents would fund their foundations (Duncan-Jones 1982, 80–81, 102–3, 132–38, 171–84). The only attested case of lending by the Roman state is an exception that proves the rule: in the crisis of 33 CE, Tiberius placed HS 100 million from the *aerarium* (state treasury) with banks in Rome to provide interest-free three-year loans to heavily indebted senators in order to avert a credit crisis (Tacitus, *Ann.* VI, 17).

The more than fifty alimentary foundations (*alimenta*) established by the emperors Nerva and Trajan in Italy to provide monthly cash allowances to rear boys and girls are typically presented as perpetual loans at 5 percent annual interest secured on farmland, but these were not like bank loans because they were not repayable. They were compensation to the owners for establishing a perpetual charge, in effect a tax, on their land. Even absorption of the total cash compensation paid out by the state over ten to fifteen years, at most around HS 40 million, the equivalent of two senatorial fortunes, will have had little impact on the Italian markets in land and credit. The closest modern analogs are the British consols (consolidated annuities) established in 1751, which paid a fixed annual return but never came due.

Endowments received resources that were used to fund various sorts of religious activities. When these resources were in the form of money, as they often were, then the funds had to be loaned out to earn interest and support the activities of the endowment. While some endowments were established by committing land, many were established with money (Laum 1914; Andreau 1977, 1; Sosin 2000). In one inscription from the reign of Antoninus Pius, the donor gave 50,000 sesterces in coins to the Collegium of Aesculapius and Hygeia near Rome with instructions to the sixty members of the association to loan out the funds and use the returns to fund their feasts and other activities (*CIL* 6, 10234; Laum 1914, Vol. 2, Latin 6; Dessau 1962–, Vol. 3, 739, #7213). This explicit injunction must have been a normal, if implicit, one for all endowments financed with a cash donation.

Some endowment accounts anticipated expenditures at or near 12 percent annually, implying that the funds had to earn at least this amount to preserve the endowment. The temples holding these aggressive endowments sometimes paid out only 10 percent, slightly less than 12 percent, to allow a margin of error on 12 percent loans (Sosin 2001). A Roman businessman looking for funds could have looked to temples in order to acquire funds for his enterprises. There were hundreds of geographically dispersed endowments (Laum

1914; Andreau 1977), although it is likely that few endowed temples would have loaned to strangers. Nevertheless, temples were an important means of pooling investment funds in the early Roman Empire. In addition to holding endowments, many temples operated banks, as will be described shortly. Unlike banks in eighteenth-century England, clustered almost exclusively in London, temples and endowments were spread among the minor cities of the early Roman Empire.

There probably were specialist brokers at Rome, even if they are hard to identify and define (Verboven 2008). Cicero's correspondence reveals three cases in the late republic of the use of brokers in Roman private exploitation of subject and allied states. The most notorious is when Cicero, as governor of Cilicia and Cyprus in 51–50 BCE , was lobbied by Brutus, that supposed paragon of republican virtue, to pressure the Cypriot city of Salamis to repay a loan it had contracted in 56 BCE at an extortionate 48 percent rate of interest from M. Scaptius and P. Matinius, Roman businessmen (*negotiatores*) resident in the province. An embarrassed Cicero then discovered that, unknown even to Salamis, the money came from Brutus (Cicero, *Att.* V, 21,10–13; VI,1,3–8; 2,7–9; 3,5–6; Andreau 1999, 15–17). Scaptius and Matinius were not acting as bankers lending from pooled deposits, nor were they Brutus's mandated agents (*institores*) since they had lent to Salamis in their own names. Thus they emerge as intermediaries, placing Brutus's money for him under their names, doubtless for a fee. The legal arrangement was possibly a societas (partnership) but probably, and much more simply, an "irregular" deposit by Brutus with them whose verbal terms specified the lending of the money to Salamis.

While the Augustan anecdote implies that some wealthy Romans still acted as brokers, literary sources and the *Digest* suggest that masters could set up slaves or freemen as *faeneratores*, money lenders, which was more discreet (Plutarchus, *De Lib. Educ.* 7 (= *Mor.* 4b). A Dacian tablet of the second century also attests a *societas danistaria*, a "money lending partnership," and such societates probably existed in first-century CE Italy too. Brokers, like most Roman businesses, operated in an informal setting, normally in the forum in the shade of a colonnade. Brokers at Rome congregated around the arch of Janus, close to the traditional location of the bankers' *tabernae* ("lock-up shops"). The Maenian column nearby was used by lenders to post notices of defaulting debtors. There was no regulation of moneylending as a profession (and no public register of debt), but many moneylenders were clearly professionals in the sense of specialists who made their living from the business and had some sense of corporate identity.

Roman banks pooled funds, although they corresponded more closely to the private banks of the eighteenth century than later joint stock banks. The Latin equivalent to the word *bank* was *mensa*, a bench, table, a translation of the Greek *trapeza* (table, bank). *Mensam exercere* meant to run a bank. But while the common Greek name for a banker, occasionally used at Rome too, was *trapezites*, the Latin *mensarius* apparently became largely restricted to disbursers of public monies and specialist money changers (*nummularii*), that is, people who actually used *mensae* in public for their business, although the rare term *mensularius* seems to have had a more general meaning.

The existence of banks in the forum at Rome is first attested in 310 BCE, a century after their development in the Greek world, by the Augustan writer Livy, who perhaps anachronistically calls them *argentariae* (*tabernae*, bankers' shops); by his day the common word for a banker was *argentarius* (silver-[coin]-man) (Livius IX,40,16; Andreau 1987a, 337–40). By the first century BCE, bankers called *nummularii* and *coactores* are sometimes attested, and also *coactores argentarii*. Andreau and Bürge take the four terms to signify four different types of bank, but it is more likely that argentarius was the generic word for banker, while *nummularius* and *coactor* referred to specific functions that an argentarius might or might not carry out as part of his general banking, and which were sometimes carried out on their own as a specialized business.

Roman banks operated under Roman private law. The *Digest* contains more than forty rulings or opinions that mention bankers or banking, almost all of which discuss the application of general principles to the everyday reality of banking procedures and hence cluster in the particularly relevant chapters (*Dig.* XIV,3 on agents, XVI,3 on deposits). There are only two legal rules in the *Digest* specific to banking: first, that women could not be bankers, probably because they were not normally allowed to act as guarantors; second, that all types of bankers had to make relevant entries in their records available in legal cases, and not just to their clients, because, as one ruling says, contracting parties often trusted them to make and keep the sole record of their transaction (*Dig.* II, 13, 4–12; Gardner 1986, 234–36). The extant rulings seem not to derive from any coherent legislation or even doctrine. Instead Roman jurists had to devise legal devices to cope with banking developments that went beyond strict Roman law.

One of these devices was the irregular deposit (a modern term). Against legal principle it was recognized that deposits could be made by informal understanding that were interest-bearing and usable by the receiver (*Dig.* XVI,3,7,2; 3,24; 3,28; XLII,5,24,2; Johnston 1999, 86–87). Another was recognition that a loan could be created by a paper transaction, that is, an entry in an account, rather than by counting out money, which a Roman legal textbook (Gaius) tries, unrealistically, to distinguish from an entry recording an actual cash payment. Although they were also applicable to private transactions, the spur to these legal adjustments must have come from banking. It seems that clients and banks could not be bothered to record every deposit through a proper contract of *mutuum* (loan), so paper transactions were common in banking, including paper transfer deposits.

A third convention was the so-called *receptum argentarii* (banker's responsibility), which allowed that once a client had instructed his banker to make defined payments on his behalf, the legal claim of the beneficiaries to these payments lay only against the banker, whether or not the client had provided the banker with the necessary funds (Andreau 1987a, 597–602; Bürge 1987, 527–36). Yet another device was the concession, established by the mid-first century BCE, that by custom, not law, claims to recover deposits and loans could be made against any of the partners of a bank set up as a societas, not just the *socius* with whom the client had dealt (*Rhet. Her.* II,19). Unsurprisingly this did not make it into the *Digest* or Gaius's textbook, along with other concessions to business realities like Roman judges accepting Roman- and Greek-style or hybrid contracts as legally binding on Roman citizens and provincials alike.

Roman bankers were professionals who made their living from banking. They used common business and accounting techniques and jargon, in which young boys were trained (Maselli 1986; Nadjo 1989; Horatius, *Ars* 325–530; Petronius 58,7). However, there was no profession in any public sense. Roman banks were not licensed or regulated, let alone guaranteed, by the state. The only exceptions were the fiscal regulations that applied to money changing (*nummularii*) because it was a state concession, and possibly also to coactores as the collectors of state sales-taxes. There was no corporate body of bankers or self-regulation. A banker was what a banker did, and a Roman chose to deal with a bank, as one legal opinion puts it, "going on its public reputation" (*Dig.* XLII,5,24,2).

There were banks in Greece before Rome came that continued in operation after the Roman conquest. The most famous banks were on Delos, where there were both temple and private banks. There appears to have been a constant number of private banks, suggesting that the banks continued to operate over time with great stability. The Temple of Apollo appeared to give loans with houses as security, which we now would regard as mortgages. There can be no doubt that these institutions were what we call commercial banks (*Inscriptions de Delos* 1926–; Frank 1933–40, v. 4, 357; Reger 1992).

Cicero (*Pro lege Manilia*, aka *De imperio Cn. Pompeii*, 7, 19) noted the interconnection of financial markets around the Roman world, describing conditions in 66 BCE by reference to events twenty years earlier:

> For, coinciding with the loss by many people of large fortunes in Asia, we know that there was a collapse of credit at Rome owing to suspension of payment. It is, indeed, impossible for many individuals in a single State to lose their property and fortunes without involving still greater numbers in their ruin. Do you

defend the commonwealth from this danger; and believe me when I tell you—
what you see for yourselves—that this system of credit and finance which operates at Rome, in the Forum, is bound up in, and depends on capital invested in
Asia; the loss of the one inevitably undermines the other and causes its collapse.

This passage clearly talks of linked financial markets. It is possible that all these
connections were made by loans from one individual to another, but it would
be unprecedented in the history of commerce. It is far more likely that Roman
loans to Asia were done at least partly through financial intermediaries such
as banks (argentarii) or joint-stock companies concerned with Mediterranean
trade (*societates publicanorum*). Even when individuals transferred money between locations, they did not appear to have the problems Voltaire did (Ligt,
2003).

Banks transmitted information, and they could transfer money. Roman
senators and even equestrians had investments all over; they needed some way
to repatriate their earnings. They might have done so like the Egyptian bank
that reported in 155 CE: "Paid into the bank of Titus Flavius Eutychides by
Eudaemon, son of Sarapion, and partners, overseers . . . for the rent of the
seventeenth year, one talent and four thousand drachmae, on condition that an
equivalent amount should be paid at Alexandria to the official in charge of the
stemmata, total of 1 tal., 4000 dr." (P. Fayum 87 in Grenfell et al. 1900, 220–22).
This document attests not only to the existence of banks, but of either branch
banks or interbank activity. This transfer might have been accomplished by the
bank sending the money to its branch in Alexandria or by having a correspon-
dent bank in Alexandria that was willing to honor obligations from the bank
of Titus Flavius Eutychides, possibly because the Fayum bank held a balance
in Alexandria for that purpose. Grenfell et al. (1900, 220) opted for the latter
choice, speaking of "mutual arrangements" between the local and urban banks.

The essence of a Roman bank, as of a modern commercial bank, was that it
accepted deposits, normally interest-bearing, from its clients, made payments
for them and lent out their pooled money at interest. Lack of documents from
Italy make it difficult to give specific illustrations of these basic functions, although there is some evidence in the Campanian tablets. Legal recognition of
irregular deposits implies that interest-bearing accounts with banks were now
commonplace. Bogaert described private banks in Roman Egypt, although
there is no way of knowing how similar banks were in Roman Italy and Egypt.
Bogaert (2000, 265–66) argued that the surviving sources limit our knowledge
of Roman banks even in Egypt: "We believe that in Egypt most bank loans,
particularly large ones, were made in Alexandria, because that is where the big-
gest banks were. . . . The fact that almost all Alexandrian documents have been
lost explains why we have so little evidence of bank loans."

An important financial service was the financing of payments by purchasers to sellers at auctions, which had an obvious practicality since prices were not known in advance. Public auctions were a typically Roman way to arrange high value sales, especially landed property and slaves, valuable goods, including luxury foods or foodstuffs in large quantities, contracts for agricultural operations, state and civic contracts for revenue-collection, building works, supplies and services, and so on. Auctions were less important in the Greek world, so Greek bankers did not normally provide this service (García Morcillo 2008). A banker who specialized in this field was called a coactor (collector), but reference to coactores argentarii show that, as with nummularii, some coactores were also general bankers and vice versa (Andreau 1987a, 139–67; Horatius, S. I,6,86; Pomponius, *Comm.* ad loc.; *Dig.* XL,7,40,8). Typically, as the tablets illustrate, the coactor paid off the vendor, whether in cash or by a credit transaction, in return for a formal acknowledgment from him that he had received from the coactor what the purchaser had paid. The coactor charged a fee (*merces*) for this service, which perhaps was meant to be 1 percent of the price (Cicero, *Rab. Post.* 30). In Roman Italy of the first century AD, sales of slaves at auction were liable to a 4 percent tax due to the state treasury, and sales of other property to a sales tax which eventually settled at 1 percent. In 57 CE Nero made the vendor, not the buyer, liable to the tax on slaves (and possibly other property), which in effect probably made coactores the collectors of this tax (Rathbone 2007b).

Most of our specific evidence for credit at auctions comes from the archive of Lucius Caecilius Iucundus (*CIL* IV, 3340,1–153), for which Andreau (1974) remains invaluable. It seems that the box had been left behind inadvertently during evacuation of the house in August 79 prior to the eruption of Vesuvius. Most of the tablets are receipts, some very fragmentary, in the form of chirographs or *testationes*, to Iucundus from the vendors of items for the price, net of costs, paid or due to Iucundus from the purchasers. The normal reading of these texts is that Iucundus was a businessman who leased and exploited public properties and concessions, but the payment for the *mercatus* is said to be on behalf of the named contractor (*manceps*) of it. These receipts all concern municipal revenues which were farmed out by quinquennial auction to contractors (*publicani, mancipes*), implying that Iucundus also acted as coactor at these municipal auctions, which made him responsible for collecting the contractors' payments on behalf of the town (*P.Fay.* 87).

Acting as collector involved Iucundus in other financial services. Some of the receipts from vendors reveal that Iucundus had made short-term loans to purchasers for the price they had bid, presumably interest bearing. A few tablets reveal that some sellers kept deposit accounts with Iucundus to which the price of items they sold was credited and from which they made withdrawals.

We have no idea how many other boxes were successfully removed from the house, let alone what they contained. Iucundus may have had all kinds of economic interests; as a banker he may have provided all kinds of services (Andreau 1999, 35).

Our evidence for the Sulpicii is similar to that for Iucundus. In 1959 a single box of tablets was found in a building, perhaps an inn, which graffiti suggest may have belonged to the Sulpicii, in the port suburb of Pompeii. This too looks like an inadvertent loss from a much bigger collection of records, perhaps in transit from the town for evacuation by ship. From the surviving fragments of those tablets, 128 texts (*TPSulp.*) have been authoritatively published in Camodeca (1999), of which 95 are well preserved. Coincidentally these texts mirror the chronological range of the Iucundus tablets, from 26/29 to 62 CE, but the majority are from 35 to 55 CE. The range of financial services attested in the tablets of the Sulpicii is much broader, perhaps because they were filed on a different principle, that is, by client or transaction. For example, five texts form a dossier relating to the grain merchant Gaius Novius Eunus. Again, it would be mistaken to make the positivist assumption that we have a representative sample of the whole business of the Sulpicii.

Interpretation of many of the transactions in the documents of the Sulpicii remains controversial. Many texts of the archive imply that the Sulpicii ran deposit accounts for their clients from which cash could be withdrawn or payments made, and particularly the following three types of document. First, the two *mandata* which authorize Sulpicius Cinnamus to make payments within certain conditions on behalf of clients, and illustrate the working of the principle of receptum argentarii (Camodeca 2003, 76–78). Second, the six texts that Camodeca calls *nomina arcaria* and often represent paper transactions into and out of clients' accounts. Third, the eight *apochae* (receipts, a Greek name), most for payments made to or from the bank, but two between third parties, where it is likely that the bank held the apochae because the transactions had been paper ones between the accounts of two clients. Unless some of the apochae issued by the bank had this function, there is no direct evidence of a client making a deposit. However, an irregular *depositum* may have generated no written record other than an entry in the bank's accounts. We also note that in these and other transactions, including those of the Iucundus archive, bankers were in effect creating credit for clients. At present, unfortunately, it is not possible to say to what extent Roman bankers allowed overdrafts, which the practice of receptum argentarii implies could occur, and, if so, under what sort of arrangements, perhaps a loan agreement.

A variety of banking activities is attested for the Sulpicii. Only one text is, like the Iucundus texts, a vendor's receipt to the bank for the price obtained at auction, but it is enough to show that the Sulpicii also acted as coactores. This is also implicit in the three contracts of sale of slaves, because slaves were normally sold by auction. As these contracts say, the vendor of a slave was liable to a penalty of double the sale price if the goods proved to suffer from undeclared faults; it appears that the bank guaranteed this sum for vendors who were its clients, that is kept deposit accounts with it.

Much of the archive has to do with lending and borrowing. The Sulpicii may have acted as brokers. On one occasion they borrowed the substantial sum of HS 94,000 for just over a month, presumably to finance smaller short-term loans. Some of the eleven contracts of loan and four acknowledgments of debt do not involve the Sulpicii; the idea that they were routed through their bank is supported by one that specifies repayment either to the creditor directly or to Sulpicius Faustus. Some scholars have been worried that no loan contract states the rate of interest and only one the date for repayment. Verboven (2003a) suggested that this was to conceal illegally high interest charges, but we imagine that these matters were fixed by informal verbal agreement based on *fides* (trust), that is a *pactum* (Camodeca 2003, 83–85; Johnston 1999, 86). Interest rates were not listed at Hoare's Bank in the early eighteenth century. Only when the full record of the loan is seen can the interest rate be calculated by modern scholars (Temin and Voth 2006).

For many of the attested loans, perhaps because the borrowers were not already clients, the Sulpicii required guarantors or pledges. For example, a local man guaranteed the loan made to a Carian ship captain. Pledges include a quantity of Egyptian wheat and beans and perhaps a shipload of wine, and for additional security the Sulpicii had the rent of space in storehouses where these pledges were kept in their name. Of the thirteen texts concerning auctions, most are to do with giving notice of intention to auction the pledges of defaulting debtors.

Almost a third of the archive relates to legal proceedings, some about financial transactions involving the Sulpicii. Twenty-two texts record the putting up or confiscation of *vadimonia*, mutual sureties offered by the parties to a legal dispute for their appearance at a hearing at the set place and date, or to remain in town. Presumably the bank did this for clients as a paper transaction, obviating, as in many of their transactions, the need to obtain and use coin. The archive provides the only evidence for the involvement of banks with vadimonia, which reminds us that there may be other services provided by Roman banks for which there is no extant evidence. The general impression is that the Sulpicii were bankers in the full sense, who ran deposit and withdrawal accounts, made paper transfers between these accounts, accepted mandates to make multiple payments, lent to third parties, acted as investment brokers, provided finance for auctions, put up court bonds and so on; perhaps they also were money changers.

Even in Egypt we lack for Roman banks the core records that survived for Hoare's bank in London, which would attest who and how many their clients were and how the clients' accounts were run, and might reveal the overall shape of the business and relative importance of different operating sectors. They also would allow historians to assess how the bankers carried risk, maintained liquidity, and made their profits. The rulings in the *Digest* expect bankers to keep accounts (rationes), apparently chronological, of receipts and disbursements (accepta et data), for which the term commonly used by legal scholars, although it appears only in one of Cicero's speeches (*Q. Com.* 1–14) and there with reference to a private individual, is a *codex accepti et expensi* (*Dig.* II,13,1,2; 14,47,1; XXXII,1,29,2; L,16,56,1; L,8,2,3). Consideration of the nature of these accounts has been enmeshed with attempts to understand what the extant Roman legal textbook of the second century CE meant in practice by nomina arcaria (strongbox entries), entries in accounts recording cash payments, and *nomina transscripticia* (transfer entries), where merely writing the entry created the loan (*litteris obligatio*), whether with regard to a person (an advance or transfer of credit as a loan) or a thing (to cover the price due from a sale) (Gaius III,128–34). It is at least agreed that the Latin verb *transcribere* in this sense, and also the noun *perscriptio*, represent the Greek term *diagraphe* (bank payment), and imply the influence of Greek banking practices on Rome.

Some of the Campanian tablets help to clarify the problem (Gröschler 1997). Several tablets that Camodeca misleadingly called nomina arcaria are testationes (witnessed statements) of loans made by entries in accounts rather than by a traditional contract. Each is titled as if it represented an extract from the lender's accounts (*tabellae* = *tabulae*) of *expensa*, and it also notes the borrower's acceptance of the sum and record of it as *accepta* (in his or her own accounts), and then documents the promise of a guarantor (*fideiussio*).

In five cases Sulpicius Cinnamus, that is the bank, is the lender; in one tablet the lender is Titinia Anthrax, and the text is overscored with the word *sol(utum)*, (re)paid. In all cases, it seems, the sum is said to have been counted from the house out of the strongbox into the recipient's strongbox as if it had been a cash transaction, but there is reason to doubt that cash had always been used. Some tablets recording other purely third-party agreements must survive in the archive of the Sulpicii because they handled the payments. So the house and strongbox cannot have been those of Titinia, and the whole image of counting the money was probably a fiction.

The testationes were a documentary safety net; counting money was the archaic legal way of making a payment or loan; this is an assertion of the reality of a paper transaction. Similarly, some of the Iucundus tablets record money (*pecunia*) as counted out (*numerata*) and others as discharged (*persoluta*), but both types are often labelled *perscriptio*, (bank) transfer, on the edge of the tablets. It is not safe to conclude that a counted sum had always been paid in cash or a discharged one by a paper entry.

We can only speculate about the types of accounts kept by Roman bankers. Our only direct evidence is that Iucundus and the Sulpicii filed, perhaps on different principles, tablets recording individual transactions and kept them for over twenty years, which seems curious. The common idea that Roman banks kept a single ledger of income and expenditure is unfeasible. For each client a separate ratio accepti et expensi was needed. One tablet notes a loan was recorded as outgoing from the account of Titinia and received in the account of the borrower, Euplia; if Euplia took the loan as cash from the Sulpicii, that will have been recorded as outgoing in her account. A client acknowledged receipt of HS 644 as payment of an auction price of HS 645, which he had received in five separate payments of uncertain interpretation: HS 200 in cash, HS 20 for judgments, HS 13 as additions, HS 51 as a debit, and the remaining HS 360 as a transfer on the day of the receipt. These probably were transactions unrelated to the auction, excerpted from the client's account because they almost exactly matched the price due to him, and that the tablet represents his agreement with the bank that the auction business was now complete.

The clients' accounts did not contain much detail of the reasons for the credits and debits recorded there. The tablets were kept because they documented the settlement of particular deals, which had often involved more than one entry in clients' accounts, and may have served the banker as extra defense against a claim under receptum argentarii that he had not made the payment instructed by his client. The bank itself, and perhaps each principal and agent, needed its own ratio accepti et expensi to record one-to-one dealings with customers. It also needed other interlocking records to run its business such as a kalendarium of loans, a register of vadimonia, a stock account of coin received and disbursed, and so on. Accounting systems of this broad type are known elsewhere in the Roman world, in the army, and on large estates in third-century Egypt (*Rom.Mil.Rec*; Rathbone 1991).

The range of services provided by the private banks in first-century Italy is quite impressive. There were no public banks (privately run concessions) in Rome and Italy that could receive tax payments, as there were in Egypt and other eastern provinces, for the simple reason that no direct taxes were levied in Italy in this period. Similarly, although the Sulpicii kept copies of contracts between others when they had facilitated the payment, they did this for their own reasons, and perhaps also as a private service to the clients like the "copy kept on land" of maritime loan contracts. There was no registration of property ownership on behalf of the state, as in Egypt and probably other provinces too. Roman law and administration operated in a quite different tradition of civic honesty compared to the prying bureaucratic registers of Hellenistic kingdoms.

Nonetheless, we may note the creeping involvement of Roman banks in collecting indirect taxes and fees for the central state and civic administrations, notably the taxes on sales at auction and revenues on auctioned concessions.

In Roman Egypt private banks are always called "the bank of A," or "of A and B," where A and B are persons' names, if necessary with the town or village also specified (Bogaert 1995). The same probably happened in Roman Italy, and it is just like the banks of eighteenth-century London known as Hoare's Bank, Child's Bank, Gosling's Bank, and so on. Almost all the Pompeian tablets are written as if Iucundus junior dealt himself with every transaction, which is quite implausible; presumably he had told his agents to have all documents drawn up in his name only. This looks like a family bank, operating over two or more generations, probably using freedmen and slave agents.

Several different and unnecessarily complex reconstructions of the family of the Sulpicii have been derived from overly positivist reading of the few extant tablets to invent a chronological line of succession. The archive attests the involvement of two brothers, the Gaii Sulpicii Faustus and Onirus, whom a funerary inscription from Puteoli shows to have been sons of a freedman, perhaps the freedman of another freedman. The protagonist in most of the tablets is Gaius Sulpicius Cinnamus, a freedman and *procurator* (legally appointed agent) of Faustus. It is likely that the bank was structured as a family *societas* which made considerable use of freedman and slave agents. In origin the family may go back to a freedman of the Sulpicii, a noble family of Rome.

The banks of Iucundus and the Sulpicii fit in with the general impression given by the literary, legal and epigraphic evidence. Banks could be formed of individuals acting in partnership (*societas*), and could use slaves and freedmen, often legally appointing them as agents (*institores, procuratores*) through the practice of *praepositio* (*Rhet. Her.* II,19; *Dig.* II,14,25,pr; 14,27,pr.; *Dig.* XIV,3,5; 3,19,1; 3). These social institutions, slavery, societas, and praepositio, as defined and regulated by Roman law in ways particular to Rome, enabled banks, as other enterprises at Rome, to develop organic and highly flexible operating structures. Note the position of manumitted slaves, that is freedmen, who bore the same main name as their ex-master, owed him respect if not services, yet legally could be treated as independent agents as described in chapter 6. Note also the first-century BCE juristic extension of partnership and agency, by which partners could contribute and profit asymmetrically, and a principal could by verbal or written *mandatum* give an agent unlimited competence or restrict it as they wished, down to a single transaction in theory, and thereby limit their own liability.

Roman banks did not necessarily have fixed business premises. Seven, then five, *tabernae* (lock-up shops) in the Roman forum had been provided specifically for bankers to lease, and this was a common arrangement in Roman towns

(Livius XXVI,27,2; Vitruvius V,1,2; *Dig.* XVII,1,32; Andreau 1987b; Jongman 1988, 220–22). The Campanian tablets show that most transactions involving these banks were agreed and recorded by people meeting in the forum, as was usual for most private and public business in Roman cities; public buildings were used in bad weather. In Rome, at least, some bankers based themselves by the wholesale and luxury foodstuff markets for the auctions. Money and records were kept at the banker's private house (*villa*), sometimes in a strong-room (*horreum*) (*Dig.* II,13,6,pr).

Most banks seem to have been local to one city or town, and it is often claimed that the Romans had no banking system (Bürge 1987, 508–9; Johnston 1999, 86). There are indications that banks in different towns were able to co-operate in making transfers, even transfers of credit. The first point to note is the ubiquity of banks. Inscriptions of the first to second centuries CE attest 47 argentarii and coactores and 12 nummularii at Rome, and 17 argentarii and co-actores and 10 nummularii in the towns of Italy (Andreau 1987a, 315). It seems that all the four hundred or so towns of Italy had at least one bank, and many had several. In the eastern provinces banks are found in settlements ranging from major cities to large villages. Not all banks were one-town banks: the Sulpicii were based in Puteoli, but may well have had a branch in Pompeii; they issued vadimonia for legal proceedings in Capua and Rome. They may have used another banker or coactor, Aulus Castricius, to handle the auction of a pledge of a defaulting debtor for them because the property was in another town. Roman jurisprudence could imagine the case of a loan spread between two banks (*Dig.* II,14,9). The mobile actors of maritime commerce needed to be able to raise cash and credit in whatever port a sudden storm might drive them, and clearly were able to do so. In the mid-first century BCE senators like Verres and Cicero had been able to transfer wealth back from Asia Minor to Rome, including changing sums out of the then existing local coinage. In the mid-first century CE the wealthy Alexandrian Tiberius Iulius Alexander made a substantial loan to King Agrippa II, some paid on the spot in cash, the bulk to be collected in Puteoli. Clearing between banks could be managed without any movement of coin by using rent payments, transfers of tax rev-enues, and so on (Rathbone 2003a).

Because of their nature the Iucundus tablets mostly concern the purchase of landed and other property, while the dealings attested in the tablets of the Sulpicii are predominantly commercial. For what it is worth, most of this lend-ing was economically productive in the sense of facilitating production and commerce. Andreau has claimed that banks were not used by the Roman elite, although he concedes that their existence in inland towns implies use by mu-nicipal elites, a rather fine distinction to draw. The witnesses to the Iucundus contracts include the local elite of Pompeian society. It is true that the only senators specifically said to have used a bank are Scipio Aemilianus and the husbands of his aunts, whose dowries he paid to them in around 160 BCE through a bank where he had an interest-bearing account, but anecdotes attest senatorial attendance at auctions, the state loans made available to senators in 33 CE were provided through banks, and slaves and freedmen of the emperor and of senatorial ladies appear in the documents of the Sulpicii (Polybius XXXI,27; Tacitus, *Ann.* VI,17 [section 3.3]; e.g. *TPSulp.* 45; 69; 73; 94).

Also, elite Roman reluctance to write publicly about their financial arrangements must be recognized: how many of the businessmen (*negotiatores*) with whom Cicero had financial dealings were bankers and brokers? The absence of senators themselves from two boxes of tablets, mostly recording minor transactions, from two perhaps middling banks in Pompeii and Puteoli is no great surprise.

We have a wider sample of the activities of the Sulpicii than of Iucundus, although still far from a complete picture. The 77 tablets from the central twenty-year period of their archive record transactions worth HS 1.28 million, an average of HS 16,623 per transaction (Camodeca 2003, 73–74). If we imagine that Cinnamus by himself was involved in one transaction on 200 days a year, the projected aggregate value of his activity per annum would be HS 3.3 million, which, at a profit margin of 2 percent would imply an income of over HS 66,000 a year. If we suppose he managed five transactions per working day and had a profit margin of 4 percent, he would have achieved a senatorial income. The preferred guesstimate must then be multiplied by the number of active partners or agents in the bank. Given that Italy had some four hundred towns at this time, of which say a hundred were large, it is unlikely that there were fewer than a thousand banks in first-century CE Rome and Italy. Even if the modal Roman bank was small, Roman banking was big business.

It is clear that Rome had a financial system that included internal and informal external sources of capital. This by itself is impressive, but still provides only limited support for economic endeavors. The question is whether Roman investors could make use of financial intermediaries, that is, whether the financial system of Rome was adequate to demands that might have been put upon it. Phrased differently, the question is whether or to what extent banks were present in the early Roman Empire.

There are many uncertainties on both sides of this comparative study, but some broad conclusions are possible. Financial intermediation was big business in first-century CE Rome and Italy. There was a wide range of institutions engaged in financial intermediation, including banks, brokers, partnerships, private individuals, and some cities. Between them they provided a wide range of services, including money changing, deposit accounts, mandated payments, transfers between accounts, credit for auctions, loans to clients and third parties, guarantees for contracts and legal appearances, and in the provinces, tax payments. There may well have been other as yet unattested services. There was no state or corporate regulation of banking, but there were professional bankers, brokers, money changers, and the like, who made their living from that business and used common operating procedures and jargon, and financial intermediation operated in a business culture based on fides (trust). In terms of table 8.1, three out of four rows were active in Rome.

We do not have much information about credit intermediation through equity ownership, but the societates publicanorum of the Roman Republic appear to have been joint stock companies with several qualities of modern corporations. The societates could outlive their principals (unlike partnerships), their shares traded at variable prices, and share ownership was extensive (Malmendier 2009). The practice attributed to Cato that I noted earlier illustrates how the societates operated. Cato insisted that people who wished to obtain money from him form a large association, and when the association had fifty members, representing as many ships, he would take one share in the company (Plutarch, *Cato the Elder*, XXI.5–6). We know that there were many societates involved with Roman tax farming and grain trading in the later republic; we do not know how long they continued in the early empire. They appear to have continued in private activities like shipping even as their role in tax collection diminished.

The early Roman Empire consequently pooled funds with the aid of financial intermediaries, that is, through many private banks. Interest rates for loans could vary, making the Roman financial market more accessible and flexible than the French eighteenth-century financial market. There were about twenty private banks in eighteenth-century London. Banks outside London were rare in the eighteenth century, and banking conditions in the rest of England probably were worse than those in the early Roman Empire.

Even if they did not have local banks, rural English people had access to Bank of England notes. The availability of a paper currency facilitated business and financial transactions even in the absence of institutional financial intermediaries. The Roman Empire lacked a national debt and a centrally chartered bank. Daily transactions outside the principal cities in the early Roman Empire probably therefore may have been more like those in eighteenth-century France, although Harris (2006, 24) asserted that "credit-money . . . enabled the Romans to extend their money supply far beyond the limits of their monetized metal."

Conditions varied in early modern Europe; Britain and Holland were more advanced in many ways than other countries. Conditions in the early Roman Empire therefore cannot be compared usefully with those in Europe because European financial institutions varied so widely. Comparing Roman financial institutions to those of specific countries, the surprising result is that financial institutions in the early Roman Empire were better than those of eighteenth-century France and Holland. They were similar to those in eighteenth-century London and probably better than those available elsewhere in England.

Unhappily, Roman banks and other financial intermediaries vanish from the historical record in the third century CE as prices began to rise (see chapter 4). Loans are contracts over time. If prices are higher when a loan is repaid, the interest received is offset by the loss of principal value. In economic terms, the real interest rate—equal to the nominal interest rate minus the rate of inflation—declined sharply and even turned negative in inflationary surges. This was a new problem for Roman banks. While we do not observe any third-century banks losing money, we infer that they accumulated losses and disappeared.

Part III

. . . .

The Roman Economy

Part III

* * * *

The Roman Economy

Introduction

■　■　■　■

Roman Macroeconomics

This final section brings together my thoughts and speculations on the implications of the preceding chapters on individual markets. When I began working on Roman economics, I did not think there was enough information to deal with macroeconomic questions of economic growth and the size of the economy. I still believe that the shortage of information makes these questions difficult and elusive. I hope that readers who have followed me so far in my intellectual journey will be encouraged to stay along for thoughts and speculations about what all the market activity of the Roman Empire meant for ordinary Romans.

I start with a review of the theory of economic growth and the problems of measuring it. Chapter 9 reveals that scholars trying to understand Roman macroeconomics are in far worse shape than economists dealing with more recent economies. I suggest some ways of using proxies for actual measures of economic growth in classical times and place them in the context of other research. It is important to understand the theory that lies behind our efforts to make sense of the scattered Roman data.

There is, however, a problem with this approach. Rome did not have an industrial revolution. Without this momentous change, Rome was subject to Malthusian pressures that limited its economic growth. Chapter 10 shows how to square this circle. It reveals even Malthusian economies can have economic growth, that is, can have rising standards of living. This can go on for a long time, even centuries, even though without industrialization, it is doomed to end. Once we understand that there is room for at least temporary economic growth in the Malthusian model, interesting questions emerge about the nature of economic growth in Roman times.

If there was economic growth, then the standard of living in Rome should have increased. How far did it go, even if it did not lead to industrialization?

Chapter 11 draws together the implications of the previous chapters to investigate the size of the Roman economy at its maximum extent. Was the Roman Empire limited to be like most other ancient empires, or should the flat line of per capita income shown in figure 10.1 of chapter 10 have a noticeable bump in the first few centuries of the Christian Era?

Chapter 9

∎ ∎ ∎

Growth Theory for Ancient Economies

The first sentence of *The Cambridge Economic History of Europe* volume on the Industrial Revolution states baldly, "The characteristic which distinguishes the modern period in world history from all past periods is the fact of economic growth" (Cole and Deane 1965, 1). The categorical assertion that economic growth started only with the Industrial Revolution makes a strong statement about ancient history. The authors did not consider that the Roman Empire lasted far longer than the United States has been in existence and that the question of economic growth under its rule cannot be decided by fiat. It would be far better to have an estimate of Roman economic growth derived from ancient sources that could be compared with more recent experience. How could we construct such an estimate?

The purpose of this chapter is to propose a few ground rules for the examination of questions relating to ancient economic growth. If we seek to investigate the possibility of economic growth in ancient times, we inevitably make analogies with modern growth and with the empirical methods and abstract theories economists have used to analyze it. I will describe some of these theories here to expose their underlying assumptions. As I will show, these theories require assumptions about ancient economies that are not comfortable to all ancient historians.

I start by discussing a few estimates of Roman economic growth by Hopkins and others to clarify the problem of measurement. This leads to a review of the empirical constructs used in modern descriptions of economic growth, a guide to historical research that occupies the major part of this essay (Solow and Temin 1978). On the assumption that the desired estimates can be constructed for ancient times, I go on to describe the theories of economic growth that are used by economists today. I then consider two aspects of these models that are critically important for ancient studies, the role of demography and of knowledge. I close with a few reflections on the application of theory to history.

When Hopkins proposed his famous taxes and trade model of the Roman economy in 1980, he argued that the authors just quoted ignored economic growth before the Industrial Revolution and that the Roman collection of taxes stimulated monetization and economic growth in the early Roman Empire:

> This simple model implies a whole series of small-scale changes in production, distribution and consumption, whose cumulative impact over time was important. There was a significant increase in agricultural production, an increase in the division of labour, growth in the number of artisans, in the size of towns where many of them lived, development of local markets and of long-distance commerce. (Hopkins 1980, p. 102)

Hopkins suggested a variety of ways to discern economic growth in this passage: the growth of agricultural production, nonagricultural production, towns, and trade. None of these indicators indicates directly how quickly the Roman economy grew. They need to be inserted into some kind of framework to result in an estimate of Roman economic growth. Hopkins's accompanying estimate of the level of production does not help because it was derived by analogy with modern conditions and does not point toward the use of ancient evidence at all. I discuss it in detail in chapter 11.

Drexhage (1991, 440–54) did not try to estimate GDP, but he estimated changes in real wages in Roman Egypt. This raises some of the same problems as estimating GDP, and real wages move with per capita GDP in the long run, even if not every year. One of his indexes showed a roughly constant real wage over several centuries, but another index showed a rising real wage. These indexes raise at least as many questions as they can answer, one of which is whether the standard of living was improving in Roman Egypt, that is, if there was economic growth.

Ward-Perkins (2005) argued that the decline of Roman civilization could be indexed by the declining availability of what he called industrial Roman pottery, that is, well-made, wheel-thrown pottery that was available widely among Roman citizens. He argued that this pottery was both better than the pottery that was made after the fall of the empire and that it was spread widely among ordinary people in the earlier period. This had not always been true, and there must have been a preceding period when Roman pottery improved in quality and became more widely available. The availability of pottery then provides an index of living standards, much as Drexhage's calculations of real wages do.

Quite different evidence has been presented recently by Greene (2000) and Wilson (2002) on technical change in Roman production. Using archaeological evidence, they show that agricultural techniques had advanced over the period of the Roman Republic and early empire. The roads and buildings of Rome are well known, and they provide corroborating evidence of technological progress. In modern times, the rate of technological progress—of which more later—largely determines the rate of economic growth. There are many steps to take between these observations and economic growth in ancient times, but the evidence nevertheless is suggestive.

So suggestive, in fact, that Saller (2005) graphed Roman "GDP per capita productivity 100 BCE—300 CE." Starting from Hopkins's estimated GDP, the line rose by "as much as 25 percent" before peaking in the first century of the Common Era and returning to its original value by 300 CE. Saller would be the first to acknowledge that this graph is only suggestive. It would be far preferable to have some actual numbers to graph. Saller's graph also makes the search for data more critical, if only to forestall the use of his suggestive graph in their place.

Scheidel (2009a) reviewed several proxies for Roman growth in response to an earlier version of chapter 10. As he noted, each of them was suggestive, but none of them were complete. I will discuss his conclusions at the end of chapter 10. The attention to economic growth in Rome has been echoed by the beginning of similar attention to Greece. Morris (2004, 2005) argued that there was economic growth in classical Greece, not very fast, but steady over several centuries. He used information on population to show the growth of the economy as a whole and information on house sizes to argue that per capita GDP was rising even as population expanded: the opposite of the normal Malthusian expectation.

This brief survey of some existing research on the level of Roman and Greek income shows that there is a variety of data that could be used to estimate Roman economic growth. There is a step needed before we begin the search for more data, however. We need to understand the methods used to measure economic growth in other times and places and the theories that underlie these estimates. This understanding will provide a guide to the usage of any new data from ancient times; the agenda for this chapter is to explain measures and theories of economic growth that are used by economists in ways that are comprehensible to ancient historians. I discuss the economic approach to using data to estimate national income, survey theories of economic growth, and finally attempt to bring theory and practice together in a way that may prove useful for ancient historians.

The first task in thinking about ancient economic growth is to find some way to tell when economic growth took place, how fast it progressed, and how far it went. An index of human welfare might seem appropriate to indicate the existence and extent of economic growth, but an index of welfare is too broad for present purposes. There are many things that affect the happiness of people, and the state of the economy is only one of them. People who have eaten to satiety are not always happier than those who eat more lightly. We all are familiar with discontent in wealthy societies and with unhappiness coming from noneconomic causes. There are even those who say that the overall psychological state of mankind is not susceptible of alteration by economic means. Each man, this theory says, will worry according to his nature. If he is poor, he may worry about his poverty. But if he is rich, he will find something else to worry about.

It is not necessary to hold to this extreme theory to see that a measure of welfare is too broad for an index of economic growth. It is enough to realize that we do not have the means to disprove such a theory to know that the link between economic growth and welfare is quite tenuous. For example, historians have been debating for many years whether workers were better off in the early years of the Industrial Revolution than they had been previously. It appears that it took longer for the fruits of industrialization to raise English wages than it did to transform the economy (Feinstein 1998; Voth 2003).

Another possible measure of economic growth is an index of structural change. The idea of an Industrial Revolution and the place of industry in the economy today suggest that industrialization can be used as a measure of economic growth. Hopkins (1980) listed several components of such an index for Rome. It is a valid measure only if there is some fixed relation between economic growth and the place of industry in the economy. The diversity of historical experience belies this simple notion. While industry plays a more important role in societies that have had an Industrial Revolution than in societies that have not, the extent of this role is determined by many as yet unknown factors, and the difference between economics that have and have not industrialized today lies more in the differences in efficiency between various sectors in the different economies than in the relative sizes of these sectors (Broadberry 1997). Just as a measure of welfare is too broad for present purposes, a measure of structural shifts within the economy is too narrow.

Since one bowl of porridge is too hot and one too cold, it is obvious that the third will be just right. The ability of the economy to produce ever more goods and services of value to its members is a more restricted measure than changes in welfare because it looks only at the goods and services produced by the economy. All other things being equal, an increase in these goods and services would increase welfare, but we do not know that other things remained the same when economic production increased. On the other hand, economic growth is a broader measure than structural change, for an economy can grow in many ways and with many different types of structural change. It is the results of structural change that concern us, and they are a good index of economic growth.

Economists speak of the output of goods and services in an economy as the national or domestic product. (National product concerns the output of citizens of a county; domestic product, output from the residents of a country.) Even though these terms apply more the modern than the ancient world, I will use them here for their obvious parallels. Ancient empires may be considered to be the analog of modern nation states. Calculating a national or domestic product for smaller areas like Italy and Egypt also may be permitted to ancient historians if it is clear that the reference is to the area of a modern nation, not a backward projection of its political integrity. By national product, economists refer to the production of goods and services used in *final* consumption, that is, goods and services that are valued by the members of the economy. This is distinguished from intermediate goods and services used in the production of other goods and services. Finally, since the national product is purchased in market economies ultimately from the factors of production— that is, labor, land and capital—economists often refer to national income interchangeably with national product. The difference is in the treatment of taxes included in the product account but not the income account. There were taxes in the ancient world, but we do not know enough about them to make separate calculations.

To speak of goods and services of value to the members of an economy raises a question of great importance for ancient history. How should we treat the consumption of slaves? From the point of view of slave owners, slaves were part of their capital, and their consumption was the cost of maintaining this capital. Clearly, the consumption of slaves was an intermediate good to the slave owner, similar in all respects to grapes for wine. To the slaves, on the other hand, their consumption represented final products of the economy, and they would have thought that it should be counted as such. In addition to deciding how to treat goods and services bought by consumers, consequently, we have to decide who the consumers are. A slave owner in the American South before the Civil War may well have had a different index of economic growth than we—believing that all men are equal and to be counted as consumers— would construct today. Jonathan Swift noted that if horses ran the country, all human consumption would be an intermediate input into the production of final goods like hay. The definition of national product reflects a construction of society.

Ancient Roman slavery was not like modern American slavery, and it depended more than its modern analog on positive rewards than the threat of punishment to motivate slaves (see chapter 6). The sharp separation between slave and free characteristic of modern slavery was not observed in ancient Rome, and some ambitious poor people sold themselves into slavery as a long-term employment contract that promised, however uncertainly, more advancement than the life of the free poor (Ramin and Veyne 1981). This action, however rare in the early Roman Empire, was more like the process of apprenticeship in early modern Europe than modern American slavery; it reveals the integration of Roman slavery with the overall labor market. Slaves must be counted as people in the estimation of GDP for the Roman world, and their consumption must be classified as final output, not as intermediate goods.

The national product might rise because of a rise in the value of the commodities and services being produced, and not because of an increase in the quantity produced. If we wish to talk of the volume of production and its relation to the quantities of factors used, we must first find a way to transform the sum of values that we have called national product into a measure that is independent of the price level, that is, into "real" national product. Given the scarcity of data for the ancient world, output typically will be measured as units of wheat or oil. These quantities then will be multiplied by their prices to get a value of production. Even though the data are constructed in a different way, the calculation of a national product in terms of its monetary value involves the same problems for ancient and modern studies.

Were there only one unalterable commodity, and consequently only one price, the problem would be trivial: dividing the value of production at different times by the price at that time would give a measure of the quantity produced. Similarly, if all prices changed together, one price would be as good as another to use for deflation, and the problem would be solved. But when there are many goods, and when prices do not move together, it is necessary to choose what price or combination of prices to use for deflation. The measure of the goods and services produced—that is, of real national product—that will emerge will depend on the choice made; there is no unique measure of real national product.

The problem may be restated as follows: when prices and quantities do not move together, it is necessary to choose a scheme where the changes in the various quantities are weighted to produce an average change. Various weighting schemes have been named after nineteenth-century investigators. A Paasche index is one that uses prices of the current year as weights; a Laspeyres index is one that uses prices of the initial year of the series as weights. In other words, a Paasche index uses the weights of the observer looking backward; a Laspeyres index uses the weights of a man at the start of the historical period being considered looking forward. As each observer uses the prices of his period as weights, each observer will give heavier weight to those sectors or products with the higher relative price, that is, the higher price relative to the prices of other products. If there is a systematic relationship between the movements of relative prices and the growth of industries, there will be a consistent difference between the two measures.

If we seek to evaluate the path of income over more than two periods, the process becomes more complex. The Laspeyres index is unchanged and poses no problems. The Paasche index will have different weights for each year, making it hard to compare progress in intermediate years. Various treatments have evolved for modern data. We often use a Paasche index, keeping the weights for a given year even as time goes on. (This produces a Paasche index for most of the data, and a Laspeyres index for the last few entries). Then the weights are updated every once in a while, forcing a recalculation of all past estimates. Alternatively, we sometimes use a series of Laspeyres indexes, each for a relatively short period of time, and just link them all together. This avoids periodic recalculations of all the data, but it loses the interpretation of a single index.

Some writers have seen the Industrial Revolution as a result of spontaneous innovations. According to this view, the pattern of demand stayed relatively stable. Innovations in some industries lowered the price of their products, and people consumed more of them. In other words, expansions took place primarily by shifts of supply curves and movements along demand curves, and this process generated a negative correlation between price and quantity changes. Those industries whose relative prices fell the most were also the industries whose output rose the most. An observer looking forward into the future would have seen rapid expansion in the industries he or she associated with relatively high prices; an observer looking back would see relatively slow expansion in the industries he or she associated with relatively high prices. The Laspeyres index would show a higher rate of growth than the Paasche index.

This discussion may appear impossibly arcane for the ancient world, but it reveals implications of practices that ancient historians frequently use. Hopkins (1980) estimated per capita Roman GDP in wheat equivalents, but the output of any ancient economy consisted of more than one good. Wheat, wine, and oil typically start the list for the Roman economy, and it goes on to include clothing, pottery, glassware, construction, etc. It is natural, as stated already, to add these outputs together by converting them all to values by means of their prices. But this is only valid if there are prices and if those prices reflect the preferences of the members of the economy. It is only valid, in other words, if there are markets and market prices. I have argued that markets were common in the ancient world, and it is possible to speak of national output if they were.

Going further, the sparse evidence of wheat prices in the late republic and early empire can be used to demonstrate the existence of a wheat market extending the length of the Mediterranean Sea. The good part of this demonstration is that it shows that markets were indeed extensive during the Pax Romana. The bad part is that it explains the well-known observation that produce prices were lower outside Rome than in the capital city; the surplus of agricultural areas had to be transported to Rome, and the price difference most probably is the cost of transportation. This means that—despite the extent of markets—prices differed across space, making it necessary to specify where production and consumption took place. This problem arises in chapter 11 where it will be discussed further.

In addition, this discussion shows that the implications of using wheat production alone as a measure of output. Such an approach assigns a high weight to wheat (and one or two other products if they are included) and a zero weight to all other products. This is an extreme form of the index-number problem just described. Poor data for ancient economies may force us to count only a few outputs, but we should not forget about the other products given zero weight in our calculation—although not in the ancient economies.

Drexhage (1991) illustrated this problem in his calculations of real wages in Roman Egypt. He calculated two indexes. The first compared wages to an index of the prices of wheat, wine, and oil. He therefore acknowledged that the Roman economy produced more than wheat, and that ordinary people consumed a variety of products. He then compared wages to an index of clothing prices, expanding from a purely agrarian economy to introduce manufactured products into his accounting. The problem that shows the importance of the theory just described is that real wages calculated the first way (relative to agricultural products) appeared to stay constant over the first three centuries of this era while real wages calculated the second way (relative to clothing) appeared to fall. This contrast exposes the need to have a way to combine the prices of different goods and services, as just discussed.

Allen (2009a) and Scheidel (2010) produced estimates of real wages as measures of Roman economic growth. Allen used data from the Diocletian Edict of 301 CE to make an isolated estimate acquiring status as a measure of economic growth by comparison of estimates for other times and places. Scheidel replicated Allen's estimates for other times and places in the early Roman Empire. The apparent stability of real wages in these years is problematical for reasons that I will discuss in chapter 10.

The important question now arises of whether the story of the growth of real economic output can be translated into a story about the growth of the conventional productive inputs. Do the historically observed increments in the supply of labor, capital goods, and land (or natural resources) "explain" economic growth? The very notion of an Industrial Revolution suggests not; historians presumably would be surprised to discover that all that happened in the second half of the eighteenth century was that the supplies of labor, capital, and natural resources began to grow more rapidly than they had done before. But even if there is more to the story than that, it is still a matter of some interest and importance to discover what part of the growth of output can be explained by the growth of inputs, and what part remains to be explained in other ways.

I first must state what I mean by explain. It is not a matter of "ultimate" explanation, of asking whether land is the mother of output and labor the father, or vice versa. If I were to say that a factor explains output if it is indispensable to the process of production, then to all intents and purposes I could explain output thrice over. Instead the notion of explanation used by economists is incremental. They want to account for changes in output by changes in the various inputs, to the extent that they can. "Account for" is perhaps more descriptive than "explain." Economists wish to account for changes in output by changes in input much as one would account for changes in the area of a rectangle by changes in the lengths of its sides. The differences are, first, that we have no prior definitional relation between output and inputs as we have between the area of a rectangle and the lengths of its sides; and, second, that we do not even know that changes in output can be accounted for completely by changes in inputs, and indeed we suspect the reverse. (I will discuss the relationship between inputs and outputs further in the next section.)

In order to perform this accounting, it is necessary to know something about the historical time paths of what economists call the "marginal products" of the factors of production. The marginal product of labor is defined as the amount produced by the last (marginal) worker. Employers in competitive markets maximize profits by hiring workers until the workers' marginal product equals the wage. We need answers—approximate answers—to questions like this: In such and such a year, if employment had been higher (or lower) by 1,000 average workers and everything else had been the same, how much higher (or lower) would output have been? It is plain that such questions can have only rough answers, if they have answers at all. How are "average workers" defined? Are we to imagine them appearing or disappearing in Rome, in Alexandria, or all over the Roman Empire in proportion to the existing supply of labor? Is everything else to be unchanged—even the stock of houses, which after all are capital goods? Some such estimates have to be produced if any analytical connection is to be made between the growth of inputs and the growth of output.

Some ancient historians will resist this idea and abandon the enterprise of thinking about the causes of economic growth in the ancient world. But while markets in the ancient world could not have operated with the same efficiency as modern markets, there is no reason to throw the baby out with the bath water. If ancient historians are willing to entertain a "modernist" view of the ancient economy, then all is not lost. We can talk of prices as representing value even if prices varied quite sharply across geographical areas. This helps us construct a national product, as discussed already. If we seek to explain any economic growth, we have to acknowledge there were markets for labor as well as for goods. For only if there was a market in which workers were free to seek the best jobs—within reason—and if wages were paid that reflected the value of their work, can we say even approximately that the marginal product of labor was uniform enough to speak of it as a single value. In chapter 5 I argued that these conditions existed in the early Roman Empire; others will have to see if this description fits other times and places in the ancient world as well.

It is hard to know whether it is better to look at regions and cities by themselves or to estimate production for the whole Roman Empire. Hopkins (1995–96) argued that consideration of the whole empire would be more accurate than local estimates, but this only is true if the errors we make in any one region are independent of those in other regions—which is very doubtful. Local estimates also can make use of local information. Yet the allure of an estimate for the whole empire may be more than anyone reasonably can resist. Maddison (2007) built up an empire estimate from estimates of provincial incomes.

If the marginal product of a factor is known or knowable, then knowing it is almost equivalent to knowing a slightly more convenient quantity, the "elasticity of output with respect to a particular factor of production," a kind of proportional marginal product. It answers in principle the question: In such and such a year, if employment had been higher (or lower) by x percent and everything else had been the same, what percentage increase (or decrease) in output would have been registered? These elasticities are natural concepts in the kind of accounting that we are trying to do. To be precise, over some interval of time, the appropriate measure of the contribution of a particular input to the average annual rate of growth of output is given by the product of the average annual rate of growth of the input and the elasticity of output with respect to that input. To ask whether the growth of productive inputs "explains" the growth of output is simply to ask whether the sum of such products is equal to the rate of growth of output itself. Following Domar (1961), the excess of the rate of growth of output over the sum of these products—if it exists—is called the Residual.

It is easy to provide definitions of the three traditional factors of production—land, labor, and capital—but hard to translate these definitions into workable rules for use. There are many factors of production, and this triad represents only a particular way of separating these myriad factors into distinct groups for analysis. The first problem is how to determine where any particular factor belongs.

"Land" consists of the sum of all natural resources possessed by an economy, that is, those earning assets not created by man. "Labor" includes that part of the population able and willing to contribute to economic production. And "capital" is the sum of earning assets created by man; it is often called "reproducible capital" to distinguish it from land ("nonreproducible capital").

Farms and other business units of the economy employ the services of these three factors to produce goods and services. The definitions have been given in terms of the stock of the three factors, that is, the amount of the factors available to the economy, but the entire stock of land, labor, and capital is not used to produce goods and services in any one year; the services of these factors are used instead. In addition to defining the stock of these factors, therefore, we must provide a means for evaluating the input of each factor to production.

I begin with labor. Labor differs from the other two traditional factors of production in at least one important way. People can improve their level of well-being by working to increase their income—their ability to purchase goods and services produced by others—and they can also increase their well-being by abstaining from work. The alternative to using land or capital is to let them stand idle, which does not increase anyone's happiness. The alternative to working is leisure, which provides pleasure directly to the workers involved.

The market for labor, therefore, is unlike the market for other factors of production. Competing against the various productive uses of labor is the additional demand for time for leisure. In general, when the price of a commodity rises, it becomes profitable for firms to substitute the production of the now higher-priced commodity for other production (or at least it never becomes profitable to switch the other way). When the price of labor rises, this effect is present: workers are inclined to substitute labor for leisure, as they can buy more of the goods they desire for a given quantity of work. However, there is also another influence at work. A higher wage means that a man doing the same amount of work as before has a higher income than before. He may want to spend this income on goods he can buy, but he may also wish to consume all or part of it in increased leisure. A rise in wages therefore may actually decrease the amount of labor supplied, if what we may call the "income effect" increasing the desire for leisure offsets the "substitution effect" by which labor is made more attractive. In this case, economists talk of a "backward-bending" supply curve of labor, because the quantity of labor supplied falls as the price rises. A backward bending supply curve can be an obstacle to economic growth, for increases in the productivity of workers can be offset by declines in the amount of labor supplied. This is an obstacle that cannot be present with either of the other factors; it is a historical question whether it was present for labor.

The historical question is compounded because the distinction between work and leisure is itself comparatively modern. Religious ritual appears as a leisure-time activity in modern life, but it was far more serious in premodern society. It is doubtful whether men who believed in the active intervention of supernatural beings in human affairs viewed religious observances as recreation. Similarly, the domestic worker producing cloth or other articles would have been hard pressed to say when the "productive" activity stopped and the duties of being a housewife or the recreation of sitting and talking began.

The process of fixing a work week is distinct from the process of varying it—they may involve entirely different forces and have quite dissimilar effects on production. Voth (2000, 2001) argued that estimates of the labor force taken from population date are misleading for the time of the Industrial Revolution. Based on the accounts of witnesses to crimes who had to state what they were doing at the time, he estimates that the hours of work rose in the late eighteenth century, producing an "industrious revolution."

Let us start the discussion of how to measure the services of labor by considering the services of a single worker, or alternatively a set of identical workers. The simplest index of labor services is the size of the labor force. This index often is the only one permitted by the data. In fact, the labor force itself often is not observed but instead derived from demographic data by assuming stable participation rates, that is, the shares of a demographic cohort that works for some kind of compensation, either for the population as a whole or for groups within the population. As the limitations of the data will remain severe, this measure will continue to be used. But let us ask, as with the measure of the national product, what is being measured.

To count the number of people who can work is to measure the potential labor input rather than the actual input: no account is taken of unemployment. It is virtually impossible to find reliable data on unemployment before the twentieth century, and no correction for unemployment is possible. It is even harder to know how many hours a day, week, or year were employed in productive work. Consequently, the measure of potential input that we use does not quite match a measure of actual output. If output is estimated by using data on capacity, as is common in many studies of the ancient world, the two measures do match.

The discussion so far has treated the problem of a homogeneous labor supply, whether composed of a solitary worker or of many identical laborers. Consider now the problem of diverse workers. The labor force will no longer be an adequate index of labor services because it does not show changes in the quality of labor. There are many ways in which workers differ from one another; we must ask if these differences are likely to change the rate of growth of the labor force and, if so, how to adjust our data. This is the same problem that Laspeyres and Paasche dealt with from prices.

Workers differ in intelligence, but in the absence of any evidence or reason to the contrary, we may assume that the distribution of intelligence among people remains constant over time. When the size of the labor force increases, the quantity of intelligent and of less intelligent people rises in proportion to the labor force. Similarly, although intelligent people can be expected to earn more than less intelligent ones, the distribution of salaries based on intelligence alone may be expected to remain constant, and the changes of any one wage can be used as an index of the movements of all wages. Therefore, we do not have to take explicit account of differences in intelligence among workers.

Second, workers differ in the skills they possess. (I include here both skills learned on the job and those that are the results of formal education.) If these skills were purely the product of experience, if everyone acquired them as he or she aged, and if the age composition of the work force remained constant, then job skills could be treated in exactly the same way as intelligence. There would always be a pool of job skills, and this pool would increase with the size of the labor force: no specific account would need to be taken of it. Although everyone does not acquire skills at the same rate, we could assume that aptitudes are constant and ignore these differences as we have ignored differences in intelligence. If the age structure changes, a simple correction could be made.

There also can be changes in the character of the labor force coming from changes in the nature of the labor market. For example, there are many barriers to labor mobility. A worker may have to travel to find the best job, and he may be unwilling or unable to do so. He may refuse to leave a traditional occupation for one he is more suited for. He may not be able to enter into the social class that is needed to fill a job he could otherwise ably perform. As a result, the labor force may not be used to its fullest capacity. If the relationship between the actual productivity of the labor force and its perfect-market potential remained constant, we would not have to worry about it; like differences in intelligence, it would remain internal to the analysis. On the other hand, if the geographical and occupation mobility of labor increased—as it did during the years before the Roman Empire—then there would be an increase in labor services in addition to the growth in the size of the labor force.

In general, there is no need to take account of the characteristics of the labor force that stay constant over time. Changes in the services of labor supplied are important to account for changes in output, and if all components of a disparate aggregate move together, we can use any one component as an index of change. On the other hand, if different components are changing at different rates, then there is an index-number problem exactly analogous to the problem in measuring the national product. Of course, it is necessary to determine the nature and identify the causes of the differences between workers to tell which is which. The historian has to decide in each case if an attribute is inborn and immutable—and will therefore vary with the size of the labor force as a whole—or is the result of changing circumstance—and will change at a rate all its own.

These problems pale to insignificance compared to the complexity of valuing the services of capital and land. There is a naive measure of labor services in the labor force. There are many difficulties with this naive index, and we try to improve on it; but it represents a fairly advanced starting point. We do not have this advantage when we discuss reproducible and nonreproducible capital, and we must start from scratch.

Let us first distinguish the two kinds of capital from intermediate goods. I stated above that goods and services produced or bought by farms or other business entities were intermediate goods. I now amend that definition to say that the goods and services that are used up within one year are intermediate goods. Goods or services that last longer than a year are to be considered to be capital, included with "capital" or with land depending on whether or not they are reproducible. Wheat bought by a mine is an intermediate product, but the mine itself is capital because it lasts more than a year.

The distinction is important. National product is measured on a yearly basis, and it should treat all years symmetrically. A Roman legion typically used most of the wheat it bought within a year, and it was left at the start of the next year in the same position that it was at the start of this year. On the other hand, a legion that built roads in one year had them on hand in the next. Rome was better off at the start of the second year than at the start of the first, and if we classified roads as an intermediate good we would observe an unexplained increase in the production of military services. To avoid this, we classify Roman roads as capital, and only their depreciation, that is, the amount by which they are used up, is subtracted from output to get value added. The undepreciated portion of the roads should be carried over from one year to the next as capital, and the excess of the production of capital over its depreciation is defined as investment and is added to consumption to give national income or product.

This discussion points to two ways of formulating a measure of the reproducible capital stock. We could add together all the undepreciated capital existing in the economy at any one time; or we could add together the investments from past years, discounting them to allow for the intervening depreciation. The two measures are conceptually the same; the problem—as always—is that prices change. The cost of building a road undoubtedly fell over time as the Romans perfected that long-lasting asset we know as a Roman road. At which price should we value the road?

As noted earlier, there is no universal answer to this question. Instead I turn to a qualitative distinction that can be made between different kinds of capital formation. As the size of the labor force—measured by one of the methods already discussed—changes, the size of the capital stock must change in order to keep constant the ratio of capital to labor. Capital formation that accompanies a rise in the labor force and serves only to maintain the existing capital-labor ratio is called "capital widening." On the other hand, capital formation that increases the ratio of capital to labor is called "capital deepening." Capital deepening can take place whether or not the labor force is increasing, and capital widening and deepening can take place simultaneously.

I suggested that a rise in the national product is a hallmark of economic growth. It is reasonable to go further and to say that a rise in the national product per capita should be the appropriate measure. This measure has the disadvantage of ignoring any increases in the population caused by economic progress, but it has the advantage of focusing attention on the increase in a typical individual's ability to consume. And if it is used, the distinction between capital widening and capital deepening is very important. In an economy with a growing labor force, some investment is required simply to maintain the existing output per capita—by maintaining the existing capital per worker—and investment to increase the output per capita must be in addition to this capital widening. A given amount of investment, therefore, will cause a smaller increase in the national income per head in a country with a rapidly growing population than in one with a less rapidly growing or stable population. Even if we cannot discover the exact rate at which the capital stock grew, therefore, it is often illuminating to know how capital formation was divided between capital widening and capital deepening.

This discussion assumes that population growth was determined separately from economic growth. Labor was an input whose size was determined previously, like capital and land. If, however, the effect of economic growth on the rate of population growth was important, then there is a more complex interaction. For example, a strict Malthusian model implies that economic growth results in a growing population rather than an increase in per capita income. I will return to this issue in more detail after discussing theories of economic growth that have been developed for non-Malthusian economies and again in chapter 10.

Let us turn our attention now to the remaining factor of production: land, by which I mean raw materials or "nonreproducible capital." Countries differ in their endowments of natural resources, and it is appropriate to take account of this fact in the explanation of economic production. But the problems of measurement encountered in the discussion of labor and capital are as nothing when compared with the difficulty of measuring raw materials. As with capital, there is no naive measure of land similar to the labor force for labor. But unlike capital, natural resources were not produced and are not reproducible, and there consequently is no easy way to value them or the cost of their production.

The crudest measure—but by the same token the easiest to use—is the area of a country, or alternatively its population density. This measure assumes that resources are spread evenly over the earth and is consequently of little help except in extreme cases, such as a comparison of nineteenth-century England and America. The quantity of one particular resource, like arable land or silver, is an alternative measure, but it is too restrictive a measure for use in any but specific, narrowly defined inquiries. And if we say that the sum of several different resources should be used, we are faced with the index-number problem deriving from the different valuation of different resources over time.

Some function of exports can also be used as an index of resource endowments. Countries tend to export the products whose production depends on the utilization of resources they possess in relative abundance, and the ratio of exports to the national product gives an index of the resource endowment. Nonetheless, the measure is seriously flawed. The United States today obviously is well endowed with natural resources, yet its exports are much smaller in relation to its national product than the exports of many less well-endowed but smaller countries. British foreign trade was large in the nineteenth century as a result of Britain's free-trade policy. And all exports fell in the 1930s, even though the world was not deprived of its natural resources in the depression in world trade. The size of a country, the nature of its mercantile policies, and the state of international affairs—as well as natural-resource endowments—affect the volume of a country's exports. Nevertheless, a better index of resource endowments is hard to find. Resources can be depleted, for example, by clearing forests that prevented soil erosion. This kind of capital consumption is not counted even in modern estimates of national products.

Suppose that, somehow, estimates are constructed of the rates of growth of real output and of the employment of the main factors of production. Without those estimates there is no possibility of even posing the quantitative question about the extent to which the growth of inputs accounts for the growth of output. Even with them, the calculation of an answer requires another ingredient as explained earlier, the marginal products or output-elasticities of each of the inputs, or at least their average values during the period of time in question. These elasticities have a status quite different from that of the rates of growth. They are not at all directly observable quantities and must be inferred.

The indirect approach to the estimation of marginal products and output-input elasticities rests on the proposition from economic theory that, under competitive market conditions, the return to a unit of each factor of production (measured in units of output) will approximate its marginal product. This is equivalent to saying that the fractional share of the return to a factor of production in the distribution of the output it has helped to produce will be an estimate of the elasticity of output with respect to that factor. This is a very strong argument, and it depends on the existence of competition. There is no reason to argue that competition was as fierce in the ancient world as today, only that it was pervasive enough to bring wages close to the marginal product of labor. Only in this "modernist" view of the ancient world does it make sense to use modern growth theory to understand and explain ancient economic growth.

The great advantage of this approach is that it requires only data on factor returns—wage rates, rents, profits—or the proportional distribution of the product of the economy or industry among the various inputs. This sort of information may be available even in the absence of usable data on the quantities of inputs and outputs. The disadvantage of the indirect approach is that its validity depends on strong assumptions: that the markets for land, labor, and capital are approximately competitive, and that they are approximately in equilibrium (that is, that factor returns do not differ from marginal products as a signal that the organization of production is in the process of adapting to change). These assumptions are not easy to swallow in ordinary times; they may be misleading in ancient times. If that is so, the data themselves may provide a warning by moving sharply or systematically. Suitably checked, this is probably the only way that the accounting exercise can be done, if it can be done at all. Antras and Voth (2003) used this indirect approach to check the validity of more standard estimates of economic growth during the Industrial Revolution.

Growth theory as a branch of economics tries to explain the relation of economic growth, defined as growth in the economy's production of goods and services, to the growth of inputs to growth, such as labor, capital and land. Old growth theory, also known as the Solow growth model, introduced a way to conceptualize the process of economic growth. Solow (1956) saw economic growth, that is, growth in the national product, as the result of combining a few aggregate inputs to production. These were labeled labor and capital. Labor consists of work efforts by workers in the economy. Capital consists of durable tools, machinery, and buildings that were produced by people some time in the past. As discussed in the previous section, it is much harder to know how to combine different kinds of capital in an aggregate measure than to combine the labor from different workers.

The Solow model has proved to be an extraordinarily useful way to describe the process of economic growth, but it had, as innovations often do, several drawbacks that cried for further improvement. The first and most important is that the long-run rate of growth was limited by the growth rate of population. The investment rate affected the rate of growth in the short run, but only the level of income in the long run. And these two factors were the only factors affecting growth.

Solow (1957) acknowledged the first problem and provided an ad hoc way to deal with it. The rate of growth of developed economies typically exceeded that of population. This gap was given a label, the growth of labor productivity. Solow expanded this concept to calculate what he called total factor productivity (TFP), and he added it to the analysis as another determinant of growth. Domar (1961) originally called it the Residual, and this terminology reminds us that TFP is a mysterious magnitude. TFP actually is the difference between the growth rate of economic output and the growth rates of its inputs, both labor and capital. That is why it is spoken of as total factor productivity, as opposed to labor productivity.

Solow's framework nevertheless provided a way to organize historical data on economic growth. Population, investment, and TFP could be listed as determinants of growth, and "growth accounting" was born. This proved to be an enormously illuminating way to summarize a vast body of knowledge and begin the process of explaining economic growth (Denison 1967; Abramovitz and David 1973). It is worth noting that this whole effort was dependent on Kuznets's pioneering work during the Great Depression measuring these economic magnitudes for the first time, summarized in Kuznets (1971).

A second problem with Solow's growth model was that it did not include any other variables. It therefore could not account for the wide differences between countries that we observe today. It also predicted that all countries would converge to the same rate of growth; different *levels* of income would reflect different rates of capital accumulation. This limitation led people to lump all other differences between countries into TFP and provide explanations outside the theory why they differed.

A third problem followed from the second. Poorer countries today are poorer according to this theory because they have less capital. The scarcity of capital in these poor countries should have generated a high rate of interest that would have attracted massive capital imports from richer countries to earn these rates and finance rapid economic growth. But we observe neither unusually high rates of interest in poor countries nor massive flows of capital from rich to poor countries.

These limitations of the Solow growth model have been relaxed in turn, giving rise to what has become known as new growth theory. Romer (1986) dealt with the first problem. He argued that TFP growth was endogenous, not exogenous, that is, determined within the growth model, not given from outside. It was generated as an externality by capital investment. The diminishing returns to investment used by Solow to find an equilibrium were private returns. Romer added a social return that did not threaten the stability of the model and which allowed income to grow faster than population in the long run. This incorporated TFP into the model, but it did not deal with the diversity of nations.

Lucas (1988) took aim at the second problem. He introduced human capital, that is, learning and skills produced by education, to the model as an additional determinant of growth. This already had been done informally in growth accounting and in economic history, but it had not been incorporated into the growth model (Easterlin 1981). Differences in education between countries then eliminated the prediction of unconditional convergence (that is, convergence to the same rate of growth by all countries), although these still left room for conditional convergence ("convergence clubs") in countries with similar education levels. The wide differences between countries now could be explained within the model by differences in educational attainment.

The third problem, the absence of high interest rates and massive capital inflows in poor countries, was confronted in a variety of ways. The difference in human capital noted by Lucas implies that the rate of return to physical capital would not differ between countries as much as in the Solow model. It was not the scarcity of physical capital that made poor countries poor, but the lack of education. More generally, international capital markets may not be able to support the capital flows predicted by the growth models. Human capital does not provide good collateral for loans; laws in poor countries may not provide security for other types of loans as well. In addition, poor countries may not be able to absorb massive additions of capital. Interest rates in poor countries may be limited by diminishing returns in the short run, even though the long-run return could be high.

These elements have been combined into the portmanteau of "social capital." This concept was introduced by Putnam (1993) and has been applied to many contexts. It refers variously to the quality of government and to civic attitudes of the population. Hall and Jones (1999) used a measure of social capital to add to the influence of education in the explanation of economic growth. They argued that education and social capital could be measured separately and had cumulative effects on growth. Social capital includes the way in which government functioned. A government that promotes peace, property rights, clear rules for commercial activity, and price stability, also encourages growth. Hopkins argued that this was the key to growth in the early Roman Empire; Easterly (2001) has argued that it is true for less-developed countries today.

New growth theories therefore provided extensions to get around the limitations of Solow's "old" growth theory, but they came at the expense of Solow's simplicity and elegance. The result was a bewildering array of new models and putative inputs to growth. Empirical investigations flowered; "growth regressions" proliferated like weeds. DeLong and Summers (1991) argued that policies determining the relative price of machinery were a prime determinant of growth. Sachs and Warner (1995) argued that openness to the world economy was a determinant of growth that was strong enough to be virtually the only determinant of growth. Acemoglu, Johnson, and Robinson (2001) argued that the legacies of colonial occupations could be good or bad for growth, depending on the health of European colonists in the seventeenth and eighteenth centuries.

The lesson for ancient history is that there are many models of economic growth being used by economists today. The tasks for ancient historians are to discover which ones—if any—are relevant to the ancient world and how one might estimate the data used in the models. The common thread running through the models of the new growth theory is the importance of knowledge and organizations to economic growth. I will discuss their role in the ancient world in more detail after considering the role of population growth in any economic growth there might have been in the ancient world.

The modern theory of economic growth emphasizes the growth of per capita income because it takes the size of the population as given. This approach may not be the best one for ancient history because a greater production might lead to a larger population instead of higher per capita income. Two hundred years ago, Thomas Malthus assured his readers that this was the inevitable result of progress. If he was right, then the size of the population is a better index of economic growth than the growth of per capita income. Economists have used this insight in several studies.

Kremer (1993) used new growth theory to explain the growth of population for the past million years. He adapted the theory just described to formulate a model in which there was what economists call linear growth. The growth of knowledge increases in such a model in proportion to the size of the population. Kremer assumed also that rising production would result in faster population growth rather than rising per capita production, and this Malthusian assumption enabled him to use population growth as an index of output, avoiding many of the measurement problems described earlier. He found that his model worked very well for all but the last half-century.

DeLong and Shleifer (1993) used a similar underlying model in their empirical description of city growth in early modern Europe. They tested for the importance of social capital as reflected in the form of city government. Absolute monarchies, they asserted, were less conducive to growth then more democratic governments. They tested this proposition by comparing the rate of population growth in different cities. Population growth, of course, was their index of increasing productive capacity. They found that their presumption indeed was correct.

As a first approximation, the same approach appears useful for ancient history. Accepting the Malthusian argument that almost all people will stay at subsistence levels of income, increasing economic productivity could lead only to population growth. This means that we can substitute demographic information for economic. There is no need to gather prices, assume that markets worked well, or evaluate the marginal product of labor. The distinction between capital deepening and widening remains relevant, however. For the Malthusian process was not in the mind of ancient producers. They may have desired to promote capital deepening, even though the dynamics of population growth led only in capital widening.

There are several problems with this approach. The first is that population data are almost as scarce as most other data for ancient times. Scheidel (2001) argued that our supposed knowledge of ancient populations is only a set of guesses that have been accepted in the literature. This may be right; we may not know the size of the imperial population. We may be able to learn about its rate of growth, which is what we need to evaluate economic growth. Settlement studies, for example, have been used to show where settlement and farming was expanding in ancient times (Alcock 1993; Cherry, Davis, and Mantzourani 1991). Such an expansion might be a good proxy for population growth.

The second problem is that the population, like the labor force, often is not homogeneous. In the ancient world, there were at least two classes: the literate elite about whom we know a great deal and the hoi polloi about whom we know only a limited amount. It is possible that only the ordinary people, mostly farmers, farm workers of various sorts, and their dependants, were subject to Malthusian constraints. The elite may have been sustained by means other than population change, and their fortunes may have been determined by other factors. It is possible that the elite's income was rising while that of subsistence farmers was not. If, for example, the overall population—that is, the population subject to taxation by the elite—was rising, and there was a roughly constant tax rate, then the income of the elite as a whole could have risen. The division of the spoils within the elite would have been determined by its internal structure (Tainter 1988).

There are implications of this view that are subject to test, although the data may not exist to test all of them. There is the matter of a rising population, as discussed under the first problem. In addition, the size of the elite needs to be restricted for this model to be valid. There may have been rules, such as primogeniture in early modern England, that can be used as evidence of limited elite membership. There also may have been downward mobility if the size of the elite grew more slowly than the population as a whole. Hopkins (1980) assumed that the tax rate was constant in his proposed model of the Roman economy, but that the elite monopolized the spoils of war. Evidence on the overall tax rate—which includes all exactions by the elite, not simply those labeled as taxes—appears scarce. And, of course, any direct observation of the income of the elite involves all the problems discussed earlier.

The third problem with population as an index of economic growth is that subsistence is a sociological construct, not a biological one. Hopkins (1980) assumed that Roman subsistence was just like subsistence in modern less-developed countries. That is, to assume the level of Roman GDP, not to calculate it. The wretched poor may always be with us, but they are not always the same. The resources that signal the right to marry, for example, are not the same in different societies. It follows that the incomes of the poor may not have been constant over long periods of time. There may have been drift in the subsistence level as culture changed. Even if subjected to a Malthusian constraint on raising income at any one time, the income of the poor may have changed slowly over time.

Just such a development took place in early modern England. Allen (2001) showed that real wages, that is, wages divided by the cost of living, of workers in London and Amsterdam rose in the three centuries before the Industrial Revolution, from 1500 to 1800, relative to those in other European cities. This was a period when most investigators believe Europe was subject to Malthusian constraints. There is no sense that English workers were limiting their family size in order to live better or educate the children they had. Yet their incomes appear to have risen relative to those in other similar countries. The interaction between productivity, population growth, and Malthusian subsistence is still unclear.

One way to rationalize this observation is to assume that Malthusian processes operated over a very long time. When conditions improved and per capita consumption rose, it took a long time for population to rise. Wrigley and Schofield (1981) argued in their classic history of English demography that just such a process explained fluctuations in income levels over the course of centuries. The result was that English (and Dutch) urban workers in the eighteenth century could be better off than their ancestors had been and also than their contemporaries in other European cities (Allen 2001). If it took decades to adjust marriage patterns and birth rates in the early modern period, it might have taken even longer for ancient populations to adjust to altered living conditions.

Not only were wages higher in Britain, it also was more urbanized than other European countries—excepting again the Dutch. More urban people meant more need for food to be sent from the agricultural sector to the cities. This food in turn must have been produced by greater efficiency to support so many more people. This is a long chain of reasoning, but it was used to generate GDP figures for the United States in the early nineteenth century, before the Census Bureau started collecting economic data (David 1967). Perhaps the growth of urban places under the Romans can be used as well to estimate economic growth. I discuss these issues further in chapter 10 with the aid of a formal Malthusian model.

There were periods of stability lasting for centuries in the ancient world. There could have been drift in the subsistence level of people during those times. It accordingly makes sense to try to evaluate changes in the standard of living in ancient times, and this task involves all the problems outlined earlier in measuring national output. To construct a real wage, one must have a cost of living. To examine consumption patterns, one must deflate the consumption bundles of different times. In all cases, the problem of which prices to use is the same for ancient and modern history.

Pottery can be used as an index of consumption levels, although it is hardly the same as an index of living standards or wages. Nonetheless, the accumulation of "consumer durables" like good pottery is a mark of rising income. This is a good index for ancient economies because pottery shards are very common. If archaeologists find high-quality pottery in households of even ordinary people, that suggests a relatively high income level in the economy as a whole (Ward-Perkins 2005).

Archaeological evidence of production techniques also are valuable, but not as close to an actual measure of economic growth. New growth theory emphasizes the role of productivity growth as an input to economic growth. It is hard to use the evidence on productivity to calculate a rate for economic growth, but a positive rate of productivity growth suggests strongly that there was economic growth in ancient economies.

Greene (2000) argued that Roman agricultural techniques improved markedly under the republic and early empire. New farming techniques fit into the general class of increasing knowledge in the new growth theory. It is reasonable to infer from changes in farm productivity to a rise in total income. Wilson (2002) extended this argument by examining productivity change in a variety of widespread economic activities such as farming, grain milling, and mining. Milling and mining were smaller parts of the Roman economy than agriculture, but the pervasive sense of productivity change supports the hypothesis of economic growth in the later republic and early empire. This evidence suggests that any gains in productivity were not one-time effects of a single innovation, but rather that new improvements in productive techniques were being made throughout the Roman economy.

Wilson (2006) summarized the economic impact of these and other changes for the increase and subsequent decrease of Roman incomes. Starting from the great Roman constructions whose remains we still see today, Wilson analyzed the component parts of these edifices, particularly concrete and brick. The large market for buildings, for both public and private purposes, created incentives for people to improve on building techniques. These techniques were not used widely before the Romans, and that suggests strongly the existence of economic growth. They also fell into disuse in Europe after the demise of the western Empire, giving evidence of economic decline.

These advances were made possible by the extension of peace and law. The growth of Roman power led to the imposition of Roman law over wider and wider areas. Communication, transportation, and a framework for absentee ownership and business spread throughout the early Roman Empire (Johnston 1999; Malmendier 2009). This development fits into the class of social capital in the new growth theory. It suggests that conditions were ripe for economic growth.

The Pax Romana extended around the Mediterranean and allowed trade and commerce to move freely. These underlying conditions lowered the costs of transporting and arranging for sale or distribution of products, allowing ordinary products, like food and pottery, to be grown or made one place and consumed another. These advances encouraged urban growth was well as regional specialization. This division of effort then encouraged technical change and generally improved the national product. It cannot tell us how fast the rate of economic growth was.

The developments of technology and of law were conducive to economic growth, but they are not direct estimates of growth. It would be good to have confirmation of growth, whether from consumption patterns or population growth, in addition to evidence on productive techniques. Evidence on the spread of new machinery or techniques strongly suggests the existence of economic growth, and it may well be one of the most promising topics to pursue.

Several conclusions emerge from this discussion. First, there are lots of economic assumptions in any estimate of economic growth. For the old, Solow growth theory, these assumptions are about the existence of functioning competitive markets. The new growth theory adds assumptions about the operation of knowledge and social capital in economic growth. All of these assumptions are problematical for ancient history, but they are integral to any estimate of economic growth. Just as one cannot make an omelet without breaking eggs, one cannot estimate economic growth without making a lot of economic assumptions.

Second, we are just at the beginning of any measurement of ancient economic growth. Far more evidence will need to be gathered to make a reasonable estimate of growth. It may seem chimerical to expose all the problems at this early stage, but that is backward. Questions are answered only if they are asked. Posing the questions of measurement properly directs the attention of ancient historians to the kind of information needed to estimate economic growth. It is the first step along a long—but potentially very rewarding—road.

Third, there is no reason to accept the statement quoted at the start of this essay as fact. There might well have been sustained economic growth in ancient times. It seems unlikely that there was growth at modern high rates, but there may have been rates comparable or better than those found in other agrarian economies. Economists have found that political stability, stable laws, cheap transportation, and widespread education promote economic growth in the modern world. Why not in the ancient world? Perhaps the statement quoted at the start of this paper will be modified to read: "The characteristic which distinguishes the modern period in world history from all past periods is the *rapidity* of economic growth."

To evaluate this claim for the ancient world, a simple Malthusian model—presented in chapter 10—helps to clarify the problems of ancient economic growth.

Chapter 10

■ ■ ■

Economic Growth in a Malthusian Empire

There is growing evidence that ordinary Romans lived well in the early Roman Empire. The existence of many cities, and particularly the large size of Rome itself, provides indirect evidence of productivity advance. More detailed evidence is emerging of improving agricultural technology, building techniques, manufacturing plants, and land use. The widespread use of African Red Slipware pottery provides evidence that even ordinary people had access to the fruits of all this technology. And the literary evidence supports the idea of prosperity by providing insights into civilized urban lives in Roman cities. As explained in chapter 9, these are all proxies for economic growth. They are not measures, but they are suggestive. How could per capita income grow in a Malthusian economy? This chapter resolves the apparent paradox of economic growth in a Malthusian world.

Even if this evidence of an improvement in general living standards is not yet convincing to everyone, there by now is enough evidence to raise the possibility that such a movement might have taken place. In the spirit of Morley's (2001) essay on the implication of a large Roman population, this chapter offers a way to understand rising per capita incomes in Rome as the accumulating evidence becomes persuasive.

It seems paradoxical that we have evidence of a rise in per capita income when we face so much uncertainty about the size of the population whose income is growing. This is only partly a matter of evidence; it also is a result of our theories. We assume that the scattered evidence of living standards can be generalized to larger groups because we implicitly or explicitly assume that people lived at roughly the same level. This does not mean that we ignore class divisions in Rome, but that we compare the lives of ordinary Romans with their predecessors. We assume this similarity of income for working families because we assume there was a labor market that brought wages into some kind of rough correspondence. I argued in chapter 6 both that we need to

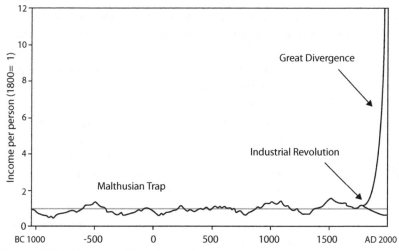

FIGURE 10.1. World economic history in one picture
Source: Clark (2007a, 2)

make such an assumption to make sense of a lot of the modern literature on ancient Rome and that this assumption is an accurate one in the early Roman Empire.

The problem with theories is that there are lots of them. We use the theory of competition between workers to support the idea that living conditions improved in the later republic and early empire, but the Malthusian theory of population change argues that our observations must be false. In that theory, changes in productivity lead to changes in the size of the population (which we cannot observe) and leave the level of per capita income (which we do observe however imperfectly) the same. The implications of this theory can be seen in figure 10.1, taken from a new economic history of the world. The level of per capita income is assumed to be roughly constant before the Industrial Revolution. Saller published a more abstract version of this graph making the assumption of constant per capita income before the Industrial Revolution more apparent. He did not allow for the fluctuations around this level indicated in figure 10.1 (Clark 2007a, chapter 1; Saller 2005). This figure has just reemerged in a new book about a "unified theory" of economic growth (Galor 2011).

The view in figure 10.1 is too reductionist for the analysis of the Roman economy. From the twenty-first century, events before 1800 appear to merge together, and it is useful to summarize them in a simple way. This tendency leads historians to interpret the Malthusian model very strictly, but there are important delays in the Malthusian system. These dynamics are integral to the Malthusian model, and historical evidence from other periods indicate that the delays can be exceedingly long—on the order of centuries rather than decades. These dynamics provide a way to acknowledge growing per capita income in the basically Malthusian world of the early Roman Empire. It also provides a way to ask if the Romans could have escaped—in some alternate history—the Malthusian constraints.

I start this argument by reviewing the evidence that per capita income was high and that it fell as the Roman Empire disintegrated. I then explain how the Malthusian model works with attention to the dynamics of how shocks affect both population size and its income over time. The model reveals how an economy could avoid the Malthusian constraints within this Malthusian model for an extended period. Breaking out—industrializing—is a different matter, and I close with some speculations about the nature of the Industrial Revolution and its relevance for Roman history.

Finley (1973) argued that the ancient economy was dominated by stagnant technology. This view became the one that historians of later periods saw when they looked back at the ancient world. In a book about the history of technology in the Western world, Mokyr (1990) spent a chapter trying to explain Roman technological stagnation.

The tide has changed in the last decade. Roman archeologists have found abundant evidence of new technologies in the Roman world, and their views are now appearing in print. Greene (2000) started the debate with a paper challenging Finley on several grounds. He argued that Finley had been misled by the literary sources; only archeology could show how technology had improved. Wilson (2008) expanded the case for a progressive Roman technology in several papers, and I follow his lead here. I discuss in turn the growth of regional specialization, the expansion of land for agricultural purposes, manufacturing, and construction.

Everyone knows about the Pax Romana. Pompey finished clearing the Mediterranean of pirates in 67 BCE and made safer transport possible. The risks before then are illustrated by the kidnapping of Caesar and its subsequent horrifying effect (Casson 1991, 181–83). The usual interest in this story is Caesar's insolence toward his captors and his subsequent revenge. I emphasize here the risk of capture that is the premise of the story. As North (1968) argued in a paper cited by the Nobel Committee in awarding him the Nobel Prize in economics, reducing the cost of defending against pirates lowers the cost of shipping.

A lower cost of shipping allowed production to be located around the Mediterranean where conditions were most suitable. Instead of growing wheat in Italy, inhabitants of Rome ate porridge and bread made from wheat grown in Sicily, Egypt, Africa, Spain, and other places. Production was scattered because it was more efficient to grow wheat in these places than in Italy. Romans did not calculate what we call efficiency; instead they purchased wheat where it was cheapest. It was cheapest in places where grain agriculture was the best use of land and labor resources (Erdkamp 2005, chapters 2, 5; Rathbone 2009, 322).

The gain to both the exporting and importing regions was shown by Ricardo in his theory of comparative advantage and explained in chapter 1. Trade that allows regions to specialize in what they produce best increases the income of both sending and receiving regions. Trade functions like an extension of resources in any one region; it loosens the constraint of limited land in an agricultural economy. One effect of Roman regional specialization was the shift in Italian farms from wheat to other crops that did not travel as well (Morley 1996; Geraghty 2007).

Roman roads performed a similar service to the economy. They were less important than a peaceful sea because overland transportation was much more expensive than water-borne transport. In addition, the roads were built for military reasons; any commercial use was incidental. The roads nevertheless made it easier for goods to get around. They promoted local specialization similar to the broad patterns just described. They also allowed goods brought from far away to reach consumers living away from seaports. Shipping and roads therefore both promoted a better life for Roman citizens.

They allowed the Romans to create the urban society that was unique in the ancient world. The agricultural system—including agriculture, trade, and coordinating institutions—was efficient enough to release substantial numbers of people from the tasks of growing food. These people could gather in cities, and they could produce other goods and services. These added products improved the quality of Roman life, and they added to per capita income.

In addition to gains from regional specialization, there was technical change in each place. Mokyr (1990, 23) opened his book on technology with a chapter that criticized Finley for being too pessimistic, but he still argued that "new ideas were not altogether absent, but their diffusion and application were sporadic and slow." Recent archaeological discoveries dispute that conclusion.

Terracing was common, extending the range of land on which crops, particularly grapes and olives, could be grown. Wine and oil presses also used the screw, enabling grapes and olives grown on new land to be processed more efficiently. The Archimedean screw was used widely in cereal agriculture to drain land, extending the range of land that could be used for this crop as well. Our evidence is spotty, but recent archaeological discoveries from many different areas suggest strongly that these innovations had diffused over large ranges of the Roman Empire (Wilson forthcoming).

Everyone knows about the Roman use of arches and concrete to construct buildings, roads, and ports. Transportation helps to achieve gains from trade as well as enhancing productivity in other ways. Aqueducts are well known, but the sophistication needed to construct them seldom is noticed. In addition to the construction of the aqueducts, the level had to be adjusted for water to flow over often large distances. Only a little thought is needed to realize that the widespread evidence of aqueducts provides evidence of the diffusion of engineering knowledge around the Roman Empire.

Water wheels also were more prevalent in Roman times than previously thought: "Today, we may state with confidence that the breakthrough of the water-powered mill did not take place . . . in the early middle ages, but rather . . . in the first century A.D., or perhaps even slightly earlier" (Wikander 2008, 149). And mass-produced Roman products were prevalent: "Pottery, glassware, bricks, coins, plate, and humble metal objects such as nails were produced in enormous quantities to standard shapes and sizes, and widely traded around the Roman Mediterranean and northern Europe" (Wilson 2008, 393).

Yet the evidence of technical change is not quite the information we need. Greater production expanded the resources available to feed people, but it could have resulted in more people rather than higher per capita incomes. As noted in chapter 9, population often is used as an indication of early growth over the long run. The Roman Empire lasted for several centuries, but the time frame of the Malthusian model is even longer. The purpose of a model is to show how individual incomes could have changed in the short run.

We need evidence on the consumption of ordinary people to show that they were better off as opposed to more numerous. Any society can support an elite that lives well; richer societies can have large elites. These elites typically are too small to affect the growth of the population as a whole, although the Roman elite was quite large. We need evidence that extends beyond the literary evidence of sumptuous Roman dinner parties and feasts.

Diet is an important part of the consumption of ordinary people and therefore a good indicator of the standard of living before the modern rise of per capita incomes. The consumption of wheat was enhanced by making it into bread rather than porridge. The Roman conquest and the resulting reduction in transportation costs led to an increasing variety of diet, including a wide range of new fruits and vegetables. More important, there is evidence of greater meat consumption in both Roman Italy and the provinces. Meat, of course, is a superior good, and its consumption rises with per capita income. There were more animal bones in the early Roman Empire than in surrounding centuries, and the number of animal bones peaks again around 500 in Roman Italy. Animals were larger in this period than before or after, adding to other suggestive evidence of improved diets and higher incomes (Jongman 2007b).

Ordinary people also had consumer durables that were better than those before or after. The most prevalent was African Red Slipware, ordinary pottery that is found everywhere in Roman settlements. The pottery was wheel-thrown and highly fired, supplying a "modern" platform on which to eat. In addition to plates, ordinary people had iron knives with which to cut their food. Good Roman pottery contrasts sharply with the friable pottery found in post-Roman Britain that was neither wheel-thrown nor highly fired. The comparison shows the decline in the living standards of ordinary people after the Romans left Britain. There must have been a previous rise in per capita income for it to fall sharply thereafter (Ward-Perkins 2005).

The omnipresent oil lamp was another consumer durable of Roman times. It extended the day and enhanced the quality of life in interior spaces for many people. The assemblages of oil lamps in many museums show their spread throughout the empire and the standardization that reveals their industrial origin (Harris 1980). Like agricultural goods, industrial goods were made in centralized locations and shipped all over the Roman world.

Evidence of widespread improvements in consumption is increasing, and Roman citizens must have had increasing incomes to buy the enhanced food and consumer durables. Jongman (2007b) cited a variety of estimates showing that real wages increased in the late republic and early empire. He surveyed the occasional evidence of documented wages, subsistence annuities, and slave prices—as an index of wages of free workers with whom Roman slaves competed. The data for any one of these measures are spotty, but the pattern of all of them is the same. This common pattern suggests that the occasional observations are capturing underlying trends whose existence is attested to by the variety of evidence that fits the pattern. Real wages rose after the Antonine Plague. Labor income was the major part of total income in the agrarian society of ancient Rome, and an increase in real wages is a good index of an increase in total income.

Allen (2009a) used data from the Diocletian Price Edict of 301 to compare real wages in Rome with those in early-modern European and Asian cities. He found that the real wage calculated from the Price Edict was close to the real wage in Florence in the eighteenth century. This is impressive for an ancient society, but it also is less than real wages at the same time in London and Amsterdam and less than Florentine real wages in the century after the Black Death. Scheidel (2010) replicated Allen's estimations for Roman Egypt.

The evidence for enhanced consumption is still very sketchy, and we hope that archaeologists will broaden the evidentiary base over time. Enough evidence has been found already to indicate that ordinary Romans lived better than ordinary people before or for many centuries after. The problem is how to square these observations with the iron law of subsistence living that is part of the Malthusian model of population change.

In particular, this evidence suggests that living standards for ordinary Romans improved in the late republic, reaching a high standard for the early empire. Given the long history of the republic, this growth did not have to be rapid to result in a substantial increase in living standards. It did, however, need to be sustained over the course of a century or more. How could these innovations result in rising living standards rather than simply more people? We need to examine the Malthusian model of population dynamics to see.

Malthus argued that the size of the population was limited by the resources available to feed it. By resources, most people now mean land, understanding that the use of land and other resources may be relevant as well. This Malthusian relation is known to economists today as the declining marginal product of labor when the number of workers on a given plot of land increases. This, of course, was Ricardo's way of making the same point at approximately the same time as Malthus, and it is Ricardo's formulation that has become central to modern economics; as the number of workers rises, wages fall and rents rise (Malthus 2004).

Wages in this summary mean "real wages," that is, the purchasing power of wages as described by Allen (2009a) and Scheidel (2010). The diet of most workers near a Malthusian equilibrium consisted largely of grain in one form or another. We therefore approximate the real wage by looking at the ratio of the money wage to an index of the price of goods workers bought, weighting grain heavily in this index. If we divide money wages by the price of grain alone, we get a measure of the marginal product of labor, since farmers typically hire workers up to the point where the last (marginal) worker produces just enough grain to pay for the wages he earns (Clarke 2007b).

Ricardo's formulation shows the need for an additional relation for Malthus to find an equilibrium point on this line. Malthus did this by specifying a relation between worker's wages—taken to be their income—and their birth and death rates. Births rise with income, both as nutrition rises and as younger marriages become feasible. Death rates fall with income as infant mortality declines and plagues, wars, and pestilence become less frequent. Modern research has confirmed the first of these relations, while generally failing to find convincing evidence of the latter (Lee 1980). For most purposes, only one relation is needed, provided the other one does not operate in the reverse direction. The full Malthusian model then was taken to restrict the range of early history. Wrigley's (1988, 29) description of the world before the Industrial Revolution is clear: "An organic economy, however advanced, was subject to negative feedback in the sense that the very process of growth set in train changes that made further growth additionally difficult because of the operation of declining marginal returns in production from the land." Clark's (2007a, 27) recent description is equally clear: "Anything that reduced the death rate schedule—advances in medical technology, better personal hygiene, improved public sanitation, public provision for harvest failures, peace and order—reduced material living standards."

The preceding discussion is summarized in figure 10.2. The horizontal axis on both graphs is the same: per capita income. The top graph shows the determination of population size. Population grows if births exceed deaths; it falls if births fall short of deaths. The equilibrium is where the birth and death rates are equal, at y^*. The bottom graph shows that the resource constraint permits only a limited population size, n^*, at this income. Note that the model works well even if there is no relation between income and the death rate. If the curve marked D in the top graph is horizontal—that is, if it shows the death rate unaffected by changing income—y^* is still the equilibrium, and the analysis proceeds as before (Lee 1980; Clark 2007a, chapter 2).

Consider the effect of a plague, like the Antonine or Justinian plagues, in this model. Let us assume that the population fell by approximately one-third, without aiming for spurious precision. The effects are shown in figure 10.3. Population fell from n^* to n_1. As population fell, income rose above the previous equilibrium income, y^*, because the marginal product of labor rises as population falls. At this higher income, n_1 in figure 10.3, birth rates exceeded death rates, as shown in the upper graph. Population grew as a result. It continued to grow until income was reduced to its previous level, y^*, where births and deaths were once again equal. As can be seen in the lower graph, per capita income was unchanged at the new equilibrium, and the population returned to its former size.

How long did this process take? From the long-run point of view of figure 10.1, this may not be important, but if it took a long time to return to y^*, then per capita incomes may have been above that equilibrium level for some time. According to Solow (2007, 39), Nobel laureate in economics, "The Malthusian process works itself out slowly. The chain of causation . . . could take years or decades to complete itself." Is this accurate, or is even this casual estimate of the delays too short?

We do not have much evidence from the Roman plagues, but we know more about the aftermath of the Black Death of 1349 in England. Immediately after the plague, money wages of farm workers shot up. As I argued for the Antonine Plague in chapter 4, the immediate effect of a plague is inflation. Wages and wheat prices both rose. Yet for the Malthusian model we need to know the path of real wages, that is, the extent to which the rise in money wages exceeded the rise in the price of grain and other consumables.

Clark (2007b) provided detailed information about the progress of English real wages after the Black Death. He showed that real wages did not rise nearly as fast as money wages in the immediate aftermath of the plague. Instead they

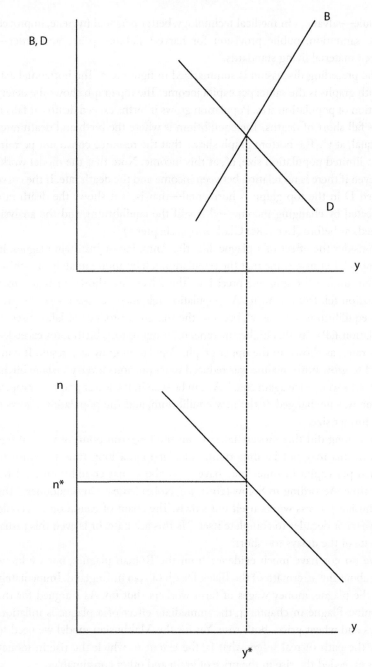

FIGURE 10.2. The basic Malthusian model

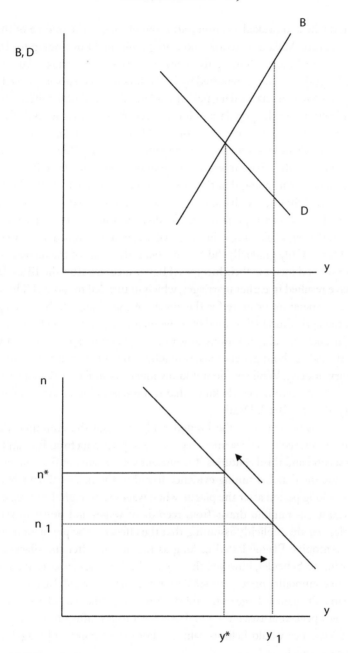

FIGURE 10.3. Effect of a plague

rose gradually and peaked a century after the plague, in the middle of the fifteenth century. Malanima (2007; 2009, 264) replicated this finding for Italian
agricultural real wages, showing that they also peaked around 1450. Allen's estimated English real wages, reported by Malanima for comparison, peaked even
later than shown in Clark's data, perhaps as late as the end of the fifteenth century. It is clear that the population did not recover to preplague levels for over
a century. It took a very long time for the Malthusian system to return to its
equilibrium. Clark was interested in the return to the equilibrium—as shown
by figure 10.1—while I am interested here in the deviations from it.

It cannot be surprising that the return to the Malthusian equilibrium took
a long time. Initially, the disruption of the plague delayed economic adjustment to the new factor proportions. As discussed in chapter 4, plagues lead
also to inflation, explaining why nominal wages rose immediately after the
Black Death. Only gradually did farmers take advantage of the increased land
per worker and increase their incomes. Higher incomes after the Black Death
may have resulted in earlier marriages, which in turn led to more children. But
it took a generation or more for the effects of this change to become apparent in the agricultural labor market. If women changed their behavior slowly,
it might take several generations to lead to population expansion. And when
we start talking about generations, it requires only a few generations to make
a century of delay. While we do not know much about family dynamics in the
late fourteenth century, we do know that real wages did not start to fall until a
century after the Black Death.

This is consistent with the limited evidence from the Antonine Plague.
Scheidel (2002) collected fragmentary wage and price data from Roman Egypt
in the second and third centuries. The ancient sources are not frequent enough
to provide the detailed timing evidence found in the medieval data, but they
suggest a long period after the plague when wages were high. If we regard the
observations as random draws from records of wages and prices in the two
centuries, we are implicitly assuming that the effects of the population decline
in the Antonine Plague lasted as long as the decline after the Black Death.
According to Scheidel, however, the rise in the real wage, that is, the ratio of
wages to commodity prices, was smaller in the ancient world. Real wages were
less than half again as large in the third century as in the second century, while
real wages peaked at twice the preplague level in the fifteenth century. More
ancient evidence would help us calibrate both the timing and magnitude of
the ancient shock.

As a matter of logic, real wages had to rise as part of the demographic process. The question for ancient history is not whether individual incomes grew,
but rather how much and for how long. Scheidel's (2010) recent estimates
of real wages in Roman Egypt fail to show any rise following the Antonine

Plague. The difference appears to come from the choice of deflator, whether wheat alone is used (to maximize the number of historical observations) or a basket of consumption goods (to maximize the fit with the modern methodology described in chapter 9). The best view at the current time is that there was a significant demographic event called the Antonine Plague, although its economic effects still are only dimly seen and apparently more modest than those of the Black Death.

Consider now a different shock to the Malthusian system. Instead of assuming that the size of the population changed, assume that the Malthusian resource constraint shifted outward. This change could come from regional specialization permitted by the Pax Romana. It could come from technological change that allowed land to be used more efficiently as described by Wilson. In any case, it shifts the line in the bottom graph of figure 10.2 to the right. For any given population size, the available land now allows the marginal product of labor and income of farm workers to be higher than before.

As shown in figure 10.4, this sets up a population expansion. In the short run, the effects of this positive shock are the same as the results of a plague shown in figure 10.3, but for different reasons. The population changed dramatically during a plague, but it changes more slowly under normal conditions. Per capita income can change more rapidly, and it increases in the short run, leaving population unaffected. But in the longer run the equilibrium has changed. The excess of births over deaths causes population to rise. Equilibrium is reached when income returns to its previous level in the upper graph, y^*. Looking at the lower graph, we see that the population is larger at the new equilibrium than before, at n_2 instead of n^*. The effect of technical change has been to increase the size of the population, not per capita income, in the Malthusian equilibrium.

Note the differences between figures 10.3 and 10.4. In both of them, income rises, setting off an increase in population. This is a rightward shift in both graphs. Although population grows in both graphs, the relation of this growth to the prior level of the population is different. In figure 10.3, the population is always lower than n^*, and the growth is only to regain the losses from the plague. In figure 10.4, by contrast, population is always larger than n^*, as technology allows for a larger population. If the shift in the resource constraint is a one-time movement, then the population settles down to a new equilibrium level, n_2, larger than n^*.

As before, the economy will not move instantly to this new equilibrium. It will take a long time, perhaps more than a century. During that time, per capita income will be high and population will be growing. If the new technology diffuses slowly or perhaps continues to improve, then the resource constraint curve will continue to shift outward for a while instead of simply jumping from

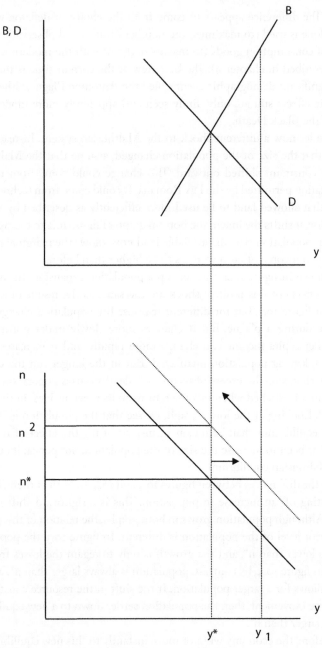

FIGURE 10.4. Effect of technical change

one position to another as shown in figure 10.4. In that case, both incomes and population will continue to increase for quite a while before the pull of the Malthusian equilibrium is felt. If the resource constraint continues to shift outward for a while, then income can stay above y^*, Malthusian subsistence, for more than a century. If productivity continues to advance indefinitely, income can stay above y^* indefinitely.

The two possibilities just mentioned can be stated as two competing hypotheses. The first hypothesis is that there was a one-time increase in productivity that had effects that gradually died out during the early Roman Empire. The second hypothesis is that there was continuing productivity growth in this time that was interrupted as the empire became less stable in the third and succeeding centuries. The long delays in the Malthusian model make differentiation between these two hypotheses difficult, but it is important to make the effort to distinguish them and to understand the nature of the Roman economy.

The two hypotheses relate to the most probable causes of increasing income. The first hypothesis of a one-time increase in productivity sees the productivity increase coming from the increase in Mediterranean trade promoted by the Romans. Making shipping safer and introducing regular sailings lowered the cost of moving even heavy and bulky goods around the Mediterranean. This allowed areas around the sea to specialize in their most productive activities and sell their products elsewhere for consumption. I showed in chapter 2 that the uniformity of wheat prices around the Mediterranean argues for a single Mediterranean market where the production of wheat could be allocated to the most productive localities.

The second hypothesis of continuing productivity growth sees this growth as coming from the improvement of technology. In this case, there is no single test of change, but rather the accumulation of evidence for technological change. Agriculture was the largest economic activity in ancient times, and improvements in agricultural productivity would have had the most impact. These changes would have required fewer agricultural workers to feed the population, allowing for the urbanization that is such a feature of the Roman world. Productivity advances in other economic processes would have had less impact, but the accumulation of productivity changes in many aspects of the economy would have increased Roman incomes.

Differentiating between hypotheses one and two is made difficult by the coincidence of shocks to the Roman economy. One might think that examination of living standards in the third century would be a way to distinguish between the two hypotheses. But in addition to the effects of technological change, there were also the effects of the Antonine Plague. In other words, the changes shown in figures 10.3 and 10.4 were superimposed on each other in the third century. The net results on population are ambiguous, but the effects on per capita income go in the same direction. This can be seen from figures 10.3 and 10.4, where both shocks increased per capita income. As a result, it will be hard to know if prosperity in the third century was the result of improving technology or declining population.

At this point in our explorations, the data are too sparse to indicate whether productivity growth was decreasing as the transition to the higher level was completed (hypothesis one) or was continuous before some kind of collapse (hypothesis two). I have tried to indicate what kind of evidence would be needed to make such a discrimination, but it may be hard to find enough data to differentiate between these two views. This lack of evidence has not kept ancient historians from debating the shape of ancient economic growth, as can be seen in two graphs from Manning and Morris (2005). The first reported Morris's (2005) data on housing sizes in Hellenistic Greece as a rough proxy for per capita income. Saller (2005) showed in a second graph an estimate of per capita income in the Roman era inferred from data indicative of trade. They both showed economic growth, but the first showed an increasing rate of growth while the second showed a decreasing rate.

Why should ancient historians be concerned about something as arcane as a different second derivative? Because these two graphs express sharply contrasting views of ancient economies. Morris's graph shows accelerating growth. Since it did not continue, it must have been interrupted by some dramatic change. Saller's graph shows decelerating growth that petered out gradually, without drama. The latter view seems more appropriate to a Malthusian process, but only in the long run; Malthus was clear that population checks could come quickly from wars or plagues.

Scheidel (2009a) made a case for hypothesis one in Roman times, a one-time increase in productivity, coming from the expansion of the Roman Republic to incorporate the whole Mediterranean. (He did not draw a speculative graph, but his argument is consistent with Saller's.) Scheidel stressed the timing of indicators of economic growth. Without explicit reference to Morris (2005), he argued that hypothesis two implied accelerating or at least continuing economic growth up to some catastrophe. He then marshaled the various indicators of economic growth described in this and the preceding chapter to argue that they peaked around the beginning of the Roman Empire. This implied that hypothesis one was correct; in his words, "a scenario of 'one-off' unsustainable growth and Malthusian pressure" (Scheidel 2009a, 69).

Scheidel presented his case forcefully, but he admitted that the underlying indexes of growth were uncertain. Jongman's (2007b) estimated consumption had different timing than the other indexes, and the shipping data are not as precise as they seem. Changes in technology could have altered the frequencies with which we find shipwrecks two thousand years later. This can be seen with a simple equation.

$$\text{Trade} = \frac{\text{Trade}}{\text{Voyages}} \times \frac{\text{Voyages}}{\substack{\text{Voyages} \\ \text{with heavy} \\ \text{cargoes}}} \times \frac{\substack{\text{Voyages} \\ \text{with heavy} \\ \text{cargoes}}}{\text{Shipwrecks}} \times \frac{\text{Shipwrecks}}{\substack{\text{Known} \\ \text{shipwrecks}}} \times \text{Known shipwrecks}$$

This long equation expresses an illuminating tautology. It shows the volume of trade, called simply "Trade" in the equation, as the product of a series of ratios. If you cancel all the magnitudes that appear in both the denominator and numerator of a ratio, the equation says only that the volume of trade equals the volume of trade. The shipwreck index is a good indicator of trade only if all the ratios in the equation stay constant. If we suspect they were not constant, the equation allows us to structure our investigation of changes in pursuit of a better index of trade.

For example, the ratio of voyages to those with heavy cargoes can change for many reasons. The most obvious is the nature of containers. Amphoras are heavy and durable. Ships containing amphoras will sink, and the amphoras will stay intact even as the ships themselves disappear. Late Romans learned to use barrels instead of amphoras to ship liquids. This was a gain to the porters who carried these containers, but it was a loss to archaeologists who could not recover evidence of barrel shipments. A rise in the ratio of total voyages to those containing heavy amphoras will change the ratio of known shipwrecks to the volume of trade. Put differently, a decline in the number of known shipwrecks might be an index of a decline in trade or of technological progress that reduced the dead weight being carried around in the form of amphoras. The shipwreck index may be a more accurate indicator of trade volumes during its rise in the Roman Republic than it is during its decline during the Roman Empire.

The ratio of voyages with heavy cargoes to shipwrecks is affected by the skill of ship captains. If the captains learned how to improve their navigation or weather prediction, this ratio might have changed. The ratio of shipwrecks to known shipwrecks similarly is affected by the skill of archaeologists in dating shipwrecks. McCormick (forthcoming) reported progress in this dimension, arguing that we now can date shipwrecks previous generations could not.

Wilson (2009a) argued that the indexes that Scheidel (2009a) used to date Roman economic growth were too fragile to bear this weight. He discussed the problems with the shipwreck data just noted and compared the overall index with an index of shipwrecks carrying stone cargoes. This rough device to correct for the bias in the index provided a different time path for the relevant wrecks. Other proxies were similarly flawed or ambiguous, and Wilson argued that the sum of the evidence was inconclusive. He concluded, "The apparent convergence of the proxies is very misleading" (Wilson 2009a, 71).

It is likely that both processes were in operation in the early Roman Empire. More evidence may produce a more precise accounting, but there does not seem to be evidence as yet or agreement that hypothesis one or two is correct while the other is wrong. Economists create these oppositions for intellectual clarity, but history has a way of splitting the difference or revealing a more complex story than either extreme hypothesis. At this stage, it is clear that there was a one-time gain from comparative advantage as the Romans promoted Mediterranean trade (see chapter 2). A unified Mediterranean market promoted regional specialization and associated income gains. There also were improvements in the technologies of agriculture and other economic activities. Wilson reminds of us of what we might call "hard" technologies that leave archaeological remains. To that should be added the "soft" technologies of attitudes and markets described in previous chapters that also contributed to economic prosperity and growth. We do not know the full distribution of these changes or the timing of their spread, but it is clear that much more was going on than simply unifying the Mediterranean world.

Whichever hypothesis is more correct, neither of them implies that economic growth could have continued from Roman times until today. Without industrialization, the Malthusian constraints described in the model of this chapter still held. They held loosely, allowing centuries of economic growth under favorable conditions, but they eventually would constrain this growth. The question therefore is not whether Malthusian constraints were present, but rather what changes in Roman times led to growth within these constraints and how far growth went. There were many shocks in the early centuries of this era, from the Antonine Plague to inflation, political instability, and invasions (see chapter 4). The purpose of this simple Malthusian model and the discussion it has generated is to clarify the complex interactions between these historical events.

We know that England began to industrialize in the late eighteenth century and that the English innovations spread throughout Western Europe in the nineteenth century. Why didn't a similar process happen in ancient times? The Malthusian model described here cannot answer such a complex question, and no answer will be forthcoming here. The model lets us understand what is similar and different in the two periods, sharpening the question. A more detailed model of technological change then is needed to compare ancient Rome and early modern England.

As described earlier, technological change can expand the resource constraint and allow both population and per capita incomes to rise. If technological change continues for a while, incomes can remain high while population rises. There are two reasons why population continues to rise. The technological change continues to shift outward the resource constraint, as seen in figure 10.4, which allows population and income to increase. In the short run, income increases, which then allows births to exceed deaths, which is how population increases. These two mechanisms can provide a stable situation where incomes are higher than Malthusian subsistence, y^*, and population is growing. The change from a static resource constraint to an expanding one has resulted in the growth of per capita incomes from y^* to its new level, accompanied by population growth.

A constant rate of technological progress therefore leads only to limited economic growth. Growth becomes a transitory phenomenon as the economy moves from a static Malthusian equilibrium to a dynamic one based on continuing technical change. This appears to describe the growth in real wages observed in preindustrial London and Amsterdam as the growth of trade in the seventeenth and eighteenth centuries expanded the English and Dutch resource constraint. Real wages in most European cities fell in this time as population grew, but not in these progressive cities. By the eighteenth century the difference between the high-wage cities and the low-wage cities on the European continent was about two-to-one (Allen 2001).

A small modification of the Malthusian model allows it to incorporate continuing economic growth. Instead of assuming that the rate of expansion of the resource constraint is constant, assume that it is proportional to the size of the population. In other words, the rate of technological progress rises when population rises. This is the assumption used by Kremer (1993) in his analysis of population growth for the last million years, by Diamond (1997) in his description of how the Neolithic Revolution set the stage for the Industrial Revolution, and by Galor (2011) in his presentation of his unified growth theory. I show in an appendix to this chapter that this assumption allows incomes and population to rise indefinitely.

This process describes the path of the Industrial Revolution. Technological improvement started to accelerate in the late eighteenth century and continued to increase as population also increased. Later, about a century after the start of industrialization, the rate of population growth diminished as the Demographic Transition took place. Women who had education could see the value of education for their children in the increasingly industrial world. They opted to have "better" children, that is, children with education and therefore "human capital," in place of having more children. In this context, the Malthusian model no longer provides many insights into the paths of industrial societies, as described in chapter 9.

This avenue was not open to Rome, at least not in the form that the

Industrial Revolution of the eighteenth century took place. Allen (2009b) showed that industrialization began in England as a result of two forces. The first was high wages. Both England and the Dutch Republic had high wages as a result of their profits from international trade. Roman Italy shared this prosperity two millennia earlier as a result of war booty and the profits from Mediterranean trade, but only England had the Industrial Revolution. Allen argued that high wages needed to be coupled with cheap power to generate industry. The coal industry of England shipped coal from the west and north of England to London. The price of fuel in London was about the same as in other advanced economies, but the price of fuel closer to the source was uniquely low. It was "the cheapest energy in the world" (Allen 2009b, 97).

The uniquely high ratio of wages to power costs gave rise to the Industrial Revolution, not only in England, but in only a specific part of England. Steam engines and iron technology improved in the north and west of England where coal was dirt cheap. The high ratio of wages to energy costs allowed England to produce goods that were competitive with goods produced elsewhere in Europe despite the high English wages. It explains why the first industrialization took place in England rather than in Holland or France. "The cheap energy economy was a foundation of Britain's economic success. Inexpensive coal provided the incentive to invent the steam engine and metallurgical technology of the Industrial Revolution" (Allen 2009b, 104).

The high ratio of wages to energy costs was not only absent in eighteenth-century continental Europe; it was absent as well in the Roman Empire. Despite the technical progress being made then that we are discovering more about, there was no possibility of escaping from the Malthusian constraints with the price ratios that existed then. However prosperous Rome may have been, it was not on the verge of having an Industrial Revolution. There was no analog of the British coal industry in antiquity and therefore no possibility that industrialization could have begun in the ancient world.

Even under hypothesis one, Romans in the early empire appear to have been living well. If this improvement came from the increase in trade, then the residents of Roman Italy may have been similar to the English and Dutch in the seventeenth and eighteenth centuries. Allen (2003) showed that the rise in Atlantic trade increased real wages in those countries before industrialization. Trade did the same for Roman Italy, and it may also, following Ricardo's analysis, have raised real wages elsewhere in the early Roman Empire. I pursue this further in chapter 11.

Any model is a simplification, and the one explained in this chapter is no exception. The exposition here does not aim to capture all the details of this economic expansion. Instead it provides a framework in which the details that emerge from various kinds of research can fit. It provides a mechanism to turn the odd facts gathered by archaeologists into a coherent picture. With more information, perhaps stimulated by having such a framework, we can aspire to constructing a more detailed model. A recent book stated, "Ancient economic history remains a largely undertheorized field of study" (Banaji 2001). I filled a small part of this lack by analyzing a simple Malthusian model. The model is designed to explain how per capita incomes could have grown in a predominantly Malthusian world. This is not possible in equilibrium, and this paper is about the behavior of this model out of the well-known Malthusian equilibrium.

There are several benefits of using a model like this one. Most important, it allows us to integrate recent archaeological discoveries about Roman technology into a coherent view of the Roman economy. It helps us resolve an apparent conflict between the observations we are accumulating about the good life of ordinary Roman citizens or at least structure our disagreements (Scheidel 2009a; Wilson 2009a).

The model also allows us to engage in a structured discussion of alternative histories, what economic historians of the modern world call counterfactuals. What would have happened if the western Roman Empire had not collapsed? We will never know. This model allows us to speculate in a coherent way about what might have been. The comparison with the Industrial Revolution showed an alternative history—about a far different time and place. It is clear that Rome could not have gone that way even if various other factors had been different. The Malthusian model will not help us identify which of those other factors were more important than others; it will help us understand the consequences of economic decline.

Even this simple model helps define questions for Roman archaeology. Hypothesis one above is that there was a single spurt of productivity change whose effects were gradually eroded by Malthusian pressures. Hypothesis two is that Roman productivity growth continued until some unrelated factors inhibited it, allowing living standards to stay high for a longer period. We need more detailed evidence than now exists to make this differentiation.

Finally, the use of this kind of model provides a bridge to help unify the study of ancient and more modern history. At the very least, it can integrate the analysis of ancient plagues with that of more modern ones. It can help us redraw graphs like the one shown in figure 10.1 to reveal accomplishments of people who lived long ago that have been largely forgotten by modern historians. And it raises questions about modern history as much as about ancient history. For all of the factors that doomed the Roman Empire must have been missing or at least modified two millennia later when the Industrial Revolution took place. A model that structures our discussion allows us to place ancient economic history into the general study of economic history.

Appendix to Chapter 10

■ ■ ■ ■ ■ ■ ■

This appendix reproduces figures 10.2–10.4 in algebraic form, allowing for the extensions of the model described in the comparison between ancient Rome and the Industrial Revolution. I represent all relations as linear, which makes the model simpler. Since it has been hard to verify the shape of these relationships in historical data, these linear equations can serve as approximations to the "true" relations in the neighborhood of equilibrium, y^* and n^*. I adopt the convention that all coefficients are positive, so that negative relations are in the sign of the equation, not of the coefficient.

Births, B, are an increasing function of income, y. $B = a + by$

Deaths, D, are a decreasing function of income, y. $D = c - dy$

Population change is the excess of births over deaths. In symbols,

$$dn/dt = B - D = a + by - (c - dy)$$
$$= (a - c) + (b + d)y$$

Equilibrium, n^* is where population change is zero, $dn/dt = 0$. Setting $dn/dt = 0$, yields:

$$(c - a) = (b + d)y$$

Solving for y yields a function to the equilibrium level of income, y^*:

$$y^* = (c - a) / (b + d)$$

As explained in the text, the first part of the Malthusian theory argues that per capita income, y, will be constant at y^*. It is necessary that $c > a$ for this to happen. Graphically, this means that the B and D curves cross each other, that is, that D starts higher than B at very low y.

The resource constraint is the second part of the Malthusian theory, and it will be presented here in three variants. The first variant is the traditional Malthusian theory, assuming a stable resource constraint:

$$n = e - f y$$

The first part of the theory gives the value of y, that is, y^*, which then gives a value of n which we can label n^*. Both points are labeled in figures 10.2 and 10.3.

$$n^* = e - f y^*$$

Figure 10.3 shows the effect of a change in the population size that moves it away from n^* while leaving the resource constraint stable. As described in the text, this leads to a temporary deviation of both population and income from their equilibrium values.

Now consider a resource constraint that expands with time:

$$n = e - f y + g t$$
$$dn/dt = g$$

This is the condition shown in figure 10.4, where the resource constraint itself has moved out. The effect, as shown in figure 10.4, is to move both n and y from their equilibrium values. There now are two equations for dn/dt, one from births and deaths and the other from the expanding resource constraint. The latter relation is dependent on y, which moves to bring the two equations into agreement. We therefore look for a value of y where they are the same by equating the two functions for dn/dt and solving for y.

$$g = (a - c) + (b + d)y$$
$$(b + d)y = g + (c - a)$$
$$y = g / (b + d) + (c - a) / (b + d)$$

The last term is the expression for y^* with a static resource constraint. Substituting that value into the equation yields:

$$y = g / (b + d) + y^*$$

Income is above the equilibrium level when the resource constraint is expanding. The faster the rate of expansion, the higher income is—and the faster the growth of population. In the lower panel of figure 10.4, that means that both n and y are expanding, and the economy is moving diagonally up and to the right from (y^*, n^*). If y exceeds that growth path, then the speed of population expansion will increase, decreasing y. If y falls short of the growth path, the speed of population growth will fall, increasing y. This is a stable growth path.

Finally, let us modify the moving resource constraint to allow for productivity growth proportional to the population. Instead of assuming a constant speed for the resource constraint, we posit that population grows both with technological change, g, and with the size of the population, n. As described in the text, this is a common assumption among modern growth theorists. It results in a constant growth rate of n for a given y, as opposed to a constant speed of change. This assumption is expressed in the following expression for the resource constraint:

$$n = e - f y + g t n$$

Differentiating this expression with respect to time gives:

$$dn/dt = ng / (1 - g t)$$

Equating this to the expression for dn/dt from births and deaths and simplifying the algebra yields:

$$y = dn/dt / (b + d) + y^*$$

This is the same equation as in the first model of a steadily expanding resource constraint, since $g = dn/dt$ in that model. Since dn/dt, the rate of increase of population, was constant in that model, y was high. Since dn/dt is increasing in this model, y is growing. This is the story of the Industrial Revolution. It was followed by the Demographic Transition, as noted in the text, which decreased the responsiveness of births to income, b, and further increased y. This marks the point where modern growth theory becomes more useful than Malthusian models.

Chapter 11

■ ■ ■

Per Capita GDP in the Early Roman Empire

Economic growth for a sustained time was possible in a Malthusian world (see chapter 10). There is indirect but compelling evidence that economic growth took place in the late Roman Republic and early empire. Not rapid growth of the modern era, but growth that appears to have progressed slowly over a few centuries. How far did this economic growth raise Roman incomes? Was the standard of living raised above its level before and after? If growth took place in Roman Italy—with its large cities and gains from war booty—did it extend to the provinces? These are questions for this final chapter.

Hopkins (1980) asked how large the Roman economy was in order to find out if taxes in the early Roman Empire imposed a great burden on the population. He argued that the Roman economy in the first two centuries of our era was large enough that the tax burden was light. He did not aim to perform a complete calculation, and he spoke of his result as a "metaphor" rather than an estimate. This classic paper has been widely quoted, and the estimated national expenditure has been quoted without the rest of the argument.

Goldsmith (1984) published an estimate of the gross domestic product (GDP) of the early Roman Empire as part of his exploration of the structure of historical economies. He was an economist like me, and he was seeking applications for the tools and skills he had developed for the analysis of modern economies. His estimate was approximately twice as large as Hopkins's.

I compared these two quite different estimates in Temin (2006a). I asked if the divergent treatments accorded with modern economic evaluations of national production as explained in chapter 9 and whether it is preferable to construct an estimate of total production from individual consumption of wheat or whether another approach is preferable.

My exploration gave rise to several other estimates of Roman GDP (Maddison 2007; Bang 2008; Scheidel and Friesen 2009; Lo Cascio and Malanima 2009a, 2009b). I survey this small literature in this chapter, distinguishing what

I call the first-generation estimates made by Hopkins and Goldsmith in the 1980s and the second-generation estimates of the last five years. The earlier group was concerned with comparisons within the Roman Empire: the distribution of income between the state and the people (Hopkins) and between the rich and the poor (Goldsmith). The later essays, stimulated in part by the kind of studies reported earlier in this book, were concerned with the comparison of the Roman Empire with more recent economies.

External comparisons have animated many of the previous chapters, and ancient historians disagree about them. It is hardly surprising that these disparate views of the Roman economy find their way into the abstruse calculations that support any estimate of GDP. The central question for this chapter is whether these views affect the presumptively objective calculations. In other words, do GDP calculations affect our views of the Roman economy or are they the result of our views?

All of the GDP estimates, mine included, rest on an exceedingly narrow evidentiary base. They are at best conjectural estimates based on a few observations, some about the early Roman Empire and some about modern economies. Not only are the assumptions needed to build on these observations open to question, but the observations themselves are subject to unknown errors. The whole exercise can yield only what Hopkins called a metaphor. The very shape of the metaphor is taken from other indications of the Roman economy, and GDP estimates reflect back these other indications. The devil is in the details, which in this chapter means the assumptions. They are the primary focus of the chapter.

The two early estimates are shown in tabular form in table 11.1. Hopkins dated his estimate quite broadly, from 200 BCE to 400 CE; it presumably represents an average of this long period. Goldsmith dated his estimate at death of Augustus. There is enough parallelism in the two estimates to place them in the same table, but the steps used by the two authors differ in some respects. The result is that several rows in table 11.1 have entries only in one of the two columns. Nevertheless, the table reveals clearly how two authors could start from almost the same data and end up with starkly different estimates.

Hopkins and Goldsmith worked from the same estimate of population size in the early Roman Empire. This makes comparison of the estimates easy, but it would not matter if they had differed in this dimension because the estimates were derived by blowing up per capita figures. Scheidel and Friesen (2009) assumed that the population was different than these authors assumed, and I will discuss later why this assumption is revealing.

Hopkins and Goldsmith also used the same estimated size of the modius, although this size figures only in Hopkins's estimate. This is only important because Hopkins started his estimates with kilograms and converted them to

TABLE 11.1.
Estimates of Roman GDP from the expenditure side

Category	Hopkins (1980)	Goldsmith (1984)
Population	54 million	55 million
Kg per modius	6.55	6.55–6.75
Price of wheat	HS 3 per modius	HS 3 per modius
Annual consumption of wheat or measured in wheat	250 kg	37.5 modii = 246–253 kg
Allowance for seed	83.3 kg	
Value of wheat production	$333.3 \times 3/6.55 =$ HS 153	$37.5 \times 3 =$ HS 112.5
Annual food expenditure		HS $112.5 \times 1.8 =$ HS 200
Annual private expenditure		HS $200 \times 1.75 =$ HS 350
Total per-capita expenditure	HS 153	HS $350 \times 1.1 =$ HS 380
Total national expenditure	HS 8,244 million	HS 20,900 million
Hopkins (1995/6), from minimum to actual expenditure	$1.5 \times$ HS 8,244 million = HS 12,500 million	

Note: Figures may be rounded to agree with sources.
Source: Hopkins, (1980; 1995/6); Goldsmith (1984).

Roman units. The two authors abstracted the same price of wheat, in sesterces (HS) per modius, from the literature. This price represents an informal average of prices in Italy; Duncan-Jones (1982, 146) said they generally were between two and four sesterces per modius. We know from Cicero's Verrine orations that HS 3 was an official wheat price in Sicily, but we also know from scattered evidence that the price of wheat could vary quite widely. The importance of this price here is that it is not the source of the discrepancy between Hopkins's and Goldsmith's estimates. It is a difference among second-generation estimates.

The next row of table 11.1 shows agreement yet again on annual wheat consumption. But appearances are deceiving, and there are many problems at this juncture. It should strike any ancient historian as odd that Hopkins stated the annual consumption in a modern unit, and indeed it is. Two aspects of this estimate are of interest. First, it is not an estimate of wheat consumption. As Hopkins stated clearly, it is total annual consumption, consisting primarily of food and textiles, measured in units of wheat equivalence. The distinction between wheat consumption and total consumption measured in wheat units is critical for the derivation of any income estimate. Second, the estimate is not from ancient Rome! It is an estimate of consumption in modern subsistence agriculture, taken from a study of modern conditions by Colin Clark and associates in the 1960s. The actual source stated that "subsistence requirements, expressed in our units of grain equivalents, are somewhere between 250 and 300 kg./person/year, varying substantially, as we have seen, with climate and average body weight" (Clark and Haswell 1967, 60).

Goldsmith estimated wheat consumption from the rations given to Roman soldiers and slaves. He assumed that these were the rations for adult men, while women and children consumed less, so that his estimate of average consumption was less than the historical rations. He supported his estimate by comparing it to fifteenth-century Florence. Note that Goldsmith estimated wheat consumption, not total consumption, while Hopkins estimated total consumption in wheat equivalents. The apparent agreement in table 11.1 is not agreement at all, and only the economist's estimate is based on ancient evidence.

Both estimates implicitly assume that consumption or wages can be generalized from a few observations to the economy as a whole. This generalization only is possible if there is a labor market equalizing wages (or at least tending in that direction). As noted in chapter 6, we can speak of a labor market if wages serve to equilibrate the demand and the supply of labor, that is, to make the desired demand for labor equal the desired supply. Workers must be free to change their economic activity and their location, and they must be paid something like their labor productivity to indicate to them which kind of work to choose. That does not mean that everyone changes jobs with great frequency; it means instead that enough people are able and willing to do so to eliminate conditions where payments to labor are either excessively higher or lower than the wages of comparable work in other locations or activities. Even in the United States today, which contains the most flexible labor market in history, wages for comparable jobs are not completely equalized across the country.

Hopkins enlarged his estimated consumption by allowing one quarter of the wheat crop for seed. This has two logical problems, in addition to the problem of knowing the yield of wheat farms in antiquity. First, the estimated consumption was in wheat units, not of wheat. The seed requirement only applies to the portion of consumption that was wheat, which was not specified by Hopkins. It appears that Hopkins treated total consumption as if it consisted only of wheat. Second, seed is an intermediate good that normally is not counted in the national product, as explained in chapter 9. GDP measures the production of goods and services for final consumption, that is, for consumption by people or by business firms (in the modern world). Wheat that is produced in agriculture and then used as seed in agriculture does not appear as a part of GDP, even though it is part of farm output (Goldsmith 1984, 273n). Hopkins was right to think that his estimate of consumption might omit parts of the national product, but he was wrong to include seed in place of the missing parts.

Goldsmith took a different approach, one more in keeping with modern economics. He stepped up his estimate by appropriate multipliers to go from wheat to all food grains, from grain to total food consumption, from food consumption to total consumer spending, from consumer spending to national expenditures. These estimates came from a wide variety of ancient and modern sources; the estimated total consumer spending was checked against the allowances of the *alimenta*.

Modern national income accounting recognizes two ways of computing national and domestic products. The first way is to count all the expenditures for final goods, that is, omitting intermediate goods used in the production of final goods. This approach is spoken of as the expenditure side, and it is the approach summarized in table 11.1. The alternate approach is to sum all the earnings in the economy, which should add up to the value of final goods if there are no taxes or accounting errors. This approach is spoken of as the income side. Its result is often labeled national income, which differs from the national product in modern data due to taxes, errors and omissions, but which should be thought of as identical in ancient times (see chapter 9).

Goldsmith tested his estimate by deriving it from income data instead of expenditure data, as shown in table 11.2. The average wage was taken to be HS 3.5 from ancient sources. Days worked per year were set as 225 because that is about what modern workers work, giving annual compensation of HS 790. Assuming that the participation rate, the proportion of people in the labor force, was 0.4, then shifting from per-worker compensation to per capita, reduces it to $790 \times 0.4 = 315$. Goldsmith then assumed that nonwage income—rents, interest, indirect taxes, and depreciation—was 20 percent of

TABLE 11.2.
Estimate of Roman GDP from the income side

Category	Goldsmith (1984)
Average daily labor compensation	HS 3.5
Working days per year	225
Average annual labor compensation	HS 790
Participation rate	0.4
Labor income per-capita	HS 315
Step-up for non-labor income	1.2
Total income per head	HS 380

Note: Figures may be rounded to agree with sources.
Source: Goldsmith (1984).

labor compensation. Multiplying HS 315 by 1.2 gives a total income per head of HS 380, the same as estimated in table 11.1 from expenditures.

Goldsmith's estimate of per capita national expenditure of HS 380, is over twice Hopkins's estimate of HS 153. In a later essay, Hopkins (1995–96) stated that his earlier estimate was a minimum estimate of subsistence, and he multiplied it by 1.5 to get a more reasonable estimate of Roman GDP, shown in the last line of table 11.1. No source was provided for this multiplier; Hopkins identified it as a "rough guess." The resulting per capita product, HS 230, is still only two-thirds of Goldsmith's estimate. If we had to choose between them, then Goldsmith's larger estimate should be preferred. It is in accord with modern economic conventions, it was derived in two ways—from the expenditure side and the income side—and it was based, at least in part, on ancient sources. However, we can do better than simply choosing between these two existing estimates.

Let us back up a bit from the specific task at hand to inquire about assumptions underlying the whole effort. We are so familiar with the concept of the "gross product" that Hopkins set out to estimate that we do not often remind ourselves about the underlying assumptions. There are two key assumptions, both connected with prices. We assume that the goods in question, wheat in this instance, were sold on competitive markets. We do not have to assume that markets were as competitive in Rome as those monitored by the Chicago Board of Trade, but we do need to assume that there is enough competition to make prices of the same good in different sales roughly the same. Only in that case does in make sense to use the few price quotations we have from ancient times as an index of prices throughout the Roman Empire.

Some ancient historians rejected my estimated GDP because they argued that there was not enough market activity in the ancient world and not enough competition around the Mediterranean to make such an estimate meaningful. This is the position taken by Finley, who asserted that, "ancient society did not have an economic system which was an enormous conglomeration of interdependent markets" (Finley 1973, 22–23). Subsequent research has exposed the presence of substantial market activity and an international division of labor that suggests the integration of distant markets, putting the burden of proof on those who are skeptical, as presented in previous chapters.

Economists make GDP estimates for less-developed countries today and medieval economies in the past, but there comes a point where the estimate loses its meaning. If ancient markets were so rudimentary, then my estimate is inappropriate. It is worth pointing out that critics who take this line also must reject most other summary statements about ancient economies—which inevitably rest on implicit assumptions of consistent economic activity.

In addition to assuming that there were markets, we need to assume that people were free to alter their consumption in order to infer that they were better off when national income increased. The relative values of different goods then reflected the relative valuation that consumers placed on them. In other words, we need to assume that people could spend the money—or wheat— that they had in any way they chose. It is not necessary that all things were for sale to anyone; there clearly were restrictions on togas with purple stripes. But there had to be a broad range of goods that people could use their incomes to purchase and consume. Only in that case can we infer any welfare comparisons from an estimate of gross product, for only in that case will it be true that a higher product will—other things being equal—make people better off.

For example, the third line of table 11.1 lists the price of wheat as being HS 3 per modius. If the few observations of wheat prices that have survived were simply random magnitudes, or if they were administrative rates set at different times or places, there would be no sense in taking an average. Another observation, or the omission of one we have, could change the average, possibly by a large amount. Only if we think wheat was sold in markets does it make sense to see the surviving observations as indications of the usual or most frequent price. Then we can generalize from the few observations we have to the prevailing price of wheat. Even this step is problematical for the price of wheat in the early Roman Empire for the reasons given in chapter 2. Wheat prices were dependent on the distance from Rome. As Scheidel and Friesen (2009, 67) reiterated, "The only thing we can be sure of is that actual prices varied quite significantly by region, being lowest in grain-exporting Egypt and highest in the capital."

The fourth line of table 11.1 shows estimated annual consumption, which is harder to measure. There is no market in consumption, and we cannot generalize easily from a few observations. Hopkins relied on modern data, but that is unsatisfactory. He assumed that almost all Romans lived at subsistence levels, and he used modern data to estimate subsistence as if it was a biological constant that had not changed in two millennia. He assumed, in other words, that subsistence was a knife edge, below which you starved, and that this boundary is the same at all times and places. Modern research, however, has shown that subsistence is not a fixed level of income (Dasgupta 1993). In other words, people do not simply die when their consumption falls below some threshold. Their ability to work is impaired when they are malnourished, their growth is stunted, and their life expectancy is reduced. No economist today takes seriously Colin Clark's estimate of consumption; it has vanished beneath the waves of current scholarship.

There are a wide variety of countries today where most people are malnourished, and developing countries differ greatly in the extent of malnourishment. The range of poverty is great, and there does not seem to be a boundary below which a country cannot fall. Bangladesh, Haiti, and Kenya are among the poorest of countries. Their per capita income was about half that of China or Egypt in the 1990s. India's per capita income fell between those of these two groups of countries. All of these countries are poor, but some are poorer than others.

Recognizing the variety of incomes in developing countries today, the question of Roman product is not whether ordinary Romans lived at subsistence level, but rather which kind of subsistence they experienced. They could have been prosperous farmers who had adequate calorie and vitamin intake and been large and healthy people as a result. Or they could have been stunted and ill from malnutrition, even while not so poor that they died or were unable to have children. The question is not whether Rome was richer or poorer than developing countries today; it is which developing country did Rome resemble most closely, at least in respect to general nutrition.

Ancient estimates of grain consumption do not help much with this question. A survey of ancient evidence concluded that "the evidence on grain consumption is very scanty—and the situation is far worse for other food items" (Foxhall and Forbes 1982, 74). The evidence is not even about consumption; it is about grain rations for Roman soldiers and Cato's slaves. We do not know if these rations were for the workers alone or for them and their households and assistants, nor do we know what other food the soldiers and slaves consumed. The rations for soldiers varied by a factor of three, suggesting that these questions are not simply theoretical. Foxhall and Forbes (1982, 64) cast further doubt on the use of rations to estimate consumption when they speculate on the process by which rations were set: "The similarity of the rations of the army and Cato's working slaves also suggests that the Romans may have used a basic 'rule of thumb' for the estimation of projected consumption similar to that suggested for the Greeks. Possibly it too originated on farms and in households and at some stage made its way to state-level usage."

One problem with using modern averages or ancient rules of thumb is that they do not allow for the possibility of economic growth. They are static estimates that apply to no specific time. At best they could provide an estimate of the average Roman income over some period; they could never reveal to us a change in that income. It would be unfortunate if the attempt to measure Roman gross product implied that there had been no change in that product over hundreds of years, except by extension of the population (see chapter 10).

We have learned more about both the ancient economy and less-developed countries today than we knew twenty years ago. We have more price data for the ancient world and more income data for modern developing countries. I employ these new data in turn, starting with the modern data, to derive two new estimates of Roman GDP. They should, like Goldsmith's estimates, agree. But, unlike Goldsmith's data, they do not correspond to the two ways national incomes and products are calculated today. Instead, they approach the estimation from two entirely different starting points.

Many historians have noted that the Romans had an urban economy. The city of Rome is thought to have had a million residents in the early Roman Empire, and there were many smaller cities throughout the Roman Empire. A conventional view is that about 10 percent of the population lived in urban areas. Perhaps that figure is just the smallest single digit that can recognize the abundant evidence of Roman cities and towns in an agrarian society. Lo Cascio (1994) and Scheidel (2001) have warned us that all demographic estimates for Rome are open to question, and this one must be highly speculative because it is highly aggregated. Even if this number is not accurate, it captures something about the early Roman Empire.

People living in cities typically do not grow their own food. An economy with a large urban population therefore has to have a more efficient agriculture; each farmer has to feed his family and part of an urban family as well. This, of course, does not deal with the question of how food gets from countryside to cities. The implication for productivity is independent of whether this was done by taxes, tribute, or trade. This reasoning has been used for early modern economies to demonstrate the extent of economic growth. David (1967) used it to estimate the rise in United States per capita GDP in the early nineteenth century. More recently, Craig and Fisher (2000, 113–18) used data on urbanization from Bairoch, Batou, and Chèvre (1988, 259) to estimate changes in per capita GDP for several European countries between 1500 and 1750.

This index puts the early Roman Empire, at roughly 10 percent urban, at the level of Britain, France, and Germany in 1600. These countries at the time appear to have been far poorer by this index than Belgium, the Netherlands, Italy, Spain, and Portugal. The urbanization rate of the early Roman Empire cannot be known with precision. The estimate of 10 percent has to be regarded, at best, as true to only one significant digit. If we assume that the early Roman Empire was between 5 and 15 percent urban, the conclusion just stated remains valid. Roman per capita GDP was near the GDP of the three main European countries of northwestern Europe in 1600, but below that of the main trading nations both north and south of these countries.

If we consider the area that is now Italy alone, Hopkins (1978, 68) speculated that it was 30 percent urbanized in 28 CE. By this measure, the center of the early Roman Empire is estimated to have been as wealthy as Belgium and the Netherlands, the richest of the trading countries of early modern Europe above Italy and the Iberian states in 1600. Like Roman Italy, they were at the center of an extensive trading network, enjoying both gains from trade and income from the management of the trade.

I drew a sharp contrast with urbanization in Italy and the rest of the empire. While Rome was the largest city in the empire, and the largest city in history for another two millennia, it was not the only city in the early Roman Empire. There were many smaller cities scattered over Europe, Africa, and Asia. There were hundreds of cities in Roman Africa alone, suggesting that I may have overdrawn the contrast between Italy and the rest of the empire. It is important to keep the distinction between the metropolis and the empire in mind.

My estimate of Roman urbanization received support from Wilson's "very tentative estimate for the urban population in the Roman world c. A.D. 150, which suggests a population of c. 7,370 living in cities of 5,000 people or more" (Wilson 2009a, 74). Taken relative to Scheidel and Friesen's (2009) estimate of 70 million people living in the Roman Empire at this time, this implies an urbanization rate of about 10 percent. (Wilson said 12.5 percent with spurious accuracy.) Their insistence on the large size of the Roman Empire reminds us of the unusually large extent of the empire and how difficult it would have been to raise 70 million incomes.

It also helps us to distinguish between Roman Italy and the empire as a whole. Only about 10 percent of the population of the empire lived in Italy, and they could easily have had higher incomes than the provinces. As just noted, we need to compare like with like. If we are to distinguish small countries in early modern Europe, then we need to compare them with Roman Italy—or even Rome itself. If we seek to compare the GDP of the Roman Empire with early modern economies, we must compare them with Europe as a whole.

Per capita GDP grew in most European countries in the years after 1600, albeit slowly during the difficult seventeenth century. Almost all Western European countries had urbanization rates above 10 percent by 1750, the principal exceptions being Germany and Scandinavia. They had not participated in the expansion of the Atlantic trade, and they remained relatively poor and rural as a result. The early Roman Empire's per capita GDP was about equal to Germany's in both 1600 and 1750. Roman Italy was between the level of Belgium and the Netherlands in 1750, which had grown apart since 1600 by the urbanization measure.

To provide a more contemporary comparison, I collected GDP data for modern developing countries in 1995. I selected countries that had population of more than 1 million and per capita GDP of less than ten thousand dollars. This provided a sample of a hundred countries. I regressed the logarithm of per capita GDP on the proportion of the population in urban areas and several regional dummies. The result showed that per capita GDP was related to urbanization. This result does not imply that urbanization caused per capita GDP to rise—the direction of causality may well run in the opposite direction—but only that higher per capita GDP is associated with increased urbanization. The regression is as follows, with t-statistics below the coefficients.

$$\text{Log per capita GDP} = 7.376 + .0267\, \text{URB} + \text{Regional Dummies} \quad R^2 = .73$$
$$(22.88) \quad (7.30)$$

Adding .267 (.0267 × 10) to the constant gives a predicted log per capita GDP of 7.643, which implies a predicted per capita GDP of \$2,085. This is comparable to India in the mid-1990s, a large country containing—like the Roman Empire—many disparate areas. This is an interesting result, which builds on Hopkins's comparison of ancient Rome and current developing countries. But the result that Roman income was like that of a current developing country has a variety of drawbacks. First, while the use of urbanization provides a way to use ancient data to refine the estimate, the effect of the ancient data is not large. The coefficient of urbanization is very small, and the estimate is close to the mean of the sample of countries used. Second, it follows that any estimate will be sensitive to the sample of countries chosen. The correlation of urbanization and per capita GDP breaks down at higher incomes, but the mean of countries clearly will be higher if richer countries are included in the sample. Third, this calculation does not provide an estimated GDP in ancient currency. It therefore can be used to compare Roman GDP with more recent conditions but not to compare GDP with other ancient magnitudes.

The previous estimate followed Hopkins's lead; the second one follows Goldsmith's, as summarized in table 11.2. I expand his calculation of the wage and explore the implications of the data for the level of the real wage, that is, the wage divided by the price of wheat. I then expand these results into an estimate of GDP and of the income distribution in the early Roman Empire.

When I started this exploration, I thought I would be able to find many more observations of Roman wages to analyze, but there are not a lot of observations, and most of them are for wages in Egypt. Given the different monetary systems used in Roman Egypt and Roman Italy, there is no thought that these wages were the same. But all is not lost. The fragmentary data that we have fit into a simple pattern that illuminates the conditions of life in ancient Rome. I rely in what follows on Egyptian wage data collected by Drexhage (1991) and Egyptian wheat price data collected by Rathbone (1997). These data have been summarized recently in Scheidel (2002). I compare these relatively abundant observations with the scatter of evidence we have about the city of Rome, mostly as collected by Duncan-Jones (1982).

The daily wage in rural Egypt from the mid-first to the mid-second centuries averaged around seven to eight obols a day. At the prevailing rate of seven obols to a drachma, the wage was approximately one drachma a day. Monthly wages were about 20 to 25 times that high, suggesting that the monthly workers were not more skilled than the daily ones. Cuvigny (1996) reported that skilled miners earned 47 drachmae a month at Mons Claudianus, approximately double the monthly rates compiled by Drexhage. The few annual wages we know of ranged from some that were 250 or 300 times the daily wage, indicating similar skills, to some that were in the range of 1,000 drachmas. The wages recorded by Cuvigny and the high annual salaries probably went to skilled workers and supervisory personnel, assuming that these wages were determined in a functioning labor market

The daily wage in Rome itself may have been about HS 3 to HS 4; Goldsmith used the average of these numbers, HS 3.5. If we convert Alexandrian drachmas to sesterces at the official rate of one-to-one, then wages in the city of Rome were three or more times as large as wages in rural Egypt. This cannot be surprising. If there was a labor market in the early Roman Empire, even an imperfect one, then this pattern is what we would expect. In less-developed countries today, wages are higher at the center of the empire than in the provinces, and they are higher in the city than in the countryside. The existence of this pattern in antiquity gives some confidence to what after all is very sparse evidence both about wages and the monetary regimes in Egypt and the rest of the Roman Empire.

Continuing this analogy, the same forces that produced higher wages in the metropolis would have generated higher prices there as well. If there had been a well-functioning labor market, the real wage, that is, the wage measured in the amount of wheat or other products it would buy, should have been similar in Egypt and Rome.

The Egyptian wheat price was about 8 drachmas for an artaba, which was the monthly ration for soldiers and other people. It then took a little over a week for a laborer in Roman Egypt to earn one artaba of wheat. We can make a similar calculation for Rome, although wages were paid in sesterces, and wheat was measured in modii. We need to know how many modii were in one artaba of wheat to make a comparison with Egypt. The artaba was a larger measure than the modius, and one artaba was the equivalent of 4.5 modii (Duncan-Jones 1982, 372).

Yet the price of wheat in Rome is difficult to use because of the prevalence of state subsidies, as discussed in chapter 2. Both Hopkins and Goldsmith stated that the price was HS 3 per modius. The cost of one artaba of wheat in Rome then would have been HS 13.5. At a daily wage of HS 3.5, that was about four and one-half days' work. This wheat price, however, was the price of wheat subsidized by the imperial authority. In other words, the cost of wheat in Rome was more than HS 3 by the amount of the subsidy. We can estimate the size of the subsidy by looking for wheat prices that do not contain a subsidy. Duncan-Jones (1982, 345) argued that "normal prices for wheat at Rome were considerably more than [HS 4]." He said that the unsubsidized price might have been as high as HS 8. If so, then it may have taken up to ten days for a Roman worker to earn one artaba of unsubsidized wheat. This is not very precise, since it is limited by the scarcity of price evidence in Rome, but it is enough to suggest that the Roman labor market might have worked exceptionally well.

Real wages, that is, wages divided by the price of wheat, in Roman Egypt and in Rome itself do not appear very different. We cannot reject the hypothesis that real wages were the same in rural Egypt and the city of Rome. This finding suggests that there was a functioning labor market that allowed workers to move to where wages were higher. It was not the case that Italian workers were impoverished relative to Egyptian, nor that Egyptian workers were exploited relative to Roman. The sparse data may even reveal that real wages were slightly higher in the city of Rome than in rural Egypt. The large difference in nominal wages translates into a smaller difference in real wages, and the best guess must be that the difference in real wages was not large. The experience of current less-developed countries suggests that there would have been a difference, as noted already, and the evidence goes in the right direction.

Scheidel (2010) disputed my estimated wage in Rome, but he confirmed my inference of similar real wages in Rome and Egypt through a comparison of his estimates for Roman Egypt with Allen's (2009a) from the Diocletian

Edict. As noted earlier, this correspondence is more troubling than comforting. Scheidel (2010) reported identical real wages in Egypt before and after the Antonine Plague in contradiction with the rise in real wages after the plague in Scheidel (2002). He used date from the earlier paper in his later paper but remained mute about the contradiction. He emphasized instead the applicability of the Diocletian Edict and implicitly the uniformity of real wages across the Mediterranean Sea.

To return to the estimation of Roman GDP, Goldsmith constructed an estimate of per capita GDP from the income side as shown in table 11.2. He used the wage in Rome. But only about one-tenth of the population of the early Roman Empire lived in Italy, and fewer than that lived in Rome. The wage data surveyed here show that wages were higher in Rome than elsewhere in the empire, implying that Goldsmith's estimate of per capita GDP was too large. It needs to be based on the average wage in the Roman Empire rather than the average wage in Rome. I retained Goldsmith's estimates of working days per year, the participation rate, and the step-up for non-labor income, changing only the estimate of the average wage.

How much lower than wages in Rome were average wages in the empire? We do not know. Wages in Egypt were only one-third as large, but we do not know if wages elsewhere were closer to those in Egypt or those in Rome. Appealing to the principle of insufficient reason, I suggested that average wages were one-half the Roman level, somewhat above the low level of Egyptian rural wages. This suggests that the GDP of the early Roman Empire was about half of that estimated by Goldsmith, or about HS 10,000 million. Surprisingly, this is almost the same as Hopkins's 1995–96 guess of HS 12,500 million. It is lower than other second-generation estimates in sesterces.

The evidence surveyed here can do more than provide another guess about the size of the Roman GDP; it can inform us about the distribution of income within the empire. We get this information by contrasting results from both ways of approaching the problem of estimation. From the modern comparison using urbanization rates, it seemed that per capita income was higher in Roman Italy than in the Roman Empire as a whole. From the comparison using ancient data on wage rates, I inferred and Scheidel (2010) agreed that real wages in Rome were equal or close to equal in Rome and at least one large province.

How can these apparently contradictory inferences be reconciled? It appears that the high income of Rome was not shared equally. Daily workers received only slightly more in real terms than daily workers outside Roman Italy. The higher incomes in Roman Italy must have been the earnings of people who were not daily workers, that is, more highly skilled workers and the owners of property. If the real incomes of richer people were higher in and around the city of Rome than in Egypt while the real incomes of the ordinary workers was the same, then the distribution of income was more unequal in Rome and Roman Italy than elsewhere in the empire. This is not to deny the presence of some very rich Romans in the provinces but rather to argue that there were only a few of them outside Roman Italy.

This suggests that the high per capita income in Roman Italy found by urbanization was the result of great fortunes of people living there. All sorts of people lived elsewhere, both rich and poor, but there was no concentration of wealth outside Italy comparable to the massing of wealth in Italy. The expansion of Roman rule had yielded great profits. It is not a new idea that these gains were captured by a few people. It may be new to learn that they were concentrated almost entirely in Rome and its surrounding countryside. They may have initiated a durable pattern of constructing luxurious villas. Two millennia later, as great wealth was being accumulated in nineteenth-century England, "millionaires made their money in the town and spent it in the country" (Crook 1999, 27). Wealthy Romans also invested in land but appear from the urbanization evidence to have retained a large presence in Rome itself.

Goldsmith (1984) argued that the distribution of income in the early Roman Empire was similar to that found in England before industrialization or in Brazil at the time he wrote. If this was true for the empire as a whole, then it follows that the distribution of income was more equal in the provinces and very highly skewed in Rome itself. Tainter (1988) argued that the concentration of wealth in the late Roman Republic led to class conflict, demagoguery, and the republic's collapse. As suggested by Tainter, the extreme income disparities in Rome itself, as opposed to conditions elsewhere under Roman rule, strengthen this argument. Phillips (2002) used the same argument to worry about the future of the American republic today.

Later estimators have all said that my estimated GDP in sesterces was too low. I used prices and wages from the provinces to be representative of the empire as a whole. If we multiply the per capita income estimate by 70 million to get aggregate income for the empire, we need to use the average price in the empire as a whole. As everyone agrees, prices were lower outside Rome and quite low in populous Egypt. But since all the estimates discussed so far were based on modern estimates of subsistence consumption, they cannot inform us of the magnitude of ancient economic growth. It is more promising to consider the alternative estimates from comparisons with early modern economies.

Maddison (2007, 43–53) started from Goldsmith after criticizing Hopkins's economics in including seeds in GDP, as described earlier. He broke down his estimates by Roman province, which added more detail, and he introduced comparison by comparing Roman GDP with early modern estimates in 1990 Geary-Khamis dollars, a hypothetical currency with the purchasing power of

1990 U.S. dollars. Purchasing power is estimated for modern countries by assuming "purchasing power parity," that is, assuming that the cost of an identical basket of internationally traded goods will cost the same around the world. In other words, the use of this unit of account implicitly assumes that the results of chapter 2 showing that the price of wheat was determined by trade across the Mediterranean were true for most items of Roman consumption. Maddison, an economist, had no trouble with this assumption; ancient historians may be suspicious. Bang (2008, 87–88) represents the opposite position. He took his cue from Hopkins, reproducing his procedures with its mistakes and accompanied by many caveats. He did not mention Geary-Khamis dollars, and he would not agree they are useful in studies of the ancient world.

Maddison's conclusions are revealing. He followed Goldsmith's lead and compared Roman incomes with those of England in 1688 when a contemporary estimate was made by valuing consumption in each period by the value of gold and then by the value of wheat. Averaging them, he concluded "that average per capita income in the Roman empire was about 40 per cent of the $1,411 in England and Wales in 1688" (Maddison 2007, 52). Since the modern estimates were in Geary-Khamis dollars, Maddison used them for Roman values.

Scheidel and Friesen drew from both ancient historians and economists. They start their estimation with their conclusion: "We merely assume that in terms of average per capital performance the Roman economy did not dramatically differ from most other pre-industrial systems and fell short of the achievements of the most advanced economies of the early modern world, those of the Netherlands and England" (Scheidel and Friesen 2009, 64). This "mere" assumption implies that Roman GDP was near subsistence and near Maddison's estimate. This becomes clear in their stated conclusions where their estimates of Roman GDP are dependent on estimated subsistence. If it was 350 kg of wheat equivalent, the Roman per capita GDP was about $610 Geary-Khamis dollars; if substance was $390—close to Maddison's $400—then Roman per capita GDP was around $700 Geary-Khamis dollars (Scheidel and Friesen 2009, 74).

They argue that their assumption of a gap between Rome and early modern Europe "does not shape our estimates . . . in an unduly arbitrary or circular way." Citing de Vries and van der Woude (1997), they elaborate as follows:

> Labeled the 'first modern economy,' the 'Golden Age' Netherlands enjoyed unusually large energy inputs, provided by fossil fuels in the form of local peat deposits, that were unavailable to other 'organic,' pre-industrial economies; attained level of formal schooling and literacy were exceptional by pre-modern standards; created a flourishing bond market; and was the first country on

record in which the share of the population engaged in farming fell below one-half. (Scheidel and Friesen 2009, 64)

There are several problems with this comparison. The main problem of this claim is that Scheidel and Friesen compare apples and oranges. As they note in the following paragraph, the Netherlands had a population of only 2 million people. How can you compare this to the Roman Empire of 70 million people, their preferred population on the eve of the plague? Rome itself had a population of 1 million, and Roman Italy had a population of around 7 million people. These entities are far closer to the early modern Netherlands than the massive Roman Empire. The Netherlands were the most advanced country in the seventeenth century, and it should be compared with the most advanced part of the Roman Empire.

Rome is smaller than the Netherlands, and Italy is larger, but they are at least the same order of magnitude. If we take Roman Italy as being comparable to the Netherlands in 1600, then the Roman Empire as a whole is comparable to Europe as a whole. According to Maddison, the population of Europe was between 60 and 70 million people, close to the 70 million maximum of the early Roman Empire. (Scheidel and Friesen were aware of this mismatch, but they compared the Roman Empire with a Europe that had the same average income after 1800 as the most advanced most advanced country in 1600. They also noted that there may have been "pockets of development such as Roman Italy or the Aegean" [Scheidel and Friesen 2009, 64]. Their reasoning is unclear.)

The putative advantages of the early modern Netherlands over Roman Italy are less clear than their advantages over the Roman Empire as a whole. Roman Italy was heavily urbanized, and it is probable that the proportion of the labor force in agriculture there was less than 50 percent. Rome did not have a bond market, but it had a more sophisticated financial system than the Netherlands (see chapter 8). It did not have peat, but it had waterwheels and needed less heat for its houses. It did not have canals, but it had roads and the Mediterranean. It had education, a functioning legal system, and an ethos of responsibility. Both places developed art and literature that still affects us today. If the previous chapters of this book are more or less accurate, then Roman Italy was comparable to the Netherlands in 1600.

The comparability is enhanced by noting that neither the Netherlands nor Rome had an industrial revolution. The Industrial Revolution took place in the north of England where the relative price of labor and power was very different than in the eighteenth-century Netherlands and ancient Rome. Dutch peat was not anywhere as cheap as English coal at the mine head, and this difference in relative prices made the early machines of the Industrial Revolution unprofitable on the European continent (Allen 2009c).

Lo Cascio and Malanima (2009a, 2009b) compared Goldsmith's and Maddison's estimates to show how similar they were. They then contested Maddison's efforts to compare Roman and early modern incomes by deflating the modern estimates by the prices of gold and wheat, arguing that gold was more expensive (and goods cheaper) than later and that Maddison had not accurately reported grain prices in early modern Europe. They followed Maddison in separating consideration of Roman Italy and the empire as a whole.

The result of these recalculations was to produce an estimate of Roman per capita GDP in 150 CE of 1,000 1990 international dollars (Lo Cascio and Malanima 2009b). This is almost twice as large as Maddison's estimates, which were the basis of Scheidel and Friesen's calculations. They follow Maddison in separating incomes in and outside Roman Italy, concluding that per capita GDP in Roman Italy was 1,400 international dollars, almost exactly equal to Maddison's estimate of per capita income in the Netherlands in 1600 of 1,381. As I argued in chapter 10, the benefits of international and interregional trade were the same in Roman Italy and the advanced countries of early modern Europe; Lo Cascio and Malanima made this same argument from a different direction.

They generalized their result to argue "that pre-modern agrarian economies underwent phases of growth and decline, but not of real long-term progress. . . . Growth was not unknown before Modern Growth, but it came about in long cycles around an overall stability of per capita income. In our view, the Roman economy was no more backward than the early modern West European economy" (Lo Cascio and Malanima 2009a, 392). In terms of the questions of this chapter, the Malthusian swing of income in the Roman Empire was as large as in early modern Europe.

Calculating Roman GDP should be a way of discovering if these two economies were equally productive. Unhappily, it appears that the answer has been prejudged before any Roman calculations are done. I therefore use a simpler and more transparent approach than that used by Lo Cascio and Malanima to confirm their results. I work backward and assume that Roman Italy was comparable to the Netherlands in 1600 and infer what the GDP of the Roman Empire might have been.

The calculations are simple, building on two observations. From Maddison (2007, 50) I take the observation that per capita income outside Roman Italy was about two-thirds of its value there. He was the only one to estimate per capita GDP by province. I couple that with the rough estimate that the population of Roman Italy (about 7 million) was about 10 percent of the Roman

Empire's population (about 70 million). Then if per capita GDP in Roman Italy was close to that of the Netherlands in 1600, per capita GDP in the Roman Empire was about 1,000 Geary-Khamis dollars. This is exactly equal to Lo Cascio and Malanima's estimate, higher than Scheidel and Friesen's high estimate of 700 for Rome and of Maddison's (2007, 382) estimate of 900 for Europe as a whole in 1600. It is almost exactly equal to Maddison's estimate of European income in 1700. Is it circular? Only if you have not been convinced by the preceding chapters about the microeconomics of Rome—or have not read them—should this short derivation seem worse than its competitors.

This easily derived estimate is the best estimate for the GDP of the Roman Empire at its peak. It can be multiplied by the size of the population to get an aggregate. As stated by Lo Cascio and Malanima (2009b): "Our discussion of the problem strongly suggests that a real difference in the level of average income between the early Roman Empire and the following European pre-modern economics did not exist at all." I look forward to more debates about how prosperous the Romans were and what their undoubted accomplishments imply for our view of their economic progress in the early Roman Empire.

References

• • •

Abramovitz, Moses, and Paul A. David, "Reinterpreting Economic Growth: Parables and Realities," *American Economic Review, Papers and Proceedings*, 63: 428–39 (May 1973).

Acemoglu, Daron, Simon Johnson, and James A. Robinson, "The Colonial Origins of Comparative Development: An Empirical Investigation," *American Economic Review*, 91: 1369–1401 (December 2001).

Akerlof, George A., "The Market for 'Lemons': Quality Uncertainty and the Market Mechanism," *Quarterly Journal of Economics* 84: 488–500 (August 1970).

———, "Behavioral Macroeconomics and Macroeconomic Behavior," *American Economic Review*, 92 (3): 411–33 (2002).

Akerlof, George A., and Rachel E. Kranton, *Identity Economics: How Our Identities Shape Our Work, Wages, and Well-Being* (Princeton: Princeton University Press, 2010).

Alcock, Susan E., *Grecia Capta: The Landscapes of Roman Greece* (Cambridge: Cambridge University Press, 1993).

Alföldy, Géza, *The Social History of Rome*, trans. D. Braund and F. Pollock (Baltimore: Johns Hopkins University Press, 1988).

Allen, Robert C., "The Great Divergence: Wages and Prices in Europe from the Middle Ages to the First World War," *Explorations in Economic History*, 38: 411–47 (October 2001).

———, "Progress and Poverty in Early Modern Europe," *Economic History Review*, 56, 403–43 (August 2003).

———, "English and Welsh Agriculture, 1300–1850: Output, Inputs, and Income," Oxford University Working Paper (2005).

———, "How Prosperous Were the Romans? Evidence from Diocletian's Price Edict (AD 301)," in Bowman and Wilson (2009a), 327–45.

———, *The British Industrial Revolution in Global Perspective* (Cambridge: Cambridge University Press, 2009b).

———, "The Industrial Revolution in Miniature: The Spinning Jenny in Britain, France and India," *Journal of Economic History*, 69: 901–27 (December 2009c).

Alonso, Nancy, *Closed for Repairs* (Willimantic, CT: Curbstone Press, 2007).

Alston, R., "Roman Military Pay from Caesar to Diocletian," *Journal of Roman Studies*, 84: 113–23 (1994).

Altman, Daniel, David M. Cutler, and Richard J. Zeckhauser, "The Changing Market for Health Insurance: Adverse Selection and Adverse Retention," *American Economic Review*, 88 (2): 122–26 (1998).

Anderson, B. L., "The Attorney and the Early Capital Market in Lancashire," in J. R. Harris, ed., *Liverpool and Merseyside: Essays in the Economic and Social History of the Port and its Hinterland* (London, Cass: 1969), 50–77.

Andreau, Jean, *Les affaires de Monsieur Jucundus* (Rome: École Française de Rome, 1974).

———, "Fondations privées et rapports sociaux en Italie romaine," *Ktema*, 2: 157–209 (1977).

———, "A propos de la vie financière à Pouzzoles: Cluvius et Vestorius," in M. Cébeillac-Gervasoni, ed., *Les 'bourgeoisies' municipales italiennes au IIe et Ier siècles av. J.-C.* (Naples: Centre Jean Bérard, Institute Français de Naples, 1983), 9–20.

———, *La vie financière dans le monde romain: les metiers de manieurs d'argent* (Rome: École Française de Rome, 1987a).

———, "L'espace de la vie financière à Rome," *L'Urbs, espace urbain et histoire*, (Rome 1987b), 157–74.

———, "Affaires financiers à Pouzzoles au premier siècle ap. J.-C.: les tablettes de Murecine," *Revue des études latines*, 72: 39–55 (1994).

———, "Commerce and Finance," in Bowman, Garnsey, and Rathbone (2000), 769–87.

———, *Banking and Business in the Roman World* (Cambridge: Cambridge University Press, 1999); French version: *Banque et affaires dans le monde romain (IVe siècle av. J.-C.–IIIe siècle ap. J.-C.)* (Paris: Seuil, 2001).

———, "Les esclaves 'hommes d'affaires' et la gestion des ateliers et commerces," in Andreau, France, and Pittia (2004), 111–26.

Andreau, Jean, J. France, and S. Pittia, eds., *Mentalités et choix économiques des Romains* (Bordeaux: Pessac: Ausonius, 2004).

Antràs, Pol, and Hans-Joachim Voth, "Productivity Growth and Factor Prices during the British Industrial Revolution," *Explorations in Economic History*, 40 (1): 52–77 (2003).

Arnott, Richard, and Joseph E. Stiglitz, "Moral Hazard and Nonmarket Institutions: Dysfunctional Crowding Out of Peer Monitoring?" *American Economic Review*, 81 (1): 179–90 (1991).

Ashton, Thomas, *The Industrial Revolution: 1760–1830* (London: Oxford University Press, (1948).

Aubert, Jean-Jacques, *Business Managers in Ancient Rome: A Social and Economic Study of Institores, 200 BC–AD 250* (Leiden: Brill, 1994).

———, ed., *Tâches publiques et enterprise privée dans le monde romain* (Geneva: Droz, 2003).

Badian, E., *Publicans and Sinners: Private Enterprise in the Service of the Roman Republic* (Ithaca: Cornell University Press, 1983).

Bagnall, Roger S., *Currency and Inflation in Fourth-century Egypt. Bulletin of the American Society of Papyrologists*, Supplement 5 (Chico, CA: Scholar's Press, 1985).

————, "Landholding in Late Roman Egypt: The Distribution of Wealth," *Journal of Roman Studies*, 82: 128–49 (1992).

————, *Egypt in Late Antiquity* (Princeton: Princeton University Press, 1993).

————, *The Kellis Agricultural Account Book* (Oxford: Oxbow Books, 1997).

————, "The Effects of Plague: Model and Evidence," *Journal of Roman Archaeology*, 15: 114–20 (2002).

————, "Prices in 'Sales on Delivery,'" *Greek, Roman and Byzantine Studies*, 18: 85–96 (1977); reprinted in R. S. Bagnall, *Later Roman Egypt: Religion, Economy, and Administration* (Aldershot, UK: Ashgate/Variorum, 2003), chap. 15.

Bagnall, Roger S., and Bruce W. Frier, *The Demography of Roman Egypt* (Cambridge: Cambridge University Press, 1994).

Bailyn, Bernard, and Lotte Bailyn, *Massachusetts Shipping, 1697–1714: A Statistical Study* (Cambridge, MA: Harvard University Press, 1959).

Bairoch, Paul, Jean Batou, and Pierre Chèvre, *The Population of European Cities: Data Bank and Short Summary of Results* (Geneva: Librairie Droz, 1988).

Ballard, Robert D., A. M. McCann et al. "The Discovery of Ancient History in the Deep Sea Using Advanced Deep Submergence Technology," *Deep-Sea Research*, 47: 1591–1620 (2000).

Ballard, Robert D., Lawrence E. Stager et al., "Iron Age Shipwrecks in Deep Water off Ashkelon, Israel," *American Journal of Archaeology*, 106: 151–68 (2002).

Banaji, Jairus, *Agrarian Change in Late Antiquity: Gold, Labour, and Aristocratic Dominance* (Oxford: Oxford University Press, 2001).

Bang, Peter F., *The Roman Bazaar: A Comparative Study of Trade and Markets in a Tributary Empire* (Cambridge: Cambridge University Press, 2008).

————, "Commanding and Consuming the World: Empire, Tribute, and Trade in Roman and Chinese History," in Walter Scheidel, ed., *Rome and China* (Oxford: Oxford University Press, 2009), 100–220.

Barro, Robert J., "Government Spending, Interest Rates, Prices, and Budget Deficits in the United Kingdom, 1701–1918," *Journal of Monetary Economics*, 20: 221–47 (1987).

Beck, Thorsten, and Ross Levine, "Legal Institutions and Financial Development," in Claude Ménard and Mary M. Shirley, eds., *Handbook of New Institutional Economics* (Dordrecht: Spring, 2005), 251–78.

Bender, Thomas, *Community and Social Change in America* (New Brunswick, NJ: Rutgers University Press, 1978).

Berliner, Joseph S., *The Innovation Decision in Soviet Industry* (Cambridge, MA: MIT Press, 1976).

Billeter, Gustav, *Geschichte des Zinsfusses im Griechisch-Römischen Altertum bis auf Justinian* (Leipzig: Teubner, 1898).

Bloch, Marc, *Feudal Society* (Chicago: University of Chicago Press, 1961).

Bogaert, Raymond, *Banques et Banquiers dans les Cités Grecques* (Leyden: Sijthoff, 1968).

————, "Liste géographique des banques et des banquiers de l'Egypte romaine, 30A–284," *Zeitschrift für Papyrologie und Epigraphik*, 109: 133–73 (1995).

———, "Les operations des banques de l'Egypte romaine," *Ancient Society*, 30: 135–269 (2000).

———, "Les documents bancaires de l'Egypte gréco-romaine et byzantine," *Ancient Society*, 31: 173–288 (2001).

Boot, Max, *War Made New: Technology, Warfare, and the Course of History, 1500 to Today* (New York: Penguin, 2006).

Borjas, George J., "Self-Selection and the Earnings of Immigrants," *American Economic Review*, 77: 531–53 (September 1987).

———, "Does Immigration Grease the Wheels of the Labor Market?" *Brookings Papers on Economic Activity*, 1: 69–133 (2001).

Bowman, Alan K., "The Economy of Egypt in the Earlier Fourth Century," in C. E. King, ed., *Oxford Symposium on Coinage and Monetary History: Imperial Revenue, Expenditure, and Monetary Policy in the Fourth Century A.D.* (Leeds: Prospect Books, 1980), 23–40.

———, "Landholding in the Hermopolite Nome in the Fourth Century A.D.," *Journal of Roman Studies*, 75: 137–63 (1985).

———, *Life and Letters on the Roman Frontier: Vinolanda and its People* (New York: Routledge, 1998).

Bowman, Alan K., Peter Garnsey, and Dominic Rathbone, eds., *The Cambridge Ancient History*, Vol. 11, *The High Empire, A.D. 70–192* (Cambridge: Cambridge University Press, 2000).

Bowman, Alan, and Andrew Wilson, eds., *Quantifying the Roman Economy* (Oxford: Oxford University Press, 2009).

Bradley, Keith R., *Slaves and Masters in the Roman Empire* (New York: Oxford University Press, 1987).

———, *Slavery and Rebellion in the Roman World, 140 B.C.–70 B.C.* (Bloomington: Indiana University Press, 1989).

———, *Slavery and Society at Rome* (Cambridge: Cambridge University Press, 1994).

Bransbourg, Gilles, "Rome and the Economic Integration of Empire," Institute for the Study of the Ancient World Papers 3, 2012. Available at http:/dlib.nyu.edu/awdl/isaw/isaw-papers/3.

Braudel, Fernand, *The Mediterranean and the Mediterranean World in the Age of Philip II* (New York: Harper and Row, 1972–73).

Broadberry, Steven N., "Anglo-German Productivity Differences, 1870–1990," *European Review of Economic History*, 1: 247–67 (August 1997).

Bruchey, Stuart, *The Colonial Merchant: Sources and Readings* (New York: Harcourt, Brace, and World, 1966).

Brunt, Liam, "Rediscovering Risk: Country Banks as Venture Capital Firms in the First Industrial Revolution," *Journal of Economic History*, 66: 74–102 (2006).

Brunt, P. A., *Italian Manpower, 225 B.C.–A.D. 14* (Oxford: Oxford University Press, 1971).

———, "Conscription and Volunteering in the Roman Imperial Army," *Scripta Classica Israelica*, 1: 90–115 (1974).

———, "Free Labour and Public Works at Rome," *Journal of Roman Studies*, 70: 81–100 (1980).

———, "Publicans in the Principate," in P. A. Brunt, *Roman Imperial Themes* (Oxford: Oxford University Press, 1990).

Bulliet, Richard W., *The Camel and the Wheel* (Cambridge, MA: Harvard University Press, 1975).

Bürge, A., "Fiktion und Wirklichkeit: soziale und rechtliche Strukturen des römischen Bankwesens," *Zeitschrift der Savigny-Stiftung für Rechtsgeschichte (Romanistische Abteilung)*, 104: 465–558 (1987).

Burnett, A. M., *Coinage in the Roman World* (London: Seaby, 1987).

Burton, G. P., "The Roman Imperial State, Provincial Governors and the Public Finances of Provincial Cities, 27 B.C.–A.D. 235," *Historia*, 53: 311–42 (2004).

Cagan, Phillip, "The Monetary Dynamics of Inflation," in Milton Friedman, ed., *Studies in the Quantity Theory of Money* (Chicago: University of Chicago Press, 1956), 25–117.

Calomiris, Charles W., "The Costs of Rejecting Universal Banking: American Finance in the German Mirror, 1870–1914," in Naomi R. Lamoreaux and Daniel M. G. Raff, eds., *Coordination and Information* (Chicago: University of Chicago Press, 1995), 257–315.

Camodeca, Giuseppi, *L'Archivio puteolani dei Sulpicii*, Vol. 1 (Naples: Jovene, 1992).

———, *Tabulae Pompeianae Sulpiciorum. TPSulp: edizione critica dell'archivio puteolano dei Sulpicii* (Rome: Ed. Quasar, 1999).

———, "Il credito negli archivi campani: il caso di Puteoli e di Herculaneum," in Lo Cascio (2003), 69–98.

Capie, Forrest, "The Origin and Development of Stable Fiscal and Monetary Institutions in England," in Michael D. Bordo and Roberto Cortés-Conde, eds., *Transferring Wealth and Power from the Old to the New World* (Cambridge: Cambridge University Press, 2001), 19–58.

Carlos, Ann M., "Historical Perspectives on the Economics of Trade Principal-Agent Problems in Early Trading Companies: A Tale of Two Firms," *American Economic Review*, 82 (2): 140–45 (1992).

Carlos, Ann M., and Stephen Nicholas, "Agency Problems in Early Chartered Companies: The Case of the Hudson's Bay Company," *Journal of Economic History*, 50 (4): 853–75 (1990).

Carswell, John, *The South Sea Bubble* (London: Cresset Press, 1960).

Casson, Lionel, "The Grain Trade of the Hellenistic World," *Transactions and Proceedings of the American Philological Association*, 85: 168–87 (1954).

———, "Harbour and River Boats of Ancient Rome," *Journal of Roman Studies*, 55: 31–39 (1965).

———, *The Ancient Mariners* (Princeton: Princeton University Press, 1991).

Chalhoub, Sidney, "Slaves, Freedmen and the Politics of Freedom in Brazil: The Experience of Blacks in the City of Rio," *Slavery and Abolition*, 10: 64–84 (1989).

Cherry, John F., J. L. Davis, and E. Mantzourani, "Greek and Roman Settlement and Land Use," in *Landscape Archaeology as Long-Term History: Northern Keos in the*

Cycladic Islands from Earliest Settlement until Modern Times (Los Angeles: UCLA Institute of Archaeology, 1991), 327–47.

Childs, Matt D., "Master-Slave Rituals of Power at a Gold Mine in Nineteenth-Century Brazil," *History Workshop Journal*, 53: 43–72 (2002).

Christiansen, Erik, *The Roman Coins of Alexandria* (Aarhus, Denmark: Arhus University Press, 1988).

Clark, Colin, and Margaret Haswell, *The Economics of Subsistence Agriculture*, 3rd ed. (London: Macmillan, 1967).

Clark, Gregory, "The Political Foundations of Modern Economic Growth: England, 1540–1800," *Journal of Interdisciplinary History* 46 (4): 563–88 (spring 1996).

——, "Farm Wages and Living Standards in the Industrial Revolution: England, 1670–1850," *Economic History Review*, 54: 477–505 (August 2001).

——, *A Farewell to Alms: A Brief Economic History of the World* (Princeton: Princeton University Press, 2007a).

——, "The Long March of History: Farm Wages, Population, and Economic Growth, England, 1209–1869," *Economic History Review*, 60: 136–89 (February 2007b).

Coates, Ben, *The Impact of the English Civil Wars on the Economy of London, 1642–50* (Aldershot UK: Ashgate, 2004).

Cohen, Edward E., *Athenian Economy and Society: A Banking Perspective* (Princeton, NJ: Princeton University Press, 1992).

Cole, Shawn, "Capitalism and freedom: Slavery and Manumission in Louisiana, 1770–1820," *Journal of Economic History*, 65: 1008–27 (December 2005).

Cole, W. A., and Phyllis Deane, "The Growth of National Incomes," in H. J. Habakkuk and M. Postan, eds., *The Cambridge Economic History of Europe*, Vol. 6, *Industrial Revolutions and After* (Cambridge: Cambridge University Press, 1965), 1–55.

Craig, Lee A., and Douglas Fisher, *The European Macroeconomy: Growth, Integration and Cycles 1500–1913* (Cheltenham, UK: Edward Elgar, 2000).

Crawford, Michael H., *Coinage and Money under the Roman Republic* (Berkeley: University of California Press, 1985).

Crook, John A., *Law and Life of Rome* (London: Thames & Hudson, 1967).

Crook, J. Mordaunt, *The Rise of the Nouveaux Riches* (London: John Murray, 1999).

Crouzet, François, "Capital Formation in Great Britain during the Industrial Revolution," in François Crouzet, ed., *Capital Formation in the Industrial Revolution* (London: Methuen, 1972), 162–222.

Cuvigny, Helene, "The Amount of Wages Paid to the Quarry-Workers at Mons Claudianus," *Journal of Roman Studies*, 86: 139–45 (1996).

Dale, Richard, *The First Crash* (Princeton: Princeton University Press, 2004).

Dari-Mattiacci, Giuseppe, "Slavery and Information: A Model with Applications to Ancient Rome," Amsterdam Center for Law and Economics Working Paper No. 2011–11 (2011).

D'Arms, John H., *Commerce and Social Standing in Ancient Rome* (Cambridge: Harvard University Press, 1981).

Dasgupta, Partha, *An Inquiry into Well-Being and Destitution* (Oxford: Clarendon Press, 1993).

David, Paul A., "The Growth of Real Product in the United States before 1840: New Evidence, Controlled Conjectures," *Journal of Economic History*, 27: 151–97 (June 1967).

David, Paul A., Herbert G. Gutman, Richard Sutch, Peter Temin, and Gavin Wright, *Reckoning with Slavery: A Critical Study in the Quantitative History of American Negro Slavery* (New York: Oxford University Press, 1976).

Davies, Norman de G., and R. O. Faulkner, "A Syrian Trading Venture to Egypt," *Journal of Egyptian Archaeology*, 33: 40–46 (1947).

Dehing, Pit, and Marjolein 'T Hart, "Linking the Fortunes: Currency and Banking, 1550–1800," in Marjolein 'T Hart, Joost Jonker, and Jan Luiten van Zanden, eds., *A Financial History of The Netherlands* (Cambridge: Cambridge University Press, 1997), 37–63.

De Ligt, Luuk, "Tax Transfers in the Roman Empire," in Lucas de Blois and John Rich, eds., *The Transformation of Economic Life under the Roman Empire* (Amsterdam: Gieben, 2002), 48–66.

DeLong, J. Bradford, and Andrei Shleifer, "Princes and Merchants: European City Growth before the Industrial Revolution," *Journal of Law and Economics*, 36: 671–702 (October 1993).

DeLong, J. B., and L. H. Summers, "Equipment Investment and Economic Growth," *Quarterly Journal of Economics*, 106: 445–530 (May 1991).

Denison, Edward F., *Why Growth Rates Differ* (Washington, DC: Brookings Institution, 1967).

Dessau, Hermann, *Inscriptiones Latinae selectae* (Berolini: Apud Weidmannos, 1962–).

De Ste. Croix, Geoffrey E. M., "Ancient Greek and Roman Maritime Loans," in Harold Edey and B. S. Yamey, eds., *Debits, Finance, and Profits* (London: Sweet and Maxwell, 1974).

De Vries, Jan, and Ad van der Woude, *The First Modern Economy* (Cambridge: Cambridge University Press, 1997).

Diamond, Jared M., *Guns, Germs, and Steel: The Fates of Human Societies* (New York: Norton, 1997).

Dickson, P. G. M., *The Financial Revolution in England: A Study in the Development of Public Credit, 1688–1756* (London: Macmillan, 1967).

Di Porto, Andrea, *Impreso collettiva e schiavo manager in Roma antica* (Milan: Giuffrè, 1984).

Domar, Evsey D., "On the Measurement of Technological Change," *Economic Journal*, 71: 709–29 (1961).

Drexhage, Hans-Joachim, *Preise, Mieten/Pachten, Kosten und Löhne im Römischen Ägypten bis zum Regierungsantritt Diokletians* (St. Katharinen, Germany: Scripta Mercaturae, 1991).

Duby, George, *The Early Growth of the European Economy* (Ithaca, NY: Cornell University Press, 1974).

Duff, A. M., *Freedmen in the Early Roman Empire* (Oxford: Oxford University Press, 1928).

Duncan-Jones, Richard, *The Economy of the Roman Empire: Quantitative Studies*, 2nd ed. (Cambridge: Cambridge University Press, 1982).

————, *Structure and Scale in the Roman Economy* (Cambridge: Cambridge University Press, 1990).

————, *Money and Government in the Roman Empire* (Cambridge: Cambridge University Press, 1994).

————, "The Impact of the Antonine Plague," *Journal of Roman Archeology*, 9: 108–36 (1996).

Easterlin, Richard A., "Why Isn't the Whole World Developed?" *Journal of Economic History*, 41: 1–19 (March 1981).

Easterly, William R., *The Elusive Quest for Growth: Economists' Adventures and Misadventures in the Tropics* (Cambridge, MA: MIT Press, 2001).

Eck, Werner, "Emperor, Senate and Magistrates," in Bowman, Garnsey, and Rathbone (2000).

Eisner, Robert, *The Total Incomes System of Accounts* (Chicago: University of Chicago Press, 1989).

Engels, Friedrich, *The Condition of the Working Class in England* (Oxford: Oxford University Press, 1993).

Erdkamp, Paul, *The Grain Market in the Roman Empire* (Cambridge: Cambridge University Press, 2005).

Feinstein, Charles H., "Pessimism Perpetuated: Real Wages and the Standard of Living in Britain during and after the Industrial Revolution," *Journal of Economic History*, 58: 625–58 (September 1998).

Fenoaltea, Stefano, "Slavery and Supervision in Comparative Perspective: A Model," *Journal of Economic History*, 44: 635–68 (1984).

Ferguson, Niall, *The House of Rothschild: Money's Prophets, 1798–1848* (New York: Penguin, 1998).

Findlay, Ronald, "Slavery, Incentives, and Manumission: A Theoretical Model," *Journal of Political Economy*, 83: 923–34 (1975).

Finley, M. I., *The Ancient Economy* (Berkeley: University of California Press, 1973).

————, *Ancient Slavery and Modern Ideology* (London: Chatto and Windus, 1980).

————, *The Ancient Economy: Updated with a New Foreword by Ian Morris* (Berkeley: University of California Press, 1999).

Finn, Margot C., *The Character of Credit: Personal Debt in English Culture, 1740–1914* (Cambridge: Cambridge University Press, 2003).

Fischer, David H., *Washington's Crossing* (Oxford: Oxford University Press, 2004).

Fisher, Irving, "The Debt-Deflation Theory of Great Depressions," *Econometrica*, 1: 337–57 (1933).

Floud, Roderick, and Donald McCloskey, *The Economic History of Britain since 1700*, 2nd ed., Vol. 1, *1700–1860* (Cambridge: Cambridge University Press, 1997).

Fogel, Robert W., and Stanley L. Engerman, *Time on the Cross: The Economics of American Negro Slavery* (Boston: Little, Brown, 1974).

Foreman, Amanda, *Georgiana, Duchess of Devonshire* (London: HarperCollins, 1988).

Foxhall, Lin, and H. A. Forbes, "Sitometreia: The Role of Grain as a Staple Food in Classical Antiquity," *Chiron*, 12: 41–90 (1982).

France J., "La ferme des douanes dans les provinces occidentales de l'empire romain," in Aubert (2003), 193–213.

Frank, Tenney, ed., *Economic Survey of Ancient Rome* (Baltimore: John Hopkins Press, 1933–40).

———, "Notes on Roman Commerce," *Journal of Roman Studies*, 21 (1937).

Frank, Zephyr, *Dutra's World: Wealth and Family in Nineteenth-Century Rio de Janeiro* (Albuquerque: University of New Mexico Press, 2004).

Frederiksen, M. W., "Caesar, Cicero, and the Problem of Debt," *Journal of Roman Studies*, 56: 128–41 (1966).

Frier, Bruce W., and Dennis P. Kehoe, "Law and Economic Institutions," in Scheidel, Morris, and Saller (2007), 113–43.

Galenson, David W., *White Servitude in Colonial America* (Cambridge: Cambridge University Press, 1981).

Galor, Oded, *Unified Growth Theory* (Princeton: Princeton University Press, 2011).

Garcia Morcillo, M., "Auctions, Bankers, and Public Finances in the Roman World," in Verboven et al. (2008), 257–75.

Gardner, J. F., *Women in Roman Law and Society* (London: Croom Helm, 1986).

Garnsey, Peter, *Famine and Food Supply in the Graeco-Roman World: Responses to Risk and Crisis* (Cambridge: Cambridge University Press, 1988).

———, *Ideas of Slavery from Aristotle to Augustine* (Cambridge: Cambridge University Press, 1996).

———, *Cities, Peasants, and Food in Classical Antiquity* (Cambridge: Cambridge University Press, 1998).

———, *Food and Society in Classical Antiquity* (Cambridge: Cambridge University Press, 1999).

Garnsey, Peter, and Richard Saller, *The Roman Empire: Economy, Society, and Culture* (Berkeley: University of California Press, 1987).

Gasnault, Pierre, *Documents Comptables de Saint-Mertin de Tours a lÉpoque Mérovingienne* (Paris: Biblioteque Nationale, 1975).

Gelderblom, Oscar, and Jonker Joost, "Completing a Financial Revolution: The Finance of the Dutch East India Trade and the Rise of the Amsterdam Capital Market, 1595–1612," *Journal of Economic History*, 64: 641–72 (2004).

Geraghty, Ryan M., "The Impact of Globalization in the Roman Empire, 200 BC–AD 100," *Journal of Economic History*, 67: 1036–61 (December 2007).

Gibb, H. A. R., *Ibn Battuta: Travels in Asia and Africa, 1325–1354* (New Delhi: Oriental Books Reprint, 1986).

Gibbon, Edward, *The Decline and Fall of the Roman Empire* (New York: Modern Library, 1961).

Goffart, Walter, *Caput and Colonate: Towards a History of Late Roman Taxation* (Toronto: University of Toronto Press, 1974).

Goldsmith, Raymond W., "An Estimate of the Size and Structure of the National Product of the Early Roman Empire," *Review of Income and Wealth*, 30: 263–88 (September 1984).

Grainger, John D., "Prices in Hellenic Babylonia," *Journal of the Economic and Social History of the Orient*, 42: 3, 303–25 (August 1999).

Greene, Kevin, *The Archeology of the Roman Economy* (London: Batsford, 1986).

———, "Technological Innovation and Economic Progress in the Ancient World:

M. I. Finley Re-Considered," *Economic History Review*, 53 (1): 29–59 (February 2000).

Greif, Avner, "Reputation and Coalitions in Medieval Trade: Evidence on the Maghribi Traders," *Journal of Economic History*, 49 (4): 857–82 (1989).

———, "Cultural Beliefs and the Organization of Society: A Historical and Theoretical Reflection on Collectivist and Individualist Societies," *Journal of Political Economy*, 102: 912–50 (October 1994).

Grenfell, Bernard P., Arthur S. Hunt, and David G. Hogarth, *Fayum Towns and their Papyri* (London: Egypt Exploration Fund, 1900).

Griffin, Miriam T., *Nero: The End of a Dynasty* (New Haven: Yale University Press, 1984).

Gröschler, Peter, *Die Tabellae-Urkunden aus den pompejanischen und herkulanensischen Urkundenfunden* (Berlin: Duncker and Humbolt, 1997).

Gutman, Herbert G., *Slavery and the Numbers Game: A Critique of Time on the Cross* (Urbana: University of Illinois Press, 1975).

Haklai-Rotenberg, Merav, "Aurelian's Monetary Reform: Between Debasement and Public Trust," *Chiron*, 41: 1–39 (November 2011).

Hall, Gwendolyn, *Databases for the Study of Afro-Louisiana History and Genealogy, 1699–1860* (New Orleans: Louisiana State University Press, 2000).

Hall, Robert E., and Charles I. Jones, "Why Do Some Countries Produce So Much More Output per Worker than Others?" *Quarterly Journal of Economics*, 114: 83–116 (February 1999).

Harl, Kenneth, W., *Coinage in the Roman Economy, 300 BC to AD 700* (Baltimore: Johns Hopkins University Press, 1996).

Harper, Kyle, "Slave Prices in Late Antiquity (and in the Very Long Run)," *Historia: Zeitschrift für alte Geschichte*, 59 (2): 206–38 (2010).

———, *River of Souls: Slavery in the Late Roman World, 275–425* (Cambridge: Cambridge University Press, 2011).

Harris, John R., and Michael P. Todaro, "Migration, Unemployment, and Development: A Two-Sector Analysis," *American Economic Review*, 60: 126–42 (1970).

Harris, William V., *War and Imperialism in Republican Rome* (Oxford: Oxford University Press, 1979).

———, "Roman Terracotta Lamps: The Organization of an Industry," *Journal of Roman Studies*, 70: 126–45 (1980).

———, *Ancient Literacy* (Cambridge, MA: Harvard University Press, 1989a).

———, "Trade and the River Po: A Problem in the Economic History of the Roman Empire," in J.-F. Bergier, ed., *Montagnes, fleuves, forêts dans l'histoire* (St Katharinen, Germany: Scripta Mercaturae, 1989b), 123–34; reprinted in W. V. Harris, *Rome's Imperial Economy: Twelve Essays* (New York: Oxford University Press, 2011).

———, "Between Archaic and Modern: Some Current Problems on the History of the Roman Economy," in W. V. Harris, ed., *The Inscribed Economy: Production and Distribution in the Roman Economy in the Light of the "Instrumentum Domesticum"* (Ann Arbor: University of Michigan Press, 1993), 11–29.

———, "Demography, Geography and the Sources of Roman Slaves," *Journal of Roman Studies*, 89: 62–75 (1999).

———, "A Revisionist View of Roman Money," *Journal of Roman Studies*, 96: 1–24 (2006).

Hay, Douglas, and Nicholas Rogers, *Eighteenth-Century English Society* (Oxford: Oxford University Press, 1982).

Heather, Peter J., *The Fall of the Roman Empire* (London: Macmillan, 2005).

Heckscher, Eli F., and Bertil Ohlin, *Heckscher-Ohlin Trade Theory*, translated, edited, and introduced by Harry Flam and M. June Flanders (Cambridge, MA: MIT Press, 1991).

Heichelheim, F. M., "Roman Syria," in Frank (1933–40), Vol. 4.

Henning, Joachim, "Revolution or Relapse? Technology, Agriculture, and Early Medieval Archaeology in Germanic Central Europe," in Giorgio Ausenda, Paolo Delogu, and Chris Wickham, eds., *The Langobards before the Frankish Conquest: An Ethnographic Perspective* (San Marino: Boyden Press, 2009), 149–73.

Hicks, John, *A Theory of Economic History* (Oxford: Oxford University Press, 1969).

Hoare, Henry Peregrine, *Hoare's Bank: A Record, 1673–1932* (London: Butler and Tanner, 1932).

Höbenreich, Evelyn, *Annona. Juristische Aspekte der stadtrömischen Lebensmittelversorgung im Prinzipat* (Graz: Leykam, 1997).

Hoffman, Philip T., Gilles Postel-Vinay, and Jean-Laurent Rosenthal, *Priceless Markets: The Political Economy of Credit in Paris, 1660–1870* (Chicago: University of Chicago Press, 2000).

Hollander, David B., *Money in the Late Roman Republic* (Leiden: Brill, 2007).

Hopkins, Keith, *Conquerors and Slaves* (Cambridge: Cambridge University Press, 1978).

———, "Taxes and Trade in the Roman Empire (200 B.C.–A.D. 400)," *Journal of Roman Studies*, 70: 101–25 (1980).

———, *Death and Renewal* (Cambridge: Cambridge University Press, 1983).

———, "Rome, Taxes, Rents and Trade," *Kodai: Journal of Ancient History*, 6/7: 41–75 (1995–96); reprinted in Walter Scheidel and Sitta Von Reden, eds., *The Ancient Economy* (London: Routledge, 2002).

Howgego, Christopher, "The Supply and Use of Money in the Roman World, 200 B.C. to A.D. 300," *Journal of Roman Studies*, 82: 1–31 (1992).

———, *Ancient History from Coins*. London: Routledge, 1995).

Husselman, E. M., "Pawnbrokers' Accounts from Roman Egypt," *Transactions of the American Philological Association*, 92: 251–66 (1961).

Inscriptions de Delos (Paris: H. Champion, 1926–).

Ionnatou, M., "Le code d'honneur des paiements. Créanciers et débiteurs à la fin de la République romaine," *Annales (Histoire, Sciences sociales)*, 56: 1201–21 (2001); cited as reprinted in Andreau, France, and Pittia 2004, 87–107.

Johnston, David, *Roman Law in Context* (Cambridge: Cambridge University Press, 1999).

Jones, A. H. M., "The Economics of Slavery in the Ancient World," *Economic History Review*, 9: 185–204 (1956).

——, *The Later Roman Empire, 284–602: A Social, Economic, and Administrative Survey* (Norman: University of Oklahoma Press, 1964).

——, "Inflation under the Roman Empire," in A. H. M. Jones, ed., *The Roman Economy: Studies in Ancient Economic and Administrative History* (Oxford: Oxford University Press, 1974), 187–227.

Jones, David, *The Bankers of Puteoli: Finance, Trade, and Industry in the Roman World* (Stroud: Tempus, 2006).

Jones, S. R. H., and Simon P. Ville, "Efficient Transactors or Rent-Seeking Monopolists? The Rationale for Early Chartered Trading Companies," *Journal of Economic History*, 56 (4): 898–915 (1996).

Jongman, Willem, *The Economy and Society of Pompeii* (Amsterdam: J. C. Gieben, 1988).

——, "Hunger and Power: Theories, Models, and Methods in Roman Economic History," in A.C.V.M. Bongenaar, ed., *Interdependency of Institutions and Private Entrepreneurs* (Istanbul: Nederlands Historisch-Archaeologisch Instituut, 2000), 259–84.

——, "The Roman Economy: From Cities to Empire," in Lucas de Blois and John Rich, eds., *The Transformation of Economic Life under the Roman Empire* (Amsterdam: Gieben, 2002), 28–47.

——, "Gibbon Was Right: The Decline and Fall of the Roman Empire," in Olivier Hekster, Gerda de Kleijn, and Danielle Slootjus, eds., *Crises and the Roman Empire: Proceedings of the Seventh Workshop of the International Network Impact of Empire*, Nijmegan, June 20–24, 2006 (Leyden: Brill, 2007a).

——, "Consumption in the Early Roman Empire," in Scheidel, Morris, and Saller (2007b), 592–618.

Joslin, D. M., "London Private Bankers, 1720–85," *Economic History Review*, 7: 167–86 (May 1954).

Karasch, Mary C., *Slave Life in Rio de Janeiro, 1808–1850* (Princeton: Princeton University Press, 1987).

Katsari, Constantina, *The Roman Monetary System: The Eastern Provinces from the First to the Third Century AD* (Cambridge: Cambridge University Press, 2011).

Kaye, J. M., *Medieval English Conveyances* (Cambridge: Cambridge University Press, 2009).

Kehoe, Dennis P., *Investment, Profit, and Tenancy: The Jurists and the Roman Agrarian Economy* (Ann Arbor: University of Michigan Press, 1997).

——, *Law and the Rural Economy in the Roman Empire* (Ann Arbor: University of Michigan Press, 2007).

Kent, J. P. C., "Gold Coinage in the Later Roman Empire," in R. A. G. Carson, ed., *Essays in Roman Coinage presented to Harold Mattingly* (Oxford: Oxford University Press, 1956), 190–204.

Kessler, David, and Peter Temin, "The Organization of the Grain Trade in the Early Roman Empire," *Economic History Review*, 60: 313–32 (May 2007).

——, "Money and Prices in the Early Roman Empire," in William V. Harris, ed., *The Monetary Systems of the Greeks and Romans* (Oxford: Oxford University Press, 2008), 137–59.

Keynes, John M., *The General Theory of Employment, Interest, and Prices* (London: Macmillan, 1936).

Kindleberger, Charles P., "Financial Institutions and Economic Development: A Comparison of Great Britain and France in the Eighteenth and Nineteenth Centuries," *Explorations in Economic History*, 21: 103–24 (April 1984).

King, Philip J., and Lawrence E. Stager, *Life in Biblical Israel* (Louisville, KY: Westminster and John Knox, 2001).

King, Robert G., and Ross Levine, "Finance and Growth: Schumpeter Might be Right," *Quarterly Journal of Economics*, 108: 717–37 (August 1993).

Kirschenbaum, Aaron, *Sons, Slaves, and Freedmen in Roman Commerce* (Washington, DC: Catholic University of America Press, 1987).

Kremer, Michael, "Population Growth and Technological Change: One Million B.C. to 1990," *Quarterly Journal of Economics*, 108: 681–716 (August 1993).

Krugman, Paul, "A Model of Balance-of-Payments Crises," *Journal of Money, Credit, and Banking*, 11: 311–25 (August 1979).

Kuznets, Simon, *Economic Growth of Nations: Total Output and Production Structure* (Cambridge, MA: Harvard University Press, 1971).

Laiou, Angeliki E., and Cécile Morrisson, *The Byzantine Economy* (Cambridge: Cambridge University Press, 2007).

Lamoreaux, Naomi R., *Insider Lending: Banks, Personal Connections, and Economic Development in Industrial New England* (Chicago: University of Chicago Press, 1994).

———, "The Mystery of Property Rights: A U.S. Perspective," *Journal of Economic History*, 71 (2): 275–306 (June 2011).

Lamoreaux, Naomi R., and Jean-Laurent Rosenthal, "Legal Regime and Business Organizational Choice: A Comparison of France and the United States during the mid-Nineteenth Century," NBER Working Paper 10288 (2004).

Landes, David S., *The Wealth and Poverty of Nations: Why Some Are So Rich and Some So Poor* (New York: Norton, 1998).

Larsen, Mogens T., *The Old Assyrian City-State and Its Colonies* (Copenhagen: Akademisk Forlag, 1976).

———, "Commercial Networks in the Ancient Near East," in Michael Rowlands, Mogens Larsen, and Kristian Kristiansen, eds., *Centre and Periphery in the Ancient World* (Cambridge: Cambridge University Press, 1987), 47–65.

Laum, Bernhard, *Stiftungen in der griechischen und romischen Antike: Ein Beitrag zur antiken Kulturgeschichte* (Leipzig: Teubner, 1914).

Lee, Ronald, "An Historical Perspective on Economic Aspects of the Population Explosion," in Richard Easterlin, ed., *Population and Economic Change in Developing Countries* (Chicago: University of Chicago Press, 1980), 517–57.

Lefort, Jacques, "The Rural Economy, Seventh—Twelfth Centuries," in Angeliki E. Laiou, ed., *The Economic History of Byzantium: From the Seventh through the Fifteenth Century* (Washington, DC: Dumbarton Oaks, 2002), 231–310.

Lendon, Jon E., "The Face on the Coins and Inflation in Roman Egypt," *Klio*, 72: 107–34 (1990).

Levine, Ross, "Financial Development and Economic Growth: Views and Agenda," *Journal of Economic Literature*, 35: 688–726 (June 1997).

Lewis, Naphtali, and Meyer Reinhold, *Roman Civilization: Selected Readings*, 3rd ed. (New York: Columbia University Press, 1990).

Libby, Douglas Cole, and Clothilde Andrade Paiva, "Manumission Practices in a Late Eighteenth-Century Brazilian Slave Parish: São José d'El Rey in 1795," *Slavery and Abolition*, 21: 96–127 (2000).

Liebenam, W., *Städteverwaltung im römischen Kaiserreiche* (Leipzig: Dunker and Humblot, 1900).

Lintott, Andrew, *Judicial Reform and Land Reform in the Roman Republic* (Cambridge: Cambridge University Press, 1992).

——, "Freedmen and Slaves in Light of Legal Documents from First-Century A.D. Campania," *Classical Quarterly*, 52: 555–65 (2002).

Little, Lester K., ed., *Plague and the End of Antiquity: The Pandemic of 541–750* (Cambridge: Cambridge University Press, 2007).

Liu, Xinru, *The Silk Road in World History* (Oxford: Oxford University Press, 2010).

Liverani, Mario, "The Collapse of the Near Eastern Regional System at the End of the Bronze Age: The Case of Syria," in Michael Rowlands, Mogens Larsen, and Kristian Kristiansen eds., *Centre and Periphery in the Ancient World* (Cambridge: Cambridge University Press, 1987), 66–73.

Lo Cascio, Elio, "State and Coinage in the Late Republic and Early Empire," *Journal of Roman Studies*, 71: 76–86 (1981).

——, "The Size of the Roman Population: Beloch and the Meaning of the Augustan Census Figures," *Journal of Roman Studies*, 84: 53–40 (1994).

——, ed., *Credito e moneta nel mondo romano* (Bari: Edipuglia, 2003).

——, ed., *Innovazione tecnica e progresso economico nel mondo romano* (Bari: Edipuglia, 2006).

——, "The Early Roman Empire: The State and the Economy," in Scheidel, Morris, and Saller (2007), 619–47.

——, ed., *La Peste Antonina* (Bari: Edipuglia, 2012).

Lo Cascio, Elio, and Paolo Malanima, "GDP in Pre-Modern Economics (1–1820 AD)," *Rivista di Storia Economica*, 25 (3): 391–419 (December 2009a).

——, "Ancient and Pre-Modern Economies: GDP in the Roman Empire and Early Modern Europe," presented at the conference on "Long-Term Quantification in Mediterranean Ancient History," Brussels (October 2009b).

Longon, Auguste, *Polyptique de l'Abbeye de Saint-Germain-des-Pres* (Geneva: Mégariotis Reprints, 1978).

Lucas, R. E. Jr., "On the Mechanics of Economic Development," *Journal of Monetary Economics*, 22: 3–42 (July 1988).

Luna, Francisco Vidal, and Herbert S. Klein, *Slavery and the Economy of São Paulo, 1750–1850* (Stanford: Stanford University Press, 2003).

MacMullen, Ramsey, *Corruption and the Decline of Rome* (New Haven: Yale, 1988).

Maddison, Angus, *Contours of the World Economy, 1–2030 AD* (Oxford: Oxford University Press, 2007).

Maeir, Aren M., "The Relations between Egypt and the Southern Levant during the Late Iron Age: The Material Evidence from Egypt," *Ägypten und Levante*, 12: 235–46 (2002).

Malanima, Paolo, "Wages, Productivity, and Working Time in Italy (1270–1913)," *Journal of European Economic History*, 36: 127–74 (2007).

———, *Pre-Modern European Economy: One Thousand Years (10th–19th Centuries)* (Leiden: Brill, 2009).

Malmendier, Ulrike, "Roman Shares," in W. N. Goetzmann and K. G. Rouwenhorst, eds., *Origins of Value: A Documentary History of Finance* (New York: Oxford University Press, 2005), 31–42.

———, "Law and Finance 'at the Origin,'" *Journal of Economic Literature*, 47: 1076–1108 (December 2009).

Malouta, Myrto, "Transactions Involving Land: Records of Amounts of Land and Value of Transactions," Oxford University, work in progress, 2011.

Malthus, T. R., *An Essay on the Principle of Population* (New York: Norton, 2004).

Manning, Joseph, and Ian Morris, eds., *The Ancient Economy: Evidence and Models* (Stanford, CA: Stanford University Press, 2005).

Maselli, G., *Argentaria: Banche e banchieri nella Roma repubblicana* (Bari: Adriatica editrice, 1986).

Masters, Brian, *Georgiana, Duchess of Devonshire* (London: Hamish Hamilton, 1981).

Mathias, Peter, "Minorities and Elites: How Do Minorities Become Elites?" in Elise Brezis and Peter Temin, eds., *Elites, Minorities, and Economic Growth* (Amsterdam: Elsevier, 1999), 115–28.

Mattingly, D. J., *Tripolitania* (London: Batsford, 1995).

Mattingly, David J., and John Salmon, eds., *Economies beyond Agriculture in the Classical World* (London: Routledge, 2001).

Mattoso, Katia M. de Queiros, *To Be a Slave in Brazil, 1550–1888* (New Brunswick, NJ: Rutgers University Press, 1986).

McCormick, Michael, *Origins of the European Economy: Communications and Commerce, AD 300–900* (Cambridge: Cambridge University Press, 2001).

———, "Movement and Markets in the First Millennium: Information, Containers and Shipwrecks," in Cécile Morrison, ed., *Trade and Markets in Byzantium* (Washington: Dumbarton Oaks, forthcoming).

Megarry, Robert, and H. W. R. Wade, *The Law of Real Property*, 4th ed. (London: Stevens and Sons, 1975).

Meiggs, Russell, *Roman Ostia* (Oxford: Oxford University Press, 1973).

Meijer, Fik, and Onnon van Nijf, *Trade, Transport and Society in the Ancient World: A Sourcebook* (London: Routledge, 1992).

Meyer, E. A., *Legitimacy and Law in the Roman World. Tabulae in Roman Belief and Practice* (Cambridge: Cambridge University Press, 2004).

Milgrom, Paul R., Douglass C. North, and Barry R. Weingast, "The Role of Institutions in the Revival of Trade: The Law Merchant, Private Judges, and the Champagne Fairs," in Daniel B. Klein, ed., *Reputation: Studies in the Voluntary Elicitation of Good Conduct*, (Ann Arbor: The University of Michigan, 1997).

Millett, Paul, "Productive to Some Purpose? The Problem of Economic Growth," in Mattingly and Salmon (2001), 17–48.

Mishkin, Frederick S., *Financial Markets and Institutions*, 9th ed. (Reading, MA: Addison-Wesley, 2010).

Mitchell, B. R., *Abstract of British Historical Statistics* (Cambridge: Cambridge University Press, 1962).

Mokyr, Joel, *The Lever of Riches: Technological Creativity and Economic Progress* (New York: Oxford University Press, 1990).

———, *The Enlightened Economy: An Economic History of Britain, 1700–1850* (New Haven: Yale University Press, 2009).

Mørkholm, Otto, *Early Hellenistic Coinage: from the Accession of Alexander to the Peace of Apamea (336–186 B.C.)* (Cambridge: Cambridge University Press, 1991).

Morley, Neville, *Metropolis and Hinterland: The City of Rome and the Italian Economy, 200 BC–AD 200* (Cambridge: Cambridge University Press, 1996).

———, "The Transformation of Italy, 225–28 B.C.," *Journal of Roman Studies*, 91: 50–62 (2001).

———, "The Early Roman Empire: Distribution," in Scheidel, Morris, and Saller (2007a), 570–91.

———, *Trade in Classical Antiquity* (Cambridge: Cambridge University Press, 2007b).

Morris, Ian, "Foreword," in Finley (1999).

———, "Economic Growth in Ancient Greece," *Journal of Institutional and Theoretical Economics*, 160: 709–42 (2004).

———, "Archaeology, Standards of Living, and Greek Economic History," in Manning and Morris (2005), 91–126.

Murphy, Cullen, *Are We Rome? The Fall of an Empire and the Fate of America* (Boston: Houghton Mifflin, 2007).

Nadjo, L., *L'argent et les affaires à Rome des origines au IIe siècle avant J.-C. Etude d'une vocabulaire technique* (Louvain: Peeters, 1989).

Neal, Larry, *The Rise of Financial Capitalism: International Capital Markets in the Age of Reason* (Cambridge: Cambridge University Press, 1990).

———, "The Finance of Business during the Industrial Revolution," in Roderick Floud and Donald McCloskey, eds., *The Economic History of Britain since 1700*, 2nd ed., Vol. 1 (Cambridge: Cambridge University Press, 1994), 151–81.

Neal, Larry, and Quinn Stephen, "Networks of Information, Markets, and Institutions in the Rise of London as a Financial Centre, 1660–1720," *Financial History Review*, 8: 7–26 (2001).

Neale, Walter G., "The Market in Theory and History," in Karl Polanyi, Conrad M. Arensberg, and Harry W. Pearson, eds., *Trade and Markets in the Early Empires* (Glencoe, IL: Free Press, 1957), 357–72.

Nishida, Meiko, "Manumission and Ethnicity in Urban Slavery: Salvador, Brazil, 1808–1888," *Hispanic American Historical Review*, 73 (3): 361–91 (August 1993).

North, Douglass, "Sources of Productivity Change in Ocean Shipping, 1600–1850," *Journal of Political Economy*, 76: 953–970 (1968).

———, *Structure and Change in Economic History* (New York: Norton, 1981).

———, *Institutions, Institutional Change, and Economic Performance* (Cambridge: Cambridge University Press, 1990).

North, Douglass, and Barry Weingast, "Constitutions and Commitment: The Evolution of Institutions Governing Public Choice in Seventeenth-Century England," *Journal of Economic History*, 49: 803–32 (December 1989).

Nussbaum, Arthur, *A History of the Dollar* (New York: Columbia University Press, 1967).

O'Brien, Patrick K., "The Political Economy of British Taxation, 1660–1815," *Economic History Review*, 41 (1): 1–32 (February 1988).

Officer, Lawrence, "The Annual Real and Nominal GDP for the United Kingdom, 1086–2004," *Economic History Services*, 2005; URL: http://www.eh.net/hmit/ukgdp/.

Parker, A. J., *Ancient Shipwrecks of the Mediterranean and the Roman Provinces* (Oxford: Tempus Reparatum, 1992).

Parker, Geoffrey. *The Military Revolution: Military Revolution and the Rise of the West, 1500–1800* (Cambridge, UK: Cambridge University Press, 1996).

Patterson, C. C., "Silver Stocks and Losses in Ancient and Medieval Times," *Economic History Review*, 25: 2, 205–35 (May 1972).

Patterson, Orlando, *Slavery and Social Death: A Comparative Study* (Cambridge, MA: Harvard University Press, 1982).

Paulson, Henry M., Jr, *On the Brink: Inside the Race to Stop the Collapse of the Global Financial System* (New York: Business Plus, 2010).

Peacock, D. P. S., and D. F. Williams, *Amphorae and the Roman Economy* (New York: Longman, 1986)

Persson, Karl Gunnar, *Gain Markets in Europe, 1500–1900: Integration and Deregulation* (Cambridge: Cambridge University Press, 1999).

Petrucci, Aldo, *Mensam exercere: Studi sull'impresa finanziaria romana* (Naples: Jovene, 1991).

———, *Profili giuridi delle attività e dell'organizzazione delle banche romane* (Turin: G. Giappichelli, 2002).

———, "L'organizzazione delle imprese bancarie alla luce della giurisprudenza romana del Principato," in Lo Cascio (2003), 99–129.

Phelps Brown, Henry, and Seila V. Hopkins, *A Perspective of Wages and Prices* (London: Methuen, 1981).

Phillips, Kevin, *Wealth and Democracy* (New York: Broadway Books, 2002).

———, *American Dynasty: Aristocracy, Fortune, and the Politics of Deceit in the House of Bush* (New York: Viking, 2004).

Piketty, Thomas, "On the Long Run Evolution of Inheritance: France 1820–2050," Paris School of Economics, Working Paper, 2009.

Pinto Vallejos, Julio, "Slave Control and Slave Resistance in Colonial Minas Gerais, 1700–1750," *Journal of Latin American Studies*, 17: 1–34 (1985).

Pirenne, Henri, *Medieval Cities* (Princeton: Princeton University Press, 1925).

Pittia, S., "L'influence des liens de parenté sur la prise de décision économique: le cas des *Tullii Cicerones*," in Andreau, France, and Pittia (2004), 21–44.

Polanyi, Karl, *The Great Transformation* (New York: Holt, Rinehart and Winston, 1944).

————, *The Livelihood of Man* (New York: Academic Press, 1977).

Pollard, Sidney, "Fixed Capital in the Industrial Revolution in Britain," *Journal of Economic History*, 24: 299–314 (1964).

Powell, Marvin A., "Money in Mesopotamia," *Journal of the Economic and Social History of the Orient*, 39 (3): 224–42 (August 1996).

Pressnell, L. S., *Country Banking in the Industrial Revolution* (Oxford: Oxford University Press, 1956).

Price, Jacob M., "What Did Merchants Do? Reflection on British Overseas Trade, 1660–1790," *Journal of Economic History*, 49 (2): 267–84 (1989).

Pryor, Frederic L., *The Origins of the Economy: A Comparative Study of Distribution in Primitive and Peasant Economies* (New York: Academic Press, 1977).

Putnam, Robert D., *Making Democracy Work: Civic Traditions in Modern Italy* (Princeton: Princeton University Press, 1993).

Quinn, Stephen, "The Glorious Revolution's Effect on English Private Finance: A Microhistory, 1680–1705," *Journal of Economic History*, 61: 593–615 (September 2001).

Rajan, Raghuram G., and Luigi Zingales, "Financial Dependence and Growth," *American Economic Review*, 88: 559–86 (June 1998).

Ramin, Jacques, and Paul Veyne, "Droit Romain et Société; les Hommes Libres qui Passent pour Ésclaves et l'Ésclavage Volontaire," *Historia*, 30 (4): 472–97 (1981).

Rathbone, Dominic, *Economic Rationalism and Rural Society in Third-Century A.D. Egypt: The Heroninos Archive and the Appianus Estate* (Cambridge: Cambridge University Press, 1991).

————, "The Census Qualifications of the *Assidui* and the *Prima Classis*," in H. Sancisir-Weerdenberg et al., eds., *De Agricultura: in Memoriam Pieter Willem de Neeve (1945–1990)* (Amsterdam: J.C. Gieben, 1993), 121–52.

————, "Monetization, not Price-Inflation, in Third-Century AD 'Egypt?'" in Cathy E. King and David G. Wigg, eds., *Coin Finds and Coin Use in the Roman World* (Berlin: Gebr. Mann, 1996), 321–39.

————, "Prices and Price Formation in Roman Egypt," in *Economie antique: Prix et formation des prix dans les economies antiques* (Saint-Bertrand-de-Comminges, France: Musée archéologique départmental, 1997), 183–244.

————, "The 'Muziris' Papyrus (SB XVIII 13167): Financing Roman Trade with India," in *Alexandrian Studies II in Honor of Mostafa el Abbadi*, *Bulletin de la Société d'Archéologie d'Alexandrie* 46 (Alexandria: Société d'Archéologie d'Alexandrie, 2000), 39–50.

————, "The Control and Exploitation of *ager publicus* in Italy under the Republic," in Aubert (2003a), 135–78.

————, "The Financing of Maritime Commerce in the Roman Empire, I–II AD," in Lo Cascio (2003b), 197–229.

————, "Roman Egypt," in Scheidel, Morris, and Saller (2007a), 698–719.

————, "Nero's Reforms of *vectigalia*, and the Lex portorii Asiae," in B. M. Levick, ed., *The Lex Portus Asiae* (Oxford: Oxford University Press, 2007b).

————, "Earnings and Costs: Living Standards and the Roman Economy," in Bowman and Wilson (2009), 299–326.

————, "Grain Prices and Grain Markets in the Roman World," presented at the conference on the Efficiency of Markets in Preindustrial Societies," Amsterdam, May 19–21, 2011.

Rathbone, Dominic, and Peter Temin, "Financial Intermediation in 1st-century AD Rome and 18th-century England," in Verboven et al. (2008), 371–419.

Reger, Gary, "Private Property and Private Loans on Independent Delos (314–167 B.C.)," *Phoenix*, 46: 322–41 (1992).

Reichskommissar für Preisbildung, "Mitteilungsblatt des Reichskommissars für die Preisbildung," 1937–38 (Bundesarchiv RD13/I).

Ricardo, David, *Principles of Political Economy and Taxation* (Homewood, IL: Irwin, 1963).

Rickman, Geoffrey, *Roman Granaries and Store Buildings* (Cambridge: Cambridge University Press, 1971).

————, *The Corn Supply of Ancient Rome* (Oxford: Clarendon Press, 1980).

Rihll, T. E., "Making Money in Classical Athens," in Mattingly and Salmon (2001), 115–42.

Riley, James C., *International Government Finance and the Amsterdam Capital Market, 1740–1815* (Cambridge: Cambridge University Press, 1980).

Rodewald, Cosmo, *Money in the Age of Tiberius* (Manchester: Manchester University Press, 1976).

Romer, Paul, "Increasing Returns and Long-Run Growth," *Journal of Political Economy*, 94: 1002–3 (October 1986).

Rosenstein, Nathan, "Aristocrats and Agriculture in the Middle and Late Republic," *Journal of Roman Studies*, 98: 1–26 (2008).

Rostovtzeff, M., *The Social and Economic History of the Roman Empire*, 2nd ed. (Oxford: Clarendon Press, 1957).

Roth, Ulrike, *Thinking Tools: Agricultural Slavery between Evidence and Models* (London: Institute of Classical Studies, 2007).

Rousseau, Peter L., and Richard Sylla, "Financial Systems, Economic Growth, and Globalization," in Michael D. Bordo, Alan M. Taylor, and Jeffrey G. Williamson, eds., *Globalization in Historical Perspective* (Chicago: Chicago University Press, 2003), 373–413.

Sachs, A. J., and H. Hunger, *Astronomical Diaries and Related Texts from Babylonia*, 3 Vols. (Vienna: Verlag Der Osterreichischen Akademie Der Wissenschaften, 1988, 1989, 1996).

Sachs, Jeffrey D., and Andrew Warner, "Economic Reform and the Process of Global Integration," *Brookings Papers on Economic Activity*, 1–118 (1995).

Sallares, Robert, "Ecology," in Scheidel, Morris, and Saller (2007), 15–37.

Saller, Richard, "Status and Patronage," in Alan K. Bowman, Peter Garnsey, and Dominic Rathbone, eds., *The Cambridge Ancient History*, 2nd ed., Vol. 11, *The High Empire, A.D. 70–192* (Cambridge: Cambridge University Press, 2000), 817–54.

————, "Framing the Debate over Growth in the Ancient Economy," in Manning and Morris, (2005); reprinted in Walter Scheidel and Sita von Reden, eds., *The Ancient Economy* (New York: Routledge, 2002), 251–69.

Sargent, Thomas J., and François R. Velde, *The Big Problem of Small Change* (Princeton: Princeton University Press, 2002).

Schaps, David M., *The Invention of Coinage and the Monetization of Ancient Greece* (Ann Arbor: University of Michigan Press, 2004).

Scheidel, Walter, "Quantifying the Source of Slaves in the Early Roman Empire," *Journal of Roman Studies*, 87: 157–69 (1997).

———, "Progress and Problems in Roman Demography," in Walter Scheidel, ed., *Debating Roman Demography* (Leiden: Brill, 2001), 1–81.

———, "A Model of Demographic and Economic Change in Roman Egypt after the Antonine Plague," *Journal of Roman Archaeology*, 15: 97–114 (2002).

———, "Human Mobility in Roman Italy, I: The Free Population," *Journal of Roman Studies*, 94: 1–26 (2004).

———, "Human Mobility in Roman Italy, II: The Slave Population," *Journal of Roman Studies*, 95: 64–79 (2005a).

———, "Real Slave Prices and the Relative Cost of Slave Labor in the Greco-Roman World," *Ancient Society*, 35: 1–17 (2005b).

———, "The Comparative Economics of Slavery in the Greco-Roman World," in Enrico Del Lago and Constantina Katsari, eds., *Slave Systems: Ancient and Modern* (Cambridge: Cambridge University Press, 2008), 105–26.

———, "In Search of Roman Economic Growth," *Journal of Roman Archaeology*, 46: 46–70 (2009a).

———, ed., *Rome and China: Comparative Perspectives on Ancient World Empires* (Oxford: Oxford University Press, 2009b).

———, "Real Wages in Early Economies: Evidence for Living Standards from 1800 BCE to 1300 CE," *Journal of the Economic and Social History of the Orient*, 53: 425–62 (2010).

Scheidel, Walter, and Steven J. Friesen, "The Size of the Economy and the Distribution of Income in the Roman Empire," *Journal of Roman Studies*, 99: 61–91 (2009).

Scheidel, Walter, Ian Morris, and Richard Saller, eds., *The Cambridge Economic History of the Greco-Roman World* (Cambridge: Cambridge University Press, 2007).

Schiavone, Aldo, *The End of the Past: Ancient Rome and the Modern West* (Cambridge, MA: Harvard University Press, 2000).

Schofield, Roger, "British Population Change, 1700–1871," in Roderick Floud and Donald McCloskey, eds., *The Economic History of Britain since 1700*, 2nd ed. (Cambridge: Cambridge University Press, 1994), I, 60–95.

Schwartz, Stuart B., "The Manumission of Slaves in Colonial Brazil: Bahia, 1684–1745," *Hispanic American Historical Review*, 54: 603–35 (1974).

Scott, William Robert, *The Constitution and Finance of English and Irish Joint-Stock Companies to 1720* (1910–12; reprint Bristol: Thoemmes Press, 1995).

Shapiro, Carl, and Joseph E. Stiglitz. "Equilibrium Unemployment as a Worker Discipline Device," *American Economic Review*, 74: 433–44 (1984).

Shelton, Jo-Ann, *As the Romans Did: A Sourcebook in Roman Social History*, 2nd ed. (New York, Oxford University Press, 1998).

Sherratt, Susan, and Andrew Sherratt, "The Growth of the Mediterranean Economy in the Early First Millennium BC," *World Archaeology*, 24: 361–78 (1993).

Silver, Morris, "Karl Polanyi and Markets in the Ancient Near East: The Challenge of the Evidence," *Journal of Economic History*, 43 (4): 795–829 (December 1983).

Sirks, Boudewijn, *Food for Rome* (Amsterdam: Gieben, 1991).

Sirri, Erik R., and Peter Tufano, "The Economics of Pooling," in Dwight B. Crane et al., eds., *The Global Financial System: A Functional Perspective* (Boston: Harvard Business School Press, 1995), 81–128.

Slotsky, Alice Louise, *The Bourse of Babylon: Market Quotations in the Astronomical Diaries of Babylonia* (Bethesda, MD: CDL Press, 1997).

Smil, Vaclav, *Why America Is Not a New Rome* (Cambridge, MA: MIT Press, 2010).

Solow, Robert M., "A Contribution to the Theory of Economic Growth," *Quarterly Journal of Economics*, 70: 65–94 (February 1956).

———, "Technical Change and the Aggregate Production Function," *Review of Economics and Statistics*, 39: 312–20 (1957).

———, "Survival of the Richest? A Review of *A Farewell to Alms*," *New York Review of Books*, 54 (18): 39 (November 22, 2007).

Solow, Robert M., and Peter Temin, "Introduction: The Inputs for Growth," in Peter Mathis and M. M. Postan, eds., *The Cambridge Economic History of Europe*, Vol. 7: *The Industrial Economies: Capital, Labor, and Enterprise* (Cambridge: Cambridge University Press, 1978), 1–27.

Sosin, Joshua, "Agio at Delphi," *Numismatic Chronicle*, 160: 67–80 (2000).

———, "Accounting and Endowments," *Tyche: Beiträge zur Alten Geschichte, Papyrologie und Epigraphik*, 16: 161–75 (2001).

Speidel, M. Alexander, "Roman Army Pay Scales," *Journal of Roman Studies*, 82: 87–106 (1992).

Spence, A. Michael, "Signaling in Retrospect and the Informational Structure of Markets," *American Economic Review*, 92(3): 434–59 (2002).

Stager, Lawrence E., "Phoenician Shipwrecks and Tyre, Ship of State," typescript (nd).

———, "The Impact of the Sea Peoples (1185–1050 BCE)," in Thomas E. Levy, ed., *The Archaeology of Society in the Holy Land* (London: Leicester University Press, 1995), chapter 20.

Stark, Rodney, *Cities of God: The Real Story of How Christianity Became an Urban Movement and Conquered Rome* (New York: HarperCollins, 2006).

Steinfeld, Robert J., *The Invention of Free Labor: The Employment Relation in English and American Law and Culture, 1350–1879* (Chapel Hill: University of North Carolina Press, 1991).

———, *Coercion, Contract, and Free Labour in the Nineteenth Century* (Cambridge: Cambridge University Press, 2001).

Stern, Ephraim, "Buried Treasure: The Silver Hoard from Dor," *Biblical Archaeology Review*, 24: 46–62 (1998).

Stigler, George J., and Robert A. Sherwin, "The Extent of the Market," *Journal of Law and Economics*, 28 (3): 555–85 (October 1985).

Stiglitz, Joseph E., "Information and the Change in the Paradigm in Economics," *American Economic Review*, 92 (3): 460–501 (2002).

Stiglitz, Joseph E., and Andrew Weiss, "Credit Rationing in Markets with Imperfect Information," *American Economic Review*, 71: 393–410 (June 1981).

Stolper, Matthew W., "Mesopotamia, 482–330 B.C.," in D. M. Lewis, John Bordman, Simon Horblower, and M. Ostwald, eds., *The Cambridge Ancient History*, Vol. 6: *The Fourth Century B.C.*, 2nd ed. (Cambridge: Cambridge University Press, 1994), 234–60.

Strachey, Lytton, *Eminent Victorians* (New York: Putnam, 1918).

Tainter, Joseph A., *The Collapse of Complex Societies* (Cambridge: Cambridge University Press, 1988).

Taylor, Lilly Ross, "Freedmen and Freeborn in the Epitaphs of Imperial Rome," *American Journal of Philology*, 82 (2): 113–32 (1961).

Tchernia, A., "Remarques sur la crise de 33," in Lo Cascio (2003), 131–46.

Temin, Peter, "Modes of Behavior," *Journal of Economic Behavior and Organization*, 1 (2): 175–95 (April 1980).

———, "Is It Kosher to Talk about Culture?" *Journal of Economic History*, 57 (2): 267–87 (June 1997).

———, "A Market Economy in the Early Roman Empire," *Journal of Roman Studies*, 91: 169–81 (2001).

———, "Price Behavior in Ancient Babylon," *Explorations in Economic History*, 39: 46–60 (January 2002).

———, "Financial Intermediation in the Early Roman Empire," *Journal of Economic History*, 64: 705–33 (September 2004a).

———, "The Labor Market of the Early Roman Empire," *Journal of Interdisciplinary History*, 34: 513–38 (spring 2004b).

———, "Estimating the GDP of the Early Roman Empire," in Lo Cascio (2006a), 31–54.

———, "Review of *The Ancient Economy*," *Journal of Interdisciplinary History*, 37: 100–102 (2006b).

———, "Mediterranean Trade in Biblical Times," in Ronald Findlay et al., eds., *Eli Heckscher, International Trade, and Economic History* (Cambridge: MIT Press, 2006c), 141–56.

———, "Land Tenure in the Roman Empire and Beyond," paper presented at the International Conference on Land and Natural Resources in the Roman World, Brussels, 26–28 May 2011.

———, "The Contribution of Economics [to Ancient History]," in Walter Scheidel, ed., *The Cambridge Companion to the Roman Economy* (Cambridge: Cambridge University Press, 2012).

———, "Price Behavior in the Roman Empire," in Francois de Callatay, ed., *Quantification in Ancient History* (Oxford: Oxford University Press, forthcoming a).

———, "Growth Theory for Ancient Economies," in Willem Jongman, ed., *Economic Growth in Classical Antiquity* (forthcoming b).

———, "Escaping Malthus: Economic Growth in the Early Roman Empire," in Willem Jongman, ed., *Economic Growth in Classical Antiquity* (forthcoming c).

Temin, Peter, and Hans-Joachim Voth, "Banking as an Emerging Technology: Hoare's Bank 1702–1742," *Financial History Review*, 13: 149–78 (October 2006).

———, "Private Borrowing during the Financial Revolution," *Economic History Review*, 61: 541–64 (August 2008).

Tenger, B., *Die Verschuldung im römischen Ägypten (1.–2. Jhr. n. Chr.)* (St. Katharinen, Germany: Scripta Mercaturae, 1993).

Thilo, R. M., *Der Codex accepti et expensi im Römischen Recht* (Göttingen, Germany: Muster-Schmidt, 1980).

Thornton, M. K., and R. L. Thornton, *Julio-Claudian Building Programs* (Wauconda, IL: Bolehazy-Carducci, 1989).

Tilly, Charles, "War Making and State Making as Organized Crime," in Peter B. Evans, Dietrich Rueschemeyer, and Theda Skocpol, eds., *Bringing the State Back In* (Cambridge: Cambridge University Press, 1985), 169–91.

Tomlin, R. S. O., "'The Girl in Question': A New Text from Roman London," *Britannia*, 34: 41–51 (2003).

Treggiari, Susan, *Roman Freedmen during the Late Republic* (Oxford: Oxford University Press, 1969).

Urbainczyk, Theresa, *Slave Revolts in Antiquity* (Berkeley: University of California Press, 2008).

Van Bavel, B. J. P., "The Organization and Rise of Land and Lease Markets in Northwestern Europe and Italy, c. 1000–1800," *Continuity and Change*, 23: 13–53 (2008).

———, "Markets for Land, Labor, and Capital in Northern Italy and the Low Countries, Twelfth to Seventeenth Centuries," *Journal of Interdisciplinary History*, 41: 503–31 (spring 2011).

Van der Beek, Karine, "Political Fragmentation, Competition, and Investment Decisions: The Medieval Grinding Industry in Ponthieu, France, 1150–1250," *Economic History Review*, 63: 664–87 (August 2010a).

———, "The Effects of Political Fragmentation on Investments: A Case Study of Watermill Construction in Medieval Ponthieu, France," *Explorations in Economic History*, 47: 369–80 (October 2010b).

Van der Spek, R., "The Effect of War on the Prices of Barley and Agricultural Land in Hellenistic Babylonia," in J. Andreau, P. Briant, and R. Descat, eds., *La guerre dans les economies antiques*, Entretiens d'Archeologie et d'Histoire, Saint-Bernard-de Comminges, Vol. 5 (Saint-Bernard-de-Comminges, France: Musée archéologique départemental, 2000), 293–313.

Van der Wee, Herman, "Monetary, Credit, and Banking Systems," in E. E. Rich and C. H. Wilson, eds., *The Cambridge Economic History of Europe*, Vol. 5 (Cambridge: Cambridge University Press, 1977), 290–392.

Vargyas, P., "Silver and Money in Achaemenid and Hellenistic Babylonia," in Joachim Marzahn and Hans Neumann, eds., *Assyriologica et Semitica: Festschrift fuer Joachim Oelsner* (Muenster, Germany: Ugarit-Verlag, 2000), 513–522.

Verboven, Koenraad, *The Economy of Friends: Economic Aspects of Amicitia and Patronage in the Late Republic* (Bruxelles: Latimus, 2002).

———, "The Sulpicii from Puteoli and Usury in the Early Roman Empire," *Tijdschrift voor Rechtsgeschiedenis*, 71: 7–78 (2003a).

———, "55–44 BCE: Financial or Monetary Crisis?" in Lo Cascio (2003b), 197–229.

———, "*Faeneratores, negotiatores* and Financial Intermediation in the Roman World (Late Republic and Early Empire)," in Verboven et al. (2008), 211–29.

Verboven, Koenraad, et al., eds., *Bankers, Loans, and Archives in the Ancient World* (Leuven: Studia Hellenistica 44, 2008).

Verhulst, Adriaan, *The Carolingian Economy* (Cambridge: Cambridge University Press, 2002).

Virlouvet, Catherine, *Tessera frumentaria: les procedures de distribution du blé public à la fin de la Républic et au début de l'Empire* (Rome: École Française de Rome, 1995).

Voltaire, *Correspondance*, Theodore Besterman, ed. (Paris: Gallimard, 1977–).

Voth, Hans-Joachim, *Time and Work in England, 1750–1830* (Oxford: Oxford University Press, 2000).

———, "The Longest Years: New Estimates of Labor Input in England, 1760–1830," *Journal of Economic History*, 61: 1065–82 (December 2001).

———, "Living Standards and the Urban Environment," in Roderick Floud and Paul Johnson, eds., *The Economic History of Britain since 1700*, 3rd ed. (Cambridge: Cambridge University Press, 2003).

Ward-Perkins, Bryan, *The Fall of Rome and the End of Civilization* (Oxford: Oxford University Press, 2005).

Watson, Alan, ed., *The Digest of Justinian* (Philadelphia: University of Pennsylvania Press, 1985).

———, *Roman Slave Law* (Baltimore: Johns Hopkins University Press, 1987).

Watson, George R., *The Roman Soldier* (Ithaca, NY: Cornell University Press, 1969).

Watson, James L., "Slavery as an Institution: Open and Closed Systems," in James L. Watson ed., *Asian and African Systems of Slavery* (Oxford: Blackwell, 1980).

Weaver, P. R. C., *Familia Caeseris: A Social Study of the Emperor's Freedmen and Slaves* (Cambridge: Cambridge University Press, 1972).

Weber, Max, *The Protestant Ethic and the Spirit of Capitalism* (New York: Allen and Unwin, 1930).

White, Eugene, "The Paris Bourse, 1724–1814: Experiments in Microstructure," in Stanley Engerman et al., eds., *Finance, Intermediaries, and Economic Development* (Cambridge: Cambridge University Press, 2003), chapter 2.

Whitman, Stephen, "Diverse Good Causes: Manumission and the Transformation of Urban Slavery," *Social Science History*, 19: 333–70 (1995).

Whittaker, C. R., "Inflation and the Economy in the Fourth Century," in C. E. King, ed., *Oxford Symposium on Coinage and Monetary History: Imperial Revenue, Expenditure, and Monetary Policy in the Fourth Century A.D.* (Leeds, UK: Prospect Books, 1980), 1–22.

Wickham, Chris, *Framing the Early Middle Ages: Europe and the Mediterranean, 400–800* (Oxford: Oxford University Press, 2005).

———, *The Inheritance of Rome: A History of Europe from 400 to 1000* (New York: Viking, 2009).

Wikander, Örjan, "Sources of Energy and Exploitation of Power," in John Peter Oleson, ed., *The Oxford Handbook of Engineering and Technology in the Classical World* (Oxford: Oxford University Press, 2008), 136–57.

Wilson, Andrew I., "Machines, Power and the Ancient Economy," *Journal of Roman Studies*, 92: 1–32 (2002).

————, "The Economic Impact of Technological Advances in the Roman Construction Industry," in Lo Cascio (2006), 225–52.

————, "Large-Scale Manufacturing, Standardization, and Trade," in John Peter Oleson, ed., *The Oxford Handbook of Engineering and Technology in the Classical World* (Oxford: Oxford University Press, 2008), 393–417.

————, "Indicators for Roman Economic Growth: A Response to Walter Scheidel," *Journal of Roman Archaeology*, 46: 71–82 (2009a).

————, "Approaches to Quantifying Roman Trade," in Bowman and Wilson (2009b), 213–49.

————, "Ancient Technology and Economic Growth," in Willem Jongman, ed., *Economic Growth in Classical Antiquity* (forthcoming).

Wolfe, Ethyle R., "Transportation in Augustan Egypt," *Transactions and Proceedings of the American Philological Association*, 83: 80–99 (1952).

Woodward, Donald, *Men at Work: Labourers and Building Craftsmen in the Towns of Northern England, 1450–1750* (Cambridge: Cambridge University Press, 1995).

Wright, Gavin, *Slavery and American Economic Development* (Baton Rouge: Louisiana State University Press, 2006).

Wrigley, E. A., *Continuity, Chance, and Change* (Cambridge: Cambridge University Press, 1988).

Wrigley, E. A., and R. S. Schofield, *The Population History of England, 1541–1871* (Cambridge, MA: Harvard University Press, 1981).

Zimmermann, R., *The Law of Obligations: Roman Foundations of the Civilian Tradition* (Cape Town: Juta, 1990).

Zimmern, Alfred, "Was Greek Civilization Based on Slave Labor?" *Sociological Review*, 2: 1–19, 159–76 (1909); reprinted in Alfred Zimmern, *Solon and Croesus* (London: Oxford University Press, 1928).

Index

• •

References to figures and tables are in **bold**.

Abbey of St. Martin de Tours, 150
ab initio, land ownership, 147
accounting techniques of banks, 178
accounts of receipts: financial intermediation and, 169
adverse selection, 98
Aemilianus, Scipio, 187
African Red Slipware pottery, 225
agents. *See* merchant-agent relationship
agriculture: labor market and, 120; Malthusian economies and, 233; prices in Hellenistic Babylon, 63; production, land ownership and, 150; techniques, growth theory and, 196–97, 217. *See also* farms and farmers
Agrippa II (king of Rome), 186
Akerlof, George A., 13; "lemons" paper, 98
Alexander, Julius, 170–71
Alexander the Great: coins, introduction of, and, 62; death of, 62–63, 65, 66, 83; price behavior in Hellenistic Babylon and, 57
Alexander, Tiberius Iulius, 186
Alexandrian tetradrachm debasement, 86, 88
alimentary foundations: financial intermediation, 175
America: market economy in, 11; South. *See* American South
American South: manumission, 127, 128; slaves and slavery, 116, 121, 123–25, 131–34, 199–200
Amschel, Mayer, 99
ancient and modern slavery, differences, 130
annona, 17; distortion of market and, 47; free men receiving, 31; Prefect of, 105–6; size of activity, 32–33
annual inflation rates, effects of, **78**
annual variation: Hellenistic Babylon, price behavior, 57

anonymous exchanges distinguished from personal exchanges, 13–14
Antonine Plague: inflation and, 74, 84, 85, 90, 227; Malthusian economies, effect on, 230–31, 233, 236; supply and demand and, 18
Antony, Marc, 111
Antwerp: masons in, 120
Appianus estates: labor market and, 119
apprentices: labor market and, 119
Apuleius, 123
aqueducts, 224
arches, use of, 223
Are We Rome?, 1
army: distinguished from private sphere, 120; land ownership and, 146; pay, in Roman Empire, 72, 76–77, 81
Asceplius, 119
Asia: horses, exports of by Turkish tribes, 11
assessment of land: ownership and, 146–47
"astronomical diary": Hellenistic Babylon and, 54
asymmetric information: banks and, 161; financial intermediation, 160–62
Atticus, 169
auctions: financial intermediation, 180–82; Greece, 180
Augustine: *City of God*, 149
Augustus: *annona* during reign of, 32; on land ownership, 144–45; wheat prices and trade and, 32–33, 51
Aurelius Adjutor, 119
Avianius, 110–11

Babylon: Hellenistic prices in, 28
"backward bending" supply curve of labor: growth theory and, 205

bakery: slaves and slavery in, 123
Bang, Peter F., 50
banker's responsibility, 178
Bank of England, 108, 165, 188
banks and banking: accounting techniques of
  banks, 178; asymmetric information and,
  161; business premises of, 185–86; Delos,
  banks in, 178; in early modern Europe,
  163–68; interest-bearing loans of, 158;
  irregular deposits, 177–78; local banks, 186;
  mensa, use of term, 176–77; merchant banks,
  161–62; pooling and pooled funds, 158,
  176–77; private banking, 165; women and, 177
barley: in Hellenistic Babylon, **55**, 58
behavior: of individuals, 7–8
bills of exchange: financial intermediation,
  163–64
Black Death of 1349: Malthusian economies
  and, 227, 230
Bloch, Marc, 151
Bologna, transportation from: wheat prices
  and trade, 45–46
Bransbourg, Gilles, 52
Brazil: manumission, 127–29; slaves and
  slavery in, 124, 128
Britain: banks and banking in, 188; rights of
  workers, 117; in Roman trade network,
  22; taxes in, 8–9; wages in, 216; wheat in,
  59–60
brokers, described: financial intermediation,
  161
Brown, James, 113
Brutus, 176
buildings: growth theory and, 197
bullion, 81; financial intermediation, 173
Bush, George W., 99
businessmen, active in grain trade, 102
business premises of banks, 185–86
business techniques of banks, 178
Byzantine system of land tenure, 150

Caesar, Julius, 171
California: gold, discovery of, 81
Camodeca, 183
Campanian tablets, 186
capital: donation of to cities, 174–75; growth
  theory and, 204–5; nonproducible,
  growth theory and, 209; overview, 96; for
  private investments, **160**; public markets,
  raised in, 162; sources of, 159–60; valuing
  services of, growth theory and, 207–14
"capital deepening": growth theory and, 208,
  214

capital markets: in Europe, 163–68
Carricius, 170–71
cash: borrowing of, financial intermediation,
  174; as wages, labor market and, 119
cashiers: in financial intermediation, 166
Castricius, Aulus, 186
Cato, 103, 129, 136, 188, 250–51
Celsus, 119
census classes: in Roman Empire, 72
childless, penalization of, 32
China: command economies in, 9; Silk Road,
  dealings with Romans over, 11
chirographum, 168–69
Chrysostom, John, 137
Cicero: credit and, 171; financial intermediation and, 172–73, 176, 178–79, 187; grain
  trade and, 104–5, 110–11; land ownership
  and, 147; Trimalchio, compared to, 2–3;
  Verrine Orations, 38, 245
Cicero, Marcus, 169
Cicero, Marcus Tullius: financial intermediation and, 168–69
City of God (Augustine), 149
civic administrations, borrowing by, 174–75
Clark, Colin, 250
Claudius: *annona* and, 32, 105–6; slave of,
  134–35
clerics: land ownership and, 153
closed model of slavery, 123, **124–25**, 125
coal industry: England, 238
coemperors: in Roman Empire, 79
coinage: financial intermediation, 173; in Hellenistic Babylon, 62; in Roman Empire, 72,
  75, 81, 89; wheat prices and trade and, 48
colonia Arausio, 145
Columella, 136
command economies, 9
commercial activity, finance for, 172–73
commodity log prices. variations: in Hellenistic Babylon, 67
Common Era: price behavior during, 61, 65
concrete, use for construction, 223–24
consumption: per capita GDP and, 246, 250;
  wheat prices and trade and, 31
contracts: financial intermediation, 168–69,
  173
corn market: wheat prices and trade and, 30
craftsmen: labor market and, 116
Crassus, Marcus, 141–42, 169
credit: financial intermediation, 166–68, 171,
  180–81, 188; in Roman Empire, 76
cruelty to slaves, 121–22
currency debasement: in Roman Empire, **71**

Dacian loan inscription, 170–71
daily workers: per capita GDP and, 256
data, prices, 27–28
Davia: wages in, 120
Debt-Deflation theory: land ownership and, 142
The Decline and Fall of the Roman Empire (Gibbon), 134
deflation, United States, 142
Delos, banks in, 178
demand. *See* supply and demand
Demographic Transition: Malthusian economies and, 237, 242
demography of slaves, 135–36
denarii, 82
descriptive regressions: Hellenistic Babylon and, 66
Didymus, 107
diet: ordinary people, consumption and living standards of, 224, 226; wheat prices and trade and, 30
Digest, 169, 178
diminishing returns: supply and demand and, 23, **24**
Diocletian's Edict of 301 CE, 39, 77, 225
distances, wheat prices and trade and, 40, **41–43, 45**; discount regression results, **45**; distance and price regression results, **48**
division of labor: supply and demand and, 21
documentation: grain trade and, 107–8
Domitian, 76
Dred Scott decision, 128
Duncan-Jones, Richard, 40
Dutch East India Company (VOC), 165–66
Dutch Republic: credit market of, 168; financial intermediation and, 165–66; wages in, 216, 238

East India Company, 100
economic structures: social structures interactions between, 100
Economic Survey (Frank), 40
economy: growth theory (*see* growth theory); slaves and, 135
education: economic activity and, 12; slaves and slavery and, 129, 131, 138
Egypt: domestic product, 199; free workers, 118; inflation in, 70, 73–74, **74**, 90; land ownership in, 148; loans, 171–72; market prices in, 76; price stability in, 73; production possibility frontier (PPF) in, 19–23; slaves and slavery in, 127; taxes in, 83–84;

wages in, 120, 254–55; wheat prices, 75; wheat prices and trade in, 39–40, 47
elite: financial intermediation and, 187
emperors: land ownership and, 144–46; in Roman Empire, 79, **80**
employment contracts: labor market and, 119
endowments: financial intermediation and, 175–76
England: banks and banking in, 188–89; coal industry in, 238; financial intermediation and, 164–65; fuel prices in, 238; grain trade and, 100; investors in, 168; Poor Laws in, 114; real wages in, 216; wages in, 8–9, 120, 238; wheat prices in, 56
enhanced consumption: Malthusian economies and, 225
equilibrium: Malthusian economies and, 231, 233, 239, 241–42
equity investments provided by financial intermediation, 162
errors in variables: for wheat prices and trade, 44
Eunus, Gaius Novius, 181
Europe: banks and banking in, 188; capital markets of, 163–68; colonies, healthiness of, 12; inflation in, 88; land ownership in, 151; mortality in, 12; per capita GDP and, 253; wages in, 216
European Price Revolution, 78
exchange ratios, 7
externalities, definition, 139

famine: wheat prices and trade and, 39
farms and farmers: growth theory and, 204–5; labor market and, 119; land ownership and, 143. *See also* agriculture
farm tenancy, 147–50
Faustus, 185
Federal Reserve (U.S.), 81, 142
fee simple, use of term, 139
fee tail, use of term, 139
feifs and feifdoms, 152–56
feoffment, 154
feudalism, 151–56
financial intermediation, 157–89; accounts of receipts and, 169; alimentary foundations, 175; asymmetric information, 160–62; auctions, 180–81; bills of exchange, 163–64; bullion, 173; cash, borrowing of, 174; cashiers in, 166; *chirographum* and, 168–69; civic administrations, borrowing by, 174–75; coinage, 173; commercial activity, finance for, 172–73; contracts and, 168–69, 173; credit, 166–68, 171, 180–81; credit

financial intermediation (*cont.*)
intermediation, 188; Dacian loan inscription, 170–71; Egypt, loans, 171–72; endowments, 175–76; equity investments provided by, 162; French credit market, 166–68; guarantors, 182; Hellenic cities, 174; informal loans, 168–72; joint-stock companies, 162–63, 165–66, 168; Keynes, John Maynard on, 158–59; land crisis of 33 CE and, 171; ledgers, 169; loans, 168–72, 182; partnerships, 173, 176; perpetual loans, 175; pledges, 182; in Pompeii, 181; public contractors, 172–73; short-term domestic loans, 166–67; slaves, sales of at auction, 182; *societates*, 172–73; Sulpicii, 181–87; tax-collecting *societates*, 172–73; trade, loans to finance, 172. *See also* banks and banking

Finley, M. I.: "Further Thoughts," 4–5, 114–15; on Malthusian economies, 222; on per capita GDP, 249; Sather lectures of, 4; on wheat prices and trade, 51

Fisher: Debt-Deflation theory, 142

fluctuations of prices: in wheat prices and trade, 48–49

food costs: in Hellenistic Babylon, 65

France: banks and banking in, 189

Frank, Tenney, 40

freedmen: acceptance into society, 133; grain trade and, 102–3

freehold, defined, 139

free workers: labor market and, 118

French credit market, 166–68

fuel prices: in England, 238

Gaius, 138, 178

GDP. *See* gross domestic product (GDP)

Geary-Khamis dollars, 261

Genoese traders, 99–100

Germany: financial intermediation and, 168

Gibbon, Edward, 134

gold: California, discovery in, 81; in Roman Empire, 75–76, 89

gold-silver ratio: in Hellenistic Babylon, 62

Goldsmith, Raymond W.: and per capita GDP, 243–48, 251, 254–57, 260

goldsmiths, 164

government interventions: in wheat prices and trade, 33, **34–35**, 37, 101

grain consumption: per capita GDP and, 250

grain trade, 97–113; agency, problems of, 106–7; asymmetric information, 112–13; documentation and, 107–8; freedmen and,

102–3; Genoese traders, 99–100; guild system and, 108–10; informal institutions and, 110–13; information, difficulties in obtaining, 104, 111–13; judges, private, 104–5; knights and, 102–3; legal institutions and, 106, 110; loans and, 106; merchants as independent companies, 103–4; Muslim traders, 100; ownership and management, separation, 103–4; receipts and, 108; reputation and, 110–11; shipping, 107–8

Great Depression: Debt-Deflation theory and, 142; growth theory and, 212

Greece: auctions in, 180; banks and banking in, 178; slaves and slavery in, 126

"Greenspan Put," 142

Gresham's Law, 81–82

gross domestic product (GDP): growth theory and, 196–97, 201, 215; per capita GDP. *See* per capita GDP

growth theory, 193, 195–219; agricultural techniques and, 196–97, 217; "capital deepening" and, 208, 214; capital, nonreproducible, 209; capital, valuing services of, 207–14; gross domestic product (GDP) and, 196–97, 201, 215; happiness and, 197–98; human capital and, 212–13; labor and, 204–7; labor productivity and, 211–13; land and, 204–5, 207–8; Laspeyres index, 200–201; Malthusian economies, 209, 214, 216; marginal products and, 203, 210–11; national product and, 200, 208; "new" growth theory, 212–14; "old" growth theory, 211–13; Paasche index, 200–201; population growth and, 209, 214–16; pottery as index of consumption levels, 217; production techniques and, 217; real wages and, 202, 216; resource endowments and, 210; "social capital" concept and, 213; Solow growth model, 211–13; stability, periods of, 216–17; structural change and, 198; technology and development of, 218; total factor productivity (TFP), 211–14; wheat prices and, 201–2; wine prices and, 202; work week and, 206

guarantors: financial intermediation and, 182

guild system: grain trade and, 108–10; labor market and, 118

Hadrian: *annona* and, 32

Hannibalic War, 173

happiness: growth theory and, 197–98

Hellenic cities: financial intermediation and, 174

Hellenistic Babylon, price behavior, 53–69; annual variation, 57; "astronomical diary," 54; autocorrelation degree and, 59–60; coins, introduction of, and, 62; descriptive regressions, 66; gold-silver ratio and, 62; inflation during, 61–63, 65; long-run trends, 56–57; market price movements, 55, 57; mint, establishment of, 62; money supply and, 63; random walks, 58; seasonal variation, 57; Seleucid state and, 61–62, 64; silver and, 61–62; supply and demand analysis and, 61–63; time-series properties, 61

Hicks, J. R., 132

high school students, examination of, 13

Hoare's bank (London), 183, 185

Holland: banks and banking in, 188–89; financial intermediation and, 165; Golden Age, 258–60; grain trade, 100; taxes in, 8–9

Hopkins, Keith: on growth theory, 201, 204, 215; and per capita GDP, 243–49, 252, 254–55, 257; price behavior and, 71–72; on transfer of Italian land, 142–46

housing boom, United States, 142

Hudson Bay Company, 100

human capital: growth theory and, 212–13

hyperinflation: in Roman Empire, 78–79

hypothetical tests, prices, 27–28

Ibn Battuta, writings of, 11

identification strategy: inflation and, 28; slavery and, 131

incentives: manumission and, 132; for slaves, 122–23, 129, 132

income distribution: per capita GDP and, 256–28

income of rich and poor, differences: per capita GDP and, 244

indentured service, 125–26

independent companies: merchants as, grain trade, 103–4

India: horses, exports of by Turkish tribes, 11

Industrial Revolution: demographics of, 259–60; early years of, workers and, 198; economic growth before, 196; growth theory and, 201–2, 226; labor markets and, 114; per capita income prior to, 221; size of Rome before, 97; technological improvement during, 237–38, 242

inflation: Antonine Plague and, 74, 84, 85, 90, 227; in Egypt, 70, 73–74, **74**, 90; in Europe, 88; in Hellenistic Babylon, 61–63, 65; index of, 28; manumission and, 131; in Roman Empire, 70–90

informal activities in Rome, 101

informal institutions: grain trade and, 111–13

informal social customs: grain trade and, 110

information: grain trade and, 104, 111–13

institutions: role of, 99

Institutions (Gaius), 138

integration: tests used to discriminate between kinds of, 8

intelligence of workers: growth theory and, 206–7

interest-bearing loans, 158

interest rates: "average" interest rates, **61**; in London, 60

irregular deposits: banks and banking, 177–78

Italy: domestic product of, 199; financial intermediation and, 168; land ownership in, 144; production possibility frontier (PPF) in, 19–20; slaves and slavery in, 136; wheat prices and trade in, 39; wheat, supply and demand for, 16–17, 20–24; wine, supply and demand for, 16–17, 19–24

Iucundus, Lucius Caecilus, 180–81, 184–86

job changes by slaves, 130

John Law, 164

joint-stock companies, 162–63, 165–66, 168

Judaean revolt: wheat prices and trade and, 47

judges, private: grain trade and, 104–5

Justinian Plague: inflation and, 85; supply and demand and, 18

Keynes, John Maynard: on financial intermediation, 158–59; on Paradox of Thrift, 142; on unemployment, 159

knights: grain trade and, 102–3; land ownership and, 153

labor: growth theory and, 204–7

labor market, 114–38; agriculture, 120; Appianus estates, 119; army, distinguished from private sphere, 120; cash as wages, 119; craftsmen, 116; farmers, 119; free workers, 118; masons, 120; miners, 119; *misthos*, 119; overview, 95; participation of slaves in (*see* slaves and slavery); rights of workers, 117; rural workers, 116, 119; salaries, division between wages and, 119; supply and demand and, 115; tenant farmers, 119; wages, variation in labor market, 116–18, 120; wheat as wages, 119. *See also* slaves and slavery

labor productivity: growth theory and, 211–13

labor specialization, 152

land: crisis of 33 CE, 171; growth theory and, 204–5, 207–8. *See also* land ownership

land ownership: *ab initio*, 147; acquisition of ownership, 147–48; agricultural production and, 150; assessment of land, 146–47; Byzantine system of land tenure, 150; *colonia Arausio*, example from, 145; Debt-Deflation theory and, 142; decline of Rome and, 149; Egypt, 148; emperors and, 144–46; Europe, 151; externalities, definition, 139; fall in land prices and, 142; farm tenancy, 147–50; fee simple, use of term, 139; fee tail, use of term, 139; feifs and feifdoms, 152–56; *feoffment*, 154; feudalism and, 152–56; freehold, defined, 139; functioning market for land and, 140; Italy, 144; knights and, 153; land tenure, complexity of, 147; loans to landowners, 145–46; lords, independent and, 155–56; *maritagium*, 153; overview, 95; *paroikoi* and, 150; population and, 151; price for land and, 140; ruling class conflict and, 141–42; Syria, 149; taxation and, 145–52; transaction costs and, 140; *usucapio*, 147; vassals and, 155; villein, use of term, 139; warfare, feudal and, 154–55; as wealth, 145

land tenure, complexity of, 147

Laspeyres index, 200–201

ledgers: financial intermediation and, 169

legal enforcement: merchant-agent relationship, grain trade, 104, 111

legal institutions: grain trade and, 106

legal systems: grain trade and, 110

"lemons" paper (Akerlof), 98

Lepidianus, Phosphorus, 134–35

less developed countries: per capita GDP and, 249

Lex Papia Poppaea, 32

libertos, 128–29

Licinia, 141–42

Livy, 177

loans: financial intermediation and, 182; grain trade and, 106; between individuals, banks and banking, 158; informal, financial intermediation and, 168–72; to landowners, 145–46

Lo Cascio, Elio, 145–47, 260–61

London: interest rate in, 60; masons in, 120

long-run trends: in Hellenistic Babylon, 56

long-run variation: Hellenistic Babylon, price behavior, 57

Long Term Capital Management, 37

lords, independent: land ownership and, 155–56

Lucas, R. E., Jr., 212–13

Lusitania (Spain): wheat prices and trade in, 36–37, 39

Macrinus, 119

macroeconomics, Roman: gross domestic product (GDP), 243–62; growth theory (*see* growth theory); Malthusian economies, 193, 220–42 (*see also* Malthusian economies); overview, 193–94; per capita GDP, 243–62 (*see also* gross domestic product (GDP)); scholarship and, 193, 195–219; size of Roman economy, 194, 243–61

Maddison, Angus: and per capita GDP, 257–58, 260

Malinowski, Bronislaw: Trobriand Islanders and, 6

Malouta, Myrto, 140

Malthusian economies, 220–42; agriculture, 233; algebraic forms, 240–42; Antonine Plague, effect of, 230–31, 233, 236; basic model, **228**; benefits of using model, 239; Black Death of 1349, effect of, 227, 230; Demographic Transition, 237, 242; Diocletian's Edict of 301 CE and, 225; equilibrium and, 231, 233, 239, 241–42; growth theory and, 209, 214, 216; income, algebraic forms, 241–42; mortality rate, reduction of, 226–27; moving resource constraint, 242; ordinary people, consumption of, 224–25; overview, 193; per capita income and, 222, 231; plagues, effect of, 227, **229**; population growth and, 226–27, 231, 233, 237, 241; productivity growth and, 233–34; real wages and, 227, 230–31, 238; regional specialization, gains from, 223, 236; shipping costs and, 222–23; shipwreck data and, 235–36; technological change, effect of, 224, **232**, 233–37; terracing and, 223; theory of comparative advantage, 223; transportation and, 223–24; world economic history, **221**

Malthus, Thomas, 214. *See also* Malthusian economies

manumission: in American South, 127, 128; in Brazil, 127–29; incentive mechanism of, 132; inflation and, 131

marginal products: growth theory and, 203, 210–11

maritagium, 153

market: use of term by economists, 10

market economy: assumption of existence of, 5–6; going from markets to, 11

market exchanges, 7–8
market prices: in Hellenistic Babylon, 57; labor market and, 117
market quotations: in Hellenistic Babylon, 55
markets in Roman Empire: adverse selection and, 98; capital, 98 (*see also* capital; financial intermediation); financial intermediation, 157–89; grain trade, 97–113 (*see also* wheat market); labor market, 95, 114–38 (*see also* labor market); land, 95, 139–56 (*see also* land ownership); and merchant-agent relationship (*see* merchant-agent relationship, grain trade); overview, 95–96; "signaling" and, 99; wheat, 95 (*see also* wheat market)
Marxism, 121
masons, 120
Massachusetts: partnerships in, 103
Matinius, P., 176
measurement of grain: grain trade and, 109
Memmius, 119
mensa, use of term, 176–77
merchant-agent relationship, grain trade, 98–100; legal enforcement, 104, 111; nature of agencies, 103; problems of agency, 106–7; punishment of agents, 104; same agent, use of by multiple senators, 111
merchant banks, 161–62
merchants, described: financial intermediation and, 161–62
miners: labor market and, 119
mint: establishment of in Hellenistic Babylon, 62
misthos, 119
monetary rule: in Roman Empire, 82
money: exchange ratios and, 7
money supply: in Hellenistic Babylon, 63
moral economy in Rome, 12–13
Morris, Ian, 4
mortality rate, reduction of: Malthusian economies and, 226–27
Moussinot, l'abbé, 167
moving resource constraint: Malthusian economies and, 242
Muslim traders: grain trade and, 100
Muziris papyrus, 172

Nasdaq Market, 163
national product: growth theory and, 200, 208
Neolithic Revolution, 237
Nero, 77; cash, need for, 82, 88; land ownership and, 146
Nerva, 175
Netherlands: "Golden Age," 258–60

New England: banks and banking in, 162
"new" growth theory, 212–14
New Institutional Economics (NIE): consideration of societies by, 11–13; described, 3–4; on merchant-agent relationship, 99–100, 103; operation of markets and, 24; supply and demand, studies on, 16, 18; transaction costs and, 22
New York Stock Exchange, 163
NIE. *See* New Institutional Economics (NIE)
Norman Conquest, 153
North America: merchant groups, 99
North, Douglass, 11
"null hypothesis," 5–6

oil lamps, 225
"old" growth theory, 211–13
On Agriculture (Varro), 140
one-to-one loans: financial intermediation and, 168–71
Onirus, 185
open model of slavery, 123, **124–25**
opsonion, 119
ordinary people, consumption of: Malthusian economies and, 224–25
ordinary workers, income of: per capita GDP and, 257
Ostia: grain information exchange in, 112; guild system in, 108–9; wheat prices and trade and, 32, 105
Ottoman Empire, 150
output of goods and services, value of: growth theory and, 199
outputs and inputs, relation between: growth theory and, 203
ownership and management, separation: grain trade and, 103–4
Oxyrhynchite nome, 107

Paasche index, 200–201
Palaemon, Q. Remmius, 129
Palestine: wheat prices and trade in, 40
pandemics. *See* Antonine Plague; Justinian Plague
Paradox of Thrift: land ownership and, 142
paroikoi, 150
partnerships: financial intermediation and, 173, 176; in Massachusetts, 103
Pax Romana: expansion of, 82; growth theory and, 201, 218; Malthusian economies and, 222, 231; operation of markets and, 24; stimulation of Mediterranean trade and, 2; transaction costs and, 22

payment for freedom: of slaves, 53
peace and law, extensions of: growth theory and, 217–18
per capita GDP, 243–62; consumption and, 246, 250; distinguishing between Roman Italy and empire as a whole, 252–53; early estimates, 244, **245**; Europe, 253; Geary-Khamis dollars, 261; grain consumption and, 250; income data, derivation from, 247, **248**; income distribution, 256–28; less developed countries, 249; ordinary workers, income of, 257; real wages and, 255; skilled workers and, 256; urban population and, 251–52; wages and, 246, 254–56; wheat prices and, 245–47, 249, 255
per capita income: Malthusian economies and, 222, 231
perpetual loans: financial intermediation and, 175
personal exchanges distinguished from anonymous exchanges, 13–14
Petronius: private merchants and, 4; *Satyricon*, 125
Piazzale delle Corporazioni, 112
pirates, 222
Pisidian Antioch: wheat prices and trade in, 39
plagues: Malthusian economies, effect on, 227, **229**. *See also* Antonine Plague; Black Death of 1349; Justinian plague
Plautius, Gaius, 170
pledges: financial intermediation and, 182
Pliny the Younger, 169, 174
Plotinus, 141
Plutarchus, 173
Polanyi, Karl: Finley, M. I., and, 4; taxonomy of interactions provided by, 6–7
political stability and instability, 71–72, 79–80, 82–84
Polybius: on coinage, 72; on wheat prices and trade, 38–39, 48
Pompeii: financial intermediation in, 181
Pompey: grain trade and, 110; pirates and, 222; wheat prices and, 37
pooling and pooled funds: banks and banking, 158, 176–77
Poor Laws: in England, 114
population: free population, numbers, 136; land ownership and, 151; numbers of people, 101; wheat prices and trade and, 31. *See also* population growth
population growth: growth theory and, 209, 214–16; Malthusian economies and, 226–27, 231, 233, 237, 241

Posidonius, 107
pottery: African Red Slipware pottery, 220, 225; availability of, 196; as index of consumption levels, growth theory and, 217
Po Valley: wheat prices and trade in, 39, 47
PPF. *See* production possibility frontier (PPF)
Price Edict (Diocletian), 39
price-making markets, 7
prices: data and hypothetical tests, 27–28; Hellenistic Babylon, 53–69 (*see also* Hellenistic Babylon, price behavior); identification strategy, explained, 28; inflation, index of, 28; for land, land ownership and, 140; Roman Empire, price behavior in, 70–91 (*see also* Roman Empire, price behavior in); of slave labor, 134; of slaves compared to wages of free workers, 137–38; stability, 73, 76, 82–83, 89; statistics, use of, 27; wheat prices and trade, 29–52 (*see also* wheat prices and trade)
Principate, 126, 173
private banking, 165, 184–85
production, change in: growth theory and, 196–97
production possibility frontier (PPF): in Egypt, 20–24; supply and demand and, 18–23
production possibility frontier (PPF) in: in Italy, 19–20
production techniques: growth theory and, 217
productivity growth: Malthusian economies and, 233–34
Pryor, Frederic L., 6–7
public contractors: financial intermediation and, 172–73
public markets, capital raised in: capital, 162
punishment: of agents, 104; of slaves, 134
purchase of freedom by slaves, 124
purchases and sales in market, 72
Puteoli, 186

random walks: Hellenistic Babylon, price behavior and, 58; in Roman Empire, 72
Rathbone, Dominic: on Antonine Plague, 86; on grain trade, 106; on inflation, 87–88; on loans to finance trade, 172; on price stability, 73–74; on wheat prices and trade, 46–47, 49, 51–52, 77
real income: per capita GDP and, 256–57
real wages: growth theory and, 202, 216; Malthusian economies and, 227, 230–31, 238; per capita GDP and, 255
receipts: grain trade and, 108

reciprocity, 6, 13
redistribution, 6
regional specialization, gains from: Malthusian economies and, 223, 236
regression analysis: for wheat prices and trade, 42–46, **45**, **48**, 51, **59**, **68**, **87**
relative variation: Hellenistic Babylon, price behavior, 57
religious ritual: growth theory and, 205
rent seeking: supply and demand and, 18
reputation: grain trade and, 110–11
resource endowments: growth theory and, 210
reverse causation: in Roman Empire, 83
Rex Gestae, 31
Ricardo, David: Malthusian economies and, 226; on production possibility frontier (PPF), 18–23; theory of comparative advantage, 223; on wheat prices and trade, 50
Rickman, Geoffrey: on price stability, 73; on wheat prices and trade, 38–40, 43, 47
rights of workers: labor market and, 117
Rio de Janeiro: slaves in, 123, 128
roads: growth theory and, 197
Roman Army, 76–77
Roman Empire, price behavior in, 70–91; Alexandrian tetradrachm debasement, 86, 88; annual inflation rates, effects of, **78**; army pay in, 72, 76–77, 81; census classes, 72; coemperors, 79; coinage in, 72, 75, 81, 89; credit in, 76; currency debasement, **71**; emperors, 79, **80**; gold in, 75–76, 89; hyperinflation (modern), 78–79; inflation in, 70–90; monetary rule in, 82; political stability and instability and, 71–72, 79–80, 82–84; price stability and, 73, 76, 82–83, 89; purchases and sales in market, 72; random walks, 72; silver in, 75–77, 81–82; taxes in, 71, 83; tax revenues in, 85–86; trade theory and, 71; Year of Four Emperors and, 86
Rothschilds, 99
ruling class conflict: land ownership and, 141–42
rural slaves, 118, 123
rural workers: labor market and, 116, 119
Russia: command economies in, 9

Salamis, 176
salaries, division between wages and, 119
São Paulo: slaves in, 128
Sather lectures, 4, 114
Satyricon (Petronius), 125
Scaptius, M., 176

seasonal variation: Hellenistic Babylon, price behavior and, 57
Seleucid state: Hellenistic Babylon, price behavior and, 61–62, 64
Seneca, 128
serfdom, transition from slave to, 137
sestertii, 33
Shakespeare, William, 151
shipping: costs, Malthusian economies and, 222–23; grain trade and, 107–8; wheat prices and trade and, 31–32, 45–46, 101–2; of wine, 108
shipwreck data: Malthusian economies and, 235–36
short-run variation: Hellenistic Babylon, price behavior and, 57
short-term debt instruments: financial intermediation and, 164
short-term domestic loans: financial intermediation and, 166–67
Sicily: wheat prices and trade in, 36–38
"signaling," 99
Silk Road, dealings with Romans over, 11
silver: in Hellenistic Babylon, 61–62; in Roman Empire, 75–77, 81–82
skilled slaves, 129–30
skills of workers: growth theory and, 207; per capita GDP and, 256
slaves and slavery, 121–38; American South, 116, 121, 123–25, 131–34; ancient and modern slavery, differences, 130; in bakery, 123; Brazil, 124, 128; closed model of slavery, 123, **124–25**, 125; creation of system, 130–31; cruelty to slaves, 121–22; demography of slaves, 135–36; economy, slaves and, 135; education and, 129, 131, 138; Egypt, 127; first slave society, Rome as, 114; freedmen, acceptance into society, 133; free population, numbers, 136; Greece, 126; hereditary slaves, 133; how slavery operated, 116; incentives for, 122–23, 129, 132; indentured service, 125–26; Italy, 136; job changes by slaves, 130; labor market, participation of slaves in, 134; life of a slave, view of, 132–33; manumission, 124, 126–29, 131–32 (*see also* manumission); modern slavery, differences from, 115; open model of slavery, 123, **124–25**; overview, 95; payment for freedom and, 53; price of slave labor, 134; price of slaves compared to wages of free workers, 137–38; punishment and, 134; purchase of freedom by slaves, 124; revolts, slave, 123; Rio de Janeiro,

slaves and slavery (*cont.*)
123, 128; rural slaves, 118, 123; sale of
slaves at auction, financial intermediation
and, 182; São Paulo, 128; serfdom, transition to, 137; skilled slaves, 129–30; slave
revolts, 123; slave systems, differences, 123–
24; timespan of slavery, 136–37; urban
slaves, 123; varieties of slavery, **124–25**;
wages for slaves, 130–31
Smith, Adam: on adverse selection, 98; on
division of labor, 21; on labor specialization, 152
"social capital" concept: growth theory and, 213
social structures: economic structures, interactions between, 100
societates: financial intermediation and, 172–73
Solow growth model, 211–13, 227
South Sea bubble, 165–66
specialist brokers: financial intermediation
and, 176
spontaneous innovation: growth theory and,
201
stability, periods of: growth theory and, 216–17
statistics: prices and, 27
Steinfeld, Robert, 117
stock market: generally, 10
stocks as securities, 166
Stoic tradition, 12
storms: prevention of shipments of wheat, 36
Strachey, Lytton, 1
structural change: growth theory and, 198
Sulpicii, 181–87
Sulpicius Cinnamus, 183
supply and demand: Antonine Plague and, 18;
curves illustrating, 15, **16, 19**; diminishing
returns and, 23, **24**; division of labor and,
21; Hellenistic Babylon, price behavior
and, 61–63; inelastic supply and, 18; labor
market and, 115; production possibility
frontier (PPF), 18–23; rent seeking and,
18; separation of, 14–21; trade, effects of
on, **21**; transaction costs and, 18, 22–23;
transportation costs and, 18; unitary elasticity and, 14, 17; wheat, in Italy, 16–17,
20–24; wine, in Italy, 16–17, 19–24
Swift, Jonathan, 199
Syria: land ownership in, 149

Tacitus, 141–42
Talmud on wheat exports, 47
taxes and taxation: in Britain, 8–9; in Egypt,
83–84; in Holland, 8–9; land ownership
and, 145–52; in Roman Empire, 71, 83,
85–86; tax-collecting societates, financial
intermediation and, 172–73
technology: change, Malthusian economies
and, 224, **232**, 233–37; development of,
growth theory and, 218; Industrial Revolution, improvements during, 237–38
tenant farmers: labor market and, 119
terracing: Malthusian economies and, 223
TFP. *See* total factor productivity (TFP)
theory of comparative advantage: Malthusian
economies and, 223
A Theory of Economic History, 132
Three Percent Consol, 164
Tiberian response, crisis of 33 CE, 81
Tiberius: land ownership and, 141–42; wheat
prices and trade and, 33
time-series properties: Hellenistic Babylon,
price behavior and, 61
Titus, 111
Torquatus, Titus Manlius, 170
total factor productivity (TFP): growth theory
and, 211–14
trade: diminishing returns and, **24**; loans to
finance, 172; supply and demand, effects
on, **21**; theory, Roman Empire and, 71
Trajan, 174–75
transaction costs: land ownership and, 140;
supply and demand and, 18, 22–23
transportation: costs, supply and demand and,
18; Malthusian economies and, 223–24
transport of wheat, 32. *See also* shipping
Triadelphus, 107
Trimalchio, 169; Cicero, compared, 2–3
Trobriand Islanders, 6
t-statistics: for wheat prices and trade, 44–49,
45, 48, 59, 68; for prices, **87**

Ulpian, 145
unemployment: financial intermediation and, 159
unitary elasticity: defined, 14; supply and
demand and, 14, 17
United States: bimetallic standard in, 81;
rights of workers, 117. *See also* America;
American South
urban population: per capita GDP and, 251–52
urban slaves, 123
usucapio, 147

Varro, 136; *On Agriculture*, 140
vassals: land ownership and, 155
vegetable oil as wages, 119
Verres, 147
Verrine Orations (Cicero), 38, 245

Vespasian, 174
villein, use of term, 139
Voltaire, 167–68

wages: in Davia, 120; in Egypt, 120, 254–55; England, nominal wages in, 8–9; per capita GDP and, 246, 254–56; for slaves, 130–31; variation in labor market, 116–18, 120
wage slavery, use of term, 121
warfare, feudal: land ownership and, 154–55
Washington, George, 121
water wheels, 224
wealth: land ownership as, 145
Western Europe, invasions of: land ownership and, 150–51
wheat: *annona* and, 17, 31–33, 105–6; in Britain, 59–60; England, prices in, 56; supply and demand for, Italy, 16–17, 20–24. *See also* wheat market; wheat prices; wheat prices and trade
wheat market: overview, 95; public and private supplies of, 106–7

wheat prices: growth theory and, 201–2; per capita GDP and, 245–47, 249, 255
wheat prices and trade, 29–52; *annona* and, 31–33, 47, 105–6; Bologna, transportation from, 45–46; distances and, 40, **41–43**, **45**, 48; in Egypt, 39–40, 47, 75; errors in variables and, 44; famine and, 39; Judaean revolt and, 47; objections to tests, 48–49; regression analysis, 42–46, 51; ships carrying, 31–32, 45–46, 101–2; Talmud on wheat exports, 47; t-statistics, 45–46; weaknesses of grain market, 49–50
Wickham, Chris, 151–52
wine: prices, growth theory and, 202; shipping of, 108; supply and demand for, Italy, 16–17, 19–24
women: in banks, 177
wool: in Hellenistic Babylon, 55–56, **56**, 64, 67
work week: growth theory and, 206
world economic history, **221**

Year of Four Emperors, 86

Creating Wine: The Emergence of a World Industry, 1840–1914, by James Simpson

The Evolution of a Nation: How Geography and Law Shaped the American States, by Daniel Berkowitz and Karen B. Clay

Distant Tyranny: Markets, Power, and Backwardness in Spain, 1650–1800, by Regina Grafe

The Chosen Few: How Education Shaped Jewish History, 70–1492, by Maristella Botticini and Zvi Eckstein

Why Australia Prospered: The Shifting Sources of Economic Growth, by Ian W. McLean

The Roman Market Economy, by Peter Temin

Printed and bound by CPI Group (UK) Ltd, Croydon, CR0 4YY

16/04/2025

14658359-0001